W9-AGX-387

THE
WEST AS
AMERICA

THE WEST AS AMERICA

REINTERPRETING IMAGES OF THE FRONTIER, 1820-1920

Edited by William H. Truettner

With Contributions by
Nancy K. Anderson, Patricia Hills, Elizabeth Johns,
Joni Louise Kinsey, Howard R. Lamar,
Alex Nemerov, Julie Schimmel

Published for the National Museum of American Art
by the Smithsonian Institution Press   Washington and London

Published on the occasion of the exhibition *The West as America: Reinterpreting Images of the Frontier, 1820–1920,* organized by the National Museum of American Art, Smithsonian Institution, and shown at

National Museum of American Art, Washington, D.C.
March 15–July 7, 1991

The Denver Art Museum
August 3–October 13, 1991

The Saint Louis Art Museum
November 9, 1991–January 12, 1992

The West as America is published with the assistance of the Getty Grant Program and the Smithsonian Institution Special Exhibition Fund.

Library of Congress Cataloging-in-Publication Data
The West as America : reinterpreting images of the frontier / edited by William H. Truettner ; with contributions by Nancy K. Anderson . . . [et al.].
p.   cm.
"Published on the occasion of the exhibition The West as America: Reinterpreting Images of the Frontier, organized by the National Museum of American Art, Smithsonian Institution, and shown at [the] National Museum of American Art, Washington, D.C., March 15–July 7, 1991, the Denver Art Museum, August 3–October 13, 1991 [and] the Saint Louis Art Museum, November 9, 1991–January 12, 1992"—T.p. verso.
Includes bibliographical references and index.
ISBN 1-56098-023-0 (alk. paper).
ISBN 1-56098-024-9 (pbk. : alk. paper)
1. Frontier and pioneer life—West (U.S.)—Exhibitions.
2. West (U.S.)—Description and travel—Exhibitions.
3. United States—Territorial expansion—Exhibitions.
4. West (U.S.) in art—Exhibitions. I. Truettner, William H. II. Anderson, Nancy K. III. National Museum of American Art (U.S.) IV. Denver Art Museum. V. Saint Louis Art Museum.
F596.W493   1991
978'.02'074753—dc20   90-41379   CIP

The paper used in this publication meets the requirements of the American National Standard for Permanence of Paper for Printed Library Materials Z39.48–1984.

Numbers in brackets [] indicate illustrations. Dimensions are in inches, height preceding width. Abbreviated notes are given in full in the References.

FRONT COVER
William Fuller, *Crow Creek Agency, Dakota Territory* (detail), 1884. Amon Carter Museum, Fort Worth, Texas.

BACK COVER
Unidentified artist, *California: The Home of the Big Tree* (detail), 1904. Library of Congress, Washington, D.C.

FRONTISPIECE
Unidentified photographer, *Charles Schreyvogel Painting on the Roof of His Apartment Building in Hoboken, New Jersey,* 1903. National Cowboy Hall of Fame Collection, Oklahoma City.

PAGE 54
Emanuel Leutze, *The Departure of Columbus from Palos in 1492* (detail), 1855. Private collection.

PAGE 96
John Gast, *American Progress* (detail), 1872. N & R Enterprises, Inc., Hampton, New Hampshire.

PAGE 148
Tompkins H. Matteson, *The Meeting of Hetty and Hist* (detail), 1857. Gordon Fraser, Minneapolis.

PAGE 190
Joseph Lee, *Residence of Captain Thomas W. Badger* (detail), circa 1871. The Oakland Museum, California.

PAGE 236
Oscar Berninghaus, *A Showery Day, Grand Canyon* (detail), 1915. The Santa Fe Collection of Southwestern Art, Chicago.

PAGE 284
Frederic Remington, *Radisson and Groseilliers* (detail), 1905. Buffalo Bill Historical Center, Cody, Wyoming.

Contents

Foreword

The essays in this book trace the way artists enlisted their talents in the service of progress during the period of westward expansion in America. The story is disturbing rather than ennobling, for it goes against our desire to see art as the voice of innate goodness and high moral values. Yet the message of this book is profound, for it shows that we find one of the most complete records of a society in its art. Hopes and dreams are there to be sure, but beneath the surface we find also the hidden agendas and ambitions that demanded some mediation, some gloss, before they could be shown to the world.

The authors contributing to *The West as America* have not been content to take images at face value, that is, as formal constructions of appealing composition and color. Rather, they have delved into the subjects, the intentions of the artists and their patrons, and the history of westward expansion to unearth a deeper, troubling story that poses questions for American society today. Many of the issues we still contend with had a beginning in the vast migration of easterners into the western wilderness a century and a half ago. That American society still struggles to adjust to limitations on natural resources, to grant overdue justice to native populations, to locate the contributions of ethnic minorities within a mainstream tradition, and to resolve conflicts between unbridled personal freedom and the larger social good tells us that we have ignored history far too long, accepting the images of the last century as reality.

The century covered here—roughly 1820 to 1920—was one of increasing religious doubt in Europe and America; the secular notion of progress offered a consoling alternative path toward perfection. Progress was dynamic, forward-looking, hopeful, and seemingly inevitable for such nineteenth-century writers as Englishman Herbert Spencer, who called it "not an accident, but a necessity . . . a part of nature." It transcended mere personal ambition, operating instead on the high public plane of society and culture, promising that today's struggles were but a prelude to tomorrow's prosperity. It implied a right of domain and "just rewards" as compensation for hardships. In this way, progress provided a natural analogue to the seemingly endless march of restless eastern settlers who moved from a less-than-perfect present toward a Promised Land of abundance.

The artists who portrayed westward expansion would have us believe that homesteaders went west not only for 160 acres to farm but for the larger purposes of taming the wilderness, Christianizing the savages, or spreading the gospel of democracy and freedom. This was construed as an American destiny made manifest through art, drawing a veil over aspects of frontier life that were unsavory or equivocal or simply mundane. Artists skated over the low points of the historical record—economic disasters, mining busts, droughts, depredations of the land, decimation of the buffalo herds, near obliteration of Indian cultures—with a consoling rhetoric of grand purpose.

The idea of progress implies some ultimate goal or at least occasional plateaus from which to gaze back with satisfaction over the path just traveled. Such a moment of reflection was offered by Frederick Jackson Turner, who wrote in 1893 that the filling of the continent from ocean to ocean had called forth aspects of character that were now to be writ large as national identity. The personal freedom of the frontiersman, trapper, cowboy, and homesteader became a mythic ideal for those in industry, labor, and politics. Turner's thesis was based on his interpretation of the 1890 census, which did more than just declare the continent fully settled. It documented what many had suspected, that the stock of the Anglo-Saxon "founders" was being rapidly diluted through immigration. The announcement that free land in the West was fully claimed, decades before

anyone had anticipated, came just at the moment that the country was discovered to be filling with a polyglot population demanding accommodation. The need to define a unique American spirit—preferably one that validated the established order—took on new urgency.

American artists responded by revising history through art, presenting in their work a privileged role for a largely eastern elite. Ignoring the much earlier Hispanic settlements and the long record of Indian tribal life, they wrote a "creation myth" for America that focused on the primacy of colonial English settlers in the New World. Already in the 1880s a few expatriate painters had settled in the old country village of Broadway in England, where they lovingly reconstructed in their art the minute details of the eighteenth-century English world they took to be the cradle of American civilization. By the end of the nineteenth century, colonial portraits were being collected for the first time as interest in early "founders" increased. At the same moment, New England folk art was discovered and celebrated for its forthright use of materials, integrity, and pure form—all taken as evidence of the simple, sturdy virtues of native stock descended from the first English settlers in the New World.

Despite this self-conscious attempt to establish a privileged bloodline for America, immigration increased apace and with it fears of barbarians at the gate—the vast influx of Mediterranean, Eastern European, Hispanic, and Asian settlers who arrived on these shores seeking freedom and economic survival. Artists did not work in isolation but were part of a wider movement of writers and thinkers in many disciplines and countries, all transfixed by the idea of progress as it applied to their own special studies. European scholars traced ancient tribal migrations throughout Asia and Europe and claimed to have proven that the New England town meeting was a latter-day descendant of the forest convocations of early Teutons, thus discovering a Nordic pedigree for democracy in America. Madison Grant published *The Passing of the Great Race* in 1916—just one of the innumerable treatises on declining Anglo-Saxon influence—in which key words were given new meanings: "original Americans" and "native Americans" refer to early English colonists, as if both Indians and Hispanics could be erased from the American past through the manipulation of language.

The theme of progress was so pervasive that it affected most intellectual movements of the last century. As Stephen Jay Gould has explained in *Wonderful Life: The Burgess Shale and the Nature of History* (1989), scientists misrepresented all evolution as steady, linear progress— one leading inevitably toward Man as its highest expression—when in fact early life teemed with alternative possibilities that were obliterated by unexplained decimations. With characteristic sensitivity, Gould has noted the powerful role that images played in persuading people to accept ideology as fact. The "branching tree" of evolution so beloved of early biologists, with its misleading visual presentation of linear progress, is just one of many "incarnations of concepts masquerading as neutral descriptions of nature," he writes. Such visual misrepresentations—biological, evolutionary, historical—provide the international background against which American artists worked, with progress accepted as a given in the development of organism, race, society, and nation. Viewed in this wider context, it seems inevitable that American artists should have depicted settlers as a crusade of easterners forging a steady stream of progress from Plymouth Rock to the Pacific palisades.

It is unnerving to discover such strategies in art, however inadvertent or conditioned by broader forces. But precisely because art possesses the power to persuade, it is a masterful

mediator between the alarming facts of history and the loudly proclaimed ideals of progress. To read these images of westward expansion closely is to discover essential truths about the cultural basis of national identity. Today, a century after America's creation myth was ushered into the world, we struggle with its inadequacies and insensitivities. By retracing the path of progress through the decades of expansion and seeing it in the context of culture and science, we can see the larger realities that lay to either side of this artificially straight line, finding there a new perspective on our past and future.

ELIZABETH BROUN
Director
National Museum of American Art

Acknowledgments

Most collaborative art-historical projects develop over a long period, but few changed course as much as *The West as America*. These changes were not in the central theme but in content and presentation—finding a way to make images express the ideas put forth in this book. Many images used in *The West as America* have been featured in previous publications and exhibitions; they have not suddenly been drawn from obscurity, nor do they reemerge free of a compelling association with a heroic West. The point of our investigation, however, is to dispel traditional ideas about images of the West, to place them in a new context designed to question past interpretations.

To make that context effective—to employ it as a means to review and rethink the meaning of familiar works by well-known artists—has not been an easy task. Not long after the book and accompanying exhibition were conceived and a core group of loans was secured, we realized that without a more challenging array of images, major works might continue to be read in a traditional way. Demystifying these works, it soon became clear, depended on a strategy of arranging them into categories that either commented on one another or that introduced popular and dissenting material. Shifting images back and forth to achieve our objective caused us to cancel loans already promised and to request new loans, in some cases from the same institutions and private collectors. To those who had to bear with this confusion, especially the directors and staffs of the Gilcrease Institute (Fred Myers, Anne Morand, Jeanne King, Sarah Erwin, and Kristi Moore) and Amon Carter Museum (Jan Muhlert, Rick Stewart, and Melissa Thompson), my sincerest apologies. I hope this book and accompanying exhibition will persuade you that method and purpose eventually triumphed.

Many museums and other institutions generously gave up one or more of their most important works for the exhibition tour. Those who were particularly helpful with such loans include Joseph Ketner, Washington University Gallery of Art, Saint Louis; Linda Mitchell Davis, member, board of directors, and Byron Price, Ed Muno, and Jacqueline Bober, National Cowboy Hall of Fame; Lawrence Dinnean, Bancroft Library, University of California, Berkeley; Holly Hotchner, Annette Blaugrund, and Richard Gallerani, New-York Historical Society; Harvey Jones, Therese Heyman, and Mickey Karpas, Oakland Museum; Elizabeth Smart and Barbara Doscher, California Historical Society, San Francisco; David Forgang, Yosemite Museum; John Wilmerding, trustee, Brian Alexander, and Eloise Beil, Shelburne Museum, Vermont; Debra Balken, Berkshire Museum, Pittsfield, Massachusetts; Andrew B. Craig III, Donald J. Brandin, and Larry Bayliss, Boatmen's Bancshares, Saint Louis; Mark J. Cedek, Saint Louis Mercantile Library Association; Peter Hassrick, Sarah Boehme, and Sue Reid, Buffalo Bill Historical Center; Theodore Stebbins, Museum of Fine Arts, Boston; Marc Simpson, Fine Arts Museums of San Francisco; Jan Driesbach and Paulette Hennum, Crocker Art Museum, Sacramento; Henry Adams, Nelson-Atkins Museum of Art; Don Snoddy, Union Pacific Historical Museum, Omaha; Michael Shapiro, Saint Louis Art Museum; Ruth Meyer, Taft Museum, Cincinnati; H. Parrott Bacot, Anglo-American Art Museum, Baton Rouge; Marsha Gallagher and David Hunt, Joslyn Art Museum, Omaha; James Nottage, Gene Autry Western Heritage Museum, Los Angeles; Patricia Trenton, Los Angeles Athletic Club; Eric Paddock, Colorado Historical Society, Denver; Michiko Okaya, Lafayette College, Easton, Pennsylvania; Jennifer Goldsborough, Maryland Historical Society, Baltimore; Hilarie Faberman, University of Michigan Museum of Art, Ann Arbor; and Marjie Sands, Spring Creek Art Foundation, Inc., Dedham, Massachusetts.

Several private collectors also made available to us key works from their collections. I am especially grateful to Elisabeth Waldo-Dentzel, E. William Judson, Elizabeth R. Moran, Donald F. Houghton, Gordon Fraser, E. G. Nicholson, Alice and Paul Elcano, Dr. and Mrs. Thornton I. Boileau, Philip Anschutz and curator Elizabeth Cunningham, Issei Fujiwara, Dr. and Mrs. Oscar Lemer, Robert E. Weinstein, and Bruce Heard.

To dealers who either contributed works of art or helpful information or assisted with private collectors, I am no less grateful. Gerald Peters and Katie Flanagan, Santa Fe, head the list, followed by John Froats, Daniel Wolf Gallery, New York; Irene Falconer, Mongerson-Wunderlich Gallery, Chicago; Frederick Hill, Bruce Chambers, and Mary Ushay, Berry-Hill Galleries, New York; Lawrence Fleischman and the late Fred Bernaski, Kennedy Galleries, New York; Ira Spanierman and David Henry, New York; Russell Burke, Altman-Burke Fine Art, New York; Stephen Good, Rosenstock Arts, Denver; Jeffrey Fraenkel, San Francisco; Carl David, David David Art Gallery, Philadelphia; Stuart Feld and Susan Menconi, Hirschl & Adler Galleries, New York; William Schaeffer, Chester, Connecticut; Mark Hoffman, Maxwell Galleries, San Francisco; and Martin Kodner, Gallery of the Masters, Saint Louis.

Scholarly assistance came from numerous individuals, but two should be singled out. Kate Nearpass, a Columbia University graduate student, shared with us her extensive files on Yosemite and big tree subjects, and Peter Palmquist, whose knowledge of photographs of early California is unmatched, patiently led us to image after image in local collections. Paula Fleming, National Anthropological Archives, and William Sturtevant, William Merrill, and John Ewers, National Museum of Natural History, Smithsonian Institution; Ellen

Schwartz, California State Railroad Museum, Sacramento; Carol Osborne, Stanford University Museum; Elizabeth Kornhauser, Wadsworth Atheneum; Gray Sweeney, Arizona State University, Tempe; and Vivian Fryd, Vanderbilt University, also deserve special mention as well as Mary Lou Gjirnes and Joan Thomas, United States Army Center of Military History; David Meschutt, West Point Museum; Tambra Johnson, Library of Congress; Jonathan Heller, National Archives; Ellen Wells, Smithsonian Institution Libraries, and Rayna Green and Deborah Warner, National Museum of American History, Smithsonian Institution; William Kloss, Washington, D.C.; Denny Carter Young, Cincinnati; Alfred Runte, Seattle; Ron Fields, University of Puget Sound, Tacoma; Joseph Baird, Tiburon, California; Katherine Littell, Twain Harte, California; Stan Hutchinson, Sierra Madre, California; Nan and Roy Farrington Jones, Ross, California; Paul Tarver, New Orleans Museum of Art; Jeff Rosenheim, Metropolitan Museum of Art; Weston Naef and Peggy Hanssen, J. Paul Getty Museum; Peter Blodgett, Susan Naulty, and Rita Mack, Huntington Library; Mark Dimunation, Stanford University; Joel Snyder, University of Chicago; George Miles, Beinecke Library, Yale University; Janet Buerger, George Eastman House; Ann M. Bolin, Lockwood-Mathews Mansion Museum, Norwalk, Connecticut; Pierre Apraxine, Gilman Paper Company, New York; Bethe B. Visick, Bureau of Reclamation, Boulder City, Nevada; Kathleen C. Eustis, California State Library, Sacramento; and Gerald Geefer, Water Resources Center Archives, University of California, Berkeley.

The list continues with Joanne Kudla and Melissa Webster, Buffalo Bill Historical Center; Bonnie Hardwick, Bancroft Library; Kay Wisnia and Aggie Mastrogiuseppi, Denver Public Library; Duane Sneddeker, Missouri Historical Society, Saint Louis; Mary Wyly, Newberry Library, Chicago; Marianna Munyer, Illinois Historic Preservation Agency, Springfield; Lance Fraser, Minneapolis; James Walter, Toledo; Richard and Selma Appel, East Lansing, Michigan; Mark Van Benschoten and Lowell McAllister, Frederick Remington Art Museum, Ogdensburg, New York; Edward Lipowicz, Canajoharie Library and Art Gallery, New York; and Caroline Welsh, Adirondack Museum, Blue Mountain Lake, New York.

My greatest debt is to my colleagues at the National Museum of American Art. Elizabeth Broun never wavered in her support of the project, except when she asked, with grace and some humor, if the checklist would ever stop changing. Cecilia Chin provided generous working space in the library, and Patricia Lynagh and Martin Kalfatovic showed unbelievable patience while I assembled a small library within their larger domain. Margy Sharpe gave life and conviction to desultory statements I provided for funding purposes. Conservator Quentin Rankin generously contributed personal time to improve the appearance of works in the exhibition. Elizabeth Anderson created a literate, intelligible manuscript from countless pages of handwritten and overwritten text and managed a reassuring smile even when she was at her wit's end. Brinah Kuss juggled contracts and budgets, somehow making things come out even. Cheryl Cibulka Gordon provided invaluable research assistance and managed loan requests, while Shelley Mead, Elizabeth Holmstead, and especially Cahssey Augenstein searched libraries and historical societies to locate images for both illustrative and exhibition purposes. Cahssey then prepared the captions for the book and put the final touches on the checklist. Kathleen Preciado, who made eight authors almost agree with one another, is the kind of editor no scholar should be without. Her skill and judgment are evident on every

page of this book. Steve Dietz solved another
category of editorial problems while Amy Pas-
tan and Lisa Vann of the Smithsonian Institution Press saw the manuscript through to its
final incarnation. Amy managed the myriad
details of producing the book and Lisa created
a layout that is both attractive and readable.

My thanks also go to the other authors
who contributed to this book and to Kenneth
Haltman, who joined us at a later stage. There
was substantial give-and-take throughout the
project; I proposed a party line (which Patricia
Hills more succinctly defined as artists involved in "persuasive imaging"), and each author gave it his or her individual interpretation.
In the process, the party line was considerably
broadened and enriched. To one of those authors I owe a special debt. Alex Nemerov,
fresh from graduate school, came to the museum in the summer of 1987. Since that time
his talent for interpreting images and his critical insights have informed every stage of this
project.

My final tribute is to Alan Wallach and
Roger Stein, friends, colleagues, and mentors,
who in the past several years have redirected
my approach to art history. Both read and
commented (at length) on the introduction. If
it only imperfectly represents their views, it is
because one does not easily turn from well-
worn grooves of scholarship.

In offering their support, Alan and Roger
as well as Betsy Broun and Alex Nemerov
helped me through a period of numbing loss,
when the companion whose warmth and spon-
taneity had always sustained me was suddenly
gone. If I have not been able to tell them how
much they have done for me, I hope they
now understand.

W.H.T.

An Overview of Westward Expansion

HOWARD R. LAMAR

In his 1930 poem, "American Letter," Archibald MacLeish declared that "America is West and the wind blowing."[1] Although this splendid line may seem poetic exaggeration today, for the United States in the nineteenth century it was almost a truism. Beginning with the Lewis and Clark expedition overland to the Pacific and back between 1805 and 1806 and continuing with the official explorations of Zebulon Pike, Stephen H. Long, John Charles Frémont, and others, Americans came to know and want the mysterious and different western lands described by these explorers.

Inventors of the West: Franklin, Jefferson, and Monroe

For the American West to come into national consciousness as a concept it had to be invented or defined, then explored, and then occupied and redefined on the basis of actual experience. None of these processes was easy or inevitable, and often they were accompanied by violence. In seeking to identify the inventors of the West as America, three patriots seem to have the greatest legitimacy as progenitors: Benjamin Franklin, Thomas Jefferson, and James Monroe.

Of the first, historian James H. Hutson has written that

although Franklin was as great a devotee of urban living as America ever produced, he was deeply involved in western matters. He once held a mortgage on the Daniel Boone family farm; as "General" Franklin, he fought the Indians in northeastern Pennsylvania; . . . his advice shaped the policy towards the American West of a British Secretary of State (Lord Shelburne, 1766–68); and he helped win the West from the British at the Paris Peace Conference of 1782. But the primary reason why Franklin should be discussed in the context of the West is that, with the possible exception of Frederick Jackson Turner, no man ever wrote on its role in shaping the character of American life with as much influence and conviction.[2]

As early as 1751 Franklin expressed his belief that the West—meaning the Old Northwest—was destined to be "a farmer's paradise" with its fertile lands, good climate, and "navigable waterways." He believed that America would be a major country because it had the resources to feed a large population, which in turn could then occupy western lands. Given this unfettered population growing by geometric increase, eventually Americans would spread west and create an empire by sheer occupation. Franklin also defined two other features that promoted the idea of the West as America. Here was a land of plenty, he said, but because livelihoods would come largely from the soil it would produce only ordinary middle-class farming people—not lords and peasants.[3] Thus Franklin declared for a demographic and democratic "manifest destiny" long before the phrase assumed the imperial and political connotations that John L. O'Sullivan, speaking in the *Democratic Review,* gave it in 1845.

In his quiet, diplomatic way, Franklin also fought relentlessly and as tirelessly to secure a larger West for Americans to expand into. He himself speculated in western land companies in the colonial period and after, and he had the pleasure of knowing that the frontier settlers of Tennessee called their new colony "Franklin." At the Treaty of Paris of 1782 the ever-practical Franklin held out for the recognition of American claims to all lands east of the Mississippi River. As much as anyone, Franklin helped give the young nation a real West.

Thomas Jefferson, the second inventor of the West as America, held views similar to Franklin's concerning America's future as a republic of small farmers, and he had an equally ardent desire to acquire still more Wests, as his administration did when it purchased the province of Louisiana from France in 1803.[4] That purchase gave the United States a claim to Oregon—our first Far West and our first opportunity to dream of being a sea-to-sea continental nation.

Long before the Louisiana Purchase, however, Jefferson had tried to shape and define older Wests to his own wishes. Even before the Revolution he and others sought to bring frontier Kentucky under Virginia's jurisdiction. If Daniel Boone was busy leading Judge Archibald Henderson's Transylvania Company of North Carolina pioneers to Boonesboro in 1775, James Harrod and Virginia pioneers were equally busy settling Harrodsburg, Kentucky.[5]

After the Revolution, Jefferson worried about land disposal and governance. He wrote the Land Ordinance of 1785, outlining a rational, scientific system of survey for new lands.[6] Although he did not write the famous Northwest Ordinance of 1787, his good friend James Monroe played a key role in creating the act that established the American system of territorial government for western regions, a system that has lasted into this century.[7]

While all the leaders of the new American nation worried about Indian policy and George Washington and Secretary of War Henry Knox, in particular, sought to devise a humane Indian policy, Jefferson went further.[8] He hoped that Indians and whites might one day intermingle and become one people. His idea of integration was bold and daring, but it had a catch: Indian Americans must become farmers. With the best of intentions Jefferson tried to force the eastern tribes to assimilate by justifying harsh treaties that acquired more and more lands for white settlers.[9] In effect, his message was assimilate or else. The Cherokee, Creek, Choctaw, and Chickasaw all heard Jefferson's message and indeed attempted to adopt white ways and Christianity, but in the end even these nations were forced from their lands and removed west.[10] By the time Andrew Jackson had become president, removal rather than as-

1. George Catlin, *William Clark,* 1832, oil on canvas, 28½ × 23½ in. National Portrait Gallery, Smithsonian Institution, Washington, D.C.

simulation had become the new policy.

Having fostered the loyalty of the first West, devised a national, scientific land system, endorsed a territorial system of government, and set an Indian policy, Jefferson then acquired the Louisiana Territory in 1803—a splendid climax to a lifetime of inventing and defining newer American Wests. Even before Jefferson purchased Louisiana he was so anxious to learn about the trans-Mississippi West that he ordered a semisecret Corps of Discovery, led by Captain Meriwether Lewis and Lieutenant William Clark to march across the continent to the Pacific [1].[11]

When Lewis and Clark finally set out on their historic trek up the Missouri, over the Rockies, and down the Columbia to the Pacific, they had three goals in mind: securing a vast potential fur trade for the United States by befriending the Indian tribes along the way [2]; seeking out fertile new lands for Jefferson's pioneering farmers to expand onto; and discover-

ing an easy route across the continent that would be the giant first step toward realizing "a passage to India," that is, commercial trade with the Far East.[12] Ironically these three aims were to prove contradictory. Developing a fur trade meant preserving Indian tribes and the wilderness; settling the vast Louisiana Purchase with farmers meant Indian displacement or assimilation and an end to wilderness; developing commerce threatened the status of both Indians and farmers.

When Lewis and Clark returned in 1806, as the first Americans to cross the continent, they rightly came to be seen as American heroes. Moreover, they produced the first map of the upper trans-Mississippi West and they reported the existence of fabulous numbers of fur-bearing animals on the Missouri and its Rocky Mountain headwaters.[13] It also looked as if they had realized Columbus's dream by finding a way to the Orient.

This is where the theme of an inevitable westward march begins to break down, for they had to tell Jefferson that incredible mountain barriers precluded any easy passage across the continent and that vast stretches of dry plains, even deserts, existed where they had hoped to find well-watered, arable soils.[14]

Regrettably Lewis and Clark had no artist or skilled draftsman with them, so the image of this newest and most distant West remained fuzzy in the eyes of the public.[15] Although Lieutenant Zebulon Pike attempted to explore the central and southern Rockies and produced a map on the Spanish Southwest, Americans would have to wait until after the War of 1812 for more information about the Far West.[16]

During his presidency James Madison was too preoccupied with Napoleonic Wars in Europe and with the War of 1812 at home to think about the Far West, but his successor, James Monroe, another inventor of the American West, had been deeply interested in the re-

gion since his youth. He had been one of the
authors of the Ordinance of 1787 and later one
of the American negotiators for the Louisiana
Purchase.[17] During Madison's troubled administration, Monroe, as secretary of war, had reorganized a collapsing American military effort
against the British. Once he became president
in 1816, Monroe sought to explore and secure
the West. In this he was aided by his aggressive secretary of state, John Quincy Adams,
and his brilliant secretary of war, John C.
Calhoun, both of whom were ardent
expansionists.[18]

In a dramatic series of moves the three
sought to fasten the nation's grip on the West
through military strategy, exploration, and diplomacy, spurred on by the knowledge that
had it not been for Jackson's victory at New
Orleans, the United States might have lost the
West to Great Britain in the War of 1812.

To secure the West militarily Calhoun
proposed an inner line of forts on the borders
of settlement in the Old Northwest, forts that
would be connected to major towns by a network of good roads. Then, very much aware
that the British still occupied parts of Wisconsin and dominated Indian affairs and the fur
trade along the Mississippi and Missouri rivers,
Calhoun and Monroe decided to send an impressive military expedition—the largest peace-
time operation in the young nation's history—
up the Missouri to the Yellowstone River to
establish an outpost there.[19] Calhoun also sent
a small reconnaissance party to the headwaters
of the Mississippi. The purpose for both
projects was to locate an outer ring of posts
and to assert American authority.[20]

The resulting Yellowstone expedition up
the Missouri under the command of Colonel
Henry Atkinson started auspiciously with
eleven hundred men and five steamboats. But
it ended ignominiously a year later, when delays stranded the expedition near present-day

Omaha, still a thousand nautical miles from its
goal. There in winter headquarters conditions
were so bad some three hundred soldiers died
of scurvy and other diseases. Revelations of
crooked contractors, bad supplies, and faulty
steamboats led Congress, already reeling under
the blow of the financial panic of 1819, to cancel the expedition.[21]

2. George Catlin, *Black Moccasin, Aged Chief* (Hidatsa), 1832, oil on canvas, 29 × 24 in. National Museum of American Art, Smithsonian Institution, Washington, D.C.; gift of Mrs. Joseph Harrison, Jr.
Lewis and Clark's visit to the Hidatsa village in 1804 was witnessed by Black Moccasin, who almost thirty years later recalled the event for Catlin.

3. Samuel Seymour, *Pawnee Council,* 1819, watercolor on paper, 5 7/8 × 8 1/8 in. Yale University, Beinecke Rare Book and Manuscript Library, New Haven.

4. Samuel Seymour, *View of the Rocky Mountains.* From James, *Account of an Expedition* (1823), pl. 3. Yale University, Beinecke Rare Book and Manuscript Library, New Haven.

To salvage what had been a grand scheme Major Stephen H. Long of the United States Topographical Engineers was ordered to go up the Platte River to the Rockies in the summer of 1820 with an absurdly small detachment of civilians, soldiers, and frontier carriers. Long was also instructed to turn south and return along the Red River, to Fort Smith, Arkansas, one of the outer ring of posts in Calhoun's defense scheme.[22]

Until recently historians have judged Major Long's expedition as a failure, for he did not actually explore the Rockies. Moreover, some scientific notes assembled during the expedition were stolen by defecting members of the party. Then, to his great chagrin, Long mistook the Canadian for the Red River and so never saw or explored one of the objectives of his trip.

Even so, for Americans interested in clarifying the image of the American West, Long's expedition was of the utmost importance. For example, the expedition party included Samuel Seymour, a British artist who sketched Indian-white treaty negotiations as well as the first drawings of the Rocky Mountains [3].[23] They provided some visual evidence of the nature and size of the central Rockies [4].

The expedition was also fortunate to have a second artist among its number—young Titian Peale, son of the famous Philadelphia artist and collector Rembrandt Peale. Although Titian was not as accomplished as his father, on the Long expedition he faithfully sketched animals and herds [5] and occasionally a landscape. He was to spend his life drawing specimens from newly discovered regions.[24]

Aided by Dr. Edwin James, the botanist on the expedition, Long produced an impressive report in 1823, which was accompanied by a map labeling much of present-day Kansas, Nebraska, and eastern Colorado as "The Great American Desert."[25] That image, in turn, had extraordinary consequences. It suggested that there were limits to the Garden of Eden Americans had previously associated with the West. The presence of a four-hundred-mile band of desert also meant that with such a physical barrier there was little need to create an outer ring of forts, for no hostile Spanish or Mexican expedition could cross it easily. Long's desert also suggested that since it was a region unfit

for agriculture, it might be suitable as a last homeland for native Americans and thus was a place to which one could remove eastern Indian tribes. Indeed, Monroe, Adams, and Calhoun were now sympathetic to the idea of removing all eastern tribes west of the Mississippi.[26] Long's report suited their purposes admirably.

One of the supreme ironies of Long's description of the Great Plains as desert was that at the very moment he wrote, Indian Americans, using the horse and the gun, had begun to move onto the plains to exploit the teeming herds of buffalo there. In the next half century they not only thrived economically, they expanded their physical territory and developed a vigorous and flexible Plains culture.[27] In time, the Plains Indians and their buffalo culture so captured the imagination of Americans that they became the Indian stereotype.

Long's report helped fix other dramatic images on the public mind as well. He described fur trappers as white savages, and, while he was no lover of native Americans, he depicted the Plains Indians as still being free and strong. Long's descriptions so captivated James Fenimore Cooper that he used the Great Plains as the setting for his novel *The Prairie* (1827). He also used Long's account of a Pawnee warrior, Petalesharro [see 128], as the model for his noble savage hero, Hard Heart. Cooper's portrayal of his famous white character, Natty Bumppo, drew on characteristics of the wilderness scout. Indeed there is convincing evidence that Cooper copied information from Long's report almost verbatim for his descriptions of the landscape in *The Prairie*.[28]

Meanwhile John Quincy Adams had negotiated the Transcontinental Treaty of 1819 with Spain by which the United States acquired Florida and the boundary between American and Spanish possessions from Louisiana to Oregon was established. In short, the United

States now had a defined trans-Mississippi West. Monroe's and Adams's vision of the West as America, however, was not just continental but hemispheric in its aim. In 1823 the president announced the famous Monroe Doctrine, declaring that European influence in North and Central America should be removed, presumably to permit democratic republics based on the American model to arise. This hands-off policy was to be used repeatedly to assert and justify the primacy of the United States in the New World.[29]

That the Monroe administration saw the West as America was demonstrated in many other ways. In 1822, under the pressure of John Jacob Astor and other fur-trade entrepreneurs, Congress ended its policy of allowing only government-designated agents, or factors, to operate trading posts in Indian country.[30]

5. Titian Peale, *Bulls,* 1820, watercolor on paper, 7⅜ × 9¼ in. American Philosophical Society, Philadelphia.

Although traders still had to secure a license and promise not to bring liquor into Indian areas, suddenly the western fur trade became a free-for-all as private firms, like the Rocky Mountain Fur Company, fiercely competed with one another to exploit the animal riches of the Upper Missouri.

Between 1822 and 1840 some three thousand trappers and traders—many associated with the loosely allied and ever-changing Rocky Mountain Fur Company, founded by Colonel Andrew Henry and William H. Ashley, or with the Saint Louis outfits dominated by French families like the Chouteaus, or with Astor's monolithic and hierarchical American Fur Company—penetrated the most obscure and remote regions of the West.[31] Moving about in small groups, on foot or on horseback, they trapped beaver and sold the skins at fur-trading posts or exchanged them for money and supplies at annual rendezvous held in the mountains. To these outdoor fairs men like Ashley brought goods from Saint Louis each summer, at first on pack animals and then by wagon. The returning caravans, laden with thousands of furs and skins, helped make Saint Louis the premier fur market in the United States.

The fur trade made fortunes for many entrepreneurs, among them Ashley, who returned to Missouri and successfully ran for Congress. But it turned others into explorers. In the winter of 1823–24, for example, young Jedediah Smith, a New York-born trader-trapper, and James Clyman discovered South Pass, Wyoming, a gentle low-lying saddleback in the Rockies by which one could not only reach the fur regions west of the Rockies but which could serve as a route to Oregon and California.[32] The South Pass crossing was so gradual that wagons could negotiate it. It was the fur trappers, rather than Lewis and Clark, who found the actual paths by which settlers could move themselves and their possessions to Oregon, California, and Utah.

This was only the first of Smith's many accomplishments. Two years later he found a route to southern California. Then he blazed a trail eastward from San Francisco Bay over the Sierra Nevada to the Great Basin and then to the annual fur-trade rendezvous in the Green River area. He also identified a path from Oregon to South Pass. In short, the ways west as well as the West itself were being opened in the 1820s and 1830s. To attribute all the discoveries to Smith would be unfair, however. Joseph R. Walker also found a way to cross the Sierra into California as did others in the 1830s.

Most mountain guides did not leave long written accounts of their discoveries, as had Major Long in 1823 or later, when Frémont tantalized the nation with his patriotic-romantic narrative of his first three expeditions.[33] But scientists, hunters, artists, and writers traveling in the trans-Mississippi West provided vivid records of what they had seen, whether through the written word or artist's brushstroke.

Splendid renditions of the West by George Catlin [see 1–2, 36, 125, 129–30, 134], Karl Bodmer [see 37, 131–32], and Alfred Jacob Miller [see 7, 133, 151] were supplemented by the writings of Washington Irving, who at the time was considered, with Cooper, to be the most famous of American writers. Irving was a cultivated easterner who wrote amusing stories about Dutch New York and had earlier written a major biography of Columbus; but in 1835, after a trip in the area of present-day Oklahoma, Irving published *A Tour of the Prairies.* A year later in *Astoria,* he tried his hand at writing the history of Astor's attempt to establish a fur-trading post at the mouth of the Columbia just before the War of 1812. In the book Astor is portrayed as a misunderstood merchant-hero.

Then in 1837 Irving published *The Adventures of Captain Bonneville,* a thinly fictionalized account of an army officer who had gone into the fur trade in the Pacific Northwest. In that volume Irving focused on colorful events, Indian battles, and wilderness scouts. As Professor Peter Antelyes notes in his recent study of Irving, the latter saw the western experience as "adventurous enterprise," a theme that other writers and artists would follow.[34]

Empresarios *and Santa Fe Traders*

While the Rocky Mountain fur trade was getting its start during the second administration of James Monroe (1821–25), two other major developments were taking place that would also contribute to the expansion of the United States. The first of these occurred in the Mexican province of Texas, where in 1821 Moses Austin, born in Connecticut but now living in the lead-mining regions of Missouri, secured a large land grant from the Spanish government to found a colony in Texas. Before he could move there, however, Austin died, leaving his son, Stephen F. Austin, to carry out the task. After further negotiations with officials of the newly proclaimed independent Republic of Mexico and the signing of the Colonization Law of 1823, Austin and other *empresarios,* as the colony leaders were called, were allowed to bring settlers, mostly Anglo-Americans from the Mississippi Valley and the lower South, to Texas.[35]

Word of the rich lands of Texas, free except for a few trifling fees, attracted so many Americans that they soon outnumbered the Mexican Texas population. Despite Mexico's abolition of slavery, white southerners brought black slaves to Texas in the thousands. In addition to responsible, serious-minded settlers with families, a set of spirited men came to coastal Texas. A potentially revolutionary group, they included adventurers, contentious lawyers, and even persons fleeing from the law.

By 1829 the Mexican government had become so concerned about conditions in Texas that it sent the respected general Luis Mier y Terán to investigate. His report was disturbing: Americans there refused to become Catholic (a proviso of the Colonization Law), give up slavery, obey the Mexican justice system, or pay customs. After a local uprising at Galveston in 1832, tensions were so great that Austin, as the recognized leader and spokesperson for all colonists, went to Mexico City to resolve matters. Austin not only failed, he was arrested and detained in Mexico City for many months.

Back in Texas there began a move toward political autonomy that grew until 1835, when Anglo Texans were in open revolt. At first it seemed as if Mexican authorities and troops would not resist. But in February 1836 a Texan force co-commanded by Colonel William Barret Travis and James Bowie, occupying the Alamo in San Antonio, was attacked by General Antonio López de Santa Anna, and all the American defenders were slain, among their numbers, David Crockett.

Despite panic among the settlers, however, rapidly assembled volunteer forces under Sam Houston eventually defeated Santa Anna and his troops at the Battle of San Jacinto in April 1836. The Lone Star State was now an independent republic, with Houston as president.[36]

At first it looked as if the inevitable march of empire would bring Texas into the Union, an event dearly hoped for by Houston and his political mentor, Andrew Jackson. But by 1836 the American abolition movement had begun in earnest and its leaders saw Texas as a new "pen to cram slaves in." Antislavery forces successfully defeated Texas's entry into the

Union with the result that Texas existed for ten years as an independent state. The turning point finally came in 1844, when James K. Polk ran on an expansion ticket that called for the annexation of Texas and reannexation of Oregon.[37] Once Polk had been elected, outgoing president John Tyler maneuvered a joint resolution through Congress to admit Texas. After voting to accept annexation, Texas became a state in February 1846.

The saga of Texas's admission introduced troubling new complexities to western expansion. Americans in Texas had taken the province of another country, not by purchase but by violence and rebellion. Mexicans were identified not only as enemies but as religiously, racially, and culturally inferior. While chanting that Manifest Destiny was to bring freedom to benighted peoples, Americans not only denied freedom to Texan Mexicans but allowed slavery to continue to exist there. Rather than unifying the nation, Texas divided it, creating a split that was to become even greater when other parts of the West, such as Kansas and Nebraska, were being organized as territories. In effect, Texas, despite all its moments of heroism and glory and its serving as a dramatic symbol of Americans expanding their democratic institutions westward, had its dark side, which would be challenged ultimately by no less than the Civil War.[38]

In 1821 William Becknell, a Missouri citizen, and a party of traders were in the Great Plains seeking to exchange goods for Indian horses. He unexpectedly encountered a military force from New Mexico who told him that the recently formed Mexican Republic had opened its borders to trade. Becknell sold his goods for a substantial profit and returned to Missouri with the glorious news that an expanded market for trade goods—especially cutlery and cloth, both strouds and velveteens—existed in New Mexico.[39]

From that happenstance an impressive trade began between Santa Fe and the border towns of Missouri. Although punctuated by ups and downs, the trade had become a million-dollar business by the 1840s and had assumed a pattern one must call classic—for it resembled the course of ancient armed caravans carrying goods across the Near East and North Africa and from Persia to Karakorum.[40]

The pattern was obvious. Each spring individual merchants would move their wagons, heavily laden with trade goods, west to a rendezvous point in Kansas. They would elect a captain and band together to make the dangerous journey through Comanche and Kiowa country. When they reached Las Vegas in eastern New Mexico, however, they disbanded and rushed pell-mell to Santa Fe, where the first-comers presumably received the best prices. After some weeks there they returned to Missouri with their wagons loaded with blankets, silver bullion, and buffalo skins.[41] They also drove so many herds of mules back that Missouri became a primary market for mules for farms and especially for southern cotton plantations.[42] The importation of silver made Missouri, unlike other border states, more commercial-minded and fonder of hard money than of paper money. Because of his support of hard money, Senator Thomas Hart Benton was nicknamed "Old Bullion" [6].[43]

The consequences of the Santa Fe-Chihuahua trade—for the American merchants soon learned that their goods also brought fantastic prices in remote inland Chihuahua—were many. Over the years the New Mexican economy became bound to that of the Missouri traders. The provincial government depended heavily on revenue derived from customs duties on the caravans. American traders began to stay year round and opened stores in Santa Fe and Taos. Inevitably they met, fell in love with, and married local Mexican women.

ifornia's Fort Sutter on the site of the future town of Sacramento.[46] These outposts of economic empire were established by the shock troops of American conquest in both New Mexico and California.

It was not long before the Bents and other Americans began to dabble in land grants, for the Mexican government had made them available in New Mexico as it had in Texas. In California, John Sutter himself secured a vast land grant from the provincial government there. The prospect of land, that obsession of frontier Americans, increased American interests in New Mexico.[47]

By the 1840s the Santa Fe trade had become so well known and important that Josiah Gregg, a trader, wrote a classic account of it, which he published under the title *Commerce of the Prairies* (1844). Here for the first time Americans began to learn about the exotic, unknown American Southwest. Gregg not only described Mexicans and their life and culture in detail, he also provided accounts of Pueblo and nomadic Indians.[48]

For Americans, New Mexico represented a totally different West from what they had known previously. Here was a frontier already with a sizable population, not only of Hispanic peoples but of sedentary, village-dwelling agricultural Indians—the Pueblo—and so-called nomadic groups—the Apache and Navaho. New Mexico gave the lie to the assertion that American pioneers were advancing into uninhabited virgin land. In fact, so many Hispanic peoples resided in New Mexico that Anglo-Americans there did not outnumber them until the twentieth century.

Let us return to the seminal years of the Monroe administration to note two other events that sparked the settlement of Oregon and the Great Basin. In 1818, in the middle of Monroe's first term, the United States and Great Britain agreed to a joint occupation of

6. George Caleb Bingham, *Thomas Hart Benton,* circa 1850, oil on canvas, 30 × 25 in. Missouri Historical Society, Saint Louis.

Whether Anglo-Americans came for adventure, to engage in the fur trade, or to settle, they soon established nuclear American communities.[44]

Symbolizing the new era in New Mexico was Fort William, or Bent's Fort, in present-day southern Colorado, built in the early 1830s on the Arkansas River by a Missouri entrepreneur, William Bent. Soon Bent's Fort became a major center of economic activity. Mountain trappers in the southern Rockies used it as a supply base. Bent, his brother Charles, and Ceran de St. Vrain traded with Indians all the way from northern Colorado to eastern Texas. Santa Fe traders made it a major stop on their trek to Santa Fe and back, picking up fur or buffalo skins. Not content with just trade, the Bents and their partners raised cattle and farmed.[45] Bent's Fort had its equivalent in Cal-

the remote Oregon Country. On the surface that agreement sounded fair and peaceable, but in 1821 the Hudson's Bay Company, now in sole command of the fur trade in Oregon, determined to keep American fur trappers out by pursuing a scorched-earth policy by trapping so many animals in the interior (present-day eastern Washington, Oregon, and Idaho) that Americans would not come into the area. The policy continued until 1845.[49]

But neither the Hudson's Bay Company nor the British government anticipated the impact on the fate of Oregon of a curious combination of American explorers, propagandists, missionaries, and settlers. Benjamin Franklin was to be proved right once again: a surfeit of people would overcome the authority of another country.

Even before Jedediah Smith made his historic trek eastward from Oregon to South Pass, Hall Jackson Kelley, a New England school teacher, had begun to praise the Oregon Country for its climate and fertility in a series of pamphlets and speeches. By 1829 Kelley had organized a society for "Encouraging the Settlement of the Oregon Territory."[50] Kelley's propaganda probably persuaded Nathaniel Wyeth, a Boston ice merchant, to go overland to Oregon in 1832 and 1834 to break into the fur trade and establish other commercial ventures.[51] Kelley's efforts were paralleled by those of Senator Benton, who had become an ardent advocate of American takeover of Oregon. Benton would employ the eloquence of the expansionist prophet William Gilpin and the reports of his son-in-law John Charles Frémont to realize his goal.[52]

Propagandists and merchants were soon joined by Jason and Daniel Lee, two Methodist missionaries, who, having read that a delegation of Pacific Northwest Indians had come to Saint Louis in 1831 seeking instruction in the "White Man's book of Heaven," were inspired

to go west to convert the Flatheads and Nez Percé.[53] Once in Oregon, Lee and his nephew chose to settle among the Chinook in the fertile, attractive Willamette Valley. Within the next two years new groups of missionaries appeared, among them Marcus Whitman and his wife, Narcissa, who established a mission at Walla Walla for the Cayuse.[54] Almost simultaneously Catholic missions were founded in the Pacific Northwest.[55]

Although the missionaries sought to save Indian souls, actually their most enduring impact was as propagandists who told Americans in the East of the attractions of Oregon. By 1838, only four years after the Lees had arrived, American settlers began migrating to Oregon. Traveling the Oregon Trail in covered wagons for a period of 150 to 180 days, they created the most familiar and classic image of pioneering in our national mythology [see 104]. All the ingredients were there: caravans of covered wagons starting out from jumping-off places in Missouri—such as Westport, Saint Joseph, and Independence—followed the Platte River Valley to the North Platte and the Sweetwater. Along the way the emigrants saw Fort Kearny, Ash Hollow, Courthouse Rock, Chimney Rock [7], Scotts Bluff, Fort Laramie and Independence Rock, South Pass, Fort Bridger, Fort Hall, the Snake River, and finally the Columbia before reaching the Willamette Valley.[56]

By 1845 some six thousand Americans had reached Oregon. Although Dr. John McLoughlin, the Hudson's Bay factor of Fort Vancouver, helped the Americans, they refused to accept British authority. In a series of meetings the Americans established their own government at Champoeg in 1843, declaring in a burst of enthusiasm that it was "strong without army or navy, rich without a treasury." Having practiced the right of popular sovereignty, they now began to petition the United

States to make them part of the Union.

The Oregon settlers certainly found Congress and the nation sympathetic to their pleas. After notably truculent demands and threats of war against Great Britain by the Tyler administration, in 1845 incoming president Polk quietly agreed to a boundary between American Oregon and British Columbia at the forty-ninth parallel.[57] Meanwhile the British, having exhausted the fur resources of the Oregon Country, voluntarily agreed to move their operations north to present-day British Columbia.

Once Oregon was annexed, national issues and local Indian problems delayed its organization as an American territory. Oregon also became part of the national debate over slavery. Proslavery forces argued that Oregon should be open to all comers, including citizens with slaves. In August 1846, however, Representative David Wilmot of Pennsylvania introduced a proviso that called for the exclusion of slavery from lands acquired from Mexico. The impasse over whether Oregon was to be slave or free lasted until 1849, when the region was finally organized as a territory.

Oregon came to represent many recurring themes in the western saga. Here was a Hudson's Bay fur-trapping, commercial frontier that Americans coveted. It was also a region still occupied by Indians whom American missionaries wanted to convert, yet violent confrontations were to occur between Indians and whites into the 1850s. With its excellent lands in the Willamette Valley, it was seen as the newest farmer paradise. Already skilled at political organization, the settlers soon created their own commonwealth, one excluding African- and native Americans. Indeed in the thirty years between the Cayuse War of 1847 and Chief Joseph's tragic retreat in 1877, Indian Americans continued to be displaced, hit by military action, and removed to reservations.[58]

7. Alfred Jacob Miller, *Chimney Rock,* 1858–60, watercolor on paper, 10¼ × 14¼ in. Walters Art Gallery, Baltimore.

In retrospect the darker side of American expansion was as present in Oregon as it had been in Texas.

By the time Monroe was nearing the end of his presidency in 1825, an area of western New York State, settled by old New England families, had undergone so many dramatic crises centering on religious doctrines and practices that it came to be known as the "Burnt-over District." Among those affected by competing religious beliefs was the Joseph Smith family, who had moved from Vermont to Palmyra, New York, in 1816. None was distressed more than a son, Joseph Smith, Jr., who in the 1820s is said to have experienced visions in which a set of golden plates was revealed to him containing the true history of the American Indians.[59] Eventually he published *The Book of Mormon* in 1830 in which he addressed many issues troubling religious people of the time. Smith had founded the Church of the Latter-Day Saints, which, like America itself, was soon moving westward, first to Kirtland, Ohio, then to Missouri, and finally to Nauvoo, Illinois, a city of ten thousand inhabitants. Smith entered politics and—given that the Mormons, as his followers were called, held the balance of power in state elections—declared himself a candidate for president in 1844. These acts of independence, his secret practice of plural marriage, and other controversies led to a series of legal actions and to his arrest. Confined to a jail in Carthage, Illinois, he was murdered there in 1844 by a mob.[60]

Brigham Young then assumed power and decided that the only salvation for his fellow Saints was to move west to the inhospitable Great Basin, where he hoped they would be left alone. Despite overwhelming hardships, between 1847 and 1849 Young managed to move the main body of the Mormons to Utah, found Salt Lake City, and create a theocracy called Deseret—"the land of the honeybee."[61]

This time American settlers had gone west not because of the "pull" factor of new lands but because of the "push" factor. The Mormons had been rejected by American mainline society, and for them the West represented exile. The theme of a free people moving west and taming the land to suit their needs is so strong that the Mormon story of exile and adaptation to a desert environment seems an anomaly. But beginning in the late 1820s the Cherokee were forcibly moved west by the Jackson administration, with the other "civilized" tribes soon to follow [see 158]. Their move too was because of push rather than pull.[62] When removal was resisted by the Seminoles in Florida, concerted military action, indeed a war lasting five years, finally led to the surrender and removal of that tribe.[63]

The Mexican War and Compromise of 1850

The Mexican War, so often seen as the climax of the spirit of Manifest Destiny, actually divided the country as few events had in the nation's first seventy years. Ostensibly it was fought because Mexico refused to acknowledge American annexation of Texas. That was hardly a basis for hostility, but when Mexican troops crossed the Rio Grande to attack American forces under General Zachary Taylor in the spring of 1846, President Polk said it was war "by act of Mexico."

The Mexican War was actually several wars. In the early stages Taylor won victories at Palo Alto and Buena Vista but bogged down in northern Mexico, fifteen hundred miles from Mexico City. Then Polk reluctantly authorized General Winfield Scott to land American troops at Vera Cruz and march them over Cortés's route to Mexico City and take the capital [see 85]. In a remarkably swift campaign Scott, using professionally trained West Point officers and volunteer troops, took Mexico City.[64] Meanwhile a bipronged interior war of sorts occurred when General Stephen W. Kearny occupied New Mexico and, leaving some forces in command, set out across Arizona to conquer California.[65] Kearny represented one interior operation; Colonel Alexander Doniphan of Missouri represented another. With a group of rambunctious, unruly volunteers, he fought the Battle of Brazito, took El Paso and Chihuahua City, and, declaring his work completed, said he was going home to "Sarah Jane and the girls."[66]

The coming of the Mexico War in California was almost as fragmented as the larger conflict. Its unfolding has all the elements of a modern covert action. The most controversial protagonist was John Charles Frémont, who was on his third exploring expedition in the West in 1845, and although a visit to California was not part of his official itinerary, nevertheless he went there in the winter of 1845–46 [8]. The California authorities viewed him and his large armed company with suspicion and ordered them to leave. Frémont moved north to Oregon, where he was overtaken by Lieutenant Archibald Gillespie with messages from Washington that war with Mexico was imminent. Frémont then retraced his steps to California, where he soon joined a group of Americans who were rebelling against Mexico under a crude banner dubbed the "Bear Flag." In effect, Frémont and the Bear Flag rebels seized northern California, while Commodores John D. Sloat and Robert F. Stockton captured the California coastal towns.[67]

General Kearny, who had hoped to be the conqueror of California, learned of Frémont's and Stockton's victories while still crossing Arizona. Then to his further chagrin, southern California not only rose in rebellion against Stockton and drove the Americans from Los Angeles, a group of mounted California lancers intercepted and attacked Kearny and his men at San Pascual. Only when Kearny's battered soldiers and Stockton's marines combined forces did the Americans finally carry the day in the war for California.

Then a tragicomic episode ensued. Stockton sailed away to return to the East Coast to receive the plaudits of eastern Americans as the "conqueror" of California. He left Frémont in charge, but since General Kearny outranked him, the latter assumed the role of commander of California. Frémont stubbornly resisted and was consequently court-martialed for insubordination and sent back to Washington.[68]

On a much larger scale there was also squabbling among the victors over the spoils of the newly acquired Mexican cession, for by the Treaty of Guadalupe Hidalgo, the United States acquired Arizona, California, Nevada, New Mexico, Utah, and part of Colorado and

8. William S. Jewett, *John Charles Frémont,* undated, oil on panel, 14⅞ × 11 in. National Portrait Gallery, Smithsonian Institution, Washington, D.C.

Texas. In fact, the country experienced such a sectional crisis about the status of its new possessions, as to whether they be slave or free, that it took the diplomacy of Calhoun, Clay, Webster, and young Stephen A. Douglas to produce the Compromise of 1850. By that act California was admitted as a free state, New Mexico and Utah were organized as territories with no real reference to slavery, Texas land claims and debts were settled, and, most controversial of all, a strong fugitive slave act was passed.[69]

For many historians, the Mexican War and the Compromise of 1850 were but preludes to civil war, and their arguments are supported by the fact that within four years the nation was again bitterly divided—this time over whether Kansas and Nebraska should be organized as slave or free territories. The result was violence in "Bleeding" Kansas, in which John Brown, Free-Soil advocates, and proslavery forces from Missouri were all guilty of murder and shootings.[70]

The California Gold Rush

In January 1848 a carpenter named James Wilson Marshall, who was constructing a sawmill at Coloma, California, for his employer, John Sutter, found flecks of gold in the millrace. After some initial skepticism, it was soon realized that gold in vast quantities existed in California's streams. The resulting gold rush brought ninety thousand persons to the region in 1849 and two hundred thousand more over the next decade [9].[71] Almost overnight California became a state and San Francisco a major port city. Further, the thousands who came so overwhelmed the Hispanic and Indian peoples of California that it seemed a very American state from the start.

9. Nathaniel Currier and James Ives, *The Way They Go to California,* 1849, hand-colored lithograph, 10¼ × 17¼ in. The Oakland Museum, California; Founders Fund.

California created an impressive new set of images associated with the West. Jefferson's agrarian empire was now overwhelmed by the belief that the West was Eldorado—a fabulous mineral empire awaiting discovery and exploitation [see 186]. Over the next half century intrepid prospectors managed to find gold and silver in Nevada and Colorado between 1859 and 1860, in Idaho and Montana in the 1860s, in Tombstone, Arizona, and the Black Hills of Dakota Territory in the 1870s, and in Alaska in the 1890s.[72] To the pioneers, farmers, and mountain guides were now added the prospectors.

Agriculture and ranching also boomed in California [see 197], along with a growing American appreciation of a wonderful climate; an infinitely varied landscape, ranging from fertile seacoast to desert to the Sierra; and fantastic natural scenery, of which Yosemite was only the most spectacular example.

As the largest city west of Saint Louis, San Francisco not only marked the coming of an urban culture to the Far West but also the rise of a regional imperial city that soon dominated the Far West economically [see 178].[73] In time, other urban oases—such as Portland, Denver, Seattle, Salt Lake City, Los Angeles, and Phoenix—or mining centers—like Virginia City, Nevada, or Butte, Montana—would be seen as much a part of the West as ranches and mines.

The California gold rush also questioned the efficiency of communication between the East and Far West. Entrepreneurs had dreamed and talked of a transcontinental railroad ever since Asa Whitney proposed one in 1844. Not only did Californians want faster transportation, various regions of the country competed to have the line benefit their section. Thus southerners advocated a railroad running from New Orleans to San Diego, the middle South hoped for a line from Memphis; and Saint Louis believed it should be the starting point for a central overland route. But the most ag-

gressive and imaginative advocate was Chicago, whose interests were represented by the dynamic and ambitious Senator Douglas.

Unable to agree on a single route, Congress finally compromised by authorizing four overland railroad surveys on the thirty-second, thirty-fifth, forty-second, and forty-seventh parallels. Headed by competent army topographical engineers, whose parties included artists and photographers, they contributed not only a wealth of new information about the western terrain but provided pictures of little-known areas [see 99]. Painting, mapping, sketching, and photographing the West were great accomplishments in nineteenth-century America, achieved as much by official government parties as by private individuals for policy and political reasons rather than for merely scientific and aesthetic concerns.[74]

Meanwhile Californians agitated for mail and passenger service. Finally, in 1857, the Butterfield Overland Mail Company was inaugurated, which promised to deliver mail from the Mississippi Valley to San Francisco in fewer than twenty-five days. Reflecting the strong southern influence in Congress and the Buchanan administration, the route went southwestward across the Great Plains, New Mexico, and Arizona to southern California and then turned north to San Francisco. As impressive and heroic as this "swing route" was, relatively few passengers and small amounts of mail reached San Francisco by overland stage before the Civil War. Indeed packet boats to the isthmus and their Pacific equivalent carried ten times more mail and passengers each month than did the Butterfield Overland. Even the romantic Pony Express, inaugurated in 1860 to deliver mail to California in ten days, proved impractical, and it was made obsolete when the telegraph joined the East and West in October 1861.[75]

Not until 1869 would the Union Pacific

and Central Pacific finally connect California to Omaha, Chicago, and the East [10], and another two decades would elapse before the other transcontinental lines were completed.[76]

Civil War and Indian War

The West played only a small role in the Civil War, yet the Lincoln government determined to keep the region in the Union and the Confederacy schemed to win it over, hoping to seize the gold regions in Colorado, Nevada, and even California.

Lincoln took the advantage when he made certain that the governments of the western territories were loyal to the Union. Then he adopted the policy of having the western areas defend themselves largely through local volun-

10. Andrew Joseph Russell, *Dodge and Montague Shake [Golden Spike Ceremony],* 1869, photograph from glass-plate negative. The Oakland Museum History Department, California.

teer regiments. He also tried to keep open central overland stage and telegraph routes to California.[77] Even so, the West was troubled by tension and conflict. In the fall of 1861 Texan forces occupied southern New Mexico and Arizona, creating the confederate Territory of Arizona. Under General Henry H. Sibley, Confederate soldiers defeated Union troops at Val Verde, occupied Santa Fe, and were on their way to gold-rich Colorado before they were defeated by hastily assembled loyal troops at the Battle of Gloreta Pass in 1863 and forced to retreat. The southern strategies to seize Colorado had failed.[78]

In contrast to the federal government's success in keeping the white West loyal, its relations with Indian tribes precipitated confrontations along a thousand-mile front. In western Minnesota the Santee Sioux had been so badly mistreated by settlers and Indian agents that they rose in rebellion in the so-called War of the Outbreak, only to be ruthlessly tracked down and some thirty-nine Indian leaders executed at a mass hanging at Mankato, Minnesota, in 1862 [11].[79]

On the Great Plains relations between white miners and settlers and Indians precipitated a raiding and shooting war. The tragic climax came when Colorado volunteers, ignor-

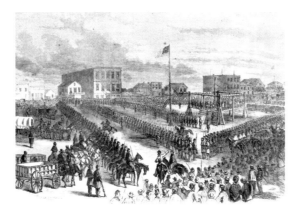

11. Unidentified artist, *Mass Hanging at Mankato, Minnesota, December 26, 1862.* From *Leslie's Illustrated Newspaper,* January 24, 1863, 285. Enoch Pratt Free Library, Baltimore.

ing sincere peace gestures by Cheyenne peoples under Chief Black Kettle, massacred more than two hundred Indian men, women, and children at Sand Creek in 1864.[80]

Meanwhile, in 1863, under the order of General James H. Carleton, Kit Carson and federal troops rounded up hostile Navaho tribespeople and marched them three hundred miles eastward to a prison-reservation on the Pecos River. After many deaths from illness and suffering near starvation, the Navaho were finally allowed to return to the Four Corners area in 1868.[81]

The Civil War ended in 1865, but the western Indian conflicts continued until 1868, when Congress finally sent out "peace commissions" to negotiate with the native Americans. Then, after Ulysses S. Grant became president in 1869, he inaugurated a "peace policy." Grant's idea was a variation of Jefferson's: civilize the Indians by placing them on reservations, where they would be instructed in Christianity and in white farming practices [see 158]. He also asked that the agents appointed be recommended by religious groups.[82]

The peace policy did not work, and new conflicts arose between the Apache and whites in Arizona and the Sioux and invading prospectors in the Black Hills. In these same years there was no peace on the southern plains, for a brutal war of attrition was fought in the Red River area in 1874–75 between whites, Comanches, and Kiowas.[83] In 1876 the Sioux fought and defeated General George Crook at Rosebud and General George Armstrong Custer at the Battle of the Little Bighorn.[84] Historians have called the fights after 1876 a mopping-up process, but resistance of heroic nature continued in 1877, when Chief Joseph of the Nez Percé marched a thousand miles trying to escape pursuing white troopers [12].[85]

During the 1880s one of the last dramatic pursuits occurred in Arizona, when Apache

warrior Geronimo finally surrendered to federal troops under General Nelson A. Miles, thereby effectively ending Apache resistance. A last military showdown came in 1890, when the Oglalla Sioux, having embraced the millennial Ghost Dance Movement, were seen as threatening the peace of the South Dakota frontier. In a series of needless confrontations, compounded by white fear and misunderstanding, shooting broke out. Among those killed were Sitting Bull and Big Foot. Black Elk, holy man of the Oglalla Sioux, later declared that at the Battle of Wounded Knee the nation's hoop was broken and the old Indian life was no more.[86]

Black Elk was speaking of more than military defeat. By the 1870s professional and amateur buffalo hunters had killed off the millions of buffalo [13]—the major food source of the Plains Indians, so that they now had to live on rations doled out at the reservations. Also in the 1870s many Quakers argued that the great enemy of peace and assimilation was tribalism.

They petitioned Congress to end the authority of the chiefs and the tribes themselves and to refuse further treaty negotiations—arguing that the Indians were not subordinate or domestic nations but individuals. A catch phrase of the time was "kill the tribe and save the individual."[87]

Finally the process toward assimilation took another giant step in 1887, when Senator Henry Dawes of Massachusetts persuaded Congress to pass the Severalty Act by which Indians were to be allotted individual plots of land, or homesteads, on which to live and farm. All surplus lands would be thrown open to whites for homesteading or purchase.[88] The dispiriting prospect of giving up an older way of life led the Sioux to embrace the Ghost Dance religion and dream that the time was near when whites would disappear and the Indians would have their lands and their culture restored to them.

The land-allotment policy proceeded apace during the 1890s. The Sioux lost more than

12. Olin Levi Warner, *Joseph, Chief of the Nez Percé,* 1889, bronze, diameter 7⅝ in. National Museum of American Art, Smithsonian Institution, Washington, D.C.; gift of Alison Warner Waterman in memory of her mother, Frances D. Warner.

13. Unidentified photographer, *Buffalo Hides at Dodge City,* circa 1874, albumen print, 4½ × 6¼ in. Kansas State Historical Society, Topeka.

eleven million acres. In the Oklahoma land runs of 1889, 1893, and thereafter the Five Civilized Tribes also lost millions of acres. The forcing of severalty on tribes continued under Theodore Roosevelt, and a new turn of the screw occurred when Congress passed a law repealing a previous stipulation that no Indian could sell an allotment for twenty-five years. Indeed after 1906 "competency commissions" toured Indian areas declaring certain Indians competent to sell their lands. By these incredibly greedy, self-serving acts, Indian Americans lost some eighty-seven million more acres, with the result that by the 1920s most Indians were living in extreme poverty on marginal lands. Thirty years after the Dawes Act and Wounded Knee the Indians were in a worse state psychologically, physically, and economically than they had ever been before.[89]

The End of the Dream

In the thirty years between 1870 and 1900 two more Wests arose to capture the imagination of the nation and indeed that of the world. The first was the coming of open-range ranching to the whole of the West but especially to Texas and the Great Plains. During the Civil War, with no market to drain off their numbers, cattle had multiplied by the tens of thousands in Texas. Since the buffalo herds were shrinking, cattle could also expand westward and northward into short-grass country. In 1867 Colonel Joseph G. McCoy persuaded Texans to drive their herds from Texas to railheads in Kansas, where they could be shipped to Chicago to meatpackers, to the northern grasslands of Montana and Wyoming for fattening, or to Indian reservations for food.[90]

Between 1867 and 1880 the seemingly romantic "long drives" over such famous trails as the Chisholm Trail helped create the most

enduring western hero—the cowboy. Although first viewed as a rough youth prone to violence, the cowboy soon came to represent a free, honorable, adventurous person, whose skill and bravery brought the herds safely to the cattle towns of Abilene, Caldwell, and Dodge City. His ability as a rider and talents with a rope found formal expression in contests, rodeos, and Wild West shows. As no other western figure, real or mythic, the cowboy captured the fancy of the American public.[91] In fact, ranching itself seized the imagination of English and Scottish investors in the 1870s and 1880s, so much so that many of the great spreads were actually owned by foreign firms.

Open-range ranching declined dramatically after a severe blizzard in 1886–87 killed many thousands of cattle. Falling prices and overgrazing, combined with quarantine laws designed to keep diseased Texas cattle from moving into Kansas and Plains settlers bent on farming rather than ranching, forced a transition to closed-range ranching [see 191 and 193]. After 1890 cattle were behind barbed-wire fences and annual hay crops were planted for their feed. But the cattle industry continued to be a major feature of the western economy and with it both the real and mythic cowboy lived on.

The nostalgia for the era of the open range was expressed in many ways: in folk songs and ballads, in verse by such poets as Badger Clark, in novels by Andy Adams, Zane Grey, Harold Bell Wright, and many others. None was more successful or more enduring, however, than Owen Wister, an aristocratic Philadelphian who graduated from Harvard at a time when Theodore Roosevelt was there. His novel *The Virginian* (1902) was not only a bestseller but was made into a play and eventually into both a movie and television series.[92]

Fictional cowboy images were reinforced

by the actual memoirs of such old trail drivers as Teddy Blue Abbott and Charles Siringo.[93] In time, their adventures were depicted on canvas by Frederick Remington, Charles Russell, and many other artists.[94] Reinforcing all these was a vast outpouring of pulp magazines featuring western stories and an emerging film genre that was distinctively American. There was also a persistence of western clothing, boots, and life-styles that has lasted to the present. The cowboy stereotype was further reinforced by the fact that in the Spanish-American War western cavalry units from Arizona and New Mexico joined the army as Rough Riders and in some cases fought with Theodore Roosevelt in his charge up San Juan Hill.[95]

Seldom have so many varied and talented persons combined to perpetuate the image of the West as America: writers and publishers, artists and cowboys, scholars and political leaders. The frontier may have been closed in 1890, but when Theodore Roosevelt became president in 1901, he was the symbol of a new American West, whose psychological influence was incredibly powerful [14].

Engineers, Preservationists, and Politicians

One of the most impressive definers of the western landscape in the late nineteenth century was John Wesley Powell, a veteran of the Civil War who in 1862 lost his lower arm at the Battle of Shiloh. In 1865 he returned to civilian life to teach science in various Illinois colleges. Always devoted to botanical and geological fieldwork, in 1867 he took his students to the Rocky Mountains. Powell was an amateur scientist, but by 1869 his expertise and knowledge of geology was so impressive that Congress funded a trip down the Green and Colorado rivers under his aegis. It took his small party of ten persons three months to get through the Grand Canyon and down the Colorado. As the first American to accomplish such a daring feat, Powell was seen as a romantic latter-day explorer.[96] This was especially the case after a second trip down the Colorado in 1871, this time accompanied by an enthusiastic young artist, Frederick S. Dellenbaugh, who painted the first pictures of the Grand Canyon. Dellenbaugh also wrote an exciting account of the trip in his book *A Canyon Voyage* (1908). Photographers E. O. Beaman and John K. Hillers were also on that historic journey [see 218]. Soon other artists and photographers—among them Albert Bierstadt, William H. Jackson, Thomas Moran—were depicting the most

14. Truman Ward Ingersoll, *Theodore Roosevelt*, 1885, photograph. Theodore Roosevelt Collection, Harvard College Library, Cambridge, Massachusetts.

spectacular landforms in the entire West [see 220].[97]

Powell's own chief aim in life was to establish a reputation as a serious scientific expert on the geology of the West. Again supported by government funds, Powell on his 1871 trip studied the arid, desiccated Colorado Plateau. Within a few years what came to be called the Powell survey began to produce much new information about western landforms. By 1879 Powell had so ingratiated himself with Congress that he persuaded it to consolidate several competing surveys into the United States Geological Survey. After Clarence King had served as its head for a year, Powell became its director, holding that position for the next thirteen years.[98]

However much one must praise Powell for his many accomplishments (he also compiled a remarkable ethnographic and linguistic survey of Indian languages), like Thomas Jefferson, he had a scheme for taming the West by using arid lands efficiently to benefit society and preserve agrarian values. Powell's theory of mastery through adaptation was echoed a generation later by Gifford Pinchot, Theodore Roosevelt's vigorous chief of the United States Forestry Service and reputed coiner of the term *conservation,* referring to the environment. A Yale graduate who had studied European forestry systems in France, Pinchot believed that by conserving natural resources in a rational, scientific way one could not only sustain the resources but through wise use provide the greatest good for the largest number of people.[99] In their joint efforts to set aside and preserve American forests and mineral regions Pinchot and Roosevelt were creating an "engineered" West as had Powell.

Another geologist who defined the West in the late nineteenth century was Clarence King, also of the Geological Survey. In 1872 King wrote a series of sketches published under

the title *Mountaineering in the Sierra Nevada.*[100] Without fully realizing what he was doing, King described what it meant to be a wilderness hiker [15]. Possessed of a fine aesthetic and personal appreciation of truly wild nature, he wrote an account that stood in contrast to the contemplative, even passive approach to western scenery and sublime natural wonders promoted by railroads and tourist agencies. Similarly Bierstadt's awe-inspiring canvases and Moran's depictions of Yellowstone and the Grand Canyon for enthusiastic clients and viewers also invited one to view and contemplate rather than act.

King's sense of joy and engagement took a very different form in John Muir, who had first visited Yosemite Valley in 1868 as a young man and who had remained in Califor-

15. Andrew Joseph Russell [also attributed to Timothy O'Sullivan], *Clarence King on Mountainside,* circa 1868, albumen print, 8¾ x 11 in. Bancroft Library, University of California, Berkeley.

nia for the rest of his life to experience nature there. For Muir, the wilderness, as represented by Yosemite and the Sierra Nevada, which he called "the Range of Light," was a holy place, where one could hike, camp, and contemplate in such a way as to realize happiness, health (both mental and physical), and even religious fulfillment.[101]

Muir eventually became the leader of a wilderness movement—which evolved into the Sierra Club—that sought to preserve natural areas from exploitation or even from the impact to human beings. Inevitably the ideas of Muir and Pinchot would clash, as they did when the federal government and the city of San Francisco sought to turn the Hetch Hetchy Valley, a part of Yosemite, into a reservoir to supply San Francisco with much needed water. A public-policy debate of the most profound sort about which "West" America would choose began in the Progressive era and continues today.[102]

Standing midway between Muir and Pinchot was Theodore Roosevelt, who himself had a deep sense of foreboding that without a frontier or wilderness experience, Americans would lose their spirit and drive—indeed their distinctive national character. Thus he promoted both the hunting life—a Darwinian survival rite—and the preservation of national forests and the enactment of game-protection laws. While endorsing Pinchot's idea of sustained yield and Powell's intelligent land use, he somehow managed to be both the symbol of a corporate, industrial, urban America and an America that harked back to an older, western frontier-oriented nation.[103] Roosevelt's close friendships with the realist Pinchot on the one hand and with the nostalgic Remington and Wister on the other were full of contradictions.

One final twentieth-century interpreter of the West as America deserves comment. In 1907 John Collier, a Georgia-born social worker employed at the People's Institute, a branch of the Cooper-Union in New York, became convinced that Americans were losing a sense of community as they grappled with the fragmenting realities of a new industrial society. Collier was startled to realize that the Italian immigrants with whom he worked in an effort to Americanize them possessed a more satisfying sense of community than did his fellow Americans. Later Collier found an even more positive sense of community in the villages of the Pueblo of New Mexico.[104] From Collier's findings and as a result of his later crusade to protect traditional Indian life-styles and lands, he brought Americans to a new appreciation of the values of another culture in their midst.

Collier's respect for native Americans and their cultures was the first step toward an eventual recognition that America itself was a persistently multiracial, multicultural country and nowhere more so than in the West, where African, Asian, Indian, and Hispanic Americans lived amid citizens only one generation away from Great Britain, Scandinavia, and the rest of Europe. In 1920 that pluralistic West was not recognized, so strong was the myth of an older Anglo America. But the West was also, as it always had been, a place to project wishes and dreams, a symbol of the unknown and of the future, when a new generation of Americans would redefine the West and in so doing reveal themselves and their own ideologies.

Notes

1. Archibald MacLeish, "American Letter," in *New Found Land: Fourteen Poems* (Boston: Houghton Mifflin, 1930).

2. James H. Hutson, "Benjamin Franklin," in Howard R. Lamar, ed., *Readers' Encyclopedia of the American West* (New York: Crowell, 1977) (hereafter cited as *REAW*), 401–4.

3. *REAW*, 402.

4. Thomas Jefferson's interest in Louisiana dated to his years as United States minister to France. By 1792, as secretary of state, he wanted the port of New Orleans and hoped a weak Spain rather than a strong Britain would govern Louisiana (Dumas Malone, *Jefferson and the Rights of Man* [Boston: Little, Brown, 1951], 312–13, 411). The purchase of Louisiana is detailed in Malone, *Jefferson the President*, 284–310.

5. "James Harrod," in *REAW*, 488.

6. Merrill Jensen, *The New Nation: A History of the United States during the Confederation* (New York: Knopf, 1950); see also Harry Ammon, *James Monroe: Quest for National Identity* (New York: McGraw Hill, 1971).

7. A convenient overview of the territorial system is to be found in Lamar, *Far Southwest*, 7–20.

8. Prucha, *American Indian Policy in the Formative Years*.

9. Sheehan, *Seeds of Extinction*; see also Thomas D. Clark and John D. W. Guice, *Frontiers in Conflict: The Old Southwest, 1795–1830* (Albuquerque: University of New Mexico Press, 1989), 28–49. Jefferson's views are also summarized in Malone, *Jefferson the President*, 273–75.

10. Malone, *Jefferson the President*, 233–53; see also Satz, *Indian Policy*; and White, *Roots of Dependency*.

11. Malone, *Jefferson the President*, 275–76.

12. Jefferson's ideas are brilliantly analyzed in Smith, *Virgin Land*, 15–50; see also Allen, *Passage through the Garden*; and Goetzmann, *Exploration and Empire*, 5–6. Lewis and Clark's expedition is detailed in Reuben G. Thwaites, ed., *Original Journals of the Lewis and Clark Expedition, 1804–6* (New York: Dodd, Mead, 1904–5).

13. Paul C. Phillips and J. W. Smurr, *The Fur Trade* (Norman: University of Oklahoma Press, 1961).

14. Allen, *Passage through the Garden*, 267, 367–68, 394–98.

15. Gary B. Moulton, ed., *Atlas of the Lewis and Clark Expedition* (Lincoln: University of Nebraska Press, 1983); see also idem, *The Journals of the Lewis and Clark Expedition* (Lincoln: University of Nebraska Press, 1986–88).

16. W. Eugene Hollon, *The Lost Pathfinder: Zebulon Montgomery Pike* (Norman: University of Oklahoma Press, 1949); and Donald M. Jackson, ed., *The Journals of Zebulon Montgomery Pike* (Norman: University of Oklahoma Press, 1966).

17. Malone, *Jefferson the President*, 269–70, 299–301.

18. Richard W. Barness, "John C. Calhoun and the Military Establishment, 1817–1825," *Wisconsin Magazine of History* 50 (Autumn 1966); Samuel F. Bemis, *John Quincy Adams and the Foundations of American Foreign Policy* (New York: Knopf, 1949–56); and Charles M. Wiltse, *John C. Calhoun* (Indianapolis: Bobbs-Merrill, 1944–51).

19. Billington, *Westward Expansion* (1982 ed.), 290–92; and Goetzmann, *Exploration and Empire*, 58–59.

20. Stephen H. Long, "Voyage in a Six-Oared Skiff to the Falls of Saint Anthony in 1817," *Collections of the Minnesota Historical Society* 1 (1860–61; reprinted 1889): 9–88.

21. The Yellowstone expedition is described in Hiram M. Chittenden, *A History of the American Fur Trade of the Far West* (Stanford, Calif.: Stanford University Press, 1954), 2:562–87.

22. James, *Account of an Expedition*.

23. John F. McDermott, "Samuel Seymour: Pioneer Artist of the Plains and Rockies," in *Smithsonian Report for 1950* (Washington, D.C.: Smithsonian Institution, 1951), 497–509.

24. Jessie J. Poesch, *Titian Ramsay Peale, 1799–1885, and His Journals of the Wilkes Expedition* (Philadelphia: American Philosophical Society, 1961).

25. See James, *Account of an Expedition* 2:361.

26. Prucha, *American Indian Policy in the Formative Years*; see also Dale Van Every, *Disinherited: The Lost Birthright of the American Indians* (New York: Morrow, 1966).

27. White, *Roots of Dependency*.

28. See James Fenimore Cooper, *The Prairie: A Tale* (1827; Albany: State University of New York Press, 1985), xv–xxxiii.

29. Dexter Perkins, *A History of the Monroe Doctrine* (Boston: Little, Brown, 1955).

30. Ora B. Peake, *A History of the United States Indian Factory System, 1795–1822* (Denver: Sage, 1954).

31. Don Berry, *A Majority of Scoundrels: An Informal History of the Rocky Mountain Fur Company* (New York: Harper, 1961); William E. Foley and C. David Rice, *The First Chouteaus: River Barons of Early Saint Louis* (Urbana: University of Illinois Press, 1983); Kenneth Porter, *John Jacob Astor: Business Man* (Cambridge, Mass.: Harvard University Press, 1931); and Dale L. Morgan, ed., *The West of William H. Ashley* (Denver: Old West Publishing, 1964).

32. Goetzmann, *Exploration and Empire,* 34ff; and Dale L. Morgan, *Jedediah Smith and the Opening of the West* (Indianapolis: Bobbs-Merrill, 1953), 78–92. Actually South Pass was discovered by returning Astorians in 1814, but the discovery was not shared at the time.

33. Jackson and Spence, *Expeditions of Frémont.*

34. Peter Antelyes, *Tales of Adventurous Enterprise: Washington Irving and the Poetics of Western Expansion* (New York: Columbia University Press, 1990), especially 1–44.

35. Eugene Barker, *The Life of Stephen F. Austin, Founder of Texas, 1793–1836* (1926; Austin: University of Texas Press, 1985).

36. T. R. Fehrenbach, *Lone Star: A History of Texas and the Texans* (New York: Macmillan, 1968); Llerena Friend, *Sam Houston: The Great Designer* (Austin: University of Texas Press, 1954); and Rupert N. Richardson et al., *Texas: The Lone Star State* (New York: Prentice-Hall, 1943).

37. Merk, *Manifest Destiny,* 61–88; see also idem, *Fruits of Propaganda in the Tyler Administration* (Cambridge, Mass.: Harvard University Press, 1971); and Thomas Hietala, *Manifest Design: Anxious Aggrandizement in Late Jacksonian America* (Ithaca, N.Y.: Cornell University Press, 1985).

38. Seymour V. Conner and Odie B. Faulk, *North America Divided: The Mexican War, 1846–1848* (New York: Oxford University Press, 1971); and David M. Potter, *The Impending Crisis, 1848–1861*

(New York: Harper & Row, 1976).

39. Moorhead, *New Mexico's Royal Road;* and Joan Myers and Marc Simmons, *Along the Santa Fe Trail* (Albuquerque: University of New Mexico Press, 1986).

40. Moorhead, *New Mexico's Royal Road.*

41. The Santa Fe Trail experience is succinctly summarized by Mark Simmons, in *REAW,* 1084–85.

42. Emmett M. Essin III, "Mule," in *REAW,* 780–82.

43. William N. Chambers, *Old Bullion Benton: Senator from the New West: Thomas Hart Benton, 1782–1858* (Boston: Little, Brown, 1956).

44. Lamar, *Far Southwest,* 36–55, 56–82.

45. David Lavender, *Bent's Fort* (Garden City, N.Y.: Doubleday, 1954).

46. Oscar Lewis, *Sutter's Fort: Gateway to the Gold Fields* (Englewood Cliffs, N.J.: Prentice-Hall, 1966).

47. Lamar, *Far Southwest,* 50–52.

48. Josiah Gregg, *Commerce of the Prairies* (1844; Norman: University of Oklahoma Press, 1954).

49. Frederick Merk, *Fur Trade and Empire: George Simpson's Journal* (Cambridge, Mass.: Harvard University Press, 1931).

50. "Hall J. Kelley," in *REAW;* see also Fred W. Powell, *Hall Jackson Kelley: Prophet of Oregon* (Portland, Oreg.: Ivy Press, 1917), 614.

51. Goetzmann, *Exploration and Empire,* 160–68.

52. William Gilpin wrote editorials in the *Missouri Argus* in support of Benton, journeyed to Oregon in 1854 with John Charles Frémont, and was to participate in the Mexican War (see Karnes, *Gilpin*). Frémont's five expeditions west all served the purposes of his father-in-law's intense desire to take Oregon and other parts of the West (see Jackson and Spence, *Expeditions of Frémont*).

53. Alvin M. Josephy, Jr., *The Nez Percé Indians and the Opening of the Northwest* (New Haven: Yale University Press, 1965), 98–101; and Robert J. Loewenberg, *Equality on the Oregon Frontier: Jason Lee and the Methodist Mission, 1834–43* (Seattle: University of Washington Press, 1976), 78.

54. Nard Jones, *The Great Command: The Story of Marcus and Narcissa Whitman and the Oregon Country Pioneers* (Boston: Little, Brown, 1959).

55. Robert Ignatius Burns, *The Jesuits and the In-*

dian Wars of the Northwest (New Haven: Yale University Press, 1966), 42–48.

56. Jay Monathan, *The Overland Trail* (Indianapolis: Bobbs-Merrill, 1947); and Unruh, *Plains Across.*

57. Frederick Merk, *The Oregon Question: Essays in Anglo-American Diplomacy and Politics* (Cambridge, Mass.: Harvard University Press, 1967).

58. Utley, *Indian Frontier.*

59. Richard Bushman, *Joseph Smith and the Beginnings of Mormonism* (Urbana: University of Illinois Press, 1984).

60. Fawn Brodie, *No Man Knows My History: The Life of Joseph Smith, Mormon Prophet* (New York: Knopf, 1971).

61. Leonard J. Arrington, *Brigham Young: American Moses* (New York: Knopf, 1985), see especially chaps. 9–12.

62. Grant Foreman, *The Five Civilized Tribes* (Norman: University of Oklahoma Press, 1934).

63. Edwin C. McReynolds, *The Seminoles* (Norman: University of Oklahoma Press, 1957).

64. A brief account of the war is Otis A. Singletary, *The Mexican War* (Chicago: University of Chicago Press, 1960). The best available biography of Winfield Scott is Arthur D. H. Smith, *Old Fuss and Feathers: The Life of Winfield Scott* (New York: Greystone, 1937).

65. Dwight L. Clarke, *Stephen Watts Kearny* (Norman: University of Oklahoma Press, 1961).

66. John T. Hughes, *Doniphan's Expedition: An Account of the Conquest of New Mexico* (1914; Chicago: Rio Grande, 1962).

67. Bernard DeVoto, *The Year of Decision, 1846* (1942; Boston: Houghton Mifflin, 1984), 234–42, 296–99.

68. Ibid., 500–509.

69. Holman Hamilton, *Prologue to Conflict: The Crisis and Compromise of 1850* (Lexington: University of Kentucky Press, 1954).

70. Eugene H. Berwanger, *The Frontier against Slavery: Western Anti-Negro Prejudice and the Slavery Extension Controversy* (Urbana: University of Illinois Press, 1967); James C. Malin, *John Brown and the Legend of Fifty-Six* (Philadelphia: American Philosophical Society, 1942).

71. Paul, *California Gold.*

72. Idem, *Mining Frontiers.*

73. A general urban history of the West is yet to be written but see Gunther P. Barth, *Instant Cities: Urbanization and the Rise of San Francisco and Denver* (New York: Oxford University Press, 1975); Robert Fogelson, *The Fragmented Metropolis: Los Angeles, 1850–1930* (Cambridge, Mass.: Harvard University Press, 1967); and Laurence Larsen, *The Urban West at the End of the Frontier* (Lawrence: Regents Press of Kansas, 1978).

74. See, for example, "Images of Progress: The Camera Becomes Part of Western Exploration," in Goetzmann, *Exploration and Empire,* 603–48.

75. Roscoe Conkling and Margaret Conkling, *The Butterfield Overland Mail* (Glendale, Calif.: Clark, 1947); and William T. Jackson, *Wagon Roads West* (New Haven: Yale University Press, 1965).

76. Oscar O. Winther, *The Transportation Frontier, Trans-Mississippi West, 1865–1890* (New York: Holt, Rinehart, & Winston, 1964).

77. Max L. Heyman, "Civil War," in *REAW,* contains a succinct account of Lincoln's policy for the West.

78. Lamar, *Far Southwest,* 109–35.

79. Utley, *Indian Frontier,* 76–81.

80. Lamar, *Far Southwest,* 240–51.

81. Ibid., 124–30.

82. P. Richard Metcalf, "Peace Policy," in *REAW,* 897–900.

83. Wooster, *Military and United States Indian Policy,* 154–59.

84. Ibid., 161–67; and Robert M. Utley, *Cavalier in Buckskin: George Armstrong Custer and the Western Military Frontier* (Norman: University of Oklahoma Press, 1988).

85. Wooster, *Military and United States Indian Policy,* 174–78.

86. Robert M. Utley, *The Last Days of the Sioux Nation* (New Haven: Yale University Press, 1963).

87. Henry E. Fritz, *The Movement for Indian Assimilation, 1860–1890* (Philadelphia: University of Pennsylvania Press, 1963).

88. Fred Nicklason, "Dawes Severalty Act," in *REAW,* 290.

89. W. T. Hagan, *American Indians* (Chicago: University of Chicago Press, 1961), 121–50; and Fred E. Hoxie, *A Final Promise: The Campaign to Assimilate the Indians, 1880–1920* (Lincoln: University of Nebraska Press, 1984).

90. Everett Edward Dale, *The Range Cattle Industry: Ranching on the Great Plains, 1865–1925* (Norman: University of Oklahoma Press, 1960); Robert R. Dykstra, *The Cattle Towns* (New York: Knopf, 1968); and Jimmy M. Skaggs, *Prime Cut: Livestock Raising and Meatpacking in the United States, 1607–1983* (College Station: Texas A & M University Press, 1986).

91. Howard R. Lamar, "The Cowboys," in Brooklyn Museum, *Buffalo Bill and the Wild West,* 57–67.

92. All these themes are discussed in detail in White, *Eastern Establishment and the Western Experience;* but see also Darwin Payne, *Owen Wister: Chronicles of the West, Gentleman of the East* (Dallas: Southern Methodist University Press, 1985); and Ben M. Vorpahl, *My Dear Wister: The Frederic Remington-Owen Wister Letters* (Palo Alto: American West Publishing, 1972).

93. Charles A. Siringo, *A Texas Cowboy* (Lincoln: University of Nebraska Press, 1966).

94. Ben M. Vorpahl, *Frederic Remington and the West: With the Eye of the Mind* (Austin: University of Texas Press, 1978).

95. The imperial implications of both Buffalo Bill and of the Rough Riders are brilliantly analyzed by Slotkin in Brooklyn Museum, *Buffalo Bill and the Wild West,* 27–44.

96. Darrah, *Powell of the Colorado;* Goetzmann, *Exploration and Empire,* 530–76; Stegner, *Beyond the Hundredth Meridian.*

97. The activities of western photographers are summarized in *REAW,* 909–12.

98. Darrah, *Powell of the Colorado.*

99. Martin Fausold, *Gifford Pinchot: Bull Moose Progressive* (Syracuse, N.Y.: Syracuse University Press, 1961). Pinchot's own ideas are well stated in an autobiography, *Breaking New Ground* (New York: Harcourt, Brace, 1941); see also Nash, *Wilderness and the American Mind* (1967 ed.), 134–40.

100. Starr, *Americans and the California Dream,* 177–81; see also Thurman Wilkins, *Clarence King: A Biography* (Albuquerque: University of New Mexico Press, 1988).

101. Nash, *Wilderness and the American Mind* (1967 ed.), 158–68; and Starr, *Americans and the California Dream,* 183–91.

102. Limerick, *Legacy of Conquest,* 293–321; and Nash, *Wilderness and the American Mind* (1967 ed.), especially 161–81.

103. Paul Russell Cutright, *Theodore Roosevelt: The Making of a Conservationist* (Urbana: University of Illinois Press, 1985); Edmund Morris, *The Rise of Theodore Roosevelt* (New York: Coward, McCann, & Geoghegan, 1979); and White, *Eastern Establishment and the Western Experience,* 171–83.

104. No full study of John Collier has yet been done but see *REAW,* 237–39; Michael Malone and Richard W. Etulain, *The American West: A Twentieth-Century History* (Lincoln: University of Nebraska Press, 1989), 136–39; and Graham D. Taylor, *The New Deal and American Indian Tribalism: The Administration of the Indian Reorganization Act, 1934–1945* (Lincoln: University of Nebraska Press, 1980).

Ideology and Image

Justifying Westward Expansion

WILLIAM H. TRUETTNER

By the late 1850s, when the Midwest and Far West had already been partially settled, Americans were generally eager to cast territorial expansion as the major accomplishment of the era. "If we boast of our own works of improvement in the West," wrote the author of an emigrant guide published in 1857,

have we not on hand a thousand proofs to sustain us? The former wild prairie, now a cultivated farm; the floating palaces upon the bosom of the river which but a little while ago rolled on undisturbed in its lonely beauty; the churches and school-houses that now stand where stood a few summers since the Indian's wigwam; the steam-cars, that fly across the land swifter than the light-footed Chippewa, the arrow from his bow, or the deer that he hunted,—are not all these proofs enough that we are justified in boasting of what we have accomplished?[1]

As a theme for this book, we might note the assurance with which the writer replaces what has been lost in the process of "taming" the West with well-recognized symbols of progress: the "wild prairie" becomes a cultivated farm, steamboats enliven a "lonely" stretch of river, religion (read Christianity) and learning replace the backward ways of the Indian, and so on. Besides extolling expansionism, the passage skillfully disguises the problems of a nation in transition—America shedding its heritage as a wilderness republic and establishing itself as an industrial democracy. Each image—the farm, steamboat, church, and schoolhouse—has been selected to convince the reader that the passage from past to present was inevitable, beneficial, and, above all, peaceful.

Guidebook writers played a major role in selling the West during the 1850s and succeeding decades. So successful were they (along with newspapers, railroads, and government land programs) that between 1870 and 1900 Americans settled more land than they had during the previous three centuries.[2] Success, however, created a new set of problems. By 1900 most of the arable land in the country had been parceled out for agricultural use. Pro-

moters of the West, who had confidently predicted that the homestead allotments would last
well into the twentieth century, were brought
up short by the turn of events. And so were a
number of early twentieth-century writers, like
Hamlin Garland and Willa Cather, who regretted America's headlong rush to the Pacific. The
latter, who had wandered along "sunflower-
bordered roads" of the "great prairie" in the
1880s, struck a particularly elegiac note in her
subsequent fiction. "Beyond the pond," she
wrote in *My Ántonia* (1918),

on the slope that climbed to the cornfield, there
was, faintly marked in the grass, a great circle
where the Indians used to ride. . . . Whenever one
looked at this slope against the setting sun, the circle
showed like a pattern in the grass; and this morning, when the first spray of snow lay over it, it
came out with wonderful distinctness, like strokes
of Chinese white on canvas. The old figure stirred
me as it had never done before.[3]

The image is strikingly different from that
in the guidebook and was surely written for a
different audience. Yet the note sounded corresponds to a certain feeling that Americans in
general had at that time for their "frontier"
past—the very one the previous writer had
confidently rejected. Symbols of time in the
Cather passage (the setting sun, the chilling
blanket of snow) that should be slowly cancel-
ing the presence of the circular Indian path are,
in fact, enhancing it. Finally it is all but released from its natural surroundings and recreated on canvas "with strokes of Chinese
white." As a work of art, the image of the circular path gains formidable power. It haunts
Cather, suddenly revealing to her America's
collective loss. Sixty years after the guidebook
passage was written, Cather renders progress a
doubtful substitute for a past symbolized only
by a circle in the snow.
    Twentieth-century historians have been no

less fascinated with the frontier—with the
changes that it did or did not produce in our
national life and its impact as a cultural deter-
minant. Many regard the concept of the frontier (an imaginary line that proceeded irregu-
larly westward for three hundred years) as the
most distinctive feature of the nation's past.[4] In
that span of time they have given most
attention to the period of 1840 to 1890, when
Americans took possession of the trans-
Mississippi West.
    Historians investigating the expansionist
impulse of those years have suggested that
Americans' view of themselves is much indebted to that impulse—that what has often
been proposed as a national character is, in
fact, an amalgam of traits assigned to the men
and women who accomplished the seemingly
impossible task of settling the West in half a
century. Aggressive individual entrepreneurship was touted as their chief attribute, as if
they had needed only land and freedom to
make their way. Belief in hard work, progress,
the future, and the providential nature of democracy was the positive manifestation of this
character; a willingness to exploit land and natural resources, dominate races with fewer technological means, and measure success in terms
of material reward was its less appealing side.
Most Americans still consider the so-called pioneer spirit of the "Old West" as the one that
"forged" the nation.[5]

East and West: Preservation versus Progress

The first frontiers, not nearly so well publi-
cized as the western frontier, were those created as successive waves of settlers abandoned
secure townsites along the Atlantic in search of
more fertile land. By 1765 settlers had reached
the base of the Alleghenies, and after the Revolution they moved beyond the mountains into

Ohio, Kentucky, and Tennessee. Occupation of the Mississippi Valley accelerated following the Louisiana Purchase of 1803.

Reports coming back from the Great Plains characterizing the land as a desert, impossible to farm or ranch, temporarily halted the next obvious step in this advance, shunting momentum toward Texas and the Mexican frontier. Wilderness scouts and government expeditions, such as those led by John Charles Frémont in the early 1840s, continued to investigate the Far West, however, raising the possibility of bypassing the Great Plains in favor of the fertile land that lay beyond. By the early 1840s, as if some invisible dam had opened just west of the Mississippi, a stream of overlanders started out for the West Coast. During the next twenty-five years the stream became a flood, augmented by miners following news of the latest gold and silver strikes. Between 1841 and 1865 some 350,000 emigrants headed west over a network of trails that led finally to Oregon or California.[6] Many thousands more went by way of the Isthmus of Panama, across which a primitive railroad had been built in the 1850s.

Not until after the Civil War were Americans willing to contemplate the more difficult task of settling the Great Plains, which required a rail network to transport produce to market and capital-intensive farming methods to offset the lack of rainfall. Thirty years after the conclusion of the war, a veneer of settlement spread over the entire area—enough to support the claim that a frontier no longer existed—even though the Census Bureau reported in 1890 fewer farms in the Far West (with the exception of California) than in the state of Mississippi.[7] The "closing" of the frontier, announced by historian Frederick Jackson Turner in 1893, clearly had a greater psychological than social or economic impact.

Literary accounts of this moving frontier were plentiful during the first half of the nineteenth century. Captivity narratives, James Fenimore Cooper's Leatherstocking Tales, Washington Irving's *Astoria* and *Western Journals,* and novels by Charles Brockden Brown and William Gilmore Simms responded to the issues faced by a young nation aggressively pursuing territorial expansion. Artistic coverage of the early frontier was, however, noticeably absent. Such subjects apparently had little academic status in an era that still acknowledged artistic tradition. But does that theory alone explain why contemporary genre painters, such as Francis W. Edmonds, Charles Bird King, John Lewis Krimmel, William Sydney Mount, and John Quidor, confronted the established social and political mores of the East while neglecting the expansionist tide in the hinterlands? Or why landscape painters who made a passing reference to expansionist themes did so with such a gentle touch? Joshua Shaw's *On the Susquehanna,* 1839, for example, depicts the banks of that river as an arcadian paradise, forever the home of the Indians who reside peacefully in the foreground [16]. In Frederic E. Church's *New England Scenery,* 1851, a covered wagon passes wistfully through a picturesque landscape, as if the pull of home is as strong as the desire to move west [17]. Other paintings, like Thomas Cole's *Hunter's Return,* 1845, or *Home in the Woods,* 1847, project a view of the frontier that preserves an ideal relationship between people and nature [18–19]. Figures are bathed in the mellow, elegiac tones of a pastoral landscape; time and progress have been subsumed in a wishful continuum with the classical world, as if America could stop dead in its tracks and remain a never-changing virgilian paradise.

The Hunter's Return and *Home in the Woods* were, in that sense, a denial of the expansionist impulse that had already sent wagon trains to Oregon and California—the same impulse that

Cole had indirectly challenged in the *Course of Empire,* 1836 (The New-York Historical Society), when warning Americans of their growing material appetite. More typically concerned with preserving the past, genre and landscape painters in the East carefully fabricated time-honored scenes—like cider making, haymaking, or rustic dances—or landscapes based on the topography of certain artistic havens (the Catskills, Adirondacks, and White Mountains) that survived more effectively on canvas than they did in real life.

When artists finally turned their sights toward expansionist subjects, they quickly jumped the Mississippi (or they were already in the West). Or they turned all the way back to exploration and discovery scenes of the seventeenth century to suggest a continuity between those historical events and the efforts then under way to settle Oregon and California. Few scenes, except those of Daniel Boone and his party by William Ranney and George Caleb Bingham, which cleverly blend hagiography and expansionist rhetoric, depict events east of the Mississippi [see 31–32].

Drawing an artistic distinction between the East and the West and how subjects were treated on either side of some imaginary dividing line is a delicate issue. Our purpose here is not to make a sectional argument nor to separate further "western" art from mainstream American art. The intent is quite the opposite: most artists who painted western scenes did so from the perspective of a New York studio. Moreover, they relied on a stylistic vocabulary drawn from the same sources used by those who painted more conventional subjects. But subjects representing westward expansion, whether painted by artists residing in the East or the West, more commonly (and more vigorously) extol the idea of progress, a concept mid nineteenth-century boosters of the West took very seriously. It was a religion, in a way, a belief in democracy and free enterprise as key factors in creating a superior civilization. And it presupposed industrial growth and territorial expansion as the means to accomplish that end.

But why should American art divide along the lines of "aggressive" and "conservative" subjects, when the East was no less committed to progress than the West? Perhaps the most

16. Joshua Shaw, *On the Susquehanna,* 1839, oil on canvas, 39 × 55½ in. Museum of Fine Arts, Boston; bequest of Martha C. Karolik for the Karolik Collection of American Paintings, 1815–1865.

17. Frederic E. Church, *New England Scenery,* 1851, oil on canvas, 36 × 53 in. George Walter Vincent Smith Art Museum, Springfield, Massachusetts.

18. Thomas Cole, *The Hunter's Return,* 1845, oil on canvas, 40 ⅛ × 60½ in. Amon Carter Museum, Fort Worth, Texas.

19. Thomas Cole, *Home in the Woods,* 1847, oil on canvas, 44 × 66 in. Reynolda House, Museum of American Art, Winston-Salem, North Carolina.

useful explanation of this seemingly arbitrary phenomenon is found in the recent description by historian Richard Slotkin of frontier social dynamics. Slotkin views the frontier world as one of "bifurcated geography," with the West (the "Wilderness") on one side, an area of abundant resources and no social organization, and the urban East (the "Metropolis") on the other side, in which order and a hierarchical society prevailed. Under this system the wilderness was there to be utilized. It provided raw material to industrial interests (in the metropolis) that effectively but "discretely" controlled the manufacturing process.[8]

This design, Slotkin believes, reveals a new psychological order on the frontier, a division "between a world of possibilities and one of actualities." On the western side of the imaginary line "lay great wealth and a suspension of the normal limitations of law and probability"—a "dreamworld" in which personal greed and the national good became magically associated. The urban East, however, operated under a different set of guidelines. Rampant development could and did produce conditions that were immediately apparent: rural land overrun

by industry, squalid urban areas, and labor unrest, all of which constituted a rebuke to capitalists, who were also major art patrons. A western scene signaling progress was tolerable because in that fictional space the implications of progress hurt no one (except Indians, foreign powers, and others who were expendable in the eyes of an expansionist society). But the same subject set in more familiar circumstances in the East rang a warning bell. It called attention to social issues that rarely surfaced in the fine arts of the era. Eastern patrons instinctively chose subjects created to preserve stereotypes for representing (or modifying) social change on both sides of the frontier. These tactfully diluted the more obvious manifestations of progress in the East.

Compare, for example, *Westward the Star of Empire,* 1867, by Andrew Melrose and *Starrucca Viaduct,* 1865, by Jasper F. Cropsey [20–21]. Both artists maintained studios in New York and celebrated in their canvases railroad-engineering feats of the midcentury: Melrose, the completion of a roadbed linking Chicago and Council Bluffs, Iowa, the eastern branch of the transcontinental line that would eventually reach San Francisco; and Cropsey, the monumental viaduct in western Pennsylvania called by admirers the "Eighth Wonder of the World." In the former, a locomotive steams through a raw cut in the wilderness, its headlamp silhouetting deer fleeing before a literal engine of progress. The light symbolizes the future, a relentless beam sacrificing everything in its path. No attempt is made to accommodate the wilderness; the painting represents the abrupt confrontation between new and old America, implying that one must make way for the other. Cropsey, however, is at pains to make the railroad fit the contour of the landscape and to diminish the impact of its mechanical presence. The train moves away from the viewer, its size is small compared to the breadth of the landscape, and many picturesque touches "naturalize" its presence. Cropsey downplays the disruptive quality of the railroad and what it portends for the future, Melrose announces its presence with unhesitating approval.

Bingham's election scenes also assume a major role in this division of artistic priorities. Three decades of increasingly open democratic practice may account for the distance between

the measured forum of debate Samuel F. B. Morse created in *The Old House of Representatives,* 1821–23, and the free-swinging street brawl offered by Bingham as a model of the frontier electoral process [22–23].[9] During the decade before Bingham painted his election series the West had become a new political arena. The true test of democracy was not only how it would address immigrant and labor issues in the East but how it would operate in an unstructured frontier community in which people were equally apprehensive of political control. Democracy had to guarantee order, but it also had to prove its value as the political medium through which progress could be achieved. Bingham's pictures, therefore, introduce all the drawbacks of an "open" system—the deals, profiteering, hustling, class influence, and disenfranchisement of minorities—but the artist ultimately channels the energy of the electorate into a pictorial design that resolves conflicting elements. His composition proclaims that the system works. What the viewer actually witnesses is the simultaneous testing and approval of democracy, on new and more hopeful ground.[10]

Similar themes were rarely presented that

20. Andrew Melrose, *Westward the Star of Empire Takes Its Way—near Council Bluffs, Iowa,* 1867, oil on canvas, 25½ × 46 in. E. William Judson Collection, New York.

21. Jasper F. Cropsey, *Starrucca Viaduct, Pennsylvania,* 1865, oil on canvas, 22⅜ × 36⅜ in. The Toledo Museum of Art; gift of Florence Scott Libbey.

22. Samuel F. B. Morse, *The Old House of Representatives,* 1821–23, oil on canvas, 86½ × 130¾ in. The Corcoran Gallery of Art, Washington, D.C.; museum purchase, Gallery Fund, 1911.

23. George Caleb Bingham, *The Verdict of the People,* 1854–55, oil on canvas, 46 × 65 in. Boatmen's National Bank, Saint Louis.

way in the East.[11] Richard Caton Woodville's *Politics in an Oyster House,* 1848, for example, is cleverly constructed to show democracy as a painstaking effort at compromise [24]. The artist takes the action off the street, confines it in a narrow space, casts it as an epicurean pastime, and finally deflects the issue to the viewer through the weary glance of the figure on the left. Even in a more one-to-one comparison—Bingham's *Country Politician,* 1849 [25], against *Politics in an Oyster House*—the Missouri artist offers a more confident appraisal of the political process. The three principals are actively engaged in debate; space in the painting is austere, clean, and open; and the central compositional motif in the painting, the potbellied stove (echoed in the prosperous girth of the man seated beside it), projects warmth and life and helps close the circle in which the men are seated. By comparison, the atmosphere of the oyster house is cluttered and hedonistic and the table separates the two figures. Bingham's picture reaffirms the process, Woodville's figures view politics with indifference bordering on cynicism.

Farming was another subject treated differently east and west of the frontier. William Hahn's *Harvest Time,* 1875, exalts prosperity and abundance; it is a glorious wide-angle view of the California landscape [26]. The benefits of sunshine and rich earth are traced through the haying, threshing (a mechanical thresher is featured), and grain-storage process—activities that require a minimum of toil and promise a golden future. New England farm scenes of comparable date by Eastman Johnson, Charles Caleb Ward, or Thomas Waterman Wood seem more like closed-off preserves of traditional life [27]. Rural folk are less often in the field than around the farmyard, pursuing individual tasks representing the time-honored rituals of farming rather than a prosperous view of the future. Even an agricultural economy fa-

voring large-scale farms over the more limited parcels of land in New England cannot explain such disparate images. Instead the answer seems to be that Hahn saw western land and resources as the fulfillment of a prophecy; while Johnson, Ward, and Wood were attempting in their paintings to guard the rural past of New England from its industrial present.[12]

Finally one must consider contrasting landscape images. Countless reasons have been advanced to explain why artists painted the Rockies, the Sierra Nevada, and other western wonderlands on such an unprecedented scale. The breadth and variety of the landscape, it has been argued, demanded a generous mode of representation; patrons with enormous homes and spacious galleries wanted grandly composed paintings to cover their walls; and Americans had a strong desire to thumb their collective nose at Europe, and especially the Alps, since at last they could boast a national asset that in sheer size and sublime effect was the superior of what they had been forced for generations to accept as an international standard. But are those the sole reasons why Albert Bierstadt's major canvases dwarfed those of Sanford R. Gifford, John F. Kensett, or Worthington Whittredge, who had observed and painted some of the same western scenery but on a more modest scale [28]? After they returned from the West, Gifford, Kensett, and Whittredge continued to supply moderately sized canvases of familiar New England haunts to patrons who also purchased Bierstadt's dramatic views of the West. The former viewed nature as if under a bell jar. They transferred to canvas images of Adirondack lakes, the Shrewsbury River, and Catskill brooks, for example, that look like carefully tended preserves of woods and waters [29]. These images freeze the landscape, as if a shutter had clicked in the artist's mind to ensure a safe and perfect recol-

24. Richard Caton Woodville, *Politics in an Oyster House,* 1848, oil on canvas, 16 × 13 in. The Walters Art Gallery, Baltimore.

25. George Caleb Bingham, *Country Politician,* 1849, oil on canvas, 20 × 24 in. The Fine Arts Museums of San Francisco; gift of Mr. and Mrs. John D. Rockefeller 3d.

26. William Hahn, *Harvest Time,* 1875, oil on canvas, 36 × 70 in. The Fine Arts Museums of San Francisco; gift of Mrs. Harold R. McKinnon and Mrs. Harry L. Brown.

27. Charles Caleb Ward, *Force and Skill,* 1869, oil on canvas, 12 × 10 in. The Currier Gallery of Art, Manchester, New Hampshire; gift of Henry Melville Fuller.

lection. Such paintings represented the past, a proscribed and ordered world, even before their final coat of varnish had dried.[13]

Meanwhile Bierstadt was remodeling and expanding the western landscape, casting it as new Eden, announcing its scenic wonders and publicizing its staggering resources [30]. Bierstadt chose to deliver the West as an aggressively fabricated national anthem, an approach his patrons would probably not have encouraged had he been picturing New York and New England landscape subjects. They were quite content to envision the West as a land of promise, but the East they wished to see rendered in a less provocative fashion. Landscapes by Bierstadt, Gifford, Kensett, and Whittredge, therefore, might hang comfortably together in nineteenth-century collections and be closely linked by us today, but to those who originally purchased them they may have represented two distinct strategies for assessing industrial development.[14]

The link between Melrose, Bingham, Hahn, and Bierstadt is meant to explain why western subjects represent a major national theme during the hundred-year span examined in this book. What was happening in the West was a phenomenon easily tracked through newspapers, periodicals, guidebooks, broadsides, and government reports, if not through an actual witnessing of events. The opportunity to represent progress through images of the West was a concept quickly grasped by artists from midcentury onward. Recognizing an iconographical trend, however, does not fully apprise us of the unique circumstances under which these paintings were produced. For perhaps the first time in modern history a corps of talented artists was available to record the intent of a government subduing an extensive area of land immediately adjacent to national boundaries. The appropriation process had the earmarks of previous colonial undertakings: native populations offered little resistance and the appropriators took for granted their right to settle the land, since it was, by their standards, rich in undeveloped natural resources.

But the conquest of the West was, in other ways, a different process. Colonial lands were usually some distance from the home country, and those who settled these remote areas rarely remained so closely tied to the political, economic, and social agenda of their place of origin. Americans moving into the lands west of the Mississippi brought with them consistent and well-defined attitudes toward democracy, progress, Christianity, and Anglo-Saxon culture. When one begins to strip away the layers of meaning that paintings of the West have acquired in our time, it can be seen that the act of representing this expansionist process is almost as unique as the events of this particular era. Furthermore, the images that evolved from an artistic appraisal of the process offer a transparent view of what was then construed as national purpose.

The soil is destined for the race using the cannon rather than the bow and arrow.

ALBERT WEINBERG, 1935

The frontier West has received most scrutiny in recent years from scholars still debating the influential work of Frederick Turner. In his frontier thesis, first presented in 1893, Turner designates the moving frontier as the most significant factor in shaping American political and social institutions and in forming a national character. Turner's thesis gained widespread acceptance during the first decades of the twentieth century, but it has since undergone extensive revision (and even rejection).[15] In one of its more recent manifestations it has been used

28. John F. Kensett, *Storm, Western Colorado,* 1870, oil on canvas, 18⁹⁄₁₆ × 28⅛ in. The Toledo Museum of Art; gift of Florence Scott Libbey.

29. Sanford R. Gifford, *White-face Mountain from Lake Placid,* 1866, oil on canvas, 11⅛ × 19⅝ in. National Museum of American Art, Smithsonian Institution, Washington, D.C.; gift of Mrs. Johnson Garrett.

30. Albert Bierstadt, *Among the Sierra Nevada Mountains, California,* 1868, oil on canvas, 72 × 120 in. National Museum of American Art, Smithsonian Institution, Washington, D.C.; bequest of Helen Huntington Hull.

to draw new and telling connections between expansionist rhetoric and American foreign-policy initiatives during the 1960s.[16] Scholars have compared Manifest Destiny to policies invoked by the federal government to justify American intervention in South Vietnam. Manifest Destiny, they argue, masked territorial ambition as a providential mission, and the Pentagon's campaign to establish democracy in South Vietnam was correspondingly a national-security ploy—a means of propping up a country considered vital to American interests in Southeast Asia.

The relationship between ideology and national self-interest has intrigued historians of American expansionism since it was first introduced by Albert Weinberg in 1935. Weinberg identified Manifest Destiny as a persistent trend in American history, one that informed activity in the nation's colonial past as much as in the era of westward expansion, and concluded, after exhaustive analysis, that the concept was essentially self-serving. "The inconsistency between the doctrines of beneficent territorial utilization and its largely unbeneficent practice," he wrote,

is probably significant of another inconsistency between ideology and motive. . . . The discrepancy is between the nationalist's pretension to interest in the *use* of territory and his fundamental *interest* in its possession. It is because of the possessive instinct and not the plough that the soil is destined for the race using the cannon rather than the bow and arrow [italics added].[17]

Weinberg stopped short of drawing a moral conclusion from his findings, preferring to expose rather than condemn expansionist ideology, but the thrust of his argument deeply affected subsequent scholarship in the field.[18] By 1955 Manifest Destiny was thought too broad a concept to explain expansionism. Instead it was maintained that "clearly conceived policies relentlessly pursued" enabled the United States to achieve its empire on the Pacific.[19] A subsequent theory, advanced by Frederick Merk in 1963, attempted to link directly the cause-and-effect relationship between Manifest Destiny literature and expansionism, citing the press and other "agencies of mass propaganda" as key factors in fomenting an expansionist mood.[20] This limited to a specific group those responsible for fanning the flames—a corps of influential politicians and industrialists—as opposed to a broad-based majority.

The propaganda generated by westward expansion and its influence on image makers of the nineteenth and early twentieth century are key issues addressed in *The West as America*. Channels connecting artists and patrons are another. Expansionist literature can be misleading on this subject since it describes a nation proceeding westward in small individual steps—using up land (or selling out for a substantial profit) and then moving on. The census of 1860 revealed, for example, that the destination of emigrants from thirty of the thirty-four states then comprising the Union was the state "immediately adjacent" to the one in which they were born.[21] Such a migration pattern suggests a grass-roots movement to expand the nation, somewhat contradicting the argument made in the preceding paragraph, which presumes a nationalistic propaganda machine operated by certain influential spokespersons of the era.

But the decision to seek frontier land was not necessarily an individual act, Slotkin explains. It came about through "the developing political economy of the Metropolis"—through the capital base that regulated demand for the

"unappropriated" resources that lay beyond (and presumably to the west of) settlement boundaries.[22] The metropolis, therefore, pulled the strings that determined not only the economic but the political and cultural development of frontier areas. Slotkin's revision of the Turner thesis is important for numerous reasons, but for our discussion it is crucial. It exposes, first of all, a controlling entrepreneurial group, which previous writers on westward expansion passed over lightly. Turner, for one, had portrayed the frontier as a racial and economic melting pot, from which emerged the self-reliant frontier "type," a designation that for a time obscured class and racial antipathies in the West. Slotkin's theory also clarifies reasons for acquiring land. Even though it was there for the taking (whether owned by a foreign power, used by an Indian tribe, or controlled by the government), most "pioneers" were prompted to act by the marketing policies of the nearest metropolis. Acknowledging this incentive considerably sharpens our understanding of the imperatives driving westward expansion.

The existence of a metropolitan-based expansion system clarifies the relationship between patrons, artists, and the images illustrated in subsequent chapters of this book. No major artist was part of the moving frontier, and historical references in paintings of the nineteenth-century West create only the illusion of authenticity. They more accurately represent the values of the metropolis and were painted by artists who were themselves urban dwellers. Most of those artists maintained studios in the East, primarily in the New York area. The western status of major exceptions—Bingham, Charles Nahl, and Charles Russell—can be discounted on the basis of background and patronage: Bingham's four years in Washington (1840–44) put him in touch with an expansionist rhetoric he never forgot, Nahl was both a product of European academies and the boom-town atmosphere of San Francisco at midcentury, and "good ol' Charlie" created a myth about himself that eastern patrons suffering from post-frontier blues at the turn of the century appear to have swallowed whole. He was no more a rustic than they were, and he understood better than they their need to surround themselves with re-creations of the Old West.[23]

Slotkin's theory, then, establishes the links necessary to place expansionism in a cultural and artistic orbit. Artistic observation was occurring from a point far behind the frontier and in association with those who stood to gain most from the westward movement—the leaders of the industrial East. In their interests, Merk, Slotkin, and others argue, the West was systematically conquered and settled. Yet the images show pioneers fearlessly leading the charge—fur trappers, riverboatmen, farmers, and cowhands. The common democratic stock of the country appears to shoulder the burden of domesticating a new land, with a grace and assurance that contradicts most of what we have learned about westward expansion in the last forty years.

The Role of Myth and Ideology

Scholars and critics who have concerned themselves with these images—from Henry T. Tuckerman in the 1860s to the 1930s, when western scenes reemerged in museums and private collections after a long period of neglect—invariably described them as works that, if not actual illustrations of historical events, captured the "true" flavor of the West for eastern audiences. Albert Christ-Janer's book on Bingham (1940), an example of this approach, repeats and accepts an earlier appraisal of Bingham's work as a "sincere, truthful interpretation of

the life of his time in Missouri."[24] Similar opinions were delivered in the years that followed on the work of George Catlin, Seth Eastman, Nahl, Ranney, Frederic Remington, John Mix Stanley, and Carl Wimar, to name only a few.[25] *Westward the Way,* the catalogue of a pathfinding exhibition of 1954, arranges images by these artists and many more into a chronological panorama of western history from 1803 to 1900. The exhibition and catalogue are perhaps the most sustained effort of western-art studies of the 1950s to match "eye-witness" texts with images "documenting" western life and landscape.[26]

A decade earlier, in 1944, art historian Edgar P. Richardson had placed a few western subjects in the context of the romantic movement,[27] and with the more informed analysis provided by Henry Nash Smith in *Virgin Land* (1950), mythical content was gradually acknowledged in images of the West. More recent surveys and studies of the popular arts have frankly admitted the ahistorical character of western subjects, describing them instead as the embodiments of myths that formed in the nineteenth century and became case-hardened in the twentieth.[28] Releasing these myths from an immediate historical context has made them no less "real" for some; reification (treating ideas as if they are the reality they purport to describe) proceeds with a vengeance among collectors, viewers, and interpreters of western art.[29] The wide-ranging belief persists that myth represents what actually was, at least in terms of what twentieth-century Americans call the "true values" inherited from the nineteenth-century West. But scholarship in the past decades has slowly isolated myth as a fable dealing only selectively with history and imposing on historical events a certain convenient interpretation.

At this level, freed from the burden of historical illustration (the true values syndrome is more tenacious) but still grappling with the significance of myth, scholarship directed toward western subjects has lingered for a decade. Useful biographical and historical information has been gathered during this interlude, and efforts have been made to fit "western" artists into "eastern" stylistic chronologies in hopes of upgrading the aesthetic rank of certain artists who have been dismissed for their narrative, "exaggerated," and presumably antimodernist style. But the myths themselves, particularly the set of beliefs informing and linking images of westward expansion, have not been investigated. Without taking that step, we limit how far we can probe the meaning of so-called western subjects.

Myth and ideology intersect continuously in western images. The former serves as a vehicle to convert traditional narratives into metaphors explaining or justifying the way in which a group (or society or nation) perceives itself. The myths present in these images are mostly drawn from accounts of frontier life that exposed the process of nation building in sometimes raw and disagreeable ways. To make them more palatable they were assimilated into a broader, more reassuring evolutionary pattern. Myth functions to control history, to shape it in text or image as an ordained sequence of events. The world is rendered pure in the process; complexity and contradiction give way to order, clarity, and direction. Myth, then, can be understood as an abstract shelter restricting debate. But myth can also function as ideology—as an abstraction broadly defining the belief system of a particular group or society.[30]

Numerous myths are present in the images presented in this book, although perhaps all are infused with what has been called the "myth of the frontier." This myth guaranteed progress without encumbering social and environmental debt. Time and again it manifests itself as a kind of illusory principle sanctioning greed, on the assumption that the supply of western resources was essentially unlimited.

Ideology, however, is the embracing factor of our investigation. In each image it serves to extol progress, "authorizing" westward expansion as a beneficial national undertaking. Ideology functions smoothly and effectively in these images to justify the headlong rush across the continent. It does so with a screen of its own—a developed language that flows effortlessly across social and moral issues, which were not unrecognized in their own time but have become the focus of recent scholarship.[31] The ideology, in effect, mounts a compelling argument on behalf of progress while masking itself as "language," as a detectable phenomenon. This often confers on images of westward expansion a quality of absolute legitimacy, as if what is being described is natural and unquestionable and therefore a fully sanctioned enterprise.

The presence of an ideology in these images does not presume a conspiracy on the part of these artists nor even a self-conscious effort to make the end result of expansionism justify the means (although many of the images actually perform this function). Nor should we assume that this ideology is immune to contemporary analysis. Ideologies, like myths, are based on a historical agenda that can be made to reveal itself. When viewed through a new perspective, images often yield this agenda—one taken for granted and therefore never acknowledged by nineteenth-century viewers.

Empire Building with Images

Thematic categories that became evident in the process of selecting illustrations for this book proved to be the most effective means of returning images to a context in which ideology prevailed, although admittedly the process has a bias of its own. One cannot discount the objectivity of past historical studies while claiming the unassailability of contemporary standards of scholarship. But establishing thematic categories is not the same as discovering the "reality" of an earlier age. It is, rather, a means of using historical data to identify and interpret expansionist rhetoric, a process that is safer, if still a bit like proceeding through a minefield.

Chronology to some extent influenced the process but more important was a common subject or belief present in groups of images, such as the Promised Land in chapter 2 or democracy-as-prosperity in chapter 4. The result is six groups of images more or less following a historical sequence but *not* meant as historical narrative. Instead they describe an arc over the years of westward expansion, rising with the Capitol murals and other history paintings announcing the onset of expansionist activities and setting beyond the heroic landscapes of Thomas Moran and Bierstadt, which signal the fulfillment of the prophecy and more indirectly the commercial value of the West. As the coda for this book, chapter 6 comprises images no less charged with ideology, but now they look backward, with a conscious obligation to preserve a frontier myth.

No overall design governs the presentation of material in each chapter, although images are consistently "read" with contemporary events and expansionist rhetoric in mind. The first chapter gathers together images that can now be seen as a prelude to expansion. The Capitol murals and a variety of history paintings helped launch expansionist initiatives toward the Southwest, Oregon, and California— initiatives that grew into one of the most extraordinary land acquisition and settlement programs in modern history [see 55–58]. Yet the paintings say nothing of the Mexican War, the contest with England over the forty-ninth par-

allel, or freebooting in California; instead they turn back to the founding of the nation, discretely paralleling the deeds of seventeenth-century explorers, in this case portrayed as high-minded representatives of European culture, and the ensuing conquest of the Southwest and Far West.

The subjects imply that a standard of civilization is being transferred from east to west, along with its capacity to uplift and benefit people in newly conquered lands. Much of this iconography reappears in subsequent chapters, where it serves to endorse expansionist activities on the frontier: Columbus becomes Daniel Boone, gesturing toward new lands [see 64]; ships crossing the ocean are replaced by covered wagons crossing the Great Plains; the founding of the colonies (models of civic order and religious toleration) anticipates the development of western frontier towns (in which the former virtue was usually emphasized); religious symbols, stressing Christianity as the foundation of an enlightened government and social code, return in numerous images; and Europeans triumph over Indians in every New World encounter, setting the stage for later confrontations.

Images in chapter 2, often contemporary with those in chapter 1, are traditionally confused with a historical narrative of westward expansion. They are nothing of the kind. In fact, they modify history with a program of their own, best seen in the paintings of Boone by Ranney and Bingham [31–32]. All images of Boone from this period project the myth created by his first biographer, John Filson, in 1784, fifteen years after Boone entered the trans-Allegheny wilderness, and subsequently refined by others, such as William Gilmore Simms and Timothy Flint. Boone emerges from their combined portraits as the quintessential pioneer, whose energy and resourcefulness (which were indeed considerable) enabled

him to extract from a succession of wilderness homesteads a generous livelihood. By midcentury his image had become a national symbol, exemplifying a spirit of adventure and accomplishment, to the first wave of pioneers crossing the Great Plains. Boone was, in this guise, the consummate empire builder.[32]

Bingham's image adds a spiritual component to Ranney's—westering becomes clearly identified with the migration of the Holy Family. The rhetoric, however, provides only more gloss; the painting substitutes a "real" Boone for one who fulfills the notion (probably for eastern audiences) of a sturdy frontier type, capable of subduing the wilderness (note the blasted trees and dark foreground) about to be entered. Christianity is reinforced by guns and axes (as it is in the Capitol mural *Discovery of the Mississippi* by William H. Powell [see 56]), and Boone's resolute advance directly toward the viewer reminds one of the onrushing locomotive in Melrose's *Westward the Star of Empire* [see 20]. Even the most steadfast believer in

Boone's virtues (his initial visit to Kentucky was prompted by real-estate speculation) begins to perceive the ideological purpose of such an image.

Further analysis, both formal and iconographical, reveals other reasons for probing the ideological content of images in chapter 2. Fur trappers, as depicted by Ranney, were pathfinders who led the way for more peaceful settlement. In fact, they were a commercial vanguard—men with no particular love of nature, who often risked everything for the high return beaver pelts brought on the European market. They were also trespassers on foreign territory, who began the process of separating Indians from their land by providing them with manufactured goods in exchange for the skins of wild animals. No wonder trappers were shown time and again looking over their shoulder, as if their anxiety echoed that of a nation overextending itself—rushing westward to conquer and exploit land rather than nurture its productive capacity [33].

31. William Ranney, *Boone's First View of Kentucky*, 1849, oil on canvas, 37½ × 54½ in. The Anschutz Collection, Denver.

32. George Caleb Bingham, *Daniel Boone Escorting Settlers through the Cumberland Gap*, 1851–52, oil on canvas, 36½ × 50¼ in. Washington University Gallery of Art, Saint Louis; gift of Nathaniel Phillips, 1890.

Nonetheless, images of fur trappers, like wagon train and railroad pictures, helped smooth the way for expansion. They perpetuated the myth that the settling of the West was peaceful, when in reality it was bitterly contested every step of the way. Slave- versus free-state rivalries caused border strife in the Midwest and raised the prospect of military intervention in Central America; territorial disputes with foreign governments were initiated

by the premature occupation of much of the Southwest, Oregon, and California; and a prolonged clash with western Indian tribes inhibited passage across the Great Plains and the eventual settling of the area. Capitalists in the East were another factor. They rushed the process of expansion, abusing people and nature, contributing to an atmosphere of violence in the West that was the antithesis of what most images represent.

No one suffered more from this "peaceful" invasion than the Indians who inhabited the Great Plains and eastern slopes of the Rockies. Few artists concerned themselves with recording the early campaigns against eastern tribes. References to these events appear mostly in literature or interpretations of literary events like Cole's *Scene from "The Last of the Mohicans,"* 1827, or Asher B. Durand's *Indian's Vespers,* 1847 [34–35]. In each, Indians are consigned to a romantic doom that left viewers untroubled, so effectively did Cole and Durand submerge the event in a wilderness landscape representing the past. When the native ground

33. William Ranney, *The Trapper's Last Shot,* 1850, oil on canvas, 18 × 24 in. W. Graham Arader III Collection.

34. Thomas Cole, *Scene from "The Last of the Mohicans," Cora Kneeling at the Feet of Tamenund,* 1827, oil on canvas, 25⅜ × 35 1/16 in. Wadsworth Atheneum, Hartford; bequest of Alfred Smith.

35. Asher B. Durand, *The Indian's Vespers,* 1847, oil on canvas, 46¼ × 62¼ in. The White House Collection, Washington, D.C.

of western tribes was challenged, however, it raised an issue still debated today.

We must recognize from the outset the effect of cultural imperialism on federal Indian policy and on portrayals by white artists of Indian life. Despite occasional concern for their plight, Indians were rarely, if ever, represented as anything but cultural alternatives of white people—either more or less children of nature—and never as individuals with a distinct set of cultural imperatives. They were subtly but effectively assigned racial stereotypes based on theories advanced in literary and anthropological studies.[33] The result was inevitable: Indians were represented with only two dimensions, a good one combining the beneficent aspects of nature with superior European cultural attributes or a bad one equating unrestrained nature with the latent savagery in white men. Racial propaganda forced even the most sympathetic artist to opt for one mode or the other. Arguments made by every white painter of Indian life from Catlin through Remington on behalf of "truthful" representation are invalidated by the attitudes with which whites regarded Indians during the nineteenth century.

Tales of atrocities and counteratrocities, of warfare and broken treaties are not the historical grounds on which to demystify images of Indian life. These have entered frontier mythology in their own way and often contribute to our misunderstanding of what these images mean. It is more useful to divide Indian subjects into groups that betray national attitudes toward these people and suggest how effectively the images were manipulated to further government objectives in the West. Catlin and King, for example, willingly contributed to a cataloging process meant to preserve an image of Indians still "untouched" by civilization but whose future was in doubt. Collecting Indian artifacts, however, did not necessarily indicate a primary interest in native races. More often it

was a means of keeping white society in touch with wilderness virtues, manifested in the culture of "good" Indians.

Yet images such as Catlin's *Horse Chief,* 1832, and Karl Bodmer's *Chan-Chä-Uiá-Teüin,* 1833, perhaps did their job too well, for they raised the spectacle of "noble savages," which some Americans were reluctant to dispatch in favor of progress [36–37]. By the 1840s, therefore, Indian images began to change, not because Indians themselves were any more or less noble but because they threatened westward migration. Either they had to be cast in the role Durand chose for them in his painting *Progress* [see 120]—as thoughtful witnesses to the passing of an age—or they had to be portrayed as belligerents, as distinctly ignoble savages, whose chief delight was attacking trappers, wagon trains, or defenseless women and children. Indian hating developed in proportion to the need to claim their land, and Indian images followed suit.[34] Contact between whites and Indians was generally shown as conflict, and violence became condoned as the triumph of good over evil. The "truth" of such images is only that white Americans finally won the battle of the West.

Violent encounters were not the only means of solving the "Indian problem," however. Image makers learned to adapt skillfully two other solutions, both of which implied eventual extinction but with a subtle difference. Paintings such as Stanley's *Last of Their Race,* 1857 [38], suggested that Indians would eventually be buried under the waves of the Pacific, while a series of paintings representing acculturation themes predicted that Indians would be peacefully absorbed into white society, thereby neutralizing "aggressive" racial characteristics. The myth in this case simply denies the Indian problem by solving it in two different ways, both of which betray the racial ideology of westward expansion: those who could

36. George Catlin, *Horse Chief, Grand Pawnee Head Chief,* 1832, oil on canvas, 29 × 24 in. National Museum of American Art, Smithsonian Institution, Washington, D.C.; gift of Mrs. Joseph Harrison, Jr.

37. Karl Bodmer, *Chan-Chä-Uiá-Teüin (Woman of the Crow Nation), Teton Sioux,* 1833, watercolor and pencil on paper, 17 × 11⅞ in. Joslyn Art Museum, Omaha; gift of Enron Art Foundation.

38. John Mix Stanley, *Last of Their Race,* 1857, oil on canvas, 43 × 60 in. Buffalo Bill Historical Center, Cody, Wyoming.

not accept Anglo-Saxon standards of progress were doomed to extinction.

Few states joining the Union after the Revolution required land ownership as a requisite for voting rights. The constitution of Vermont (which became a state in 1791), for example, guaranteed universal manhood suffrage, and as western states were added during the first half of the nineteenth century they followed this practice.[35] We commonly think of this as a political phenomenon rising under the Jackson administration, but, in fact, it had already gained considerable momentum by the 1830s, and the West during the 1840s became a testing ground for democratic practice.[36]

The East had evolved from a republic to a democracy with national parties and local political systems engineering a gradual transition. Western states, like Missouri, acquired democracy all at once, as a direct challenge to the spirit of free enterprise that guided the westward movement. Bingham's classic election scenes, the centerpiece of chapter 4, confront and attempt to resolve the imposition of political control on a frontier society.

No stranger to politics, Bingham incorporated in his series references to specific issues and campaign excesses that as a Whig candidate he had witnessed in local elections.[37] Campaign practices are paraded in a humorous and appealing (if also condescending) way to make us believe we are seeing democracy in an unexpurgated state—to convince us that the artist is telling the truth.[38] What the viewer actually perceives is that the system can tolerate error without collapsing. Bingham is demonstrating democracy's ability to flex—to accommodate inequities and yet overcome them. His pictorial scheme, a masterful organization of competing elements, suffused with redeeming color, guarantees this outcome.[39] Indeed it could be argued that Bingham had little choice. Democracy was both catalyst and justification for westward expansion. If it did not work in a

society that valued individual freedom as much as (and sometimes more than) political union, progress would amount to chaos. So in pictorial and formal terms Bingham carefully defines democracy as attendant to progress (and therefore a loose rein on free enterprise).

The theme of democracy is also applied to two related groups of paintings in chapter 4, one devoted to domestic life, the other to commercial and industrial ventures on the frontier. Both invoke prosperity as a function of the democratic system, following the premise that freedom fosters progress and that the measurable component of progress is economic gain. A sequence of domestic scenes begins with Bingham's squatters [39], who jealously guard their land holdings but have made little progress in raising themselves above subsistence level, and ends with views of California estates representing the economic and cultural benefits of progress. Joseph Lee's portrait of the Badger residence relentlessly tallies the civilized amenities of life in the San Francisco area while ignoring less attractive aspects of urban life [40].

39. George Caleb Bingham, *The Squatters,* 1850, oil on canvas, 23⅜ × 28¼ in. Museum of Fine Arts, Boston; bequest of Henry L. Shattuck in memory of the late Ralph W. Gray.

40. Joseph Lee, *Residence of Captain Thomas W. Badger, Brooklyn, from the Northwest,* circa 1871, oil on canvas, 26¼ × 42 in. The Oakland Museum, California; gift of the Oakland Society of Pioneers.

41. Thomas Moran, *The Grand Canyon of the Yellowstone,* 1872, oil on canvas, 84 × 144¼ in. United States Department of the Interior, Office of the Secretary, Washington, D.C.; on loan to the National Museum of American Art.

The other group of paintings ranges from riverboating and ranching scenes (images guaranteeing the geographical benefits of the West) to views of factories and towns that convey the energy and bustle of progress. Each is a carefully edited statement linking democracy to the bountiful supply of resources in the West and the triumph of free enterprise. They support the myth that there was enough for everyone: industrial initiative and inexhaustible resources denied labor struggles and the wasting of nature. Cities are models of organization and industry, exploitation of land and natural resources is featured with engaging naïveté [see 190], and industrial pollution is offered as a picturesque accessory to the landscape. These paintings convert frontier life to a national idiom of prosperity and promise.

Chapter 5 focuses on a series of landscape clusters that represent in succession, the Green River bluffs of Wyoming, the Colorado River and Grand Canyon, Donner Pass, and the big trees of California. The major oil paintings in each cluster portray their subjects as both edenic wonders and emblems of national pride. The latter is particularly evident in the expansive scale of the landscapes and in the rich supply of "nature" they offer. These paintings collectively measure national success in the most American of all symbols, the wilderness, and yet they simultaneously designate nature as the font from which all future benefits will flow. In this sense they complete the cycle of westward expansion initiated by the Capitol murals, a view seconded by a critic in 1876 who praised Moran's *Grand Canyon of the Yellow-*

stone, 1872 [41], which then hung in the Senate lobby, opposite *The Chasm of the Colorado,* as "the only really good picture to be found in the Capitol" [see 220]. The same critic disparaged Emanuel Leutze's Capitol mural, *Westward the Course of Empire,* as too melodramatic—indicating a changing taste but also a search for a new symbol of national achievement [see 100].[40]

By 1867, according to a *New York Tribune* correspondent, some combination of the physical attributes of the West had already become a national symbol. "Its mines, forests and prairies await the capitalist," he wrote. "Its dusky races, earth monuments and ancient cities importune the antiquarian. Its cataracts, canyons and crests woo the painter. Its mountains, minerals and stupendous vegetable productions challenge the naturalist."[41] Major landscapes of the West had become purveyors of expansionist ideology presumably because of their capacity to offer a multiple interpretation of western resources. As images substituting for the real world, they did not "preserve" nature as had the landscapes of Gifford, Kensett, and Whittredge. Instead they argued a different point of view—that America could have it both ways, that an empire could be built that did not destroy nature or the social fabric already under stress from expansionist activities.

That a market for scenes of commerce and industry coexisted with a taste for heroic landscapes is evidence of how Americans regarded western scenery during the last decades of the nineteenth century. Moran could paint the wonders of Yellowstone and factories pouring smoke across the Rockies without apparent conflict [42]. Moreover, during the years that Bierstadt, Hill, Keith, Moran, Whittredge, and others were painting majestic views of the West, countless photographers "documented" as progress activities now regarded as environmental disasters [43]. Millions of board feet

42. Thomas Moran, *Smelting Works at Denver,* 1892, watercolor on paper, 13¾ × 16⅝ in. The Cleveland Museum of Art; bequest of Mrs. Henry A. Everett for the Dorothy Burnham Everett Memorial Collection.

43. Unidentified photographer, *Oxen Logging,* undated. Oregon Historical Society, Portland (3651).

were being removed from Pacific Coast forests each year, hydraulic-mining techniques washed away mountainsides in California, plows tore up the thickly tufted buffalo grass of the Great Plains, and raw frontier towns, which grew up and were abandoned in the space of several years, littered the landscape. National parks and scenic wonders acclaimed in paintings were also subjected to overuse and abuse, effectively challenging the belief that the wilderness was a resource claiming Americans undivided attention.

What made these landscapes ideological statements, however, is precisely their ability to encompass seemingly different views of nature—to argue for a resolution of conflict. Current approaches to landscape painting tend to isolate the transcendental and material. We see landscapes the way we view nature, conditioned by twentieth-century environmental concepts. It is difficult to transport ourselves back to a time when nature, at least in an allegorical sense, was capable of providing whatever society required.

The last chapter of this book heads off in a somewhat different direction. The images are no less ideological, but they no longer convey a single-minded faith in expansion and progress. By the 1890s a diminishing frontier and the mounting effects of eastern industrial development had begun to act on one another. Historians like Turner warned that the amount of arable land in the West was finite and without a frontier America might face a future less bright than the one optimistically predicted earlier. Although Turner's concerns were premature and founded on an agrarian bias, they nevertheless had a major impact on social scientists and politicians who believed that an important safety valve, "free" land, had been removed from the American economic system.

Indicative of this concern was a desire to review and canonize the frontier past, to reex-plain the sequence of events that had caused the rapid expansion during the previous half century. Images in the first five chapters of this book serve as metaphors of progress. They represent events that were underway or had occurred in the recent past; they reveal a strong sense of the present and the future, with only a perfunctory lament for a "disappearing America." In chapter 6 one sees many of the same subjects through the wrong end of a telescope. The historical perspective has increased and the metaphor has changed, from progress to tradition. The past is now a more discernible medium than the present or future, the past of frontier "virtues" is played, with telling objective, against the industrial present of 1900.

Recalling the past for Remington, Russell, Charles Schreyvogel, and their colleagues became an industry and an obsession. Their claims for verisimilitude (and similar testimony from those who viewed the paintings) rested on little more than studio images cleverly manipulated to convey an "authentic" version of Old West [44]. But it was enough to make early twentieth-century writers brand as authentic all images of the American West, and "authenticity" remains one of the most difficult issues to resolve. On one hand, a specific group of converts, which includes readers of western novels, viewers of western films, and collectors of western art, is still abroad. They find no reason to doubt what they read and see. Another group has relaxed its views on authenticity enough to admit the presence of artistic style but so far has failed to note the ideological content of western images. Art historians generally fall into this camp. We strenuously promote the artistic virtues of Remington, Russell, and their predecessors, leaving them as not particularly interesting characters in a company of eastern artistic swells.

More serious attention might be given to western art if it were restored to a national context, which, in fact, seemed to be the concern of artists painting western subjects at the turn of the century. The authority they claimed on behalf of their subjects was part of a very real effort to assess the frontier past and revitalize it for national consumption. This involved recycling numerous visual (and written) accounts of the frontier, extracting from them characters and events that would codify the "virtues" of the national past. The ideology used to justify expansion suddenly achieved permanent status. With no more frontier or at least with the concept in jeopardy, images were now called on to relay the ideology of the past to future generations.

Chapter 6 begins with a group of historical images specifically designed to carry out this mission. These images often repeat subjects that appear in earlier chapters: *The Discovery of San Francisco Bay* and Radisson and Groseilliers exploring the Saint Lawrence, for example, are scenes recycled from material presented in the first chapter. The paintings speak not of the actual events but to the memory of those events and its impact on viewers at the turn of the century. Heroic views of lone Indians, intended to expiate the sins of the past hundred years of frontier life, constitute another group of images in this chapter. They reward Indians for sustaining countless indecencies at the hands of whites by allowing them a share of the frontier past. The most lethal evocation of that past, however, appears in a group of paintings translating frontier "virtues" into a martial system for maintaining class and racial lines in industrial America. These paintings indicate the devastating consequences of reading as historical narrative or myth images charged with an ideology that continues to infuse our national life.

A National Role for Western Art

The point of this discussion is not to condemn motives that prompted territorial acquisition in America during the nineteenth century. But the role of images in guiding national behavior is another question. Images of the frontier are among the most potent and moving invented by American artists during the nineteenth century. Decade after decade they return with new force and meaning for our national life. So efficiently do they function as ideological statements that we grasp their import without even realizing it, making them devastating as hidden

44. Unidentified photographer, *Charles Schreyvogel Painting on the Roof of His Apartment Building in Hoboken, New Jersey*. From *New York Herald,* March 23, 1903, 3. National Cowboy Hall of Fame Collection, Oklahoma City; Carothers Collection.

persuaders but even more intriguing as works of art.[42] What is the source of these images, how does one establish their meaning, and to whom was their message directed? What cultural agenda makes them equally compelling as national symbols and as works of art?

In art-historical studies of the past several decades nineteenth-century images of the American West have often been neglected in favor of eastern landscape subjects and genre scenes thought to reveal more accurately national aims and ideals.[43] Perhaps it is time to reinstate western images as an alternate version of those same aims and ideals. The former set of images admitted progress as an inevitable but carefully controlled aspect of the national environment, the latter more openly advocated a "productive" and powerful America. The majority of images illustrated in this book favor the western version of progress, and, for better or worse, they seem to represent the star that most Americans followed during the second half of the nineteenth century.

Notes

1. N. H. Parker, *The Minnesota Handbook for 1856–57* (quoted in Ekirch, *Idea of Progress in America* [1951 ed.], 90).

2. Walter LaFeber, *The New Empire: An Interpretation of American Expansion, 1860–1898* (Ithaca, N.Y.: Cornell University Press, 1963), 12.

3. Willa Cather, *My Ántonia* (1918; Cambridge, Mass.: Riverside Press, 1946), 62.

4. R. G. Ferris, ed., *The American West: An Appraisal* (Santa Fe: University of New Mexico Press, 1963), 6. Others, however, have recently challenged many traditional assumptions of frontier scholarship (see Cronon, "Revisiting the Vanishing Frontier").

5. Robert G. Athearn, *The Mythic West* (Lawrence: University Press of Kansas, 1986), 223–75.

6. Unruh, *Plains Across,* 20.

7. Billington, *Westward Expansion* (1967 ed.), 753.

8. Slotkin, *Fatal Environment* (1985 ed.), 41, 45.

9. The difference in the way each artist interprets the political process is, of course, a convention representing a cultural belief rather than "reality." Lukas Vischer, a Swiss visitor to Washington, D.C., in 1825, describes behavior in the House of Representatives as "chaotic," rude, and obscene, hardly the impression one obtains from Samuel F. B. Morse's painting (see Christian F. Feest, "Lukas Vischer in Washington: A Swiss View of the District of Columbia," *Records of the Columbia Historical Society of Washington, D.C.* [1973–74]: 87–88). William Kloss very kindly supplied this information.

10. See Gail E. Husch, "George Caleb Bingham's *The County Election:* Whig Tribute to the Will of the People," *American Art Journal* 14, no. 4 (1987): 4–22.

11. Alfred Jacob Miller's, *Election Scene, Catonsville, Baltimore County,* circa 1860 (The Corcoran Gallery of Art, Washington, D.C.), is a notable exception.

12. See Patricia Hills, "Images of Rural America in the Work of Eastman Johnson, Winslow Homer, and Their Contemporaries: A Survey and Critique," in Hollister Sturges, ed., *The Rural Vision: France and America in the Late Nineteenth Century* (Omaha: Joslyn Art Museum, 1987), 63–82.

13. The literature to support this interpretation is

growing. It begins with Alan Wallach's article "Cole and the Aristocracy," *Arts* 56 (November 1981): 94–106; and includes Kenneth Myers, *The Catskills: Painters, Writers, and Tourists in the Mountains, 1820–1895* (Yonkers, N.Y.: Hudson River Museum, 1987); and Beth Ellis, "Cape Ann Views," in John Wilmerding, *Paintings by Fitz Hugh Lane* (Washington, D.C.: National Gallery of Art, 1988), 19–44. The remarks of the Reverend Samuel Osgood and Henry T. Tuckerman on John F. Kensett's late landscapes are helpful (see Oswaldo Rodriquez Roque, "The Last Summer's Work," in John Paul Driscoll and John K. Howat, *John Frederick Kensett (1816–1872): An American Master* [Worcester, Mass.: Worcester Art Museum, 1985], 149, 152, 155, 157). So are those of Leo Marx in Danly and Marx, *Railroad in American Art,* 197. We must also ask why Cropsey and Sanford R. Gifford repeated so often familiar views of New England and New York State, if not to fix a constantly changing scene.

14. The following nineteenth-century collectors each owned a major western painting by Albert Bierstadt as well as eastern scenes by Gifford, Kensett, or Whittredge: Alvin Adams, Samuel P. Avery, Thomas B. Clarke, W. W. Corcoran, Joseph Harrison, Collis P. Huntington, Legrand Lockwood, Marshall O. Roberts, James H. Stebbins, and A. T. Stuart. I am grateful to Nancy Anderson and Colonel Merl Moore, who helped compile this list.

15. See Cronon, "Revisiting the Vanishing Frontier"; and Clyde A. Milner, ed., *Major Problems in the History of the American West* (Lexington, Mass.: Heath, 1989).

16. The most notable examples are Drinnon, *Facing West;* Slotkin, *Fatal Environment;* and idem, *Regeneration through Violence.*

17. Weinberg, *Manifest Destiny,* 99, 457.

18. Ibid., 8.

19. Norman A. Graebner, *Empire on the Pacific: A Study in American Continental Expansion* (New York: Ronald Press, 1955), 3, 226–28.

20. Merk, *Manifest Destiny,* 55.

21. Billington, *Westward Expansion* (1967 ed.), 9.

22. Slotkin, *Fatal Environment* (1985 ed.), 43.

23. When asked who purchased his paintings, Charles Russell replied in 1919, "Pittsburghers most of all. They may not be so strong on art but they are real men and they like real life" (quoted in Dippie, *Looking at Russell,* 73). I am grateful to Alex Nemerov for calling my attention to this quote.

24. Albert Christ-Janer, *George Caleb Bingham of Missouri* (New York: Dodd, Mead, 1940), 138.

25. McCracken, *Catlin and the Frontier,* 16; McDermott, *Eastman;* Jeanne Van Nostrand and Edith M. Coulter, *California Pictorial* (Berkeley: University of California Press, 1948), 66, 72, 110; Grubar, *Ranney,* 13–14; Harold McCracken, *The Frederic Remington Book: A Pictorial History of the West* (Garden City, N.Y.: Doubleday, 1966); Kinietz, *Stanley,* 17; and Rathbone, *Wimar,* 28.

26. Perry T. Rathbone, ed., *Westward the Way* (Saint Louis: City Art Museum of Saint Louis, 1954).

27. Edgar P. Richardson, *American Romantic Painting* (New York: Weyhe, 1944).

28. See especially Hills, *American Frontier;* and Goetzmann and Goetzmann, *West of the Imagination.*

29. Richard Slotkin, "Myth and the Production of History," in Bercovitch and Jehlen, *Ideology and Classic American Literature,* 74.

30. Ibid., 70; see also Barthes, *Mythologies,* 142–43.

31. See T. J. Clark, *The Painting of Modern Life* (New York: Knopf, 1985), 8.

32. There were, in fact, several versions of the Daniel Boone myth in circulation at midcentury (see Smith, *Virgin Land* [1970 ed.], 3–58).

33. See Said, *Orientalism.*

34. Herman Melville, *The Confidence-Man: His Masquerade* (New York: Dix, Edwards, 1857), 227.

35. The lower houses, at least in bicameral legislatures, were popularly elected.

36. Billington, *Westward Expansion* (1967 ed.), 748–49, contends that western states "expanded belief in popular rule" by vesting unusual power in legislatures, extending the election process to cover more public offices, and requiring fewer voting restrictions.

37. Barbara S. Groseclose, "Painting, Politics, and George Caleb Bingham," *American Art Journal* 10 (November 1978): 5–19, notes Bingham's focus on specific campaign excesses in the election scenes. But Husch, "Bingham's *The County Election,*" provides a broader

view of the same issues and a generally more positive reading of the series.

38. Note, for example, the various triangles linking the principal figures in the foreground of *The Verdict of the People* [see 23], all of whom register different reactions to the announcement of election results.

39. Alan Wallach and Elizabeth Johns have convinced me that eastern patrons would probably have been amused by Bingham's frontier "characters."

40. Gerdts and Thistlethwaite, *Grand Illusions,* 114.

41. Quoted in Danly and Marx, *Railroad in American Art,* 16.

42. Slotkin, *Fatal Environment* (1985 ed.), 16–17.

43. In the book *America as Art,* for example, chapters on genre and landscape painting are called respectively, "The American Cousin" and "The Virtue of American Nature." Images of the West, however, never quite enter the mainstream of "national" art (see Taylor, *America as Art*).

Prelude to Expansion

Repainting the Past

WILLIAM H. TRUETTNER

The *West as America* begins with representations of events that long precede the actual occupation of the trans-Mississippi West and yet are not the earliest paintings included in this book. To connect these events with images of westward expansion will require us to modify our concept of a linear past. But as outlined in the introduction, the iconographical source for the paintings considered in subsequent chapters is less likely to be found in representations of rural life in the East than in "historical" scenes painted at midcentury. The latter designated precolonial and colonial events as initial steps along an ordained path directing American settlement westward. For nineteenth-century viewers, these images were programmed to collapse time and redefine the past. New chronologies, events, and personalities were invented, all subject to an acknowledged formula for recreating the past.

This campaign was orchestrated less by artists than by patrons and an expansionist ideology, which served to explain expansionist activity in the best possible light. It also informed artistic interpretation of the westward movement, encouraging the use of subjects and styles that effectively encoded expansionist aims. To our eye, the subjects of the paintings addressed in this chapter never utter a direct word about events that were determining the future course of the nation. But to those witnessing these events, the language used in the paintings rang with clear and determined purpose.

It is our task to exhume that language—to arrive again at an awareness of the subjects, themes, and aesthetic strategies nineteenth-century audiences understood and took for granted when viewing works of art. That does not mean, however, we have a unique ability to recall the circumstances of time and place. The one "fact" recent scholarship has taught us is that our inability to perceive historical "truth"—our avowed aim in studying the past—is shared with our ancestors, who had similar difficulties viewing their own or previous times with an objective eye. To drop the argument there, however, makes it difficult ever to retrieve useful knowledge of the past or of this particular group of paintings. Recent scholarship must be used as a guideline for further investigation, while never accepting it as the last word. Changing methods and the application of new values reveal "empirical fragments" of history that cohere in new ways but are themselves a warning against building too confidently on shifting ground.[1]

Interpreting history paintings, then, is a task requiring a qualification of sources as well as new lines of inquiry. It also involves recognition of another factor in current historical studies. The reexamination of national aims and goals and their foundation in expansionism (or "conquest," as it is now more frequently called) has behind it the moral impulse of contemporary scholars who find many good reasons to challenge the so-called success of nation-building practices of the nineteenth century.[2]

Historical analysis begins on at least two different levels. Our own—how we as contemporary Americans view our national past—and the viewpoint of audiences for whom the "historical" work was created. Ideological arguments condemned today were often the mainstream beliefs accepted in the past as the proper way to conduct national affairs. One could maintain that within this majority were a good many people who were unaware that these arguments were framed for political and commercial advantage. To obtain a clearer picture of an age their passive belief should be discounted against the presence of strong, if minority, dissent. But that only reduces the morality gap, it does not make it go away.

Rather than condemning our ancestors, it is perhaps safer to expose the way in which they made history—never forgetting that our own efforts may someday be subject to a similar process. History painting provides an in-

triguing view of history making in the nineteenth century, perhaps because the medium was used so often and effectively to convey national objectives. In turn, the "success" of history painting during those years was apparently a function of its unique and virtually unlimited resources. It drew on, for example, a

45. Peter F. Rothermel, *Columbus before the Queen,* 1842, oil on canvas, 62⅜ × 50 in. National Museum of American Art, Smithsonian Institution, Washington, D.C.

46. Anthony Van Dyck, *Charles I*, 1635, oil on canvas, 107 × 83½ in. Musée du Louvre, Paris.

distinguished artistic repertoire—grand figures and compositions from European old masters and the classical past gave it status and monumentality. It possessed extraordinary narrative capability. One could tell a story, draw a conclusion, and pronounce judgment all in the same frame. And, like literary myths, safely surrounded by metaphorical one-way glass, it was difficult to argue with.[3]

Now, we contend, that glass admits two-way vision.[4] Not because we can distinguish reality where our ancestors could not, but because new methods of research and a changed moral stance enable us to see what nineteenth-century viewers took for granted—the projection in pictorial language of a national ideology.

Once we unlock ourselves from a concept of history as fact and historical scenes as mirrors of the past, our task is to rediscover the purpose of history in nineteenth-century America and how it was used in works of art. This requires focusing on paintings and sculptures as both aesthetic and cultural objects and determining how style reinforced content. If the method is valid, we should begin to understand "historical" art as a means by which individuals or groups committed to certain nationalistic purposes argued their interests in pictorial language.

The Fiction of Historical Images

Two examples reveal the synthetic or constructed nature of history as it was used by nineteenth-century artists. *Columbus before the Queen,* 1842, by the Philadelphia painter Peter F. Rothermel, ostensibly portrays the exchange between Isabella and the future explorer that at least figuratively gave birth to America [45]. The queen, whose hands are dramatically crossed beneath a large jeweled pendant, listens

sympathetically to Columbus's plea for funds to launch his expedition to the Americas. A charged look passes between Isabella and Columbus, suggesting a romantic complicity in New World discovery. The globe is strategically placed between the two figures, on the drapery extending from the dais on which the queen stands. On Isabella's right is Ferdinand, less convinced of Columbus's project and attended by an openly suspicious counselor. With awe clearly written across his upturned features, a scribe connects the two groups visually, counteracting the king's skepticism. Behind is a looming, cathedrallike space into which a prophetic light pours from a high window.

The scene is more or less taken from Washington Irving's biography of Columbus, a diligent effort, published in 1828, to glorify

Columbus's enterprise and vision.[5] Rothermel, however, telescopes Irving's text to revive an apocryphal seventeenth-century tale in which Isabella offers her jewels to finance Columbus's voyage (which one takes to be the meaning of Isabella's gesture), when, according to Irving, she made the gesture under very different circumstances.[6] The interior is another problem. Columbus first encountered Ferdinand and Isabella at the royal residence in Córdoba, not in a Gothic cathedral or the ecclesiastical space depicted by Rothermel. One hopes also that everyone at the meeting was dressed in fifteenth-century costume and not in the Van Dyck mode chosen by Rothermel [46].

Not only did Rothermel adjust Irving's account, he added additional interpretations from the Columbus legend. The queen's jewels were never pledged to finance Columbus's voyage. Irving admits that the money came from the royal treasury, and recent scholars suspect that the real source was Moorish plunder, since Granada had been retaken by Spain only a short time before Columbus met Ferdinand and Isabella. The presence of the globe in the foreground, mounted on a base with finely detailed astronomical markings, raises other issues. The few terrestrial globes that existed in Columbus's time were simple spheres on which land masses were crudely indicated. The design of Rothermel's globe, with its elaborate meridian table, was probably taken from an early nineteenth-century model. Rothermel uses its modern appearance to great advantage, however. The globe functions to reinforce a rational, scientific justification for Columbus's voyage, its gleaming, precise surface an emblem of clarity in a world of superstition. Note that the globe is placed on top of a wrinkled map (the flat world?) and beside numerous discarded books scattered about the floor as if the knowledge they contain has been superseded by the authority of the globe.

Rothermel appears to be alluding to Irving's narrative, in which much is made of Columbus's debate with professors at the University of Salamanca: the former (Irving maintains) propounded his theory of a spherical world against the established flat-earth concept. That debate, however, was not about the shape of the world (which additional research would have told Irving and Rothermel, had they not been so anxious to settle it in favor of Columbus). Most learned people of the fifteenth century accepted it as round, but they disagreed on the distance Columbus would have to travel to reach the New World. The professors thought it was much further than did Columbus, and they turned out to be right.[7]

Details—authentic or manufactured—only create historical ambience for a more important objective, however: Rothermel's wish to give the scene a human and individual touch and yet to construe in divine terms the relationship between Isabella and Columbus. Isabella stands before her throne and above the stylish nun who attends her, in a manner reminiscent of a seventeenth-century saint. Light floods down on her to emphasize her elevated status. Columbus, meanwhile, is delicately profiled against the mysterious gloom of the cathedral background, which forms a giant halo around his head. The implication is obvious: Columbus's mission was to carry divine authority from the Old World to the New.

Unfortunately the articles of agreement drawn up between Ferdinand and Columbus do not exactly bear out Rothermel's interpretation. They say nothing about religion, a missionary objective, a desire to enlighten "backward" people and lands. They read more like a corporate document. Columbus was appointed admiral of the sea and governor-general over all mainlands and islands he discovered or acquired; he was to receive one-tenth of all natural resources obtained from those lands; and if he decided to underwrite one-eighth of the cost of the expedition, he was entitled to one-eighth of the profits. New World exploration during the fifteenth and sixteenth centuries was not carried on for altruistic reasons; it was a means of developing trade and commerce and of expanding the royal domain. Salvation came later when it could enhance conquest.[8]

In a practical sense *Columbus before the Queen* tells very little about the circumstances under which the navigator launched his expedition. But it discloses much about how mid nineteenth-century Americans (and the pious Philadelphia banker Edward S. Whelen who commissioned the picture) chose to interpret the founding of the New World. Not only was America the beneficiary of divine succession, it drew on a tradition of knowledge and experience, symbolized in the refined appearance of Isabella and Columbus, for its subsequent achievement (a point Rothermel also makes by employing the technique and poses Van Dyck used for portraying English aristocrats [see 46]). America culled the best from Europe, the painting implies, while rejecting despotic kings and scheming advisors (like Ferdinand and his counselor), who eventually led their countries into gradual decline.

Emanuel Leutze's *Storming of the Teocalli by Cortez and His Troops,* 1848 [47], follows its literary source more closely than *Columbus before the Queen.* The painting is based on a passage from William H. Prescott's *Conquest of Mexico,* a richly detailed account, published in 1843, of how the explorer Hernán Cortés vanquished the Aztec empire. Leutze has boldly envisioned a bitter contest between the Spaniards and the Aztecs on one of the upper terraces of the Teocalli, a sacred pyramid in the heart of the Aztec capital (present-day Mexico City). The composition divides along the middle on an imaginary line that carries one from the dead Spaniard on the steps in the fore-

ground up through a series of grotesque figures to the architectural motif capping the highest terrace of the pyramid. Arranged on the left are the Spaniards, whose angle of advance assures them ultimate triumph; the Aztecs defend the altar on the right, above which a priest raises a child already sacrificed. On a diagonal leading to the terrace above, a soldier prepares to dispatch another Aztec child, Leutze's way of revealing parity or a reminder to mid nineteenth-century audiences that the Spaniards were not above reproach. This theme is played several times more, most conspicuously at far left, where a Dominican monk offers last rites to a dying Indian (who rejects them), while behind him a soldier pulls valuable beads off the neck of an already dead Indian [48].

The architectural stage on which the battle rages is one of the most intriguing parts of the composition and not simply the product of Leutze's imagination. Several years earlier the writer and amateur archaeologist John Lloyd Stephens and architect Frederick Catherwood had investigated Mayan temple sites in the Yucatán. Catherwood published a volume of lithographs in 1844, which contained detailed renderings of the ruined temples.[9] From those lithographs, Leutze copied the giant serpent head in the right foreground [49], the heads inserted over the doorway and at the base of the tower, and the decorative designs bordering the terraces of the great pyramid. The entire architectural stage appears to be freely adapted from a number of Mayan temples, not one of which closely matches the altarlike appearance of Leutze's structure.

Assuming for the moment that Catherwood's drawings are reasonably accurate, Leutze's revisions betray attitudes more common to the nineteenth rather than the sixteenth century. Mayan temples are generally more delicately conceived, with deeply undercut, almost lacy, facades, in which strong horizontal

47. Emanuel Leutze, *The Storming of the Teocalli by Cortez and His Troops*, 1848, oil on canvas, 84¾ × 98¾ in. Wadsworth Atheneum, Hartford; The Ella Gallup Sumner and Mary Catlin Sumner Collection.

48. Emanuel Leutze, *The Storming of the Teocalli by Cortez and His Troops* (detail).

49. *Teocallis, at Chichén-Itzá*. From Catherwood, *Views of the Ancient Monuments* (1844), pl. XXII. National Museum of American Art/National Portrait Gallery Library Smithsonian Institution, Washington, D.C.

50. *Las Monjas, Chichén-Itzá*. From Catherwood, *Views of the Ancient Monuments* (1844), pl. XXI. National Museum of American Art/National Portrait Gallery Library, Smithsonian Institution, Washington, D.C.

elements are broken by angular or vertical lines, deep insets, and corners whose undercut decorations challenge the mass of the building [50]. The squat, powerful look of Leutze's structure is more menacing, more purposefully conceived as a primitive barricade against light and reason. Its low proportions are ugly and uninspiring; the detail has no distinction, no overall linking design that gives life and meaning to the whole; and the tower, with its cruelly distorted human faces bathed in a diabolical red light, is an appalling tribute to the dark side of humanity.

If one harbored any illusions about the Aztec empire, Leutze was determined to destroy them. And so, in his own way, was Prescott (an acquaintance perhaps of Amos Binney, the wealthy Boston scientist who commissioned *The Storming of the Teocalli*).[10] Prescott's concern about the legitimacy of the Spanish conquest of Mexico lies between every line of his three volumes, but occasionally it surfaces in forceful statements that leave no doubt as to his position. "We cannot regret the fall of an empire," he writes,

which did so little to promote the happiness of its subjects, or the real interests of humanity. . . . The Aztecs were emphatically a fierce and brutal race, little calculated, in their best aspects, to excite our sympathy and regard. . . . They ruled over their wide domains with a sword, instead of a sceptre. They did nothing to ameliorate the condition, or in any way promote the progress, of their vassals. . . . How can the interests of humanity be consulted, where man is levelled to the rank of the brutes that perish?[11]

Regardless of their level of civilization, Prescott went on to argue, the Aztecs were not Christian and therefore had no prospect of rising higher. A conquering nation, so long as it was Christian, had every right to subdue them. The point of Leutze's picture was not lost on contemporary critics. They recognized the passage in Prescott from which it came, and one openly declared that the subject represented "the final struggle of the two races—the decisive death-grapple of the savage and the civilized man . . . with all its immense results."[12]

What else did Leutze use to argue his point? The advancing Spaniards in black armor resemble human dreadnoughts; the technology of civilization entitles them to victory. The Aztecs battle in comparative disarray, half-nude as befitted "savages," wearing jewels, brightly colored clothes, and fanciful helmets, an ensemble meant to display decadent, pleasure-loving ways. Leutze has also been prolific in his artistic borrowing. The Massacre of the Innocents is surely one source, martyrdoms another, both of which convey a note of Christian sacrifice to the fierce battle.

In another passage Leutze raises (literally) the sacrifice issue again and turns it more conclusively against the Aztecs. Prescott describes in detail (in some of the most widely read chapters of the *Conquest of Mexico*) the Aztec method of sacrifice and the numerous victims. No practice, he maintained, illustrated more widely the moral gap between the invading Europeans and resident natives, a judgment Leutze played on in the vignette in which the Aztec priest holds aloft a partially disemboweled child.[13] Like much of Leutze's Aztec world, however, the vignette is a distortion to prove a point. Aztec children were rarely sacrificed and only in times of drought. Young male adults were the usual victims.

Despite all of Leutze's historical adjustments, few took issue with the picture. Contemporary critics applauded it for the "truth of the representation" and as a legitimate pictorial complement to Prescott's reporting of the scene.[14] The "work stamps itself on the recollection with so much vividness and reality," concluded another reviewer.[15] Surely Leutze's

Düsseldorf style accounts for some of that impression. The vigor and substance of his figures, their direct flow of energy, are almost cinematic. Textures, details, and lurid color enforce the effect; Leutze's facility collapses time and distance, bringing the past to the present with a formidable power.

But technical sleight of hand alone would never have convinced Leutze's contemporaries that the painting was a faithful representation of the past. There had to be a context into which the painting fitted, a contemporary situation that made them understand and accept the terms under which Leutze invented the scene. One of those is suggested by a remark made by Prescott when recounting the Aztec ritual preceding and following human sacrifice. "There were," he writes,

some occasions when preliminary tortures, of the most exquisite kind . . . were inflicted, but they always terminated with the bloody ceremony above described. It should be remarked, however, that such tortures were not the spontaneous suggestions of cruelty, as with the North American Indians; but were all rigorously prescribed in the Aztec ritual.[16]

North American Indian "savagery" already had a foundation in captivity narratives and historical reports of white settlement east of the Mississippi; by 1848 western fur trappers and settlers in the Southwest and Far West added new chapters to these tales of horror. Contemporary viewers must have had little trouble shifting the scene from the Aztecs to the Comanche, Sioux, Blackfoot, and other western tribes considered especially fierce adversaries of white encroachment. One can almost read into Leutze's painting a gratuitous violence stemming not so much from Prescott's text as from the record of Indian-white encounters during the nineteenth century. In 1848 Leutze—or mainstream expansionists— might well have believed that the worst was yet to come. *The Storming of the Teocalli*, therefore, represented the future as well as the past.

Contemporary audiences must have also associated the subject of the painting with the storming of the Castle of Chapultepec, a battle in 1847 that led to the speedy conclusion of the Mexican War [51]. Fought just outside the center of Mexico City, on a hill once crowned by an Aztec palace, the battle gave substance to the rallying cry of American forces, "To the Halls of the Montezumas."[17] It also provided General Winfield Scott's army access to the Mexican capital. Subsequently, through the Treaty of Guadalupe Hidalgo, the United States claimed most of what we refer to today as the Southwest. History was repeating itself. What Spain took from the Aztecs, America had now taken from Spain, by right of conquest once again blessed by Prescott. At pains to ex-

51. Britt and Major after Tompkins H. Matteson, *Storming of the Castle of Chapultepec, by the American Army under General Scott, September 13, 1847.* From *Pictorial Brother Jonathan* (July 4, 1848). Library of Congress, Washington, D.C.

plain and justify Spanish conquest of the New World, he fashioned a doctrine that appears to have less application to the sixteenth than to the nineteenth century. "With the right of conquest," he contended,

came also the obligation, on which it may be said to have been founded, to retrieve the nations sitting in darkness from eternal perdition. This obligation was acknowledged by the best and the bravest, the gownsman in his closet, the missionary, and the warrior in the crusade. However much it may have been debased by temporal motives and mixed up with worldly considerations of ambition and avarice, it was still active in the mind of the Christian conqueror.[18]

One does not have to search far for contrary evidence. Writing from the South Seas in 1620, a missionary father stated: "If the Spaniard does not see any advantage he will not be moved to do good, and these souls will perish without remedy if it is understood that no profit will be drawn from going there."[19]

Was Prescott stretching to vindicate Cortés or was he being chased by another ghost—his own conscience? The question, after all, was much more germane to the United States, which would soon engage Mexico under a similar pretext, soundly denounced by the Boston circle around poet and essayist James Russell Lowell, whom Prescott must have known well.[20] *Conquest of Mexico* was basically about progress: how a more advanced civilization was entitled to conquer one of lesser achievement, a principle Prescott desperately wanted to apply to a democratic nation bent on expansion. The best he could do was temper his principle with "humane" judgment.

STORMING OF THE CASTLE OF CHAPULTEPEC, BY THE AMERICAN ARMY UNDER GENERAL SCOTT, SEPT. 13, 1847.

History as Theater

Roy Strong begins a chapter of *Recreating the Past* (1978), his influential study of Victorian history painting, with a recollection of Norma Shearer playing Marie Antoinette in a Hollywood movie of the 1930s.[21] Hollywood's effort to reproduce the pomp and ceremony of the French court remains an experience that no one, then or now, would ever confuse with an "authentic" view of life in the past. But no such thoughts, Strong contends, inhibited history makers of the nineteenth century. The Scottish novelist Sir Walter Scott and the English historian Thomas Carlyle had convinced a new literate middle class that the past could indeed be recreated, that it could be presented as a passionate spectacle in which was preserved the spirit (or "truth") of characters, actions, and events. Moreover, historical subjects served as a kind of genealogy for this class. By providing a means of proceeding back and forth through history they ensured a continuum of ideas, aims, and goals that enabled one to see the present in terms of the past and vice versa. This continuum—based on social and economic objectives shared by the middle class—became gospel. History, therefore, was both a chain of events and a system of values, created by and for the convenience of a group of people who henceforth had a special interest in directing history in Europe and America.

History paintings, like nineteenth-century historical novels, offered a convenient way of reviving the past. They functioned as dioramas in which one could quite literally read history, both as direct observation and as a measure of growth and progress. Dry documents and dead bones were revived in dynamic tableaux that effectively passed for the real thing. What is real about them to our eyes is a few details

52. John Ferguson Weir, *An Artist's Studio,* 1864, oil on canvas, 25½ × 30½ in. Los Angeles County Museum of Art; gift of Jo Ann and Julian Ganz, Jr.

53. Robert W. Weir, *"Westward the Star of the Empire Takes Its Way" / in Progress at the National Capitol by E. Leutze,* 1861–62, ink on paper, 5 × 7⅞ in. Arthur J. Phelan, Jr., Chevy Chase, Maryland.

lifted from an engraving or another pictorial or written source. But nineteenth-century viewers saw them very differently. Accurate portraits, settings, and costumes gave authenticity to further invention, in which the artist attempted to convey what a character might actually feel in a given situation. The key to everything was setting the stage correctly. If properly done, the actors would follow "with colour in their cheeks, with passions in their stomach, and the idioms, features, and vitalities" of live and truthful characters.[22]

Witnessing this transformation in pictorial terms is less easy than describing it, but a comparison between two historical subjects by John Ferguson Weir and Robert W. Weir at least gives us insight into the two-step process. *An Artist's Studio,* 1864, is actually a portrait by John Ferguson of his father, the history painter Robert Weir, seated at a desk in his West Point studio [52]. A large easel, on which a painting is displayed, stands at the center of the room, but the father retires in a corner, engaged in scholarly pursuit. The success of the picture on the easel depends as much on what Robert Weir has obtained from historical sources (like the countless props lining the walls and studio surfaces) as on the act of reproducing the images developed from his studies. The paintbrush that has slipped to the floor before the easel is perhaps unwitting testimony to a hierarchy of artistic values represented by the picture. Fidelity to the past was not a matter of sleight of hand but of thorough and conscientious study.

A quite different and less formal way of showing how history painters made history is revealed in Robert Weir's small but lively drawing [53] of Leutze painting *Westward the Course of Empire.* The prescribed sketching trip to the Rockies preceded execution of the mural, so that Leutze could "witness" overland travel. But in Weir's drawing more emphasis is

placed on the artist imagining and reproducing the psychological implications of the scene. Robert Weir converts the process of history painting into pure theater. Standing before the mural on a scaffold-stage, his maulstick held across the mural surface and his brush poised, Leutze is acting the role of artist. Spectators, comfortably seated, sipping wine or brandy, have gathered together to watch his performance. Enhancing the stagelike atmosphere, the mural is brilliantly lit in an otherwise dark interior; the cartoon rests on an easel at the left, a resource to be given life and energy in its final incarnation.

But what kind of "life and energy"? Weir unwittingly reveals Leutze embarked on a purely imaginary venture (note the distance between the cartoon and the artist). The dimension the artist seeks to incorporate in the final version of the mural is not historical fact but drama of his own invention. Leutze performs for his audience; he is the vehicle through which we gain insight into the aspirations and ideals of an era but not a figure who recounts straightforwardly a narrative of contemporary events.

The final step in this argument involves recognizing the distance Robert Weir's drawing imposes between the viewer and the mural itself, which is described only as a vague outline. The real subjects of the drawing are the figures observing Leutze painting the mural. But a further retreat is implied by considering the interior as a tableau in itself. The viewer, at that point, is actually three steps removed from the mural, screened each time by a perspective that deliberately blurs historical truth. Comparing the oil painting of Weir's father to the sketch of Leutze painting the mural is now more revealing. The oil painting begins to look more "official"—a masterfully contrived version of how history was supposed to be made. Robert Weir's sketch of Leutze suggests a different view. Robert seems to reject the concept of history as carefully controlled narrative, acknowledging it instead as an ambivalent and willful act.

Loading the Image

Once John Ferguson Weir's reading of history or "historical" images is understood, the way is open to investigate the paintings collected in this chapter as evidence of a determined, if largely unrecognized, effort to offer as fact images charged with a potent ideology. Allusions to this ideology and its expansionist overtones have already been made in the discussion of *Columbus before the Queen* and *The Storming of the Teocalli*. The task is now to discover how mid nineteenth-century historical images became so effective a medium for conveying national aspirations.

The concepts of progress and expansionism had been clearly associated in America since the end of the eighteenth century, but not until politicians began to envision the country as a continental empire did they become inextricably bound. By the 1820s President John Quincy Adams and others had designated the Pacific Coast as the "natural" boundary of the nation, although most of it was still under Mexican control (Mexico had won independence from Spain in 1821). And two decades later expansionists conceived of Manifest Destiny as a theme for annexing what they had come to believe as rightfully theirs.

Destiny in this case meant mission, an exalted effort to carry forth guarantees of democracy, freedom, and economic opportunity to new domains. James K. Polk won the presidency in 1844 on a platform of Manifest Destiny and two years later declared war on Mexico. In 1847 a New York newspaper editor sanctioned the war in these words:

> The [Mexican] race is perfectly accustomed to being conquered, and the only new lesson we shall teach is that our victories will give liberty, safety, and prosperity to the vanquished, if they know enough to profit by the appearance of our stars. To *liberate* and *ennoble*—not to *enslave* and *debase*—is our mission. Well may the Mexican nation, whose great masses have never yet tasted liberty, prattle over their lost phantom of nationality. . . . If they have not—in the profound darkness of their vassal existence—the intelligence and manhood to accept the ranks and rights of freeman at our hands, we must bear with their ignorance.[23]

Six years later, in 1853, the signing of the Gadsden Purchase filled out the nation's "natural" boundaries.

Expansionism without progress was, of course, difficult to justify. A nation had to be better if it grew bigger, richer, and more powerful. But better how? And at whose expense? Americans for two centuries have debated the concept of progress and what it means. Until the end of the nineteenth century, however, that debate rarely addressed underlying political and moral issues.[24] Opponents of expansionism were mostly an undercurrent in the mid-nineteenth century; they were fortunate if they managed to raise doubts in the minds of more naive defenders of progress.[25] Those less innocent in their belief knew that a strong campaign to bolster the public conscience was required. God, morality, political and economic theory, science, and racial arguments were all used to prove that territorial acquisition would strengthen America.

These justifications were sometimes mounted separately but more often together under the aegis of "history." "The primary use of history [during the nineteenth century] was social," a recent scholar has written. Its purpose was "to strengthen society by supporting the basic principles in which men believed . . . personal morality, the existence of God, the greatness of America."[26] The last involved teaching patriotism, which "was largely a matter of making American history known so that its greatness would be apparent." That "greatness" was best understood as the pursuit of liberty.[27]

Put in such terms, the study of history appeared altogether admirable; but the course of the nation through the nineteenth century was less so. There was, in effect, a moral contradiction between pursuing liberty on behalf of an expanding democratic society while simultaneously denying freedom to those occupying lands the United States had recently conquered. To resolve the contradiction, to justify disrupting the moral framework of the nation (and decades of conflict), a higher cause had to be invoked. Manifest Destiny became that cause. It assumed the burden of establishing social priorities by implicitly denying status to those not in sympathy with an Anglo-Saxon vision of progress. Once conquest could be regarded as a providential mission, Americans proceeded westward with a formidable ideological weapon.

Nineteenth-century historians had firm foundations on which to build an argument for expansionism. The English preacher Richard Price had observed in 1784:

It is a conviction I cannot resist, that the independence of the *English* colonies in America is one of the steps ordained by Providence. . . . It is scarcely possible they should think too highly of their own consequence. Perhaps, there never existed a people on whose wisdom and virtue more depended; or to whom a station of more importance in the plan of Providence has been assigned.[28]

The chosen people concept became embodied in the next century in a host of American insti-tutions devoted to expansionist activities. Commerce, for example, was touted as a means of "diffusing civilization." It did so

by giving to savage tribes whom it visits, new ideas of comfort, and by thus forming them to habits of industry. It diffuses civilization by diffusing knowledge, and by imparting the improvements of the more intelligent and favored nations to those who are less so. It promotes the spirit of improvement, not only in these ways, but by bringing different nations into contact with each other, and compelling the ignorant to see their ignorance, and the uncivilized to acknowledge their inferiority.[29]

Racial bias and ambiguous references to "improvement" are hallmarks of expansionist literature. In the name of enlightenment—a "superior" race lifting the burdens of ignorance and poverty from an "inferior" people—a catalog of evils was committed. Yet history could justify them all by tracking the course of human events from one generation to the next. The gradual improvement of life, measured by those in control of the historical process, was self-evident.

History as a means of gauging advancement in the nineteenth century is further revealed in the subjects most frequently chosen by artists and writers. History painters, for example, selected subjects that revealed an "upward" path to their audiences. Discovery and exploration scenes from Columbus through La Salle marked the first step in civilizing the continent. The founding of the colonies was next, followed by events preceding the Revolution and the war itself. Post-revolutionary expansionism, personified by Daniel Boone, David Crockett, and other trans-Allegheny frontier heroes, was the next category, followed by Missouri and California scenes by George Caleb Bingham and Charles Nahl. The last gasp of midcentury history painting were the images of westward expansion created by Leutze and Albert Bierstadt.

The predictability of the sequence is revealing. One is led from great moment to great moment, literally across the continent, in a march demonstrating the progress of America as a free and independent people and as a nation accumulating innumerable resources [see 122]. The events up to and including the Revolutionary War remarkably parallel those treated extensively in George Bancroft's ten-volume history of the United States, published between 1843 and 1874 (in which the American Revolution was judged of secondary importance only to the birth of Christ).[30]

"National Pictures"

The growth of interest in nationalistic history paintings can be documented by a survey of midcentury exhibition records. Before 1840 only a few examples were exhibited, by 1850 the number had increased dramatically and remained high through 1860, after which it leveled off and subsequently declined.[31] At midcentury discovery and exploration scenes were one of the most popular categories of history painting. Another was, not surprisingly, events leading up to and the settlement of the original colonies. Both categories were featured in the murals commissioned by Congress in 1836 to fill the four remaining spaces in the rotunda of the Capitol (murals by John Trumbull already occupied four of the original eight spaces). The murals themselves can be considered an institutionalized form of transmitting to the public expansionist policies formulated by the federal government.

Chief among congressional tastemakers in the 1830s were Edward Everett, scholar, orator, and statesman from Massachusetts, and

Gulian C. Verplanck and Gouverneur Kemble, both associated with Irving in the Knickerbocker circle and congressional representatives from New York. Everett was chairman of the House Library Committee, through which passed all projects involving decoration of the Capitol during the late 1820s and early 1830s, and Verplanck served an overlapping term on the influential Buildings Committee. Dedicated advocates for the arts and connoisseurs (Verplanck and Kemble were collectors), all three were closely associated with the leading painters and sculptors of the day.

Everett's patriotism and dedication to expansionism are so well known that they need little corroboration. Early in his career, at the Harvard commencement of 1824, he prophesied:

Should our happy Union continue, in no great futurity this great continent will be filled up with the mightiest kindred people known in history; our language will acquire an extension which no other ever possessed; and the empire of the mind, with nothing to resist its sway, will attain an expansion, of which, as yet, we can but partly conceive.[32]

Later, during his short tenure as secretary of state, he proved to be a firm supporter of the Monroe Doctrine and "the law of American growth and progress." He proclaimed in a speech of July 4, 1853, "The pioneers are on the way. Who can tell how far and fast they will travel? Who, that compares the North America of 1753 . . . with the North America of 1853, . . . will dare to compute the timetable our railway progress . . . ?"[33]

Verplanck supported Andrew Jackson in the presidential elections of 1828, but his nationalism generally took a more scholarly turn. He promoted American arts and letters and encouraged writers to explore themes and subjects that he believed made the nation unique.

His views were delivered in numerous speeches and essays, which generally probed past events for patriotic meaning. The subject of one of Verplanck's "historical discoveries" was

the commemoration of some of those virtuous and enlightened men of Europe, who, long ago, looking with a prophetic eye towards the destinies of this new world, and regarding it as the chosen refuge of freedom and truth, were moved by a holy ambition to become the ministers of the Most High, in bestowing upon it the blessings of religion, morals, letters, and liberty.[34]

Those "blessings," as we have seen, set America above all other nations, obliging citizens to share with less fortunate neighbors the "benefits" of Christianity, democracy, and freedom.

Kemble, the most avid collector of the three, owned numerous old master paintings as well as works by American artists. He served

54. John Ferguson Weir, *The Gun Foundry*, 1864–66, oil on canvas, 46½ × 62 in. Putnam County Historical Society, Cold Spring, New York.

two terms in Congress (1837–41) and was a delegate to the Democratic national convention that nominated Polk. Kemble was also a promoter of the railroad that crossed the Isthmus of Panama and a proprietor of the West Point Foundry Association, which produced and sold to the federal government military ordnance (including cannons) of exceptional quality. The foundry was later featured in *The Gun Foundry*, 1864–66, a major work by John Ferguson Weir [54].

To the Joint Committee on the Library fell the task of designating artists to fill the four vacant rotunda panels. Chaired by Everett, but with ample advice from Verplanck, the committee in 1836 awarded two panels to Washington Allston and one each to two of four other major contenders: John Gadsby Chapman, Henry Inman, John Vanderlyn, and Robert Weir. Allston demurred, too preoccupied with a monumental history painting, *Belshazzar's Feast*, 1817–43 (The Detroit Institute of Arts), but probably also mindful of a previous exchange with Verplanck, who had advised him that religious scenes would not be appropriate as mural subjects.[35] The four winners (Inman and Weir were protégés of Verplanck, Vanderlyn was a close friend of Allston, and Chapman had illustrated Bancroft's *History of the United States*) were offered a choice of subject, so long as it illustrated an event "civil or military, of sufficient importance to be the subject of a national picture, in the history of the discovery, or settlement of the colonies."[36] The code words were, of course, "national picture" and "history." A national picture guaranteed an endorsement of current political aims, and history was the yardstick validating those aims.

Apparently by chance the murals represent a sequence of exploration, discovery, and settlement. But the outcome must have been managed more carefully than records indi-

cate.[37] The triumphant nature of the exploration and discovery scenes by Vanderlyn and
William H. Powell (the latter was awarded Inman's contract after the artist's death) in which
Columbus and De Soto lay claim to the New
World are further evidence of a "historical"
viewpoint [55–56]. Columbus is conceived in
the same manner as the aristocratic figure in
the Rothermel painting. His right to conquer,
as an agent bringing civilization to the New
World, is taken for granted. Indians flee, his
men grub for gold in the sand (at far left), but
he remains above it all, his gaze fixed on the
future. Powell is more forthright. With a supporting cast of monks and soldiers, De Soto
parades through an Indian village on horseback
(the image of the Spaniards most frightening to
the Aztecs and Incas). If religious conversion
fails, the viewer observes, cannons are not far
behind. History was a process by which the
strong were entitled to conquer the weak; it
also enabled Powell's contemporaries to view
expansionism in the best possible light. A critic
writing for the *National Intelligencer* in 1853

praised Powell's selection of subject:

The discovery of the Mississippi by De Soto may be
said to be the starting point in the history of that remarkable region, which has already astonished the
world by its growth, its vigor, and its vast resources, and which is destined to be perhaps in less
than two centuries the citadel and centre of the
world's civilization and the world's freedom.[38]

The two settlement scenes, Weir's *Embarkation of the Pilgrims,* 1843, and Chapman's
Baptism of Pocahontas, 1840, are less directly
concerned with conquest than with the establishment of freedom and a national religion
[57–58]. Weir's painting represents the moment
when the pastor and friends of the *Speedwell*
passengers (subsequently the Mayflower Pilgrims, after they changed ships) offer prayers
for a successful voyage. More than prayers will
guide the *Speedwell,* however. The rainbow at
left, the light that plays on the uplifted head of
the pastor (and on the scripture), and the
armor on the deck indicate that the voyage is a
crusade to carry the word of God to the New

55. John Vanderlyn, *Landing
of Columbus at the Island of
Guanahani, West Indies, October
2, 1492,* 1846, oil on canvas,
144 × 216 in. United States
Capitol, Washington, D.C.

56. William H. Powell,
*Discovery of the Mississippi by
De Soto A.D. 1541,* 1853,
oil on canvas, 144 × 216 in.
United States Capitol,
Washington, D.C.

57. Robert W. Weir, *Embarkation of the Pilgrims at Delft Haven, Holland, July 22d, 1620*, 1843, oil on canvas, 144 × 216 in. United States Capitol, Washington, D.C.

58. John Gadsby Chapman, *Baptism of Pocahontas at Jamestown, Virginia, 1613*, 1840, oil on canvas, 144 × 216 in. United States Capitol, Washington, D.C.

World. In short, the voyage already had divine blessing. It was also, in the words of another *National Intelligencer* critic, a reminder of "the great events which grew out of principles imparted by the actors in it to their descendants, and which finally led to that separation from the dominion of the Old World which made us an independent people."[39]

Chapman's *Baptism of Pocahontas* allegedly recorded the first conversion of an American "savage" to Christianity—or as the artist stated it in his description of the mural, Pocahontas

stands foremost in the train of those wandering children of the forest who have at different times . . . been snatched from the fangs of a barbarous idolatry, to become lambs in the fold of the Divine Shepherd. She therefore appeals to our religious as well as our patriotic sympathies, and is equally associated with the rise and progress of the Christian Church, as with the political destinies of the United States.[40]

Chapman meant by this remark that Christianity was the ordained religion of progress and

that as the nation expanded and prospered only those who shared the faith would benefit.

Before leaving the Capitol, we should also examine several commissions awarded by Montgomery Meigs, an army officer and engineer who became supervisor of the Capitol extension program in 1852. Meigs served much of his term under Jefferson Davis, secretary of war to President Franklin Pierce and a tacit, if not open, supporter of the filibuster William Walker, a half-mad lawyer and journalist, whose territorial ambition outshined that of all other Americans during the 1850s.[41] Meigs turned for advice to the familiar trio—Everett, Kemble, and to a lesser extent, Verplanck— who persuaded him to engage American artists to decorate the new complex.

In brief, Meigs commissioned from Thomas Crawford (whom Everett had recommended) the eastern pediment of the new Senate chamber. Disdaining allegories and classical subjects, Meigs urged Crawford to select subjects from the American past. "In our history of the struggle between civilized man and savage," Meigs wrote to Crawford, "between the cultivated and the wild nature are certainly to be found themes worthy of the artist and capable of appealing to the feeling of all classes."[42] The subject decided on, The Past and Present of America and the Decadence of the Indian Race—in which a personification of America separates a decadent past, symbolized by a despondent Indian, from a prosperous future, represented by a soldier, merchant, schoolmaster, mechanic, and, at far left, the anchor of hope—is about as direct an exposure of expansionist priorities as one can find in a midcentury public monument [59].

Meigs also commissioned from Crawford "Armed Freedom," 1863, the sculpture that stands atop the Capitol dome [60]. Jefferson Davis recommended that the cap worn by the figure in its initial stage be replaced with a helmet, more appropriate to a triumphant nation.[43] An enormous painting of one of those "triumphs," *The Storming of Chapultepec,* 1857–62 [61], by James Walker, which hung in the Senate wing for many years, was also commissioned by Meigs as well as the quintessential expansionist mural, *Westward the Course of Empire* [see 100], by Leutze. When the execution of the mural and payment for it lapsed into the Civil War years, Meigs justified the expense by claiming that completing the Capitol decorations would give "the people" a "welcome assurance" of confidence and strength in their government.[44] What he really meant was that westward expansion would eventually diffuse sectional conflict, a view advocated by many who backed construction of a transcontinental railroad a few years later.[45]

Themes of Conquest

The images that remain to be discussed in this chapter fall roughly into categories or follow

59. Thomas Crawford, *Progress of Civilization,* 1863, marble, length 720 in. United States Capitol, Washington, D.C.

60. Thomas Crawford, *Statue of Freedom,* 1863, bronze, height 234 in. United States Capitol, Washington, D.C.

themes dictated by concepts of history prevalent at midcentury. The post-Trumbull Capitol murals serve as iconographic models for these categories, although they are not necessarily prototypes, since several paintings in each category predate the murals. The categories themselves, however, now become more central to the argument than do the individual paintings. As groups of paintings, they reveal a consistent ideology linking a number of related subjects. By comparing the groups to each other, one begins to understand the sequential nature of such images—that they represented not so much individual scenes or events as steps in the nation's progress.

Each can be discounted as representing a specific time or place, using the method employed earlier when analyzing the paintings by Rothermel and Leutze. But those same paintings make positive and effective arguments in advancing an expansionist ideology. As works of art, they have a special advantage. Aesthetic strategies could be devised to support ideological arguments. Further, the major oils have an insulating factor: they raise themselves above the debate over expansionism while using language understood by contemporaries. They rarely, for example, openly advocate territorial

expansion, commercial opportunity, or dispossession of native races. They are not broadsides; they never "expose" contemporary life. Instead they turn back the clock and present their arguments as part of a distant past, in which they gain time-honored legitimacy. The stylistic vocabularies employed by each artist also rely on the past. Classical vistas, old master compositions, and antique figures reoccur time and again. Subjects and styles create a patina hard to penetrate. To do so, one has to doubt the authority of the past as well as the legitimacy of a political experiment held aloft as the premier American virtue. Arguments were rarely, if ever, made against progress; they were only made on behalf of modifying progress.

The categories are not mutually exclusive; each shades a bit into the next. Yet they represent three major ways of understanding and justifying expansionism. And, in turn, they provide an iconographic direction for subsequent chapters in this book, in which artists chose a more contemporary strategy for treating a similar idea. Grouped in the first category—Encountering the New World—are pictures by Leutze, Thomas Moran, Rothermel, Joshua Shaw, and Robert Weir, all of which announce the proprietary rights of Europeans in the New World. Some do it by constructing a link between Europe and America, implying the passage of civilization westward, like Rothermel's *Columbus before the Queen* or Leutze's *Departure of Columbus from Palos* [see 45 and 64]. But the paintings by Moran and Shaw make the most breathtaking assumptions of superiority [62–63]. Their subjects are closely related. Neither has a text, since both are conceived (hypothetically) from the Indian point of view. The New World and its inhabitants are not seen from the deck of a ship but from the shore, from which the approach of European explorers is observed.[46]

61. James Walker, *The Storming of Chapultepec*, 1857–62, oil on canvas, 90 × 93½ in. United States Capitol, Washington, D.C.

62. Thomas Moran, *Columbus Approaching San Salvador,* 1860, oil on canvas, 24 × 45 in. Thomas Gilcrease Institute of American History and Art, Tulsa.

63. Joshua Shaw, *Coming of the White Man,* 1850, oil on canvas, 25¼ × 36⅜ in. The Elisabeth Waldo-Dentzel Collection, Northridge, California.

Both subjects are prophetic: the ships appear like stars in the East, announcing the presence of an awesome new divinity in the celestial brightness of the sails on the horizon and redeeming path of sunlight. The V of birds in the sky of Shaw's painting also establishes the scene as a paradigm of migration—the passage westward toward new land—and perhaps refers to the ark from which Noah released a dove to determine the proximity of land newly emerged from the Flood. In dignified but apprehensive formation, the Indians in Moran's painting anticipate the landing of the ship. The island (San Salvador) on which they stand is a tropical paradise, with mountains, lush forests, delicate flowers, and a splashing waterfall. Its

promise of richness and abundance is carefully reinforced by Claudian space; deep, saturated tones; beguiling patterns of sunlight; and by docile natives, who have already accepted their supporting role.

In Shaw's painting the warm light strikes the four principal figures with almost tangible force. One is led to believe that the Indians—in this case, primitive half-naked savages (a scalp lies on the flat rock in the very center of the painting)—have been converted simply by witnessing the appearance of the ship. The composition is again Claudian, this time employing the master's combination of space and light for its redemptive value. Neither picture, of course, describes the Indians' viewpoint; both

64. Emanuel Leutze, *The Departure of Columbus from Palos in 1492*, 1855, oil on canvas, 48 × 72 in. Private collection. Courtesy of the America-Japan Quincentenary Foundation. (Detail illustrated on p. 54.)

artists postulate the European presence as the basis for raising the spiritual and material circumstances of native Americans.

The Departure of Columbus from Palos, 1855 [64] (once in the collection of Charles W. Gould, who also owned Asher B. Durand's *Progress* [see 120]), represents a more conventional approach: the viewer is led by the extended arm of the explorer in the direction of the New World.[47] Irving's account of the departure from Palos is brief, mentioning only "the tears and lamentations" of those left be-

hind.[48] Leutze has included vignettes registering a range of emotions, in particular those of the young men in the small boat on the right, who seem ready to capitalize on the anticipated loneliness of the beautiful young woman seated before them. This touch of Düsseldorf narrative, which gives a familiar domestic air to the scene, is played off against the grave and prophetic gesture of Columbus, who assumes the role of martyr, prepared to sacrifice himself on the open sea. Echoes of Carl Friedrich Lessing's *Hussite Preaching,* 1836 (Kunstmuseum,

65. Peter F. Rothermel, *De Soto Discovering the Mississippi,* 1843, oil on canvas, 50 × 63 in. Saint Bonaventure University Art Collection, New York; gift of Dr. T. Edward Hanley.

66. Robert W. Weir, *The Landing of Hendrick Hudson,* circa 1835, oil on canvas, 33 × 48 in. Private collection.

Düsseldorf), as well as scenes of Christ performing miracles are evident.[49] The picture could also be viewed as a mock Crucifixion: the mast and spar behind Columbus form a cross, while other vignettes recall the Passion cycle. A young boy in a Judas-like gesture kisses Columbus's hand; two young men behind Columbus, who draw down on the main halyard, are reminiscent of figures in Deposition iconography; and the young lady in white, who gazes longingly at Columbus, could be construed as Mary Magdalene. Whatever the meaning of these figures, the painting is saturated with religious symbolism. Columbus assumes the role of a minor divinity, the most legendary figure in New World iconography.

Rothermel's *De Soto Discovering the Mississippi,* 1843, and Robert Weir's *Landing of Hendrick Hudson,* circa 1835, are two more views of European explorers helping themselves to the New World but in very different ways [65–66]. Rothermel makes much out of a discovery that did not exactly fire De Soto's imagination; the explorer only wished to cross the river to cities of gold he hoped were on the other side. But the Mississippi in 1843 was one of the major pathways west (which is perhaps why the picture was an Art-Union selection the next year; see chapter 2), and so it took on momentous proportions under Rothermel's brush. De Soto is another Van Dyck courtier posing on a foreground stage that includes Indians lifted from Tiepolo or another European source.[50] The European explorer towers over the Indians, who appear to be both his guides and servants. The darker male (also a European convention) gestures toward the deep vista with which Rothermel attempted to immortalize De Soto's discovery. The viewer, in turn, passes from civilization to savagery to the land, a sequence that, followed in reverse order, will redeem the New World.

The first owner of *The Landing of Hendrick Hudson* was Gulian Verplanck, who apparently commissioned it from Weir.[51] Hudson was supposed to have landed on a point in the river that subsequently belonged to Verplanck's Dutch ancestors.[52] Verplanck's view of Indians, which was more humane than that of his ancestors, may be why Weir included a Penn's

Treaty vignette on the shore between the standing Indian and the Dutch longboat [see 81].[53] Hudson, with arms outspread, seems ready to embrace the standing Indian, who raises ears of corn in a sign of friendship. No one cowers or is struck blind as in Shaw's painting; Weir invites the viewer to believe that the two principals are about to meet as equals. The key to the painting, however, is conveyed by the position of Hudson's longboat. At the center of the composition, moving on a major diagonal from the *Half Moon* to shore, Weir established Hudson as the emissary from civilization, about to land on Indian territory. The Indians welcome the intrusion, acknowledging Hudson's role in the attitude with which they draw his boat toward shore.[54] A later version of the painting [67] follows more closely the

67. Robert W. Weir, *The Landing of Henry Hudson,* circa 1838, oil on canvas, 68 × 108 in. David David Art Gallery, Philadelphia.

encounter theme detailed in the Moran and Shaw paintings. A ghostly rendition of the *Half Moon* sits offshore, causing curiosity and astonishment among the Indians on the high foreground bank and in canoes slowly moving toward the sailing vessel. Weir also includes a formation of shore-bound birds similar to those in the Shaw painting.

The iconography of these encounter paintings is most conveniently summed up as voyages of discovery. Wagon trains and railroads are the successors of sailing ships, and Daniel Boone and fur trappers claim territory in the name of Columbus, De Soto, and Hudson.[55] One era made way for another, the sequence implies, and the course of civilization continued westward.

Into the second category of paintings—Savagery versus Civilization—fall images closely related to those in the first category. The major difference is that the establishment of European civilization on the new continent is now taken for granted; conquistadores, missionaries, and colonists confront a race they must instruct and control. Rothermel and Chapman lead off with works that impose a courtly solution on the problem. The noble conquerors, in this case Cortés and John Smith, extend to the vanquished a guarantee of "generous" treatment that implies a recognition of Indian "royalty" and a desire to temper it with the advantages of civilization. Rothermel's *Surrender of Guatemozin,* 1845 [68], and Chapman's *Coronation of Powhatan* [see 70] consider this issue somewhat differently.

Rothermel's picture is extraordinarily rich in color and texture, as if echoing the high ceremonial occasion described by Prescott and the noble attributes of the principal subjects.[56] Additional authority is given the subject by linking it to monumental baroque compositions, such as Diego Velázquez's *Surrender at Breda,* 1634–35 [69], which in mood and arrangement

constitutes a likely precedent. Following Velázquez's lead, perhaps, Rothermel also uses compositional devices to distinguish the victor from the vanquished (note the position of the lances). *The Surrender of Guatemozin* reads from left to right: the viewer emerges from the smoke and destruction of battle to encounter Guatemozin's wife (Montezuma's daughter), who stands at the crucial dividing line between dark and light, distraught and facing neither direction. Profiled against the light background, her husband reluctantly approaches Cortés but does not return his overture. The angle of Guatemozin's scepter neatly divides savagery and civilization. Seated beside Cortés is his Indian mistress, dark and sensual compared to the European woman who stands (predictably) above her. Behind and above Cortés, a courtier plants the standard of Castile, and at the right edge of the picture a spar crossing a mast effects an unmistakable cross, the concluding symbol on the path the Aztec leader must follow. Rothermel signifies the course with movement upward from lower left to the standard and cross, which mark the ultimate triumph of Cortés's campaign. The destruction of Aztec civilization is designed to lead to a glorious Christian future.

Reading further in Prescott, however, one finds that Cortés and his soldiers, who had not located a royal treasury that met expectations, tortured Guatemozin in an attempt to make him reveal where more gold was hidden.[57] Very little was subsequently found. Not long after, Guatemozin was condemned as a rebel and executed. Even Prescott thought the charges unfair. But historians and history painters had larger issues at stake; one infamous act did not erase the long-term benefits of European civilization and Christianity.

Chapman's *Coronation of Powhatan,* 1836 [70], painted a few years before the *Baptism* mural [see 58], recounts an incident in which

68. Peter F. Rothermel, *The Surrender of Guatemozin,* 1845, oil on canvas, 37½ × 49 in. Kennedy Galleries, Inc., New York.

69. Diego Velázquez, *Surrender at Breda,* 1634–35, oil on canvas, 120¾ × 154½ in. Museo del Prado, Madrid.

John Smith was sent to flatter the old chief (Powhatan was Pocahontas's father) with a crown and other presents, contained in the trunk at left. In exchange, Smith and his colonists at Jamestown hoped Powhatan would lead them to the Monacons, a neighboring tribe who were reputed to have "boundless wealth." Borrowing from a baroque coronation scene, Chapman shows Powhatan eyeing the crown cautiously, although he finally allowed it to be placed on his head. He later re-fused to guide Smith's men to the Monacons, however, thereby resisting the trappings of power and luxury offered as a bribe by the Europeans.

On the surface, it appears that Powhatan and his followers have been portrayed in a favorable light—until one reads a subsequent commentary in *Graham's Magazine,* in which Powhatan is described as a "sturdy old republican . . . having no notion of a crown."[58] The Powhatan incident now takes on a different

70. John Gadsby Chapman, *Coronation of Powhatan,* 1836, oil on canvas, 22½ × 29 in. Gerald Peters Gallery, Santa Fe, New Mexico.

meaning. Chapman's contemporaries probably read the subject as America versus Europe, the disdain of the New World for the despotic and decadent ways of the Old (note that the Indians stand or sit at the edge of the forest; nature is on their side). Powhatan's costume supports this interpretation. Taken from a European illustration rather than a specific example Chapman could easily have found in this country, it was probably meant to dignify Powhatan, to lift him above the realm of an ordinary "savage" so that he could represent America. As easily as garments could be changed, white artists manipulated Indian images to suit their pictorial needs. Indians could be conquered for their own good, as many images in the category Encountering the New World suggest; they could be sacrificed for a greater cause, as Leutze and Rothermel advocate in their Aztec subjects; or they could be reinvented to defend the spirit of democracy, as did Chapman and subsequent painters. Rarely, if ever, were they represented in any other way.

The "sturdy old republican" Powhatan appears in another guise in Victor Nehlig's *Pocahontas and John Smith*, 1870 [71]. Presiding over the imminent death of John Smith, the chief exhibits a barbarous nature that links him to Leutze's Aztecs.[59] His family watches the procedure indifferently, while warriors actively encourage Smith's destruction. The figure in the foreground, about to deliver the fatal blow, closely resembles the club-swinging priest in *The Storming of the Teocalli* [see 48]. A very young Pocahontas stops the blow, thus redeeming the scene for nineteenth-century white viewers. Pocahontas's early association with Jamestown colonists, these viewers believed, led her to reject the "savage" ways of her tribe. A formal acceptance of Christianity followed; she was baptized (as we noted in Chapman's mural) and eventually married the Englishman John Rolfe. Thus Indians, even from

71. Victor Nehlig, *Pocahontas and John Smith*, 1870, oil on canvas, 89 × 74½ in. Brigham Young University Fine Arts Museum Collection, Provo, Utah.

72. Jusepe de Ribera, *Martyrdom of Saint Bartholomew*, circa 1616, oil on canvas, 80 × 60 in. H. Shickman Gallery, New York.

73. Joseph Mozier, *Pocahontas*, 1859, marble, height 48 in. Hirschl & Adler Galleries, Inc., New York.

circumstances as inhumane as those presided over by Powhatan, were thought capable of redemption and, of equal importance, acculturation.

Nehlig too offers Christianity as an art-historical solution. The picture is constructed like a Last Judgment scene, with activity radiating out from Powhatan, whose evil command is overturned by Pocahontas. The artist may have considerably rearranged the progression of events, but the "judgment" finally carried out by Pocahontas nonetheless gains meaning from the compositional strategy. Nehlig also gives John Smith the appearance of a martyred saint to convey more forcefully his pending sacrificial role [72].

The sculptor Joseph Mozier approached the issue another way, depicting Pocahontas as a child of nature, as guileless as the fawn that nuzzles her leg [73]. A cross, held in her right hand, signifies her "natural" Christian instinct, not derived from European contact but from dwelling in a world in which God's presence prevailed. Nature, however, also had a dark side, which could foster passion and cruelty in pagan hearts. The version of nature one used depended on which message was to be conveyed.

Fewer representations of contact among Indians and Europeans employ a Spanish California iconography, since that area had to become a state (1848) before it gained a "colonial" status. Nevertheless, *Father Serra Celebrating Mass in Monterey*, circa 1870 [74], painted by Leon Trousset, is similar in theme to the Rothermel and Chapman paintings, which precede it. Trousset signals his view of Spanish-Indian encounters with the relentless arrangement of soldiers surrounding Serra. The viewer is reminded of wagons circled on the prairie, prepared to defend against marauding tribes.

Junípero Serra was indeed an active colonizer; he established nine Franciscan missions in California in a span of thirteen years. But his zeal as a missionary did not preclude concern for his Indian subjects, whom he often protected from the military attachment that accompanied his exploration of Upper California. The rigid classification of faithful plotted by Trousset seems out of touch with the missionary era. Creeping through the underbrush or kneeling behind the "stockade" of Spanish soldiers, the Indians invented by Trousset are like dispossessed victims of Anglo California. They remind one of Indians described by Helen Hunt Jackson in *Ramona* (1884) rather than those mentioned in the memoirs of Francisco Palóu, Father Serra's biographer and contemporary.[60]

By the 1870s landscape had begun to play a major role in historical paintings. One senses

74. Leon Trousset, *Father Serra Celebrating Mass in Monterey,* circa 1870, oil on canvas, 24 × 32 in. California Historical Society, San Francisco.

75. Thomas Moran, *Ponce de León in Florida, 1514,* 1878, oil on canvas, 63½ × 115 in. National Cowboy Hall of Fame Collection, Oklahoma City.

76. Robert W. Weir, *Embarkation of the Pilgrims,* 1857, oil on canvas, 48 × 71½ in. The Brooklyn Museum; A. Augustus Healey Fund and A. Augustus Healey Fund B.

it with Trousset, although nature is still dominated by the figures. Moran, however, sets the scene of his painting in a woodland glade that dwarfs the figures [75]. The Spanish explorer Juan Ponce de León, who had accompanied Columbus on his second voyage, stands before a large tree in the center of a sunlit clearing; he is the connecting link between savagery and civilization. His soldiers maintain martial order, while the Indians, except for one leader who advances to meet him, recline indifferently. The arrangement decides who will prevail (although contemporary accounts reveal

that Ponce de León was rebuffed by Indians during his entire journey across the Florida Peninsula).

The landscape itself and its relation to events are the most compelling aspects of the painting. The towering forest, resonant with deep green foliage and golden highlights, suggests the fecundity and promise of the New World and the untold riches that lay in its dark and unexplored corridors (note the soldier in the very center of the composition who peers tentatively into the gloom). The Spaniards, as the more formidable military force, also appear

77. Peter F. Rothermel, *Landing of the Pilgrims,* 1854, oil on canvas, 41⅛ × 54⅞ in. Lafayette College, Easton, Pennsylvania; Kirby Collection of Historical Paintings.

to possess the energy and technology needed to wrest from the land its vast potential. Tall trees reinforce the soldiers' ranks, and a shaft of light marks their entrance into the forest. No such formal elements validate Indian life. Two Indians recline in the foreground, near the swamp; the rest seem content to remain in their smoky forest den. They are not committed to progress, the painting implies; the land will never improve under their aegis.[61]

In the third category of paintings—Founding a New Nation—the emphasis is more specifically on settlement, although themes of ap-

propriation and Indian-European relations are no less present. The images generally attempt to establish a political and religious foundation for domestic life in the New World, as if that base could be perennially shifted westward. Many settlement images, such as Bingham's *Family Life on the Frontier* [see 167] and John Mix Stanley's *Oregon City on the Willamette River* [see 173], are spiritual descendants of colonial scenes. By midcentury the colonial era had, in both pictorial and written accounts, gained the status of high patriotic myth.[62] Major oils incorporating this myth projected a

strong nationalism and the concept of settlement as religious mission.

In Robert Weir's Capitol mural [see 57], a
later version of which is illustrated here, the
Pilgrims are shown embarking from Delft [76];
Rothermel's *Landing of the Pilgrims*, 1854,
brings them to a stormy and forbidding New
England shore [77]. The scene is based on the
first two stanzas of a popular poem of 1826:

The breaking waves dash'd high
On a stern rock-bound coast,
And the woods against a stormy sky
Their giant branches toss'd;

And the heavy night hung dark,
The hills and water o'er
When a band of exiles moor'd their bark
On the wild New England shore.[63]

Alone in the New World, "exiled," exposed to nature, without resources other than
their own extraordinary courage, "pioneer"
Pilgrims disembarking on one of many "unfriendly" shores are conjured in poem and
painting. They face a difficult uphill journey,
Rothermel reminds us, with his high cliff that
towers above those on land. Yet they are in-
domitable. The female who strides valiantly
forward symbolizes that spirit, bringing to the
New World the civilized virtues needed to
found a new colony. The aura of the group is
that of Israelites—a chosen people—safely
landed in Canaan. The scene anticipates William Ranney's *Advice on the Prairie* [see 95], in
which latter-day pilgrims cross the Great Plains
to Oregon and California, and a sturdy group
of "pioneer women" who appeared in the
1920s [78].

78. Bryant Baker, *Pioneer
Woman*, 1927, bronze, height
32¼ in. National Museum of
American Art, Smithsonian
Institution, Washington,
D.C.; gift of the artist.

The record of the Pilgrims' first years at Plymouth is indeed impressive; their staying power in the face of a harsh winter (perhaps alluded to in the ominous cloud behind the central couple) is a legitimate tale of heroism. Their pioneer spirit, however, is subject to qualifications that apply to most phases of westward migration. The Pilgrims, it turns out, were interlopers, claiming land that did not belong to them. Their original destination was Virginia, but they were blown off course and forced to settle where they came ashore. Nor had they set off on their own. They were part of a capitalist venture; wealthy English merchants had advanced them funds to settle in the New World. The success of the Pilgrims (in ten years they were free of debt and relatively prosperous) encouraged New England immigration on a much larger scale. Had the Pilgrims been alone in the New World, however, they probably would not have survived their first winter. They were townspeople—laborers and shopkeepers (unlike the gentlefolk Rothermel depicts)—unused to foraging in the wilderness. A local tribe, the Wampanoags, taught them to hunt and plant corn, and with them the Pilgrims celebrated the first Thanksgiving. That event never appeared in colonial history scenes until late in the nineteenth century, when Indians could safely be credited for

79. Frederic E. Church, *The Hooker Company Journeying through the Wilderness from Plymouth to Hartford in 1636*, 1846, oil on canvas, 40¼ × 60³⁄₁₆ in. Wadsworth Atheneum, Hartford.

certain significant deeds. One often attains a clearer perception of period bias through what was not painted rather than what was.

Frederic E. Church's *Hooker Company Journeying through the Wilderness,* 1846 [79], continues the spread of Puritan hegemony through New England, although less aggressively than the Rothermel picture. Thomas Hooker and a group of dissidents at odds with the Massachusetts Bay Colony moved to Hartford in 1636, then a remote settlement beyond the New England frontier. Church depicted the journey as a biblical passage through a splendid, backlit landscape, reminding one of Bierstadt's 1867 processional *Emigrants Crossing the Plains* [see 104]. Both parties travel west toward the setting sun, which casts a mellow, providential light across each scene. In both pictures, peace and serenity prevails.

Hooker and his party, however, had a difficult passage through what one eighteenth-century historian called a "hideous and trackless wilderness."[64] And, once again, Puritans were settling land to which they had no claim. Hooker's destination was a tract held both by the Massachusetts Bay Colony, from which the Hooker party was attempting to extricate itself, and a Dutch company, whose claim everyone wished to ignore. Moreover, the land was inhabited by the Pequot, whom the Pilgrims and other settlers were bound to antagonize.[65] Settlement precipitated the Pequot War fought in 1637, a particularly bloody encounter in which the tribe was all but destroyed. Two years later, at Hooker's instigation, a group of colonists in Connecticut drew up "Orders" proclaiming self-government and independence from the Massachusetts Bay Colony. In short, the pattern of settlement was neither peaceful nor "ordained," until glossed by an artistic strategy. Church's painting compels one to read colonial history as a preview of expansionism, while the artist imposes on that "his-

tory" the values of mid nineteenth-century Americans seeking to justify contemporary expansionist policies.

The final picture in this group, Leutze's *Founding of Maryland,* 1860, is perhaps this chapter's most conspicuously patriotic image [80]. One is reminded of Thanksgiving and the Fourth of July, all rolled into a single high-spirited festival. Backed by a large wooden cross, a priest (in the stance of a blessing Christ) says mass while simultaneously conferring approval on the meeting of Sir George Calvert, first Lord Baltimore, and an Indian chief (friendly Algonquins surrounded the original colony). A circle forms around the group, composed of soldiers, settlers, and Indians, an alliance of interests that would surely benefit the colony, if not the Indians. The halberds held aloft by the soldiers signify their martial preoccupation, the elegant couple between the soldiers and the Indians represents civility and refinement as the mediating factors between the military and the natives. The latter make available the bounty of the sea and land—oysters, tobacco, and game. The standard of Lord Baltimore is raised above the crowd, a patriotic vignette in which one could substitute the Stars and Stripes.

As a prototype for *The Founding of Maryland,* Leutze probably had in mind *Penn's Treaty with the Indians,* 1771–72, by Benjamin West [81]. Here too the principal figures form a circle in the center of the composition, with seated or kneeling figures occupying the corners of the picture. The backgrounds have been transposed, so that the harbor is on the right in Leutze's picture, while a half-constructed house is prominently situated on the left (where it looms dangerously close to the point of the spear held by the Indian in the foreground). Another art-historical borrowing may associate the relationship of the Old Testament figures Abraham and Melchizedek [82] to that of Lord

80. Emanuel Leutze, *The Founding of Maryland,* 1860, oil on canvas, 52 × 73 in. The Maryland Historical Society, Baltimore.

81. Benjamin West, *Penn's Treaty with the Indians,* 1771–72, oil on canvas, 75½ × 107¾ in. The Pennsylvania Academy of the Fine Arts, Philadelphia; gift of Mrs. Sarah Harrison (The Joseph Harrison, Jr., Collection).

82. Peter Paul Rubens, *The Meeting of Abraham and Melchizedek,* circa 1625, oil on wood, 26 × 32½ in. National Gallery of Art, Washington, D.C.; gift of Syma Busiel.

Baltimore and the Indian chief.[66]

Both *The Founding of Maryland* and *Penn's Treaty* attempt to establish equity between Indians and Europeans on the basis of two non-events.[67] In that sense both are political allegories, but they argue their cases very differently. *Penn's Treaty* is an eighteenth-century commentary on a seventeenth-century "event," composed and painted in a muted classical style. Leutze's ideology evolves from a period of high expansionism; his style is one of richly detailed drama.

The absence of a cross or religious symbol in West's picture can, of course, be explained by Quaker belief; and the presence of one in Leutze's picture by Lord Baltimore's faith and the fact that the colony was founded as a haven for Catholic dissenters. But the conspicuous size and placement of the cross in Leutze's picture attests more to a mid nineteenth-century conviction of settlement as a divinely ordained mission (note the size of the cross in Leutze's *Westward the Course of Empire* [see 100]). Conversely, the absence of the cross in West's painting points to a more reticent, contractual approach to justifying colonization. Military symbols are also absent from *Penn's Treaty,* again, one could argue, on the basis of Quaker

belief. But there is no evidence that Lord Baltimore maintained a corps of mercenaries. One may thus conclude that the soldiers in the background of *The Founding of Maryland* acknowledge the role of the military in colonization.

The difference in the way Indians are treated in the two paintings is especially revealing. West's Indians are grave and dignified, as numerous as Penn's party, equally deliberate in their approach to treaty making, and models of domestic virtue. Their image—the rational Indian—is a stereotype of the Enlightenment, but it is more appealing to our beliefs than that employed by Leutze, to whom the concept of equal representation never occurred. Behind Lord Baltimore is a tight arrangement of soldiers and colonists; behind the Indian chief and his attendant is one male "savage," contemplating a dismal future and a chorus line of alluringly bare-breasted females—heathen providers of earthly pleasure. The Englishwoman on their left recoils from them but consents to accept a gift, a gesture signifying cultural and racial differences.

So trivialized in our view are the Indians in Leutze's canvas that they have no future, despite the pact that the picture is meant to commemorate. "Our view," however, misses the point that Leutze was adjusting his image to fit a prescription for the settling of the West. Prosperous "pioneers" would control "savages" so that a Christian civilization would prevail. Supporting that scenario were historical concepts endowing a more "advanced" and "humane" society with the right to conquer those it considered inferior.

The rhetoric of expansionism reappears in scenes of westward migration and Indian and frontier life, in landscapes, and in re-creations of the "Wild West." Because these paintings rely heavily on an elaborate narrative and stylistic structure to make themselves understood, they meet resistance from the modernist camp, which requires us to look for simpler and more direct solutions to the problems of picture making. Historical paintings as well as western genre and landscape subjects have been condemned in the past for the weight of their rhetoric, as if that quality alone precludes them from further notice.[68] Yet no understanding of these paintings—their content, historical perspective, or formal structure—is possible if we ignore the message they sent to nineteenth-century audiences. Only when we gain that understanding can we begin to isolate and judge the impact of artistic strategies that not infrequently converted rhetoric into enduring works of art.

Notes

1. Alan Trachtenberg, "Myth, History, and Literature in *Virgin Land,*" *Prospects* 3 (1977): 127–28.

2. See Limerick, *Legacy of Conquest.*

3. In fact, many did argue with history painting but not on the basis of content. Critical reviews of its artistic caliber were often scathing (see Gerdts and Thistlethwaite, *Grand Illusions,* 61–118; and Miller, *Patrons and Patriotism,* 45–57, 66–78).

4. Slotkin, *Fatal Environment* (1985 ed.), 45.

5. Washington Irving, *The Life and Voyages of Christopher Columbus* (London, 1828).

6. Samuel Eliot Morison, *Admiral of the Ocean Sea: A Life of Christopher Columbus* (Boston: Little, Brown, 1942), 103.

7. Ibid., 89. A separate issue is whether Washington Irving or Peter F. Rothermel ever questioned the apocryphal tale of the debate or did they simply accept it as one more indication of a heroic Columbus. At no time, before or after, was the explorer's reputation higher than during the mid-nineteenth century. I am grateful to Deborah J. Warner, curator of the history of science, National Museum of American History, Smithsonian Institution, for identifying the globe in the Rothermel painting and for pointing out how it differs from those in use at the end of the fifteenth century.

8. Jennings, *Invasion of America* (1976 ed.), 34.

9. Catherwood, *Views of the Ancient Monuments.*

10. Amos Binney (1803–1847) was a Harvard-educated medical doctor who never practiced medicine but instead pursued a business and scientific career. He was successful in real estate, a zoologist of international reputation, and an avid collector of American art. He commissioned scenes of American history from Daniel Huntington, Emanuel Leutze, Rothermel, and Luther Terry. His status in Boston scholarly and social circles must have put him in touch with William H. Prescott (see Amos Binney, *The Terrestrial Air-Breathing Mollusks of the United States* [Boston: Little, Brown, 1851], xxvii–xxviii). I am grateful to Elizabeth Kornhauser, who is currently preparing a catalogue of the Wadsworth Atheneum's American painting collection, for furnishing the material on Binney.

11. Prescott, *Conquest of Mexico* 3:188–89.

12. *Literary World,* September 8, 1849, 204.

13. Prescott, *Conquest of Mexico* 1:93–96.

14. *Bulletin of the American Art-Union* (New York) 2 (July 1849): 7.

15. *Literary World,* September 8, 1849, 204.

16. Prescott, *Conquest of Mexico* 1:95. Sixteenth- (or seventeenth-) century European accounts of conquest generally contain a franker admission of economic motive than westward-expansion literature. Conquest accounts also indicate a preference for converting native races rather than destroying them. An alarming amount of westward-expansion literature condones the opposite. "All we can do," wrote the well-known journalist Samuel Bowles in 1869, "is to smooth and make decent the pathway to his [the Indian's] grave" (see Bowles, *Our New West,* 158).

17. Marching inland from Vera Cruz, Winfield Scott's soldiers imagined themselves in the footsteps of Hernán Cortés (see Johannsen, *Halls of the Montezumas,* 155).

18. Prescott, *Conquest of Mexico* 2:42.

19. Quoted in Jennings, *Invasion of America* (1976 ed.), 34.

20. A number of Whigs, in addition to the Boston literati, were opposed to the war (see Merk, *Manifest Destiny,* 89–143), and Prescott had reservations (see Johanssen, *Halls of the Montezumas,* 245–48).

21. Roy Strong, *Recreating the Past: British History and the Victorian Painter* (New York: Thames & Hudson for Pierpont Morgan Library, 1978), 47.

22. David Levin, *History as Romantic Art* (New York: AMS Press, 1967), 9.

23. Quoted in Merk, *Manifest Destiny,* 122.

24. An expansionist society "never admits that it is doing violence to its moral instincts," wrote H. H. Powers in 1900 (see "The Ethics of Expansion," *International Journal of Ethics* 10 [1900]: 292).

25. American studies professor Lee Clark Mitchell notes the apprehension with which certain groups of Americans viewed the effects of progress during the nineteenth century and recounts their attempts to forestall change. Many of these attempts, however, can also be interpreted as ways of accommodating progress, of accepting the inevitable while restructuring the past into a form that could be conveniently lamented and preserved (see Lee Clark Mitchell, *Witnesses to a Vanishing America* [Princeton: Princeton University Press, 1981], xii–xvi).

26. George H. Callcott, *History in the United States, 1800–1860: Its Practice and Purpose* (Baltimore: Johns Hopkins University Press, 1970), 177, 180.

27. Ibid., 186–87.

28. Quoted in Ernest Lee Tuveson, *Redeemer Nation* (Chicago: University of Chicago Press, 1980), 158.

29. Quoted in Ekirch, *Idea of Progress in America* (1951 ed.), 98.

30. George Bancroft, *The History of the United States of America from the Discovery of the Continent,* ed. Russel B. Nye (Chicago: University of Chicago Press, 1966), xxv.

31. William H. Truettner, "The Art of History: American Exploration and Discovery Scenes, 1840–1860," *American Art Journal* 14 (Winter 1982): 9 n. 10.

32. Quoted in Paul Revere Frothingham, *Edward Everett: Orator and Statesman* (Boston: Houghton Mifflin, 1925), 84.

33. Quoted in Weinberg, *Manifest Destiny,* 197.

34. Gulian C. Verplanck, *Discourses and Addresses on Subjects of American History, Arts, and Literature* (New York: Harper, 1833), 11.

35. Miller, *Patrons and Patriotism,* 51.

36. Ibid., 56.

37. Vivien Fryd's forthcoming book, "Course of Empire: Art in the United States Capitol, 1815–1860," discusses in great detail the expansionist overtones of the Capitol murals. She very kindly allowed me to read relevant passages in her manuscript while I was preparing this chapter.

38. *National Intelligencer* (Washington, D.C.), April 25, 1853, 2.

39. *Daily National Intelligencer* (Washington, D.C.), December 22, 1843, 3.

40. John Gadsby Chapman, *The Picture of the Baptism of Pocahontas* (Washington, D.C.: Peter Force, 1840), 5.

41. As a southern legislator, Jefferson Davis was committed to an expansionist role to support the extension of slavery. William Walker invaded Nicaragua with a band of American mercenaries in 1855 and the next year established himself as president. Cornelius Vanderbilt, whose commercial interests in Central America Walker threatened, soon toppled his regime.

42. Quoted in Russell F. Weigley, "Captain Meigs and the Artists of the Capitol: Federal Patronage of Art in the 1850s," *Records of the Columbia Historical*

Society of Washington, D.C. (1969–70): 289–90.

43. Miller, *Patrons and Patriotism,* 75.

44. Montgomery Meigs to Simon Cameron, secretary of war, June 20, 1861 (quoted in Fairman, *Art and Artists of the Capitol,* 202).

45. See Bowles, *Our New West;* and William M. Thayer, *Marvels of the New West* (Norwich, Conn.: Henry Bill, 1888).

46. A similar iconographic trend simultaneously appears in scenes set in the Far West. The pictures represent "The Coming of the White Man," but they rarely portray Indians as subservient as those in the Thomas Moran and Joshua Shaw paintings. Henry Farny, Charles Russell, and John Mix Stanley, for example, often show Indians apprehensive of and resistant to white encroachment, although the outcome of any encounter is never in doubt.

47. *Oil Paintings from the Estate of the Late Charles W. Gould* (New York: American Art Association/Anderson Galleries, 1932), nos. 80, 98.

48. Washington Irving, *History of the Life and Voyages of Christopher Columbus* (Philadelphia: Lea & Blanchard, 1839), 1:79–80.

49. Gerdts and Thistlethwaite, *Grand Illusions,* 144.

50. Rothermel apparently disdained Indian materials in Philadelphia collections (Academy of Natural Sciences, American Philosophical Society, and Peale's Museum) in favor of more exotic trappings. The effect he sought was probably based on distinctions made by Prescott and other history writers. Sixteenth-century Indians were more dignified than the bloodthirsty types encountered in the nineteenth century.

51. Robert Weir mentions delaying work on the "Hudson picture" in a letter to Gulian Verplanck, January 17, 1835 (see Gulian C. Verplanck Papers, New-York Historical Society, New York).

52. *Important American Paintings, Drawings, and Sculpture of the Eighteenth, Nineteenth, and Twentieth Centuries* (New York: Christie's, 1988), no. 169Q.

53. Sara King Harvey, "Gulian Crommelin Verplanck: A Forgotten Knickerbocker" (Ph.D. diss., University of Chicago, 1934), 4–5.

54. Henry Hudson was searching for a Northwest Passage on his third voyage. According to official logs, the Indians he encountered along the river were both friendly and unfriendly. Some he traded with, others were killed in skirmishes (see Milton W. Hamilton, *Henry Hudson and the Dutch in New York* [Albany: University of the State of New York, 1964], 20–30).

55. Mid nineteenth-century writers frequently linked the two eras. William Gilmore Simms, for example, claimed that Daniel Boone, standing on Cumberland Mountain, must have "felt very much as Columbus did, gazing on his caraval on San Salvador . . . or Vasco Nuñez [Balboa], standing alone on the peak of Darien, and stretching his eyes over the hitherto undiscovered waters of the Pacific" (quoted in Drinnon, *Facing West,* 132). Not to be outdone, Senator Thomas Hart Benton of Missouri wrote: "Pierce the Rocky Mountains, and hew the highest crag into a statue of Columbus, pointing the Old World on the way to the Indies!" (quoted in T. Poesche and C. Goepp, *The New Rome; or, the United States of the World* [New York, 1853], 11). This last quote was very kindly supplied by Albert Boime.

56. Prescott, *Conquest of Mexico* 3:180–82.

57. Ibid. 3:203–5.

58. *Graham's Magazine* (Philadelphia), 20 (March 1842): 12.

59. In this case Powhatan is dressed in a Plains costume perhaps to emphasize his "savage" demeanor.

60. *Ramona,* a popular novel dramatizing the miserable circumstances of California Indians after 1848, created immediate concern for their welfare. See also Herbert Eugene Bolton, ed., *Historical Memoirs of New California by Francisco Palóu* (Berkeley: University of California Press, 1926).

61. The landscape aspect of this argument is raised again in chapter 5, in which scenic views of the West are reexamined as emblems of commercial enterprise.

62. Daniel J. Boorstin, *The Americans: The National Experience* (New York: Random House, 1976), 325–90.

63. See Mark Thistlethwaite, "Peter F. Rothermel: A Forgotten History Painter," *Antiques* 124 (November 1983): 1019. Despite the implication of poem and painting (the full text is included in Thistlethwaite's article), the Pilgrims did not disembark from the Mayflower as one group; they went ashore in small parties over a period of several months.

64. Quoted in Kelly, *Church,* 6–9. Kelly also cites a passage from a mid nineteenth-century author who describes Thomas Hooker's band as "serious, hardy, enterprising hopeful settlers, ready to carve out, for themselves and their posterity, new and happy homes in a wilderness—there to sink the foundations for a chosen Israel—there to till, create, replenish, extend trade, spread the gospel, spread civilization, spread liberty." No doubt contemporary patrons of art in Hartford saw themselves as descendants of these virtuous Pilgrims. Church's painting was purchased by the newly founded Wadsworth Gallery (now the Wadsworth Atheneum) soon after it was completed.

65. Jennings, *Invasion of America* (1976 ed.), 197–201.

66. Melchizedek was a priest-king in Canaan whose primary occupation of the land was recognized by Abraham.

67. Leutze has apparently telescoped several events from early Maryland history. Sources such as J. Thomas Scharf's *History of Maryland* (1879; Hatboro, Pa.: Tradition Press, 1967), describe a mass celebrated by Father White in 1634 and subsequent visits by Lord Baltimore to local tribes. A "romantic" novel about the "old colony" cited in Tuckerman (see Henry T. Tuckerman, *Book of the Artists* [1867; New York: James F. Carr, 1966], 338) may have been another source for ambience and details. William Penn's legendary meeting with the Delaware seems to have taken place under circumstances very different from those depicted by West (see Harry Emerson Wildes, *William Penn* [New York: Macmillan, 1974], 180-81; and Ann Uhry Abrams, *The Valiant Hero: Benjamin West and Grand-Style History Painting* [Washington, D.C.: Smithsonian Institution Press, 1985], 195).

68. See Milton Brown's comments on Leutze in *American Art* (New York: Prentice-Hall, 1979), 228; and those of Lloyd Goodrich on Bierstadt in *Art of the United States, 1670–1968* (New York: Whitney Museum of American Art, 1966), 25.

2

Picturing Progress in the Era of Westward Expansion

PATRICIA HILLS

America is the country of the Future. From Washington, . . . through all its cities, states, and territories, it is a country of beginnings, of projects, of vast designs, and expectations. It has no past: all has an onward and prospective look. . . . Gentlemen, there is a sublime and friendly Destiny by which the human race is guided.

RALPH WALDO EMERSON, 1844

Pictures *are more powerful than* speeches. . . . *Patriotism, that noblest of sentiments, for it is a sentiment as well as a principle, and governs more in that capacity than in the other, is kept alive by art more than by all the political speeches of the land.*

AMERICAN ART-UNION *TRANSACTIONS*, 1845

In 1850 Andrew Jackson Grayson commissioned William S. Jewett to paint *The Promised Land—The Grayson Family* [83].[1] Grayson wanted Jewett to commemorate the historical moment in 1846 when he, his wife, and son reached the summit of the Sierra Nevada that overlooked the Sacramento Valley. Grayson insisted Jewett render the view he recalled, and the two men met in late May near Poverty Flat and traveled up Canyon Creek to where Grayson decided the "spot" had been.[2] It must have been a congenial adventure, for they had much in common. Grayson and his family had journeyed west from Independence, Missouri, in April 1846—traveling part way with emigrants who included the ill-fated Donner Pass party.[3] Several business ventures and land speculation had paid off handsomely for Grayson, but he was increasingly drawn to ornithology.

Jewett, a New York artist who exhibited at the National Academy of Design and the American Art-Union, arrived in San Francisco in May 1849 after sailing on the *Hope* around

Cape Horn with a group planning to invest in business or mining. The artist was soon persuaded by New York friends to set up his easel, and he discovered that portraiture in San Francisco could bring a good income.[4] He accepted Grayson's offer and headed off to the mining country around Sacramento, where he sketched the river diggers. Thus from his own experience he knew the Sacramento Valley to be teaming with land speculators and gold hunters.[5]

Jewett's assignment was not to paint the reality of 1850 but Grayson's memory of a symbolic moment four years earlier—before the gold rush had brought in speculators and scoundrels, entrepreneurs and hussies. The picture thus became a careful construction and collaboration. Drawing on the legacy of conversation pieces—family scenes of eighteenth-century English gentry posed before their country manors—Jewett painted a group portrait blending biblical allusions with landscape and history painting to validate western expansion as enlightening and ultimately rewarding.[6] A Holy Family image has been modified for the occasion: Grayson dons a buckskin coat and leggings over his starched white shirt and cravat; Mrs. Grayson wears a dress appropriate to a middle-class parlor while holding her son on her knee; and their son sports a regal, ermine-trimmed robe. The costumes announce the metaphoric message: Grayson is prepared to deal with city affairs (starched shirt and cravat) but is equally at home on the frontier (buckskin, telescope, gun, and dead game); his wife will bring gentility and nurturing ways to the new settlement (her sober dress, shawl, and maternal gesture); and the son, the next generation, will be heir to that wealth (the red, ermine-trimmed robe). The parents survey the distant valley with its golden meadows; their view commands not their personal property but the limitless horizon of California. The

son, on the other hand, gazes at the painter. It is Jewett, after all, who gives visual permanence to the memory and the scene.

The painting was justly famous in its own time. When exhibited at the First Industrial Exhibition of the Mechanics' Institute in 1857 in San Francisco, it was described as a subject

particularly interesting to Californians. . . . The early pioneer has survived the perils of his arduous journey, and, feeling that his family is safe and his object attained, calmly and joyfully surveys the scene. The composition representing the high idea of the progress of civilization westward will render this picture of ever-increasing value in the history of the arts in California.[7]

Portraits incorporating imagery so clearly suggesting the "high idea of the progress of civilization westward" would appeal to the successful entrepreneurs attending that First Industrial Exhibition who favored pictures historicizing the roles of the early white pioneers.

Two years later, when Grayson had become a naturalist and artist himself, Jewett's painting helped Grayson reconstruct that epiphanic moment in lyrical terms:

The broad valley of the Sacramento and the far-off mountains of the coast range, mellowed by distance, and the delicate haze of Indian summer lay before me—whilst the timber growing upon the borders of the Rivers Las Plumas and Sacramento, but dimly seen at that distance, pointed out our course. I looked upon the magnificent landscape with bright hopes for the future.[8]

But painted in 1850 *The Promised Land* also served to gloss over California events of 1846—the year John Charles Frémont stirred up American pioneers to revolt against the Mexican authorities and to set up the Bear Flag Republic at Sonoma.[9] Our concern, however, is not with how reality diverged from the memory of discovery or the propaganda of the

83. William S. Jewett, *The Promised Land—The Grayson Family,* 1850, oil on canvas, 50⅞ × 65 in. Berry-Hill Galleries, New York.

westward movement but how the strategies of persuasive imaging maintained a specific reading of history and reinforced the ideology of expansion. For the message of the picture—the future of American progress—was not confined to the Grayson-Jewett production. That message sprang from a deep well of economic and expansionist interests, and it permeated the images of the 1840s through the 1860s.

The Rhetoric of Progress

In the mid-1840s many national leaders, whether writers, merchants, patrons of the arts, or entrepreneurial adventurers, viewed America as the country of the future. To these nationalistic and forward-looking gentlemen,[10] expansion was a prerequisite to America's destiny as an international leader. Cultural nationalism became a necessary corollary. Culture, that is, the arts, had a role to play in this destiny by actively strengthening allegiance to the American Union and encouraging a commitment to the course of future expansion.[11] Along the way money was to be made; indeed, in the spirit of Calvinism, the very acquisition of personal wealth bore witness to the rightness of the westering enterprise.

Expansionists took as their motto the first line of George Berkeley's poem "Verses on the Prospect of Planting Arts and Learning in America," written about 1726. As often happens in history, this appropriation occurred even though Berkeley had in mind something quite other than westward expansion. The Irish philosopher and Anglican dean had written his poem on the eve of launching a scheme to establish an experimental college in Bermuda. His plan entailed converting and educating American Indians, people he considered emi-

nently worthy of "enlightenment." Like other eighteenth-century intellectuals yearning for a golden age, Berkeley viewed the New World as the "seat of innocence, Where nature guides and virtue rules . . . Not such as Europe breeds in her decay." In the sixth and final stanza he declares America as the culmination of history:

> *Westward the course of empire takes its way;*
> *The four first Acts already past,*
> *A fifth shall close the Drama with the day;*
> *Time's noblest offspring is the last.*[12]

"Westward the Course of Empire"—the phrase, not the poem—resounded throughout the period from the 1840s to the 1870s; and the rest of Berkeley's text, along with its historical and philosophical context, was conveniently forgotten in the rush westward to settle the continent. To expansionists, America was not the finale of history, as Berkeley's poem proclaimed, but proof of perpetual progress, of infinite beginnings, of inexhaustible future wealth. After all, they daily experienced an America on the move—an expanding economy, new markets, growing population, social mobility, and technological innovations that speeded communication and transportation.[13]

These material circumstances provided the conditions for the growth of the *idea of progress* in America, but its intellectual roots are found in the European Enlightenment.[14] Drawing on these eighteenth-century sources, the French historian François Guizot connected progress with civilization; he argued in *Histoire générale de la civilisation en Europe* (1828) "that the first idea comprised in the word *civilization* . . . is the notion of progress, of development. It calls up within us the notion of a people advancing, of a people in a course of improvement and melioration." Guizot continues:

Two elements, then, seem to be comprised in the great fact which we call civilization;—two circumstances are necessary to its existence—it lives upon two conditions—it reveals itself by two symptoms: the progress of society, the progress of individuals; the melioration of the social system, and the expansion of the mind and faculties of man.[15]

Guizot's ideas would in time apply to the American situation; we have only to look at Progressivism of the 1890–1920 period to see a concerted effort toward "the melioration of the social system."

But to expansionists in 1845–75, "progress of society" meant conquest and nation building. Expansionist rhetoric ignored "the progress of individuals . . . the expansion of the mind," except toward the end of the era. It had to be so. To talk about the progress of individuals in a post-Enlightenment age meant dealing with equality and justice—notions severely compromised in those days of slavery, Indian removal, exploitation of Hispanics and Asians, and limited rights for women. Instead, as historian Arthur Ekirch observes, "To the actuality and ideology of American expansionism the idea of progress lent a comforting aura of historic inevitability and of righteous respectability."[16]

The rhetoric of historic inevitability was much in evidence in the mid-1840s—in the speeches of expansionists then campaigning to push American claims for Oregon above the forty-ninth parallel, to annex Texas, or to underwrite new railroad routes.[17]

Journalist William Gilpin, supporter of Missouri senator Thomas Hart Benton, traveled the Oregon Trail in 1843 and returned to Jefferson City, Missouri, in 1844, more of an expansionist than even Benton. To agitate for

the American settlers in their claims for the Oregon Territory against the British, Gilpin returned to the East in 1845 and prepared several documents, which were widely circulated in Washington, D.C., and printed in official Senate reports.[18] In addition to extolling Oregon as farm country, he saw the territory as a major gateway to the Far East—to the islands of the Pacific and China. His most famous report, read to the Senate on March 2, 1846, exemplifies nineteenth-century rhetoric raised to a fever pitch:

Two centuries have rolled over our race upon this continent. From nothing we have become 20,000,000. From nothing we are grown to be in agriculture, in commerce, in civilization, and in natural strength, the first among nations existing or in history. So much is our *destiny*—so far, up to this time—*transacted,* accomplished, certain, and not to be disputed. From this threshold we read the future.

The *untransacted* destiny of the American people is to subdue the continent—to rush over this vast field to the Pacific Ocean—to animate the many hundred millions of its people, and to cheer them upward . . . to teach old nations a new civilization—to confirm the destiny of the human race . . . to emblazon history with the conquest of peace . . . and to shed blessings round the world!

Divine task! Immortal mission! Let us tread fast and joyfully the open trail before us! Let every American heart open wide for patriotism to glow undimmed, and confide with religious faith in the sublime and prodigious destiny of his well-loved country.[19]

Gilpin's words, which helped persuade the Senate to ratify the treaty establishing the northwest boundary of the United States at the forty-ninth parallel, have come down in history as the paradigmatic expansionist proclamation.[20]

Later this same rhetoric would be appropriated in support of a vast national system of railroad routes, with some of the most persistent oratory published in *DeBow's Review,* a southern magazine established in 1846 by James DeBow, an ardent expansionist and president of the Tennessee Pacific Railway. In 1859 DeBow published "Westward the Star of Empire," an article by Jessup Scott, Whig editor of the Toledo *Blade.*[21] Extolling the virtues of expansionism, Scott wrote:

The westward movement of the Caucasian brand of the human family from the high plains of Asia, first over Europe, and thence, with swelling tide, pouring its multitudes into the New World, is the greatest phenomenon of history. What American can contemplate its results, as displayed before him, and as promised in the proximate future, without an emotion of pride and exultation?[22]

While Scott had in mind the settling of the Mississippi Valley, it would have been clear to DeBow that the superior technological prowess of the railroad would be the engine for continued westward movement.[23]

With such language coming from the secular pulpits of Manifest Destiny, how was a painter to represent expansionism? How can one say "*Pictures* are more powerful than *speeches,*" as J. T. Headley wrote in the American Art-Union *Transactions* for 1845? In the words leading up to Headley's statement, he reveals why he believed in the power of images:

Some one has said, give me the writing of the *songs* of a country, and you may make its laws. I had almost said, give me the control of the *art* of a country, and you may have the management of its administrations. There can be no greater folly than that committed by our statesmen, when they treat art and literature as something quite aside from great national interests. . . . Art is too often looked upon as an abstract thing, designed only for men of

taste and leisure. . . . Every great national painting of a battle-field, or great composition, illustrating some event in our history—every engraving, lithograph and wood cut appealing to national feeling and rousing national sentiment—is the work of art; and who can calculate the effect of all these on the minds of our youth?[24]

The men who ran the American Art-Union, staunch supporters of the federal Union, knew full well that not only must painters be encouraged to paint such pictures, but an organized effort was required to promote and distribute patriotic images to as many Americans as possible in order to, in the words of Gilpin, "animate the many hundred millions."

The content—the Progress of Civilization—existed before a subject matter and iconography was fully worked out to visualize such concepts. Yet artists had been assigned their task. Eventually the subjects settled into three groups: the acquisition of new lands (including lands taken by force), scouts and the overland journey to the West, and the technological superiority of the railroad.

The full message of these pictures of "progress" can be understood from the artist's choice of landscape models, from the privileging of certain figures or groups within compositions, from gestures and expressions unique to those figures, and from the inclusion of significant motifs. These paintings did not *illustrate* westward expansion; they actively endorsed the concept by visualizing the excitement of virgin lands, picturesque pilgrimages of stalwart men and women, or awesome and powerful railroad trains. Images of progress—pleasurable, heroic, or majestic—persisted in the collective memory of middle-class easterners long after the brutal consequences of land grabs, railroad scandals, and racialist policies had become evident.

The Mexican War

At the heart of the debate among expansionists in 1845 was the issue of slavery. The question was: Would the annexation of Texas lead to war with Mexico, and if so, would any newly acquired territories be slave states or free?

The United States did go to war. "Military exercises" by both sides along national borders escalated and active fighting began on April 25, 1846. With meager support from Washington, Generals Zachary Taylor, Winfield Scott, John E. Wool, and Stephen W. Kearny nevertheless succeeded in routing the Mexican army in a series of victories. The storming of the fortress at Chapultepec broke the final resistance, and United States troops entered the Mexican capital on September 14, 1847; the war concluded, the Treaty of Guadalupe Hidalgo was ratified by the Senate on March 10, 1848, thus securing an additional 1.2

84. Adolphe-Jean-Baptiste Bayot after Carl Nebel, *Battle of Palo-Alto.* From Kendall, *The War between the United States and Mexico Illustrated* (1851), pl. 1. Library of Congress, Washington, D.C.

million square miles, which included parts of Colorado and Texas as well as Arizona, California, Nevada, New Mexico, and Utah.

Technical innovations that emerged during the war include the first war photography and mass-produced, colored lithographs, the most notable by German artist Carl Nebel and the American James Walker.[25] Nebel had spent nearly five years in Mexico in the 1830s, but he returned to Mexico City in 1847 during the American occupation.[26] Although it is unlikely that he saw any fighting, he teamed up with journalist George Wilkins Kendall, who had seen combat and had sent dispatches back to the *New Orleans Daily Picayune*.[27] Together they produced a deluxe album, *The War between the United States and Mexico Illustrated* (1851), containing twelve hand-colored lithographs.

The first in the series, *Battle of Palo-Alto,* represents the decisive battle of May 8, 1846, when General Taylor faced Mariano Arista, the Mexican general, at Palo Alto, just above the Rio Grande [84]. The battle produced the first heroes, "Old Rough and Ready" Taylor and Major Samuel Ringgold, who died at his post directing artillery fire.[28] The album begins with this event even though neither artist nor writer had been to the site. Nebel's image includes anecdotal scenes in the foreground and a line of mountains falsely inserted across the horizon (the battle site was a flat plain). Accurately represented, however, is the grass fire in the middle distance that delayed Taylor's advance and helped screen Arista's retreat.[29] Yet the viewer is reassured of American strength by the massive line of infantry and cavalry advancing along the road and the long-range cannons aimed at the distant Mexican troops. While the scene is full of movement and historical incident, the long road pulling our eye back to the distant (if nonexistent) purple mountains presents an image of the vast, transversible spaces made available by the Mexican adventure.

Walker, who was living in Mexico City at the outbreak of the war, escaped and joined the advancing army of General William Jenkins Worth as an interpreter. He painted the storming of Chapultepec, relying on his own field sketches and perhaps a camera but also on descriptions from a military participant.[30] In New York in 1848 he arranged for the printers Sarony and Major to publish the single-sheet chromolithograph, *The Storming of Chapultepec* [85]. In this image Walker brings order to the chaos of the battlefield; the calculated rows of soldiers advancing toward the battlements and holding high the American flag invoke a rational purpose. In the distance small figures storm the citadel that will soon fall to American military skill and valor.

Walker kept his small oil sketches with him, ever ready to enlarge one should a commission come. While unexciting in terms of dramatic, individual action, the twelve panels, entitled *Scenes of the Mexican War,* circa 1848–50, impress the viewer as "real" scenes representing the collective effort involved in warfare—the logistics of massing troops and advancing them to strategic places in preparation for battle [86]. The storming of the white citadel on the hill would have appealed to those viewers whose imaginations were already being fanned by the expansionist creed "to emblazon history with the conquest of peace."[31] In sum, the many lithographs of the Mexican campaigns visualized seemingly limitless, open lands—western lands that beckoned the pioneer and promised peaceful passage.

The American Art-Union as Patron for Expansionist Ideology

During the 1840s the most important patron of eastern artists was the American Art-Union, an organization that purchased, exhibited, and distributed to the public through lottery works by American artists.[32] Historians have estimated that during its thirteen-year active life an estimated three million visitors viewed its exhibitions. The committee of management consisted of leading New York merchants, bankers, and lawyers.[33] The name they chose for the organization was entirely fitting, for they believed that what was "American" was the "Union," that is, a united United States. Typical members of the committee were artist Francis W. Edmonds, a banker and director of the New York and Erie Railroad; former mayor and indefatigable theatergoer Philip Hone, a prominent Whig, who counted among his friends

85. After James Walker, *The Storming of Chapultepec, Sept. 13th, 1847,* 1848, chromolithograph (hand-colored), 23⁹/₁₆ × 35¹⁵/₁₆ in. Amon Carter Museum, Fort Worth, Texas.

86. James Walker, *Scenes of the Mexican War,* circa 1848–50, oil on canvas, twelve panels, 11¼ × 18 in. each. United States Army Center of Military History, Washington, D.C.

Henry Clay, William Henry Seward, and Daniel Webster; poet and newspaper editor William Cullen Bryant, who served as president from 1844 through 1846; art collector, merchant, and Illinois Central Railroad director Jonathan Sturges; merchant Charles M. Leupp, who served as a director of the Tradesmen's Bank and the Erie Railroad; Marshall O. Roberts (who joined the committee in 1846), a railroad promoter and shipbuilder, who made a fortune during the Mexican War; Abraham Cozzens, an amateur artist and prominent art collector, who served as president from 1850 until the Art-Union folded in 1852; and Harvard- and Yale-educated William J. Hoppin, who edited the Art-Union *Bulletin.*[34]

In 1847 many of the older Art-Union artists (John Gadsby Chapman, Asher B. Durand,

Edmonds, Daniel Huntington, and Thomas P. Rossiter) and New York writers (Bryant, Hoppin, Henry T. Tuckerman, and Gulian C. Verplanck) joined with these merchants, bankers, and railroad directors (Cozzens, Leupp, and Sturges) and founded the Century Club. Most had been members of the Sketch Club, meeting in each other's homes for talk, sketching, and refreshments; the Century, however, was to be a permanent place with a library and dining room, where men devoted to arts and letters could retire for pleasant study or conviviality. The Century provided a place where artists and patrons could mingle on a basis of social equality, thereby modifying the commercial, artist-patron aspect of the Art-Union. But the Art-Union and the Century were close not only in membership but also in physical proximity; during the first two years the club leased space next door to the Art-Union's exhibition rooms.[35] Overlapping social and patronage networks typified the urban art scene before art dealers became prominent.[36]

These gentlemen promoted an art that was distinctly *American*—by encouraging artists to paint native subjects, by buying these paintings both for the lottery and their personal collections, by distributing to subscribers engravings of their favorite images, and by praising such pictures in the *Bulletin.*[37] Through shrewd recruitment of agent-secretaries in distant towns and cities the Art-Union grew to 18,960 subscribers in 1849, the year 460 artworks were distributed to the lucky winners. In 1843 the officers proudly announced: "The largest part of the works . . . [for that year's lottery was] illustrative of American scenery and American manners. The Committee would be happy to distribute none others."[38] Their stable of artists included Tompkins H. Matteson, William Sidney Mount, William Ranney, and Richard Caton Woodville. Of George Caleb Bingham, they boasted: "Bingham acknowledges his indebtedness to us as the first patron of his higher efforts, and his main-stay in all attempts beyond the line of portraiture."[39]

Richard Caton Woodville's *War News from Mexico,* painted in 1848 and exhibited at the Art-Union in 1849, was the first major picture with a specific, topical subject to be promoted by the Art-Union [87].[40] In the context of the many lithographs and illustrations of the Mexican War, two features of Woodville's painting stand out: it does not represent a battle nor offer a sentimental image of the war, such as Matteson's *Fall of Major Ringgold at the Battle of Palo Alto* or *Heroine Martyr* [88–89].[41]

The boisterous masculinity of the white men gathered on the porch and specific clues in Woodville's picture alert us to its pointed ideological content. Moreover, its influence as a

potent image cannot be disputed; thousands saw the original oil painting, which hung in the Art-Union's galleries, and the large folio engraving after the picture was distributed to some fourteen thousand subscribers [90]. When reproduced as a small engraving for the *Bulletin,* the editor announced:

The large engraving for the members of 1851, will be executed by Mr. Alfred Jones, after Woodville's celebrated painting of *Mexican News,* in the posses-

87. Richard Caton Woodville, *War News from Mexico,* 1848, oil on canvas, 27 × 24 in. National Academy of Design, New York.

88. Tompkins H. Matteson, *The Fall of Major Ringgold at the Battle of Palo Alto*. From *Columbian Magazine* 6 (July 1846): facing 48. The Newberry Library, Chicago.

89. Unidentified artist, *Heroine Martyr*. From Percival, *Friendship's Gift* (1848), facing 101. Library of Congress, Washington, D.C.

90. After Richard Caton Woodville, *Mexican War News*, 1853, hand-colored engraving by Alfred Jones, 20½ × 18⅜ in. Mongerson-Wunderlich Gallery, Chicago.

sion of George W. Austin, Esq. This painting was exhibited for several months in the Gallery of the Art-Union, where it was greatly admired. It represents a group gathered around the porch of a country inn and post-office, listening to the reading of a newspaper, which contains an account of one of the battles in the late war with Mexico. . . . The slouching barkeeper, the tavern-haunting scapegrace who finds something in the news to arouse him from his ordinary indifference, the deaf man, the exultant boy who is swinging his cap in the background, and the poor old negro upon the steps, are all treated with extraordinary fidelity to nature.

The subject of this print is perfectly AMERICAN in its character.[42]

Woodville's painting incorporates numerous details that would appeal to expansionists in 1851, when such issues as the extension of slavery into the western territories were being debated. Even without the title, the handbill calling for volunteers, tacked to the front pillar of the porch, establishes the historical moment—the Mexican War. The porch, a vernacular classical portico with the sign "American Hotel" nailed to its pediment, situates the place—the Union. The occupants of this crowded porch-Union include a heterogeneous mix. The old gent, who wears out-of-fashion knee stockings and breeches, represents the conservatives who have trouble understanding the full import of the news. The young man seated at the left represents potential volunteers; he flings out his right hand holding a penknife—an instrument he might be willing to exchange for a more lethal weapon. The youth flinging his cap will join up. In the center an enthusiastic patriot holds the newspaper that brings the tidings of the recent victories. Since the paper is folded and the hotel also functions as a post office, one assumes that the news came through the mails—another system of communication rapidly developing in these years.[43]

The war's inextricable link to the extension of slavery accounts for the presence of the African-Americans in the lower-right corner of the picture. Their peripheral location (below other figures) indicates their marginal status.[44] The black man wearing a bright red shirt sports a gold earring, surely a symbol of his freed status. His hat and jug represent his work and leisure; the peacock feather suggests his aspirations to an independent and perhaps stylish life. He holds his cup close to his chest, protective of its contents—of what he has already achieved. He awaits not just the outcome of the battles of war but the future of free black labor. The black child standing in tatters represents the immediate issue of slavery. By the time the engraving was distributed the Compromise of 1850 had decided the fate of both free blacks and slaves for another decade.

Earlier, in April 1849, the *Bulletin* heralded Woodville's next subject in a short notice about American artists living abroad: "Woodville is also at Düsseldorf, painting a subject which he calls 'Old '76 and Young '48'—a volunteer relating to his old grandfather his adventures in Mexico. From Woodville's well known power in the expression of character and feeling, we may expect something highly interesting in this picture." The Art-Union promoters were not disappointed when *Old '76 and Young '48* went on exhibition in New York in the early summer; rather than entering the lottery for December, however, the painting was held for the engraver [91].[45]

For the composition, Woodville relied on a drawing of 1844 called *Soldier's Experience* [92]. The messages in both are similar: a wounded soldier, returned home, relates his military exploits to his grandfather, a veteran of the Revolutionary War. The differences, however, are telling. The earlier scene is set in a humble interior, with bare wood floors, a wood-burning stove, and rustic furniture; the grandfather sits in an armchair directly in front of a simply framed print labeled "1776," and his musket and tricornered hat hang on the wall. The other figures consist of the soldier's mother and father, and a sleeping dog lies curled on the floor.

In contrast, the interior shown in *Old '76 and Young '48* is crowded with the artifacts of comfortable bourgeois living, including oriental rugs, marble fireplace mantle, brass andirons and fire tongs, Queen Anne-style leather armchair, Chippendale ottoman, and elaborate dishes and glassware. The picture-buying Art-Union audience would find such furnishings compatible with their own. The "Old '76" grandfather sits beneath an elaborately framed print of John Trumbull's *Signing of the Declaration of Independence* hung over the mantle and a sculpture bust of George Washington placed above a bookcase. The tightly knit group of father, mother, and younger sister stare intently at the handsome young man, who emphatically

91. Richard Caton Woodville, *Old '76 and Young '48,* 1849, oil on canvas, 21 × 26⅞ in. The Walters Art Gallery, Baltimore.

92. Richard Caton Woodville, *Soldier's Experience,* 1844, watercolor on paper, 10¼ × 11¾ in. The Walters Art Gallery, Baltimore.

gestures toward the portrait of his grandfather in his Continental uniform on the side wall. Even the dog is alert to this family and national drama.

The more explicitly drawn symbols and title of the painting clarify Woodville's message: "Young '48," like many poets and politicians throughout the war, was not just relating his own experiences, he was justifying them in terms of Revolutionary War goals.[46] South Carolina novelist and poet William Gilmore Simms had praised the Mexican War volunteers and compared them with such southern Revolutionary heroes as Francis Marion, William Moultrie, and Thomas Sumter. But Simms went even further back in time for validation; according to historian Robert W. Johannsen, Simms's collection of poems, *Lays of the Palmetto: A Tribute to the South Carolina Regiment, in the War with Mexico,* "were laced with the chivalric ideal and the valor of knights."[47] Chivalry and its wartime codes were not far from Woodville's notions of suitable subject matter for pictures; in 1847 he had painted *The Cavalier's Return* (New-York Historical Society), another Art-Union picture.[48]

Contemporary observers noted the presence of the black servants in the shadows on the right—one liveried black manservant, one turbaned black woman, and another black man. The Art-Union *Bulletin* referred to them as "several black servants, whose lively curiosity has gathered them in a group at the door."[49] Their positioning, however, suggests the uncertain consequences of the war's aftermath to the status of black Americans. They anxiously stand in the doorway, on the threshold between the security of this white middle-class household, to which allegiance means servitude, and the freedom of the outside. In the foreground at the right, on a line immediately before the three servants, the soldier has thrown his sword, perhaps meant as a motif to remind the audience of the chivalric crusade but perhaps also as an augury of the impending Civil War, the result of which would decide the fate of the African-Americans.[50]

The 1850s: Daniel Boone, the Boone Type, and the Promised Land

William Ranney was one of the first Art-Union regulars to try his hand at western subjects. He

had fought in the Texas army in 1836 and had returned to the New York area, eventually settling in West Hoboken, New Jersey. There he painted coastal scenes, then Revolutionary subjects with themes that would appeal to an audience eager to equate the Mexican conflict with a more acceptable, patriotic history. Perhaps spurred by news of California gold, Ranney turned his attention to subjects of westward expansion, blending history painting with contemporary events.

Boone's First View of Kentucky, 1849, exhibited at the Art-Union in 1850 and engraved for the May 1850 issue of the *Bulletin,* brought Ranney added fame in this expansionist era [93]. Drawing on the imagery of discovery pictures, Ranney painted an episode from the life of the scout and land speculator Daniel Boone. The Boone narrative (more legend than history) was popularized by John Filson, another land speculator, when he included Boone's "autobiography" in his *Discovery, Settlement, and Present State of Kentucke* (1784).[51] Subsequent writers produced their own variations, but Ranney seems to have drawn on the version closest in time—John Peck's *Life of Daniel Boone,* published in 1846.[52]

Ranney staged the reputed moment described by Peck when Boone and his companions "discover" new fertile lands for exploration and settlement. Long after the painting had gone off to a lottery winner in Zanesville, Ohio, and after the Art-Union had folded, the contemporary art critic Henry T. Tuckerman kept alive the imagery of the picture by writing about it for *The Home Book of the Picturesque* (1852):

There hung, for many months, on the walls of the Art-Union gallery in New-York, a picture by Ranney, so thoroughly national in its subject and true to nature in its execution, that it was refreshing to contemplate it. . . . It represented a flat ledge of rock,

93. William Ranney, *Boone's First View of Kentucky*, 1849, oil on canvas, 37½ × 54½ in. The Anschutz Collection, Denver.

the summit of a high cliff that projected over a rich, umbrageous country, upon which a band of hunters leaning on their rifles, were gazing with looks of delighted surprise. The foremost, a compact and agile, though not very commanding figure, is pointing out the landscape to his comrades, with an air of exultant yet calm satisfaction; the wind lifts his thick hair from a brow full of energy and perception; his loose hunting shirt, his easy attitude, the fresh brown tint of his cheek, and an ingenuous, cheerful, determined yet benign expression of countenance, proclaim the hunter and pioneer, the Columbus of the woods, the forest philosopher and brave champion. The picture represents Daniel Boone discovering to his companions the fertile levels of Kentucky.[53]

We might add the obvious: Boone, the elder man, stands like Moses pointing out the Prom-

ised Land to the advanced guard of his people.

A striking change occurs, however, when the work was engraved for the Art-Union *Bulletin*. In the illustration the face of the Boone figure lacks identifying clues and he merges in with the support group, while the central, virile young man dominates the picture. Symbolizing those who will settle the land when Boone is long gone, he has removed his hat as if on holy ground. He holds his gun like a standard-bearer in procession; his crusade will be one of peace; the Promised Land awaits him. Ranney's picture reassures the public that westward expansion will be achieved without further conflict.

Another Ranney painting, *The Scouting Party* [94], was illustrated in the September

1851 issue of the *Bulletin* as a wood engraving, significantly placed next to an engraving after Thomas F. Hoppin's *Emigrants' Last Look upon Home*. When sold at the American Art-Union liquidation sale in 1852, Ranney's painting was described as "a party of trappers with their horses on a high bluff watching the movements of Indians who are betrayed by fires in the prairie below."[54] Trappers who followed scouts such as Boone were the vanguard of trade and commerce; romantic representations of these frontier entrepreneurs had immediate appeal for the merchants and railroad developers of the 1850s.[55]

After scouts and trappers came the pioneers; Ranney's *Advice on the Prairie,* 1853, represents the next chapter in his series [95]. According to family history, the man sitting on his camping gear and gesturing to make a point is Jim Bridger, known as the "Daniel Boone of the Rocky Mountains."[56] After a career of trapping in the 1820s and 1830s he became a scout; in 1843 he led the missionary party of Marcus Whitman to Oregon and later

94. William Ranney, *The Scouting Party,* 1851, oil on canvas, 22 × 36 in. Thyssen-Bornemisza Collection, Lugano, Switzerland.

in 1843, with partner Louis Vasquez, opened a trading post on the Oregon Trail called Fort Bridger. Pioneers who traveled west in the early 1850s gave colorful accounts of Fort Bridger and Bridger's persuasive advice on propitious routes, and any one of their published narratives could have served as a literary source for Ranney.[57] Behind the scout, Ranney has constructed the primary expansionist image—a self-sufficient family unit: capable, healthy, and strong, confident of achieving their destination. Their cohesion and purpose is expressed as a pyramidal figural group. Motifs suggested by Christian art symbolize their mission: the mother holds her infant as if display-ing the Christ Child in a Renaissance altar-piece, and two white horses flank her like angel sentries.

In 1851 George Caleb Bingham, an artist and Whig politician from Missouri, began an-other Boone picture—*Daniel Boone Escorting Settlers through the Cumberland Gap* [96]. The picture narrates the passage of Boone and his party of pioneers through the famous fissure in the mountains of eastern Tennessee near the Kentucky border. Its reputation as one of the gateways to progress had extraordinary staying power.[58]

Bingham's Boone leads his people forward through a hostile environment like a latter-day

95. William Ranney, *Advice on the Prairie,* 1853, oil on canvas, 40 × 54 in. Private collection.

96. George Caleb Bingham, *Daniel Boone Escorting Settlers through the Cumberland Gap*, 1851–52, oil on canvas, 36½ × 50¼ in. Washington University Gallery of Art, Saint Louis; gift of Nathaniel Phillips, 1890.

Moses en route to the Promised Land. Contemporary viewers would see Boone's companion, the woman on the white horse, as symbolizing the gentle, civilizing influences necessary to develop frontier culture. The rocks and trees part like the Red Sea, and an eerie glow proceeds them and shines on their advance. The theatrical, almost supernatural, lighting reminds one of the passage in Exodus (13:21): "And the Lord went before them by day in a pillar of a cloud, to lead them the way; and by night in a pillar of fire."[59] Bingham's stage-set tableau had little relationship to the reality of overland migration in the early 1850s, when the trip to California could take five or six months of grueling hardship.[60]

Always ready to couch the rhetoric of westward expansion in biblical terms, expansionists used the term *Promised Land* to reinforce their belief that the western lands were God's gift to Caucasian Americans as Canaan was to the Jews. An example of this merging of promotional and biblical rhetoric was C. W. Dana's introductory remarks to the 1856 book that he hoped would spur emigration, *The Garden of the World, or the Great West*. The book begins:

The *Land of Promise,* and the *Canaan* of our time, is the region which, commencing on the slope of the Alleghanies, broadens grandly over the vast prairies and mighty rivers, over queenly lakes and lofty mountains, until the ebb and flow of the Pacific tide kisses the golden shores of the El Dorado.

With a soil more fertile than human agriculture has yet tilled; with a climate balmy and healthful, such as no other land in other zones can claim; with facilities for internal communication which outrival the world in extent and grandeur,—it does indeed present to the nations a land where the wildest dreamer on the future of our race may one day see actualized a destiny far outreaching in splendor his most gorgeous visions.[61]

Reading such passages, the reader would quite naturally envision Moses at the head of a procession, leading his people into a land of milk and honey.

Dana's book singles out each new western state and territory for praise—Ohio, Indiana, Illinois, Michigan, Wisconsin, Iowa, Missouri, Kansas, Nebraska, Minnesota, Texas, New Mexico, Utah, Oregon, Washington Territory, and California. The author emphasizes the natural resources, farming opportunities, urban amenities, and benevolent territorial governments while minimizing the dangers inherent in emigration and frontier living.

Small, emblematic illustrations reinforce

Dana's narrative. Each represents a state or territory and includes a centered medallion containing an image flanked by schematic scenes. The orderliness of the overall composition persuades the viewers of the "inherent" plan and purpose to the westering project. For example, in the illustration *Oregon* men cut giant trees at the left, while the rugged mountain scenery is shown at the right [97]. In the medallion an industrious farmer plows the land in a field where trees have already been cleared. In the background an Indian witnesses the pioneer's work and further back a steamship moves through the harbor against the setting sun. Such images propagandized and rationalized expansionism every bit as much as the lengthy narratives.

Dana also took the opportunity in his book to endorse the Free-Soil movement. In the chapter on Kansas more than seventeen pages are devoted to promotional text obtained from the New England Emigrant Aid Company Society, an organization chartered in April 1854 by Eli Thayer, a Massachusetts Free-Soiler, for the purpose of sending anti-slavery northerners to Kansas.[62] The Free-Soil movement did not just adhere to the Jeffersonian agrarian ideal, the movement's leaders realized that a free labor market in the West was crucial to their long-range economic view of national development.[63]

At the end of his book Dana reprinted a speech by Thomas Hart Benton in the House of Representatives in 1855, advocating the Pacific Railroad bill.[64] Earlier, from 1853 to 1855, with Benton's encouragement and a mandate from Congress, Secretary of War Jefferson Davis dispatched seven expeditions to chart the most economical and practical route for a transcontinental railway, while two more surveyed the Pacific Coast.[65] Twelve artists accompanied the expeditions, creating a new category of western pictorial imagery.

97. Unidentified artist, *Oregon*. From Dana, *Garden of the World* (1856), fig. 24. Office of Horticulture Branch Library, Smithsonian Institution, Washington, D.C.

John Mix Stanley, the best known of these artists, traveled along the northern route with Isaac I. Stevens, an army engineer and the first territorial governor of Washington.[66] Stanley sketched the topography along the forty-seventh and forty-ninth parallels, but he also made mental notes of scenes with pictorial possibilities. *Scouts in the Tetons,* circa 1854–63, is one of these [98]. Alert soldiers, their Winchesters at their sides and mounts in readiness, scan the plains for danger. In the distance at the left, rows of orderly tents, the encampment of the survey engineers, signal that all is planned, regular, and rational. The pyramidal form suggests the figures' authority over the landscape and asserts the control the government had in settling the West.

Stanley's views were finally published as chromolithographs in 1860, in the last of the twelve volumes that cataloged survey findings.[67] His *Teton Valley* [99] compares with *Scouts in the Tetons* in its representation of the landscape as broad, flat plains ringed by distant buttes. The dramatic element has, of course, been eliminated, not just because these were topographical views but because the promoters of the transcontinental railroad wanted to assure readers that the western terrain was a picturesque Eden with gently rolling hills, readily adaptable to agriculture, pasturage, and railroad

98. John Mix Stanley, *Scouts in the Tetons,* circa 1854–63, oil on canvas, 24 × 34⅛ in. Thomas Gilcrease Institute of American History and Art, Tulsa.

99. After John Mix Stanley, *Teton Valley*. From Stevens, *Explorations for a Route for a Pacific Railroad* (1860), facing 117. Smithsonian Institution Libraries, Washington, D.C.

routes.[68] Benton had already persuaded Americans that along the route through the Rockies in southern Colorado there was "not a tunnel to be made—a mountain to be climbed—a hill to be crossed—a swamp to be seen—or desert, or movable sand to be encountered, in the whole distance."[69]

Emanuel Leutze's Westward the Course of Empire

While the major patronage for expansionist pictures in the 1840s came from the group of merchants and railroad boosters directing the American Art-Union, in the 1850s the government began to serve as an important patron. Not only did artists accompany the railroad surveys, but the United States Capitol building in that decade underwent expansion, providing new decorative commissions for painters and sculptors. The most important expansionist mural painting of that era was surely Emanuel Leutze's *Westward the Course of Empire*, 1862 [100].

In July 1862 the *Atlantic Monthly* published Nathaniel Hawthorne's account of a recent trip he had taken to Washington. Hawthorne first encountered Leutze on a scaffold in a Capitol staircase preparing his epic painting *Westward Ho!* After viewing an oil study of the final composition, Hawthorne concluded:

The work will be emphatically original and American, embracing characteristics that neither art nor literature have yet dealt with, and producing new forms of artistic beauty from the natural features of the Rocky-Mountain region, which Leutze seems to have studied broadly and minutely. . . . It looked full of energy, hope, progress, irrepressible movement onward, all represented in a momentary pause of triumph; and it was most cheering to feel its good augury at this dismal time, when our country might seem to have arrived at such a deadly standstill.[70]

Hawthorne was not a typical spokesperson for the northern cause; he regarded the war with a somewhat ironic detachment,[71] yet he must have seen beyond the conflict to the time when to be "American" meant looking west, beyond sectional conflicts.

Leutze's artistic campaign to paint a grand national theme for the extension of the Capitol had begun in January 1854, when Captain Montgomery C. Meigs, in charge of the Capitol commissions, wrote to Düsseldorf to ask if Leutze would be interested in submitting "suitable designs" for the halls and marble stairways. Within a month Leutze had replied, listing appropriate subjects, one of which was "Emigration to the West." Delighted that opportunities were opening up for American artists, Leutze wrote: "Give us a chance, and my word on it we'll do what Europe cannot do even with her best artists (and I can say so because I know them all most of them personally) we will paint 'American pictures.' "[72]

Leutze's cultural nationalism had been earlier encouraged by American Art-Union directors. They had bought his work for their personal collections and had designated two of his

100. Emanuel Leutze, *Westward the Course of Empire Takes Its Way [Westward Ho!]*, 1862, water-glass painting, 240 × 360 in. United States Capitol, Washington, D.C.

paintings for engraving and distribution.[73] Moreover, Leutze had recently had success with his "American" picture par excellence, *Washington Crossing the Delaware,* exhibited in New York and Washington in 1852.[74] Patriotic pictures of George Washington flourished in the aftermath of the Mexican War, and a number of senators and representatives who viewed *Washington,* became enthusiastic about Leutze's ability to construct grand historical compositions.[75]

Meigs finally succeeded in winning approval for Leutze's Capitol commission in June 1861, after writing to the new secretary of war, Simon Cameron.[76] In the wartime climate,

Meigs pitched his appeal to the patriotism of the project:

The people of the country have so responded to the call of their Government that danger to the Capitol has now passed away, and it is a question worthy of consideration whether the Government by pursuing in some degree the project of completing its Capitol would not give to the people a welcome assurance of its confidence in its own strength and in its patriotism of its people.[77]

Meigs regretted the delays in the stairway decorations and ended his letter by stating he "would be gratified . . . to see in this time of rebellion one artist at least employed in illustrating our western conquest."[78]

Much has been written about the mural itself and the two studies that proceeded it, particularly the version Leutze gave to William Seward, one of his Washington fans [101]. Leutze went west in 1861 to sketch the Rocky Mountains and experience overland travel. Back in Washington he finished a final study that combined three different kinds of pictures: an elaborately staged tableau set on the peak of a mountain, with stereotypical representations of pioneer men and women, mountain guides, wagons, and mules; a realistic view of San Francisco Bay through the Golden Gate, the predella along the bottom; and an elaborate border across the top and sides. Centered in the top border, a bald eagle holds an unfurling scroll on which is lettered "Westward the Course of Empire Takes Its Way," while Indians seek to escape the scroll and maze of winding plant tendrils. The sides include iconographical motifs drawn from classical and biblical literature, making up an imaginative typology for westward expansion—Hercules, the Argonauts, Moses, a raven with manna in its beak, a dove with a branch, Columbus, "the spies of Escholl bearing the fruits from Canaan," and the Three Magi. The sides also contained medallion portraits of Daniel Boone and explorer William Clark.[79]

The progress of the mural was charted in Washington, New York, and even Boston papers. Not surprisingly, the *New York Evening Post,* of which William Cullen Bryant was editor, was the most faithful in its praise of Leutze's project. When the finished mural opened to the public in December 1862, the *Evening Post* was enthusiastic.[80]

The finished mural differs from the study in its elaborated decorative border and the broader landscape setting to accommodate more pioneers and mountain peaks. But the key addition to the completed work is the black man in the foreground leading a woman on a mule. That the study of 1861 without the African-American won the approval of Secretary of War Cameron is hardly surprising considering that he was an expansionist opposed to the emigration of blacks into the western territories.[81]

When Leutze decided to add the figure of the African-American is unclear. A surge of sympathy for slaves and freed blacks arose in the art world during the 1860s. Such feelings reached a crest in 1867–68 and undoubtedly touched Leutze.[82] In 1868 critic Anne Brewster, writing for *Lippincott's Magazine,* describes meeting Leutze and asking him:

"There is a group almost in the centre of your picture—a young Irish woman seated on an ass holding a child—the ass is led by a negro. Did you not mean this group to teach a new gospel to this continent, a new truth which this part of the world is to accept—that the Emigrant and the Freedman are the two great elements which are to be reconciled and worked with? The young, beautiful Irish woman, too, is she not your new Madonna?

The artist's face glowed . . . the hard ridges on the brow and cheeks grew soft, and his eyes fairly laughed with joy at my comprehension of his thoughts. In the flush of his pleasure he told me I ture. . . . I learned afterward that although my interpretation was original so far as I was concerned, it had been made by others and approved of by the artist.[83]

Following the Civil War, however, the question of parity for black labor intensified, and while a significant number of blacks emigrated west, they encountered the same prejudices as they had in the East.[84]

Westward Migration after the Civil War: Covered Wagons

With the Civil War concluded, the theme of westward expansion increasingly appeared in

pictures and books. Some writers encouraged emigration of settlers or cataloged the scientific, natural, and mineral resources of the country, while others lured travelers to new adventure and scenic wonders. Pictures of covered wagons—bumping down mountain passes, crossing ravines, fading into the distant sunset—satisfied the expansionists' immediate cravings for picturesque evocations of the journey.

In 1865 Samuel Bowles, editor of the Springfield (Massachusetts) *Republican* went westward accompanied by Schuyler Colfax, speaker of the House of Representatives. The fruits of his trip were articles he sent back to Springfield, later published as *Across the Continent* (1865). Journeying by Concord coach [see 183] over the Great Plains and visiting the miners of Colorado and the Mormons of Utah, the Bowles party passed many wagon trains, described by the author:

The wagons are covered with white cloth; each is drawn by four to six pairs of mules or oxen; and the trains of them stretch frequently from one-quarter to one third of a mile each. As they move along in the distance, they remind one of the cara-vans described in the Bible and other Eastern books.[85]

Bowles, like George Caleb Bingham, knew his audience; and biblical allusions would stir their imaginations and sanction the moral rightness of the overland journey. But the large fold-out, colored map tipped into Bowles's book also brought that audience to practical terms. By indicating the rivers, major mountain ranges, and the route the party traveled, such maps rationalized the journey and made it measurable in space and time.

A similar mapping occurs in William H. Jackson's *California Crossing, South Platte River,* 1867 [102]. Jackson's fame rests primarily on

his photographs, particularly those done for the Hayden survey during the 1870s, but earlier, in 1866, he went west with a wagon train as a driver of an oxen team.[86] Along this trip he sketched, and it was probably from sketches (and perhaps photographs) that he put together *California Crossing.* The details of pioneer life are spread across the front plane of the picture; as the wagons head across the Platte River, they converge only to fan out again in the distance. The painting also reminds us of the moving panoramas presented in theaters in the East, where real people, wagons, and accessories were placed on the stage and behind them moved a canvas with a painted western landscape.[87]

While Jackson provides us with a broad spectacle of achievement, Currier and Ives offer a sense of romance in their lithograph of 1866 called *The Rocky Mountains—Emigrants Crossing the Plains,* designed by Fanny Palmer, one of the few women who pictured the theme of western expansion [103]. Wagon trains roll over gentle hills and past majestic mountains and welcoming Indians on horseback. Such concoctions pleased the folks back home who bought such inexpensive prints as emblems of pride in the expanding nation.

In 1870 Fitz Hugh Ludlow published in book form the results of his trip to California in 1863 with Albert Bierstadt. Entitled *The Heart of the Continent,* the account vividly describes the scenery and wagon trains. As he and Bierstadt approached the Platte, wrapped in a "misty veil," Ludlow pictures for his readers the mirage that held the party spellbound: "Hot sun and mirroring sand had wrought up the scanty materials of the stream into a dream of beauty which had no geometric reasons."[88] Later they passed

a very picturesque party of Germans going to Oregon. They had a large herd of cattle and fifty wagons, mostly drawn by oxen. . . . The people themselves represented the better class of Prussian or North German peasantry. A number of strapping teamsters, in gay costumes, appeared like Westphalians. Some of them wore canary shirts and blue pantaloons; with these were intermingled blouses of claret, rich warm brown, and the most vivid red. All the women and children had some positive color about them, if it only amounted to a knot of ribbons, or the glimpse of a petticoat. I never saw so many bright and comely faces in an emigrant train.[89]

Bierstadt, who made sketches along the route of the trip, seems to have sought inspiration in the mirage as much as in the German wagon train when he painted his grand picture, now called *Emigrants Crossing the Plain,* 1867 [104].[90] The large canvas combines elements of the sublime and the picturesque: we feel the infusing warmth of the setting sun and are awed by the spectacular hues streaking across the sky to illuminate the sheer cliffs rising at the right.

102. William H. Jackson, *California Crossing, South Platte River*, 1867, oil on canvas, 22 × 34 in. Thomas Gilcrease Institute of American History and Art, Tulsa.

103. Fanny Palmer, *The Rocky Mountains—Emigrants Crossing the Plains*, 1866, hand-colored lithograph, 17½ × 25¾ in. Amon Carter Museum, Fort Worth, Texas.

But the sparkling touches of color accenting the common aspects of pioneer travel and the fattened cattle and sheep are what finally reveal Bierstadt as a master of persuasive imagery. Pictures constructed in this way brought to life for nineteenth-century viewers the westering experience.

Appearing immediately after the Civil War, *Emigrants Crossing the Plain* begs comparison with George Inness's idyllic *Peace and Plenty*, 1866 (The Metropolitan Museum of Art, New York), a painting suggestive of the attempts to heal the wounds of strife. Inness's eastern scene offers a harvest of plentiful grain stacked in the foreground along the riverbank; one contemporary review referred to the scene as "a land overflowing with milk and honey" and noted that "here, in this land, man may dwell in peace, bless God, and be content."[91] Bierstadt's painting offers a similar message, except that the harvest will be the strong, healthy children of the pioneers.

Fattened cattle also figure prominently in *View of Denver, Colorado*, painted about 1865–70 [105]. Located on the South Platte, Denver was settled in 1858 as a gateway through the Rocky Mountains. In 1867, when the town became the capital of Colorado Territory, with William Gilpin as governor, it was already thriving.

Cowhands leading short-horned cattle through the dusty plains to the West to improve the stock are the subject of Otto Sommer's *Westward Ho!* painted about the same time [106]. The largest cattle drives, however, went in the opposite direction; in the winter of 1866–67 the first "long drive" occurred when cowhands moved cattle from Texas north to the stockyards in Sedalia, Missouri. Other stockyards sprang up in Abilene, Kansas, where seventy-five thousand head were driven in 1868. Between 1868 and 1871, 1.5 million were herded north to be slaughtered for eastern markets.[92] But typical of a producer society, which the era was, images of cattle going westward to produce had greater appeal than cattle coming back east to be consumed.

In 1869 Frederick B. Goddard published *Where to Emigrate and Why*, with sections on the resources and opportunities of all the western and southern states and territories, including Alaska, which was purchased by the federal government in 1867. The author clearly had in mind foreign readership for he explains in detail American democratic institutions. His paean to immigration dissolves into an endorsement of emigration:

During the last two years more than six hundred thousand sturdy immigrants have landed upon our shores, and there is no ebb to the flowing tide. Our land is ringing with the din of her internal improvements; cottages are springing up far away to the west upon sunny acres where, but yesterday, roamed the Indian and the buffalo. Grand lines of railroad are stretching out across the continent—iron

monsters resting upon either ocean, swallowing the values of one hemisphere to void them upon the other—revealing what our first Great Emigrant, Columbus, vainly sought to manifest in the gloom of earlier ages—that the shortest way to the Indies was *via* America.

Goddard sums up: "And all we have, and are, or may be, as a nation, we offer to share with the struggling millions of the earth."[93]

   Goddard's text, interspersed with Alfred R. Waud's illustrations, makes the West into a place of domestic bliss. Waud's frontispiece pictures before-and-after scenes: "Where to Emigrate" consists of a hearty pioneer family encamped on a riverbank [107]. "And Why" depicts the same scene developed into a peaceful agricultural village, with fields of wheat being reaped in the foreground, a general store with a female customer, houses, and a church; a steamboat paddles along the river and a train crosses a viaduct in the distance. In the middle of the book another illustration, *A Prairie*

104. Albert Bierstadt, *Emigrants Crossing the Plains,* 1867, oil on canvas, 60 × 96 in. National Cowboy Hall of Fame Collection, Oklahoma City.

105. William O. Bemis, *View of Denver, Colorado,* circa 1865–70, oil on canvas, 46 × 62 in. Unlocated.

106. Otto Sommer, *Westward Ho!* 1867–68, oil on canvas, 44 × 74½ in. The Los Angeles Athletic Club.

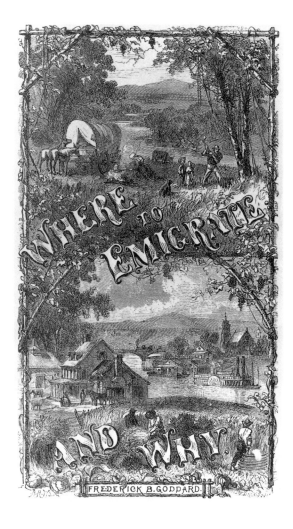

Home, also by Waud, represents a prosperous farm with fields in the process of being harvested and children (another pioneer harvest) fishing in a picturesque lily pond [108]. While the men would be interested in farming opportunities, details of the Homestead Act, and expected wages in each state or region, the women had to be convinced that home in the West differed little from home in the East. Such pictures countered negative accounts of sod houses and parched lands on the prairies; they satisfied homemakers that comfort and security awaited them.

The Triumph of the Railroad

All the reports of scientific expeditions and surveys, all the books designed for emigrants, all the speeches about Manifest Destiny eventually served the railroads in their campaigns for popular and government support. While some railroad presidents, directors, and stockholders were driven only by the urge to make quick personal fortunes in railroad stocks and land speculation and development, others, such as expansionist William Gilpin, even while he was growing moderately rich, believed that the fortune of the country as a world commercial power depended on an efficient network of railroads across the continent. Such individuals took the long view of fortune and finance.

When Samuel Bowles was in San Francisco in 1866, he had pleaded for the railroad project; it was not simply commerce, agriculture, and mining that suffered from delays in

107. Alfred R. Waud, *Where to Emigrate and Why.* From Goddard, *Where to Emigrate and Why* (1869), frontispiece. Library of Congress, Washington, D.C.

108. Alfred R. Waud, *A Prairie Home.* From Goddard, *Where to Emigrate and Why* (1869), facing 252. Library of Congress, Washington, D.C.

building the transcontinental railroad, but society, religion, and family bonds:

You will feel hearts breaking, see morals struggling slowly upward against odds, know that religion languishes; feel, see and know that all the sweetest and finest influences and elements of society and Christian civilization hunger and suffer for the lack of this quick contact with the Parent and Fountain [the eastern states] of all our national life.

"To build the railroad," Bowles concluded, "is the cheapest, surest and sweetest way to preserve our nationality, and continue the Republic a unit from ocean to ocean."[94] His traveling companion, Speaker Colfax, concurred and delivered a similar plea when the party stopped in Virginia City. Even though Colfax had become involved in 1866 with enriching himself from the profits of Crédit Mobilier, the construction company set up by railroad developers and Boston financiers to build the Union Pacific Railroad at immense profits to themselves, his faith in the railroad as a national unifier was no doubt sincerely felt.[95]

Despite two decades of Manifest Destiny rhetoric and railroad boosterism, artists were slow to bring the railroad to the front and center of their oil paintings. Works done in the 1840s by Thomas Cole, Thomas Doughty, and others represent trains nestled within the Catskills or New England landscape.[96] Even Inness, when commissioned in 1855 by the Lackawanna Railroad to paint the roundhouse of the Delaware, Lackawanna, and Western Railroad at Scranton, Pennsylvania, distanced the train from the viewer.[97] And similarly, Asher B. Durand situated his train in the far-middle ground in *Progress* [see 120].[98] Thomas Prichard Rossiter, however, painted *Opening of the Wilderness*, circa 1858 (Museum of Fine Arts, Boston), with four trains surrounding a roundhouse, ready to steam off to new lands.[99]

Against this artistic tradition of demurring trains, *On the Road*, 1860, by the little-known Philadelphia artist Thomas P. Otter, makes its entrance [109]. Otter seems to have painted primarily landscapes and moonlit coastal scenes in the 1860s but was ambitious enough to send pictures to the Boston Athenaeum and National Academy of Design as well as to the annual exhibitions of the Pennsylvania Academy of the Fine Arts. Less is known about the provenance of *On the Road*, certainly his chef d'oeuvre. But even from the slim record, two men stand out as likely patrons: Matthias W. Baldwin and Joseph H. Harrison, Jr., both locomotive manufacturers for the Baltimore and Ohio Railroad.[100] In 1859 Baldwin bought Otter's *Beach by Moonlight* (unlocated), which hung at the Pennsylvania Academy's annual that year, and Harrison bought the artist's *Wood Scene* (unlocated) from the academy's 1867 annual.

Since *On the Road* differs so radically from Otter's other known work and the locomotive he pictures seems to be modeled on the Tiger, designed by Baldwin's company, one might surmise that Otter painted it as a commission or on speculation that it might appeal to someone like Baldwin [110]. The inclusion of the lumbering Conestoga in the foreground qualifies the painting as a westering image; the message asserts the technological superiority of the steam locomotive moving westward like an arrow in contrast to the wagon following an indirect route along a dried riverbed. Otter bears witness to the conception of the image by carving his initials into the milestone in the foreground.[101]

Andrew Melrose, who lived for a time in West Hoboken, Ranney's hometown, painted *Westward the Star of Empire*, 1867, even though there is no clear evidence that he had spent any time in the West [111]. In contrast to the wagon train in Bierstadt's painting, Melrose's

railroad disrupts nature and bears down on the viewer, its bright headlight glowing like a jewel. Deer scatter toward the left, but the field harbors no refuge, for it has been cleared of trees; the stumps catch the light of the waning sun as it sinks behind the cabin in the distance.

Thomas Nast's frontispiece for Albert D. Richardson's *Beyond the Mississippi* (1867) also depicts a locomotive charging mercilessly toward the forest animals and an Indian family, which splits apart in its eagerness to escape [112].[102] The iconic placement of the locomotive in a central medallion, with partial medallions containing western scenes at the sides and bottom, reminds us of those illustrations in Dana's *Garden of the World,* except for Nast's sheer ambition to include everything: wagon

109. Thomas P. Otter, *On the Road,* 1860, oil on canvas, 22⅛ × 45⅜ in. The Nelson-Atkins Museum of Art, Kansas City, Missouri (Nelson Fund).

110. Jonathan Ord, *Baldwin Locomotive—"The Tiger,"* circa 1856, chromolithograph, 21½ × 37 in. Kenneth M. Newman, The Old Print Shop Inc., New York.

trains, stagecoaches, trains, telegraph wires and poles, schematic renderings of New York and California. Above it all speeds Mercury, god of travelers and of communication, a classical reference to sanction the great migration westward and bring the blessings of the gods themselves.

Richardson's book differs from Bowles's in its pitch toward the traveler seeking adventure and in its ample illustrations, but he too praises the railroad. Richardson reminds his readers that the race to finish the lines of track by both the Union Pacific and Central Pacific was furiously competitive, since each would own and run as much track as each could lay. Moreover, additional government subsidies were based on the track owned. "Each company," Richardson noted, "acquires absolutely thirteen thousand acres of land per mile along its line. . . . No other enterprise in our country was ever so magnificently endowed."[103]

Richardson returned to the West the following year to observe Irish workers laying track 240 miles west of Omaha:

We found the workmen, with the regularity of machinery, dropping each rail in its place, spiking it down, and then seizing another. Behind them, the locomotive; before, the tie-layers; beyond these the graders; and still further, in mountain recesses, the engineers. It was Civilization pressing westward—the Conquest of Nature moving toward the Pacific.[104]

An illustration, *Building the Union Pacific Railroad in Nebraska,* designed by Waud, pictures what Richardson has reported [113]. It emphasizes the labor required to lay ties and then tracks; another, depicts Chinese labor employed on the western branch. But images of labor in the West are virtually nonexistent; patrons preferred portraits of entrepreneurs or

111. Andrew Melrose, *Westward the Star of Empire Takes Its Way—near Council Bluffs, Iowa,* 1867, oil on canvas, 25½ × 46 in. E. William Judson, New York.

glorious landscape constructions uncompromised by labor problems.

The most colorful visual imagery of the railroads came from Currier and Ives, a firm that prided itself on its topicality and which shifted from the subject of covered wagons to trains in the late 1860s. Fanny Palmer developed designs for the print *Across the Continent: "Westward the Course of Empire Takes Its Way"* [114]. An initial sketch of 1862 suggests a more rugged landscape, with a mountain range on the left. But when published in 1868, the lithographer eliminated the mountains, allowing the route of the railroad to advance unimpeded

over a vast open plain.[105] This compositional change effectively resolved for the viewer the perceived difficulty of overland travel. Later, when the transcontinental railroad was a fait accompli, Currier and Ives published such dramatic train pictures as *Prairie Fires of the Great West,* 1872 [115].

Picturesque landscape elements aroused the imaginations of those who bought Currier and Ives prints of the railroad traversing the country. But far more potent flights into the technological sublime were encouraged by the photographs of railroads under construction, especially those taken as part of the promotional campaigns of the lines. Thomas C. Durant, vice president and financial wizard of the Union Pacific Railroad, the man who in 1863 had set up the Crédit Mobilier, organized in 1866 the Hundredth Meridian Excursion Party. This consisted of more than two hundred guests, including the "principal railroad men and leading capitalists throughout the country," senators, an English earl, a French mar-

112. Thomas Nast, *Beyond the Mississippi*. From Richardson, *Beyond the Mississippi* (1867), frontispiece. Smithsonian Institution Libraries, Washington, D.C.

113. Alfred R. Waud, *Building the Union Pacific Railroad in Nebraska*. From Richardson, *Beyond the Mississippi* (1867), facing 567. Smithsonian Institution Libraries, Washington, D.C.

114. Fanny Palmer, *Across the Continent: "Westward the Course of Empire Takes Its Way,"* 1868, hand-colored lithograph, 17⅝ × 27 ⅛ in. Joslyn Art Museum, Omaha; gift of Eugene Kingman.

115. Unidentified artist,
Prairie Fires of the Great West,
1872, hand-colored litho-
graph, 9¼ × 12⅜ in. Library
of Congress, Washington,
D.C.

quis, reporters, and photographers; entertaining the group were caterers, two brass bands, and friendly Pawnee scouts.[106] Free-lance photographer John Carbutt came away with about three hundred stereograph photographs of the excursionists and the landscape viewed along the journey [116].[107]

In 1868 the Union Pacific hired Andrew Joseph Russell, who recorded with his camera the step-by-step building of the Union Pacific as it approached Promontory, Utah.[108] Russell's spectacular photographs of major engineering feats, such as the trestle bridge at Promontory, declared that no ravine was so deep that it could not be traversed [117]. The Union Pacific was pleased; in 1869 it published a deluxe, leatherbound album, *The Great West Illustrated,* of fifty albumen prints taken by Russell. Later William H. Jackson would photograph the Cañon of the Rio Las Animas in Colorado, convincing viewers that no mountain was so rugged or steep that it could not be circumvented by the engineering skills of the railroad [118]. And California landscape photographer Carleton E. Watkins would photograph a portion of railroad track leading to the Pacific; his *Cape Horn, near Celilo, Oregon,* 1868, bears witness to the capacity of technology (both the railroad and the camera) to control nature while conjuring visions of sublime beauty [119].

On May 10, 1869, the ceremonial golden spike was driven into the last tie at Promontory, where the Union and Central Pacific met. Russell's photograph of the work gangs, waving bottles as officials from the two railroads shook hands, was engraved and published in *Harper's Weekly* on June 5, 1869 [see 10]. Like all railroad photographs of the era, whether circulated as stereographic views, issued as deluxe albums, or engraved for the popular press, they ultimately celebrate the sheer power of American capital and business enterprise.

The Progress of Empire and the Indians

In the illustration *Building the Union Pacific Railroad in Nebraska,* published in Richardson's book, and in Palmer's lithograph *Across the Continent* [see 113–14], Indians stand at the edge of the picture observing the "progress of civilization." They are included not simply because Indians actually did show up at the scenes of railroad construction but because Indians and their nontechnological life had become the very measure by which whites could gauge the "progress" of their civilization.[109] In Thomas Crawford's pedimental group for the Capitol building [see 59], the Indian sits "contemplating the progress of civilization."[110] And in Durand's *Progress,* 1853, commissioned by railroad financier Charles Gould, Indians stand amid wild nature looking out on a vista that includes telegraph poles and wires, steamships, and the railroad [120].[111]

119. Carleton E. Watkins, *Cape Horn, near Celilo, Oregon,* 1868, albumen print, 15¾ × 20½ in. Stanford University Libraries, Special Collections, California.

120. Asher B. Durand, *Progress,* 1853, oil on canvas, 48 × 72 in. The Warner Collection of Gulf States Paper Corporation, Tuscaloosa, Alabama.

The theme of the Indians' wonder at the progress of civilization is a leitmotif in the literature of Manifest Destiny. In reality, however, the Indians did not stand passively by as technology rolled on. They organized and fought back. Official railroad historian Edwin L. Sabin in his book *Building the Pacific Railway* (1919) displays his biases when recounting "the bloody year" of 1867:

This was the year when the northern Plains Indians made one last concerted effort to halt the forward march of empire: When all along the Smoky Hill emigrant route through Kansas into Colorado, and all along the great Overland route on the north, through Nebraska, ranchers and stage hands fought from sod walls and galloping coaches for their lives; when Custer rode and Hancock marched and Sherman raged; when the advance of the Kansas Pacific crumpled and the Union Pacific nevertheless did its 260 miles of track, 1600 miles of line, 3000 miles of reconnoissance, in defiance of the very devil.[112]

Army cavalry protected the train crews, but Sioux and Cheyenne continued to attack and derail train cars throughout 1867 and 1868.

Not everyone denounced the Indians' actions. Former abolitionist and Indian-rights advocate Wendell Phillips delivered a speech in July 1869 congratulating the Indians for tearing up the rails and thereby discovering the "vulnerable spot in the tyrant."[113] Thomas Nast lampooned Phillips in his *Harper's Weekly* illustration entitled *All Hail and Farewell to the Pacific Railroad* [121].

Nevertheless, the powerful technology of expansionist whites plus longstanding disunity among Indian nations guaranteed territorial advance that the Indians could not counter. This state of affairs comprises the subject of John Gast's *American Progress,* 1872, painted to the specifications of publicist George A. Crofutt, in need of a chromolithograph to promote his travel guide [122].[114] Crofutt subsequently

"ALL HAIL AND FAREWELL TO THE PACIFIC RAILROAD."
WENDELL PHILLIPS.

121. Thomas Nast, *All Hail and Farewell to the Pacific Railroad.* From *Harper's Weekly* 13 (July 10, 1869): 436. Smithsonian Institution Libraries, Washington, D.C.

commissioned a steel engraving based on Gast's painting and used it as a frontispiece for his later tourist guidebooks, such as *New Overland Tourist and Pacific Coast Guide* of 1878–79. His conception for the image draws on the old rhetoric of Manifest Destiny, a still persuasive harangue for publicists urging western travel. The central figure he describes as a

beautiful and charming female . . . floating westward through the air, bearing on her forehead the "Star of Empire." She has left the cities of the East far behind, crossed the Alleghanies and the "Father of Waters," and still her course is westward. In her right hand she carries a book—common school—the emblem of education and the testimonial of our national enlightenment, while with the left hand she unfolds and stretches the slender wires of the telegraph, that are to flash intelligence throughout the land.

122. John Gast, *American Progress,* 1872, oil on canvas, 12¾ × 16¾ in. N & R Enterprises, Inc., Hampton, New Hampshire. (Detail illustrated on p. 96.)

But not everyone was destined to share this national enlightenment:

Fleeing from "Progress," and toward the blue waters of the Pacific, which shows itself on the left of the picture, beyond the snow-capped summits of the Sierra Nevadas, are the Indians, buffalo, wind horses, bears, and other game, moving westward—ever westward. The Indians, with their squaws, pappooses, and "pony-lodges," turn their despairing faces toward the setting sun, as they flee from the presence of the wondrous vision. The "Star" is *too much for them*.[115]

Crofutt reiterates the commonly held belief that the Indians as a race were vanishing, unable to cope with the advance of white civilization.

Exterminationist rhetoric was not quite so sugar-coated. Following General George Armstrong Custer's "last stand" at the Battle of the Little Bighorn on June 25, 1876, sentiment ran high to eradicate the lot of them.[116] But Custer himself went to his death believing that the Indians could be civilized and peace on the plains established because of the railroad. In an essay published just before his fateful end, he praised the railroad:

The experience of the past, particularly that of recent years, has shown too that no one measure so quickly and effectually frees a country from the horrors and devastations of Indian wars and Indian depredations generally as the building and successful operation of a railroad through the region overrun. . . . So earnest is my belief in [its] civilizing and peace-giving influence.[117]

Custer died in 1876, the year the nation celebrated the centennial of the Declaration of Independence. A new iconography began to assert itself in images of progress, including the Crofutt-Gast collaboration: the motif of the book carried by the personification of empire—"the emblem of education and the testi-monial of our national enlightenment."

Domenico Tojetti, an Italian artist who settled in San Francisco with his family at age sixty-four, emphasized cultural symbols in his allegorical *Progress of America,* 1875 [123]. The personification of America wears a liberty cap, and flying putti dip down to crown her with a laurel wreath and lead her chariot decorated with the American eagle and drawn by two white horses. Four maidens accompany her, representing agriculture, medicine, the arts, and mechanics. In the right background, two Raphaelesque women follow holding a tablet; behind these two steams a railroad locomotive. To the left, a group of Indians and buffalo flee the advance of this personification of civilization.

When reviewed in the local San Francisco *Daily Evening Bulletin* in October 1875, a critic wrote that "the story not only suggests the progress of a great country, but it has about it the flavor of the Centennial."[118] Indeed, in the decade of America's centennial, the focus of the idea of progress shifted subtly from Manifest Destiny to the progress of society that the French philosopher Guizot had referred to as "the melioration of the social system." Education, already suggested in the motifs of the Gast and Tojetti paintings, moved to the forefront of reformers' concerns.

Liberal thinkers and activists had long felt that in a democratic nation true progress depended on universally available education. Horace Mann, in the Annual Report of the Massachusetts Board of Education (1848), of which he was secretary, discussed "intellectual education as a means of removing poverty, and securing abundance."[119] And J. H. Stearns, writing in *Merchants' Magazine* in 1853, urged: "Intelligent laborers . . . can add much more to the capital employed in a business than those who are ignorant."[120] By the turn of the century progressive reformers were advocating ex-

123. Domenico Tojetti,
Progress of America, 1875, oil
on canvas, 71½ × 102 in.
The Oakland Museum, Cali-
fornia; Kahn Collection.

124. George Willoughby Maynard, *Civilization,* 1893, oil on canvas, 54¼ × 36 in. National Academy of Design, New York.

tensive training in the trades for the working poor and newly arrived immigrants. Only a few progressives had in mind universal education in the liberal arts—Guizot's *"progress of individuals . . . the expansion of the mind and faculties of man."* Most progressives simply intended to make capitalism more efficient.[121]

A final image epitomizes this shift. In 1893, fifty years after Gilpin rode the Oregon Trail, George Willoughby Maynard painted *Civilization,* which was exhibited at the Columbian Exposition in Chicago that year [124]. Here the personification of civilization, a comely white woman wearing a classical, white chiton, points to her book: civilization, she declares with her gesture, is knowledge. The image was one of four murals that Maynard executed for the Library of Congress, itself a place of learning constructed when expansion within the continent had come to an end. The four murals were entitled *Adventure, Discovery, Conquest,* and *Civilization.*[122] Thus by 1893 it was recognized that the earlier era of Manifest Destiny was not yet "civilization." Civilization was what came from education, from books. Her very Anglo-Saxon whiteness reminds us of a last question, a question often sidestepped by our nineteenth-century artists. Would all the people, including blacks and Indians and newly arrived immigrant groups, share in that book of knowledge as the country moved into the twentieth century?

Notes

Just as westward expansion was a collective effort, requiring the energies of vast numbers of people, whatever their motives, goals, or dreams, so too is the art history of westward expansion. My undertaking of this assignment depended on scholars who have researched and synthesized the primary-source material, museum curators who have organized exhibitions that included long-forgotten works, and dealers and private collectors who have shared their finds. I want to acknowledge the late John I. H. Baur, who encouraged me to curate an exhibition for the Whitney Museum of American Art in 1973, entitled *The American Frontier: Images and Myths;* the National Endowment for the Humanities, which awarded me a summer stipend in 1976 to conduct further research on the topic of artists in the West; and Peter Hassrick, who invited me to teach at the Summer Institute of Western American Studies at the Buffalo Bill Historical Center in Cody, Wyoming, in June 1981. There I had the good fortune to meet the other teachers, William H. Goetzmann and Alvin M. Josephy, Jr., as well as Nancy K. Anderson, a student in the program and a contributor to this volume. Thanks, too, to David Hall for facilitating my research and to Kevin and Andy Whitfield for helping me keep my perspective.

1. The epigraphs are quoted from Ralph Waldo Emerson, "The Young American," *Dial* 4 (April 1844): 492; J. T. Headley, *Transactions of the American Art-Union for the Year 1845* (New York, 1845), 14–15.

For a discussion of William S. Jewett, see Evans, "Promised Land," 1–11; and idem, "Some Letters of Jewett."

2. Evans, "Promised Land," 4–6, discusses the site at length and concludes that the "spot" became "overwhelmingly important as a symbol transcending any particular place on the map."

3. According to Evans, "Promised Land," 2, Grayson "chose a more fortunate route" than did the Donner party.

4. Jewett wrote home, "Many of my old New York friends are here and they have all insisted so strongly upon my sitting up my easel right amongst all

this crazy stuff that I have at last done so and am at work quite in earnest as it is impossible to get up to the mines if I should ever choose to go—I shall give my pencil the preference until all is safe. . . . Society has great hopes of *me* here and think I am a lucky fall to them, gentle men desire their portraits to send home to their families and I am likely to be full of work" (quoted idem, "Some Letters of Jewett," 160).

5. For a discussion of the reality and myth of the California gold rush, see Starr, *Americans and the California Dream,* chap. 2.

6. Jewett may have seen the engraving after William Ranney's *Boone's First View of Kentucky,* published in the May 1850 issue of the *Bulletin of the American Art-Union* (New York).

7. Quoted in Evans, "Promised Land," 7–8.

8. Quoted in Van Nostrand, *First Hundred Years of Painting in California,* 61 n. 102.

9. The Bear Flag revolt hastened United States military conquest of California, which was completed during the Mexican War.

10. All the major writings, speeches, and paintings were authored by men. For the various responses of women see Sandra L. Myres, *Westering Women and the Frontier Experience, 1880–1915* (Albuquerque: University of New Mexico Press, 1982). I want to thank Julie Schimmel for bringing this book to my attention.

11. The management of the American Art-Union had no doubt of the nation's position in world affairs. William J. Hoppin reported in the *Transactions of the American Art-Union for the Year 1846* (New York, 1846), 17: "We are one of the four leading powers of the world, equal to any of them in the average of intelligence and enterprise. Have we done our share of this labor in the cultivation of High Art? Sir, we have hardly commenced to do it."

12. Alexander C. Fraser, ed., *The Works of George Berkeley, D.D.* (Oxford, 1901), 4:364–65.

13. According to Charles Frankel, "The Idea of Progress," in Paul Edwards, ed., *The Encyclopedia of Philosophy* (New York: Macmillan and Free Press, 1967), 6:483: "The emergence of this idea is the product of a variety of circumstances, such as the accumulation of an economic surplus, the increase of social mobility, and the occurrence of major inventions that have dramatically increased human power over nature. Over

and above these, however, the idea of progress is peculiarly a response to the emergence of the unique social institution of organized scientific inquiry."

14. Ekirch, *Idea of Progress in America.* Ekirch builds on the study of J. B. Bury, *The Idea of Progress: An Inquiry into Its Origin and Growth* (1920; New York: Dover, 1955).

15. François P. Guizot, *General History of Civilization in Europe from the Fall of the Roman Empire to the French Revolution,* 3d American ed. (1838; New York: Appleton, 1842), 23, 25. Also quoted in Ekirch, *Idea of Progress in America* (1969 ed.), 22.

16. Ekirch, *Idea of Progress in America* (1969 ed.), 41.

17. I use the word *speech* broadly; even though the words of the expansionists generally reached the public through essays and written reports, their hortatory quality brings to mind speeches.

18. For the events in William Gilpin's life that led to his "untransacted destiny" statement, see Karnes, *Gilpin,* 105–37.

19. William Gilpin, *Mission of the North American People: Geographical, Social, and Political* (1860; New York: Lippincott, 1873), 124. As a wealthy manufacturer's son, Gilpin would also have had a classical training; Kevin Whitfield reminds me that Gilpin's speech echoes a famous celebration of Roman imperialism in Virgil's *Aeneid,* bk. 6.

20. Gilpin would have preferred a more aggressive stance, with the boundary set at 54°40', but most others, including Thomas Hart Benton, were satisfied with the treaty. The first use of the phrase "Manifest Destiny" is credited to John L. O'Sullivan, in his unsigned editorial for the July–August 1845 issue of the *Democratic Review.*

21. Smith, *Virgin Land,* 149–51, 159–62, discusses James DeBow and Jessup Scott.

22. *DeBow's Review* 27 (August 1859): 125–36.

23. As Smith, *Virgin Land,* 150, points out, DeBow in time realized the political and economic consequences of expansionism: "Southern leaders were eventually forced to recognize that the notions of the course of empire and of the coming dominance of the West were implicitly free-soil."

24. *Transactions of the American Art-Union for the Year 1845* (New York, 1845), 14.

25. See Rick Stewart, 40–39, in Sandweiss, Stewart, and Huseman, *Eyewitness to War.*

26. For information on Carl Nebel, see Ben W. Huseman, ibid., 110 n. 1.

27. Stewart, ibid., 5, discusses the speed with which news of the war returned to the United States through the use of telegraphy, the penny press, and lithography.

28. For the heroicization of Samuel Ringgold in contemporary theater and song, see Johannsen, *Halls of the Montezumas,* 124–27.

29. See Eisenhower, *So Far from God,* 76–80.

30. In 1847 James Walker painted two versions of the Battle of Chapultepec to please the two generals, John Quitman and Gideon Pillow, who each claimed the final victory. The Quitman version is currently in the collection of Mr. and Mrs. David Carter, San Antonio; the Pillow version is unlocated; both served as the basis for lithographs (see Huseman, in Sandweiss, Stewart, and Huseman, *Eyewitness to War,* 329–35).

31. In 1857 Walker was commissioned to paint the Battle of Chapultepec for the Capitol. Intended as part of a series of historical paintings for the Capitol extension, the painting was to represent General Quitman's attack from Tacubaya Road. Captain Montgomery C. Meigs, in charge of the commissions, became displeased with Walker and refused to accept the final painting; Walker sued and was awarded six thousand dollars (see Marian R. McNaughton, "James Walker: Combat Artist of Two American Wars," typescript in the Army Art Archives, United States Army Center of Military History, Washington, D.C). I am grateful to Alex Nemerov for providing me with this information.

Goetzmann and Goetzmann, *West of the Imagination,* 99, sum up the Mexican War pictures: "Thus, what were essentially wartime propaganda pictures and personal souvenirs, directly served the great national objective of Manifest Destiny. They glorified the 'transacting' of William Gilpin's 'untransacted destiny,' but they also created a demand for more and more information about the Far West."

32. For information on the American Art-Union, see the records at the New-York Historical Society as well as Baker, "American Art-Union"; Mann, *American Art-Union;* and Miller, *Patrons and Patriotism,* 160–72.

In 1838 New York portrait painter-entrepreneur James Herring set up a gallery to provide exhibition space for younger artists and "for the lovers of Art a place of resort, where they might expect to find a rich variety of subjects for study or for sale" (quoted in Miller, *Patrons and Patriotism,* 160). When Herring's first gallery for this purpose failed, he decided to model a new organization on the art unions of Europe, which he called the Apollo Association for the Promotion of the Fine Arts in the United States. The goals were to assist artists and elevate the public taste, accomplished by taking money from the pool of membership fees (five dollars per subscriber each year) and purchasing art, which then went on exhibition. At the end of each year members had a chance to win one work at a lottery. In addition, all members received at least one engraving. In 1842 a newly installed committee of management reorganized the association and renamed it the American Art-Union.

33. Baker, "American Art-Union," 216, estimates the number who attended. During these years the population of New York was about 400,000, yet an annual average of 250,000 (58 percent) visited. Granted the repeat visitors, the figures are impressive.

34. Biographies of many of these men can be found in *Dictionary of American Biography* and *The National Cyclopaedia.* I am grateful to David Shapiro for providing me with an offprint he authored, "William Cullen Bryant and the American Art-Union," in Stanley Brodwin, Michael D'Innocenza, and Joseph G. Astman, eds., *William Cullen Bryant and His America* (New York: AMS Press, 1983). Four issues of the *Crayon,* volume 3 (February, April, June, and August 1856), focused on the art collections of, respectively, Jonathan Sturges, Abraham Cozzens, Charles M. Leupp, and Marshall O. Roberts.

35. See Allan Nevins, "The Century, 1847–1866," in *The Century, 1847–1946* (New York: Century, 1947), 3–24.

36. For a history of Sketch Club activities, see James T. Callow, *Kindred Spirits: Knickerbocker Writers and American Artists, 1807–1855* (Chapel Hill: University of North Carolina Press, 1967). Recent studies have also focused on such networks (see Carrie Rebora, "The American Academy of Fine Arts" [Ph.D. diss., City University of New York, 1989]; Annette Blaugrund, "The Tenth Street Studio Building" [Ph.D.

diss., Columbia University, 1987], focuses more specifically on artists' networks).

37. Beginning publication in 1848 and issued from April through December, the *Bulletin* at first merely listed works on exhibition. It later printed lengthy articles on art subjects. In the same month that the first *Bulletin* was issued, April 1848, discussions were held at the Century regarding the desirability of a regular publication; see typescript, "Louis Lang's Art History of the Century Association from 1847 through 1880," Century Association Archives, New York, 3. I am grateful to W. Gregory Gallagher, librarian of the Century, for bringing this manuscript to my attention.

38. Quoted in Baker, "American Art-Union," 152. An analysis of the engravings distributed to the entire membership better gauges the cultural nationalism of the organization than does a study of all the paintings bought for exhibition and the lottery, since encouragement of emerging talents motivated a goodly number of such purchases. Of the thirty-six engravings issued between 1840 and 1851, three referred to American historical events, eight were American genre scenes (some referring to contemporary events), thirteen illustrated American fiction, and two were American landscapes; four more referred to events from Roman or European history about patriotism or civic virtue that the management would consider "American."

39. *Bulletin of the American Art-Union* (New York) 2 (October 1849): 12. They also took credit for advancing the careers of portrait painter George Baker and landscape painters Frederic E. Church and John F. Kensett.

40. Ranney's *Dead Charger* (unlocated), shown in 1846 at the American Art-Union, was inspired by the Mexican War; according to Johannsen, *Halls of the Montezumas,* 126–27, the horse is Davy Branch, the mount of Major Ringgold, who fell at the Battle of Palo Alto. In 1848 Henry Peters Gray painted *The Wages of War* (The Metropolitan Museum of Art, New York), an allegorical painting, which could have referred to the Mexican War or the revolutions of Europe.

41. *Heroine Martyr* appeared in *Friendship's Gift,* which was edited by Walter Percival and published by John P. Hill in Boston. The engraving accompanies an antiwar poem, "The Heroine Martyr of Monterey," by the Reverend J. G. Lyons, about a Mexican woman

who tended both the American and Mexican wounded on the battlefield before being killed by a fuselage from the Mexican side.

42. *Bulletin of the American Art-Union* (New York) (April 1, 1851): 17. Alfred Jones was also a member of the Century, having joined in 1847; George W. Austin joined in 1851.

43. Bryan Wolfe has linked the picture to the development of the penny post in his article "All the World's a Code: Art and Ideology in Nineteenth-Century American Painting," *Art Journal* 44 (Winter 1984): 328–37. According to the *Literary World* 9 (December 13, 1851): 47 (quoted in Mann, *American Art-Union,* 24), the scene represents "a southern tavern."

44. I discuss the peripheral placement of both women and African-Americans in nineteenth-century genre painting in *Painters' America.*

45. Smaller than *War News,* the engraving distributed to members measured 7½ by 9⅝ inches.

46. It is no coincidence that Ranney, known for his western scenes, painted at this time historical pictures of George Washington and Revolutionary subject matter that were shown at the American Art-Union: *Washington's Mission to the Indians in 1753,* circa 1847 (unlocated); *First News of the Battle of Lexington,* 1847 (North Carolina Museum of Art, Raleigh); *Veterans of 1776 Returning from the War,* circa 1848 (unlocated); *Washington Rallying the Americans at the Battle of Princeton,* 1848 (Princeton University). Ranney's *Marion Crossing the Pedee,* 1850 (unlocated), was engraved by the American Art-Union and distributed in 1851. It is also possible, however, that Richard Caton Woodville was making a covert reference to the European revolutions of 1848.

47. Johannsen, *Halls of the Montezumas,* 212–13.

48. Although Woodville painted these works in Düsseldorf, friends from his hometown of Baltimore had fought in the war and Major Ringgold had hailed from there (see Francis S. Grubar, "Richard Caton Woodville: An American Artist, 1825 to 1855" [Ph.D. diss., Johns Hopkins University, 1966], 139 and 166 n. 28).

49. A reviewer for the *New York Herald* called it "an excellent composition, and well done," and Walt Whitman called it a "pleasing piece . . . the mother and the old '76er are beautifully done; the whole picture is

good, and free from that straining after effect," but neither mentioned the African-Americans in the picture (quoted ibid., 138).

50. In the following year, 1852, when the American Art-Union was forced to sell off all its holdings, the disposition of Woodville's *War News from Mexico* and *Old '76 and Young '48* tells us of the sustaining power the pictures had for New York's merchant Unionists. The man involved with extending an efficient mail service, Marshall O. Roberts, came to possess *War News*. *Old '76* was bought by successful shipbuilder William Webb, whose commercial interests would have dictated strong Unionist and expansionist endeavors and who would have found appealing the theme of patriotic unity. In 1862 Webb loaned the painting to the Artists' Fund Society, at which time it was recycled as a Union Army picture with the title *The Spirit of '76 and '62.*

51. See Smith, *Virgin Land*, 51–58; Glanz, *How the West Was Drawn*, 1–25; and Slotkin, *Regeneration through Violence*, chap. 12.

52. For the best discussion of Ranney's painting, see Glanz, *How the West Was Drawn*, 16. See also Linda Ayres, "William Ranney," in Amon Carter Museum, *American Frontier Life.*

53. Henry T. Tuckerman, "Over the Mountains, or the Western Pioneer," in *The Home Book of the Picturesque; or American Scenery, Art, and Literature* (New York: Putnam, 1852), 117. Also quoted in Glanz, *How the West Was Drawn*, 17.

54. Quoted in Cowdrey, *American Academy of Fine Arts and American Art-Union*, 2:295.

55. In reality trappers were considered a disreputable lot (see Bernard DeVoto, *Across the Wide Missouri* [Boston: Houghton Mifflin, 1947]).

56. See Grubar, *Ranney*, 41, no. 68.

57. J. Cecil Alter, *Jim Bridger* (1925; Norman: University of Oklahoma Press, 1962), 231–39, quotes several firsthand accounts by forty-niners.

58. In his famous essay of 1893, Frederick Jackson Turner wrote: "Stand at the Cumberland Gap and watch the procession of civilization, marching single file—the buffalo following the trail to the salt springs, the Indian, the fur-trader and hunter, the cattle-raiser, the pioneer farmer—and the frontier has passed by" (see "The Significance of the Frontier in American His-

tory," in *Frontier and Section: Selected Essays of Frederic Jackson Turner* [Englewood Cliffs, N.J.: Prentice-Hall, 1961], 44).

When the Art-Union declined to purchase the painting, George Caleb Bingham took it to the French firm of Goupil, Vibert, and Company, which agreed to engrave it for distribution. Bingham was disappointed that Goupil reproduced the image not as a fine-arts engraving but used the cheaper lithographic process. The lithograph had much less of the concentrated power of the original, since the scene opens up at the right so that the forward thrust is less forceful. For the chronology of the painting's making and Bingham's ambitions for it, see Bloch, *Bingham: Evolution of an Artist* 1:120–23.

59. The Moses typology seems obvious, and I mentioned it in *American Frontier*, 6. Glanz, *How the West Was Drawn*, 19–24, analyzes in detail Bingham's painting, its symbolism, and its lithograph; see also Elizabeth Johns, "The 'Missouri Artist' as Artist," 93–139, in Shapiro, *Bingham.*

60. See Martin E. Schmidt with Dee Brown, *The Settlers' West* (New York: Scribner's, 1955).

61. Dana, *Garden of the World*, 13.

62. Billington, *Westward Expansion* (1974 ed.), 514. Dana also published the constitution of the American Settlement Company, the aim of which was to settle "a tract of land in the Territory of Kanzas, in order to assist in making it a free state" (Dana, *Garden of the World*, 221).

63. See Foner, *Free Soil.*

64. Between 1848 and 1853 Benton was a consistent advocate of the transcontinental railway, and the speech he made on the floor of the Congress took up thirty-five pages of Dana's book. He had not been west himself, but he drew generously on the reports of his son-in-law John Charles Frémont and those returning from the railroad surveys; but by and large his rhetoric was based on what he wanted to believe. While Benton at first advocated that the railroad be a government project, by 1853 he had become persuaded that private enterprise should tackle the task. For Benton's role in developing a "Passage to India," see Smith, *Virgin Land*, 19–34.

65. See Goetzmann and Goetzmann, *West of the Imagination*, 107. For a more detailed account of the

railroad surveys, see William H. Goetzmann's two books: *Army Exploration in the American West, 1803–1863* (1959) and *Exploration and Empire* (1966).

66. See "John M. Stanley and the Pacific Railroad Surveys," in Taft, *Artists and Illustrators of the Old West.* Taft's endnotes to the chapter, 252–78, review extensively the contributions of all the artists to the survey.

67. See Stevens, *Explorations for a Route for a Pacific Railroad.*

68. To promote lands along the Illinois Central Railroad the land commissioner of Chicago advertised in 1861 in *Godey's Ladies Book* with illustrations of fertile farm lands along the railroad and farmers reaping with the most up-to-date equipment. Modernized equipment, however, rarely made it into the oil paintings of the period.

69. Quoted in Smith, *Virgin Land,* 32.

70. Nathaniel Hawthorne, "Chiefly about War Matters," *Atlantic Monthly* 10 (July 1862): 46. During Hawthorne's month-long stay the painter and writer became friends and Leutze painted a sympathetic portrait of Hawthorne (see Groseclose, *Leutze,* no. 219).

71. This thesis is persuasively advanced by George M. Fredrickson in *The Inner Civil War: Northern Intellectuals and the Crisis of the Union* (New York: Harper & Row, 1965), 1–3.

72. Emanuel Leutze to Montgomery C. Meigs, February 14, 1854, Records of the Architect of the Capitol, Washington D.C. I wish to thank Barbara Wolanin, curator for the architect of the Capitol, for sending me a photocopy of this letter.

73. The Art-Union exhibited eighteen paintings by Leutze from 1839 to 1852 and issued the large folio engraving of Leutze's *Sir Walter Raleigh Parting with His Wife* (unlocated) in 1846 and a smaller engraving of *The Image Breaker* (Noah Cutler, Philadelphia) in 1850. When Andrew Warner, the corresponding secretary, urged young Americans to study in Düsseldorf, it was partly for the chance to get to know such a sterling role model. Furthermore, Abraham Cozzens, the Art-Union's president in 1850–51 was both the namesake of Leutze's son and owner of several Leutze paintings including his own portrait (The Century Association, New York).

74. See Raymond L. Stehle, "*Washington Crossing the Delaware,*" *Pennsylvania History* 31 (July 1964): 269–

94. The most complete resource for scholarship on this painting is Spassky, *American Paintings in the Metropolitan* 2:13–24.

75. At the time, April 1852, Pennsylvania senator James Cooper introduced to the Senate a resolution to commission Leutze to paint two paintings, another *Washington Crossing the Delaware* and *Washington Rallying the Troops at Monmouth,* and G. P. A. Healy to paint *The Battle of Bunker Hill* and *The Throwing Overboard of the Tea in Boston Harbor* (see Fairman, *Art and Artists of the Capitol,* 134–38). All these pictures need to be understood in the climate of Unionists seeking to avert a war of secession.

76. It may well be that Jefferson Davis, secretary of war from 1853 to 1857 and in charge of the Capitol extension building program, may have discouraged such pictures—particularly those depicting westward expansion—when it became evident to him that such expansion would be on the basis of Free-Soil principles. As Ekirch, *Idea of Progress in America* (1969 ed.), 34, has observed, "In the South the necessity of defending slavery imparted in many quarters a generally conservative, backward-looking philosophy of life opposed to the concept of progress entertained in the other parts of the nation." But Leutze had other friends in Washington who would no doubt help with the efforts of Captain Meigs, most notably William Henry Seward, a Republican senator from New York and a leading Free-Soil expansionist. Leutze painted portraits of Seward as well as members of his family in 1859 and 1861.

77. Quoted in Fairman, *Art and Artists of the Capitol,* 202.

78. On July 9, 1861, Leutze and Meigs concluded an agreement for Leutze to paint the twenty-by-thirty-foot mural for a sum of twenty thousand dollars. The letter of agreement is quoted ibid., 202.

79. Leutze wrote notes on the iconography, published in Justin G. Turner, "Emanuel Leutze's Mural *Westward the Course of Empire Takes Its Way,*" *Manuscripts* 18, no. 2 (September 1966): 14–16. Glanz, *How the West Was Drawn,* 77–81, relates the iconography to the millennialism of the abolitionists.

80. Stehle, "*Westward Ho!*" 310–13, notes the reviews but does not quote at length from any of them.

81. According to Foner, *Free Soil,* 267, Scott Cameron "wished to keep Negroes out of the territo-

ries, because the white laborer 'must be depressed wherever the Negro is his competitor in the field or the workshop.' " The racialist premises of Cameron's beliefs are complicated (see Eric Foner, "Racial Attitudes of the New York Free Soilers," *New York History* 46 [October 1965]: 311–29; and George M. Frederickson, *The Black Image in the White Mind: The Debate on Afro-American Character and Destiny, 1817–1914* [Middletown, Conn.: Wesleyan University Press, 1971]).

82. Eastman Johnson painted several pictures valorizing blacks, including *A Ride for Liberty—The Fugitive Slave,* circa 1862 (The Brooklyn Museum); John Quincy Adams Ward sculpted *The Freedman* in 1862–63 (Cincinnati Art Museum); and in 1864 John Rogers began mass-producing his plaster-sculpture group *The Wounded Scout: A Friend in the Swamp,* depicting a strong black youth helping a Union soldier. I deal with such images in a paper, "Eastman Johnson: The Civil War and Reconstruction," delivered at the College Art Association annual meetings, February 1986, and subsequently at Boston University, Stanford University, and the Brooklyn Museum.

83. Anne Brewster, "Emmanuel Leutze: The Artist," *Lippincott's Magazine* 2 (November 1868): 536.

84. See Limerick, *Legacy of Conquest,* 277–80; Limerick includes a useful bibliography on the subject.

85. Bowles, *Across the Continent,* 14.

86. See Naef and Wood, *Era of Exploration,* 219.

87. See Angela Lynn Miller, " 'The Imperial Republic': Narratives of National Expansion in American Art, 1820–1860" (Ph.D. diss., Yale University, 1985), particularly chap. 8.

88. Ludlow, *Heart of the Continent,* 110.

89. Ibid., 110–11; first noted by J. Gray Sweeney, "The Artist-Explorers of the American West, 1860–1880" (Ph.D. diss., Indiana University, 1975), 167. Albert Bierstadt was born in Germany and studied in Düsseldorf and would thus be attracted to a party of German pioneers. Many, however, believed that Germans made superior immigrants, such as E. Pershine Smith in 1858, because they "become either artisans or cultivators of their own land at once" (quoted in Foner, *Free Soil,* 232).

90. This could be the painting *Emigrants Crossing the Plains—Sunset,* owned by Bierstadt, as noted by Tuckerman, *Book of the Artists,* 393, or *Emigrants Cross-*

ing the Plains, listed in Tuckerman's appendix, 625, as belonging to Marshall O. Roberts.

91. Quoted in Spassky, *American Paintings in the Metropolitan* 2:254.

92. See Billington, *Westward Expansion* (1974 ed.), 583.

93. Goddard, *Where to Emigrate and Why,* 12. The author emphasized the largesse of the Homestead Act, "one of the most beneficent enactments of any age, or country, and one which has done more than any other to honor the American name, and make it loved throughout the earth." For a realistic appraisal of the Homestead Act, see American Social History Project under the direction of Herbert G. Gutman, *From Conquest and Colonization through Reconstruction and the Great Uprising of 1877,* vol. 1 of Bruce Levine et al., *Who Built America?: Working People and the Nation's Economy, Politics, Culture, and Society* (New York: Pantheon, 1989), 518–19.

94. Bowles, *Across the Continent,* 255–57.

95. See ibid., 408–12. Massachusetts congressman Oakes Ames had been distributing Crédit Mobilier stock to influential government officials, who were reaping inflated dividends (see Stewart H. Holbrook, *The Story of American Railroads* [New York: Crown, 1947], 171; Arthur M. Johnson and Barry E. Supple, *Boston Capitalists and Western Railroads: A Study in the Nineteenth-Century Railroad Investment Process* [Cambridge, Mass.: Harvard University Press, 1967], 216; and Matthew Josephson, *The Robber Barons: The Great American Capitalists, 1861–1901* [1934; New York: Harcourt, Brace, 1962], 75–100).

96. See Thomas Cole, *River in the Catskills,* 1843 (Museum of Fine Arts, Boston), and Thomas Doughty, *A View of Swampscott, Massachusetts,* 1847 (Worcester Art Museum, Massachusetts).

97. *The Lackawanna Valley,* 1856–57 (National Gallery of Art, Washington, D.C.); reproduced and discussed in Nicolai Cikovsky, Jr., "George Inness's *The Lackawanna Valley:* Type of the Modern," in Danly and Marx, *Railroad in American Art,* 71–91.

98. Reproduced and discussed in Kenneth W. Maddox, ibid., 51–69.

99. See Susan Daly, ibid., 1–50. The painting most likely was the result of the Baltimore and Ohio Railroad's "artists' excursion" of 1859, when well-

known artists, including Kensett, Louis Lang, Louis K. Minot, Thomas Rossiter, and James Suydam, were guests.

100. See Gemmill, "Ferreting out Thomas P. Otter," 19–40. Their respective firms were Baldwin Locomotive Works of Philadelphia and Eastwick and Harrison (see Edward Hungerford, *The Story of the Baltimore and Ohio Railroad, 1827–1927* [New York: Putnam, 1928]).

101. For the railroad enthusiasts who thrilled to the picture of a locomotive at full throttle, see John F. Casson, *Civilizing the Machine: Technology and Republican Values in America, 1776–1900* (1976; New York: Penguin, 1977), 172–80.

102. See Richardson, *Beyond the Mississippi.*

103. Ibid., 461. The author wrote for the *New York Tribune* and traveled west with the Bowles-Colfax party, also railroad enthusiasts, in the summer of 1866.

104. Ibid., 567.

105. The two sketches are reproduced and discussed in Peters, *Currier & Ives* 1:114.

106. See Sabin, *Building the Pacific Railway,* 279–85. Thomas C. Durant went so far as to stage a mock Indian battle for the excursionists to view. See also Taft, *Photography and the American Scene* (1938 ed.), 278.

107. For photographers who recorded the building of the transcontinental railroad, see Naef and Wood, *Era of Exploration,* 42–49.

108. See ibid., 201–18. Therese Thau Heyman notes, 202: "The railroad images include a great many sequence shots, which would provide a record of the actual construction had they been exposed on motion-picture film. Over 200 large glass-plate railroad views, 10 × 13 inches, are in the collection of The Oakland Museum History Department." For a critical assessment of Russell's photographs of the Union Pacific Railroad, see also Nancy Rich, "Politics and the Picturesque: A. J. Russell's *Great West Illustrated,*" *Views* 10, no. 4 (Summer 1989): 4–6; and 11, no. 1 (Fall 1989): 24.

109. See Roy Harvey Pearce, *The Savages of America: A Study of the Indian and the Idea of Civilization,* 2d ed. rev. (1953; Baltimore: Johns Hopkins University Press, 1965).

110. A succinct study of this theme is provided by Maddox in Danly and Marx, *Railroad in American Art,* 51–69.

To nineteenth-century racialists, Indians were also the measure of whites' supposed superiority. In describing Horatio Greenough's statuary group *The Rescue Group* installed on the Capitol steps, the *Bulletin of the American Art-Union* (New York) (September 1851): 97, quoted the *Home Journal:* "The thought embodied in the action of the group, and immediately communicated to every spectator, is the natural and necessary superiority of the Anglo-Saxon to the Indian. It typifies the settlement of the American continent, and the respective destinies of the two races who here come into collision. You see the exposure and suffering of the female emigrant—the ferocious and destructive instinct of the savage, and his easy subjugation under the superior manhood of the new colonist."

111. Maddox has found one of the earliest images of the "Indian contemplating the progress of civilization," published in 1844—the subject of a frontispiece of S. G. Goodrich's *Pictorial History of the United States* (see reproduction in Danly and Marx, *Railroad in American Art,* 62).

112. Sabin, *Building the Pacific Railway,* 234

113. *Harper's Weekly* 10 (July 10, 1869). Wendell Phillips charged: "For seventy years and more the Indian has begged this great nation to attend to his wrongs. His cries have been unheard. Ruthless and unheeding we have trampled him down. Today the worm turns and stings us.

"Last year [1868] Indians destroyed locomotives and shot conductors. Timid [Thomas C.] Durant forbade the telegraph wires to report the fact. He trembled for his road. To-day fifteen thousand warriors on the war-path—a thousand miles of exposed road. . . . Would our words reach every Indian chief. We would tell him, lay down your gun, but allow no rail to lie between Omaha and the mountains." At least, Phillips adds, until the Indians' grievances are addressed.

114. Fifer, *American Progress,* 201–5.

115. Crofutt, *Crofutt's New Overland Tourist and Pacific Coast Guide.*

116. According to Slotkin, *Fatal Environment* (1986 ed.), 427, Generals William Tecumseh Sherman and Philip Henry Sheridan considered a war of extermination both inevitable and desirable.

117. Quoted ibid., 427. Slotkin adds: "But the point of the adventure tale is to provide a validating

myth for a systematic restatement of the Northern Pacific's propaganda" and that was "that the Indian is an
obstacle to progress and to progress's most essential
work, the railroad."

118. *Daily Evening Bulletin* (San Francisco), October 23, 1875, 2.

119. Quoted in Ekirch, *Idea of Progress in America*
(1969 ed.), 196.

120. Quoted ibid., 197. Ekirch's chapter "Education: The Universal Utopia" is useful on this subject.

121. Research on this topic is vast and constantly
being revised; for the most recent assessments, see
Blaine A. Brownell, "Interpretations of Twentieth-
Century Urban Progressive Reform," in David R. Col-
burn and George E. Pozzetta, *Reform and Reformers in
the Progressive Era* (Westport, Conn.: Greenwood Press,
1983), 3–24.

122. See Lois Marie Fink and Joshua C. Taylor,
Academy: The Academic Tradition in American Art
(Washington, D.C.: National Collection of Fine Arts,
1975), 207.

3

Inventing "the Indian"

JULIE SCHIMMEL

No sooner had the first representation of American Indians appeared on canvas than the question was raised as to whether or not it was accurate. From that day until the present it has been the issue most frequently debated in judging portraits of Indian life. During the nineteenth century, in particular, questions about accuracy superseded judgments about artistic merit, so convinced were critics and commentators on Indian habits and customs that "real" Indians could be isolated and identified.

A journalist writing for the *Missouri Republican* in 1848, for example, described "a home scene" of Indian life by Seth Eastman as if it were possible for an artist to create without a point of view. The painting, he wrote, was "quite unlike the vast mass of Indian pictures it has been our bad luck to see—for it is true. There is no attitudinizing—no position of figures in such a group that you can swear the artist's hands, and not their own free will, put them there."[1] Yet George Catlin's self-portrait

among the Mandans, painted just a decade later, suggests just how much "attitudinizing" permeated the relationship between whites and Indians [125]. Catlin stands dressed in a contrived buckskin outfit that makes of western garb a fashionable eastern suit. Poised with brush in hand before his easel, he paints the Mandan chief Máh-to-tóh-pa as a reflection of his own self-conscious, controlling image. The artist's stance among a spell-bound crowd of half-nude Indians leads the viewer to believe that nothing but reality is being recorded, but Catlin's relationship to his subjects comes straight from the drawing rooms of eastern society, as Indians are submitted to a portrait process that cherishes individuality, material status, and vanity—all notions less highly regarded in Indian culture.

Whether from the spheres of religion, politics, commerce, or ordinary walks of life, white Americans perceived Indians through the assumptions of their own culture. As a result, Indians were seen in terms of what they might become or what they were not—white Christians. Or Indians were not seen at all, at least in terms of the cultural organization particular to Indian tribes or in terms of the negative impact white contact had on Indian culture. In 1874 *Harper's Weekly* published *Two Bits to See the Pappoose,* an illustration by Paul Frenzeny and Jules Tavernier [126]. The accompanying text reads:

To those who have never come into contact with Indians on their native plains, the sight of the squaws and pappooses is something very droll and interesting. The poor creatures crowd about the railroad stations on the arrival of the trains, and pick up many a penny by showing off their babies to the lady passengers.[2]

The author of this text, with an attitude shaped by ethnocentric standards of behavior, can only perceive what is inappropriate. Where tragedy was visible, only a comedy was seen. No one comprehended that begging was the result of white destruction of tribal life, in which traditional means of support could no longer function.

By the time American artists first ventured forth to paint Indians in western territories, the latter had long been perceived in the light of contrasts made between white and tribal cultures. As historian Patricia Limerick states in *The Legacy of Conquest* (1988): "Savagery meant hunting and gathering, not agriculture; common ownership, not individual property owning; pagan superstition, not Christianity; spoken language, not literacy; emotion, not reason."[3] Whether the comparison was represented overtly or not, Indians were judged according to these contrasts, as Fanny Palmer's well-known Currier and Ives lithograph of 1868 makes clear [see 114]. America's growth is expressed in terms of the Indians' decline. On the left, a white community bustles with

activity. The major features of the town are the public school, the foundation of "enlightened" citizenry; the woodsmen, who prepare the way for future settlement; and the telegraph and railroad lines, the technological lifelines of civilization. These last two forms of invention—communication and transportation—most explicitly separate the two Indians on the right from civilization. Astride their horses, which suggest their nomadic life-styles, partially obliterated by smoke from the train, they stand rooted, while lines of so-called progress reach toward the horizon.

As a result of the implicit or explicit comparison of Indian and white cultures, Indians were commonly judged as "good" or "bad." The duality is well expressed in 1859 by Henry A. Boller, a Northwest fur trader:

I could "paint" you, were it not for the constant interruptions . . . two pictures:
The One would represent the bright side of In-

125. George Catlin, *Catlin Painting the Portrait of Máh-to-tóh-pa—Mandan,* 1857–69, oil on composition board, 15⅜ × 21⅞. National Gallery of Art, Washington, D.C.; Paul Mellon Collection.

dian Life, with its feathers, lances, gayly dressed & mounted "banneries", fights, buffalo hunting &c.

The other, the dark side, showing the filth, vermin, poverty, nakedness, suffering, starvation, superstition, &c. *Both would be equally true—neither exagerated, or distorted; both totally disimillar!*[4]

Noble but Savage

Artists drew on both interpretations but more often at first (particularly in the 1830s and 1840s) on an idealized Indian representing the "natural" man conceived by whites as an alternate role model—the independent male who lived beyond the bounds of civilization but who embodied wilderness "virtues." The "dark side," the superstitious, godless "savage" in conflict with white civilization (and a hierarchy of Anglo-Saxon values), emerged in significant numbers on canvas in the 1840s and has persisted to the present.[5]

Paintings by Charles Bird King from the 1820s and by Karl Bodmer, Catlin, and Alfred Jacob Miller from the 1830s portray Indians as separate from white civilization, as if colonization had not yet introduced epidemics, alcoholism, and tribal disintegration caused by removal from traditional to distant lands. Artists

126. Paul Frenzeny and Jules Tavernier, *Two Bits to See the Pappoose*. From *Harper's Weekly* 18 (October 24, 1874): 880. Library of Congress, Washington, D.C.

ignored current realities in favor of earlier literary and artistic traditions, which placed Indians in remote and pristine environments. Here were earthly paradises, where life, supported by the beneficence of nature, proceeded in an orderly fashion. At one with their surroundings, Indians were seen as innocent, simple, devoid of guile and deception.

While rarely revealing the ideas that formed their attitudes, painters drew on well-established European intellectual constructs regarding primitivism and the Noble Savage.[6] First developed in the late sixteenth century, the concept of the Noble Savage was used by eighteenth-century writers and philosophers such as Rousseau, Voltaire, and Diderot to criticize contemporary French morals and practices. In this context the Noble Savage was the rational individual, who, as historian Robert F. Berkhofer, Jr., notes, "pointed to the possibility of progress by civilized man if left free and untrammeled by outworn institutions."[7] By the end of the eighteenth century the Noble Savage suggested other meanings. Previously viewed as an enlightened savage, he could now also be pictured as a "primitive," a man of intuition and emotion. At the beginning of the nineteenth century American painters suggested both concepts in their paintings of Indians. Particularly in portraits, we are shown well-formed heads with high foreheads and prominent noses, which recalled to nineteenth-century audiences men of Roman physique and virtue. The light of intelligence can be seen in their eyes. As romantic savages, Indians appear equally to be men of emotion and sensibility, their intelligence shaped as much by intuition as by reason.

Charles Bird King was among the first to paint numerous portraits of native Americans. King had studied for seven years with Benjamin West in England, where the young artist might well have absorbed sentiments regarding the Noble Savage. Having been commissioned initially by the Department of War and subsequently by the chief of the Bureau of Indian Affairs, Thomas L. McKenney, King painted about 143 portraits of Indians between 1821 and 1842. Among his subjects was Hayne Hudjihini, who, according to an inscription on the back of one of five versions of her portrait, was the youngest of the five wives of an Oto chief who brought her to Washington, D.C., in 1822 [127].[8] An Indian commissioner described her as "young, tall, and finely formed, her face . . . was the most beautiful we had met with."[9] One suspects that her appearance appealed to Washingtonians to the degree it approached the standards of beauty held for white women. But her beauty was not all that attracted her audience. Through her conventional pose and rose-colored dress, King suggests a demure women. Even the soft, white fur she wears is far removed from the fierce looking pelts more commonly shown on Indian subjects. Yet the so-called primitive side of her life is not absent from the artist's brush or the viewer's mind. Among Indian sexual mores, none was more titillating to whites than polygamy. In the text accompanying her portrait, published in *The Indian Tribes of North America* (1837–44), author James Hall commented that Hayne Hudjihini's husband had concluded that his wives' "caprices" were the result of "so many mistresses and but one master."[10] Hayne Hudjihini must have appealed to her white viewers as a morally inferior savage who was yet ennobled by simplicity and nature.

The consummate Noble Savage portrait, *Young Omahaw, War Eagle, Little Missouri, and Pawnees,* was completed in 1822 in King's Washington studio [128]. The painting subsumes Indians and their individuality in the artistic tradition and romantic sentiments of the late eighteenth century. Derived from a con-

127. Charles Bird King, *Hayne Hudjihini (Eagle of Delight),* circa 1822, oil on panel, 17½ × 13⅞ in. The White House Collection, Washington, D.C.

128. Charles Bird King, *Young Omahaw, War Eagle, Little Missouri, and Pawnees*, 1822, oil on canvas, 28 × 36⅛ in. National Museum of American Art, Smithsonian Institution, Washington, D.C.; gift of Helen Barlow.

vention of multiple portraits of the same or different subjects, the four heads, despite the painting's title, are probably based on the likenesses of two Pawnee chiefs, Petalesharro, chief of the Pawnee Loups, and Peskelechaco, chief of the Republican Pawnees, whom King painted when they traveled to Washington with a tribal delegation in late 1821.[11] The partly shaven heads are capped with deer-hair crests, with loops of wampum hanging from their pierced ears. One wears a silver peace medal bearing the image of President James Monroe. The Indians' bare shoulders, buffalo-skin robes, and body decorations imply that they are "primitive," yet their impressive physiques and countenances suggest more. Having seen the Pawnee delegation of which Petalesharro and Peskelechaco were members, one observer pointed to just those features that probably inspired King's multiple portrait: "All of them were men of large stature, very muscular, having fine open countenances, with the real noble Roman nose, dignified in their manners, and peaceful and quiet in their habits."[12] Conceived as Roman nobles, these are men to be admired for physical prowess as well as rea-

son. They represent a race that could perhaps be persuaded by rational argument as well as the formidable presence of the United States government to abandon tribal tradition for a more civilized life-style.

Catlin's 1834 portraits of the chief of the Osage, Clermont, and his wife, Wáh-chee-te, reveal other preconceptions about savage life [129–30]. The two adults assume conventional poses. Catlin's loose brushwork, pastel pinks and blues, and mottled sky suggest romantic portraiture styles of the day, such as those found in the work of fellow Philadelphia paint-

ers John Neagle and Thomas Sully. But Catlin's subjects are placed outdoors; their home is not in the city but in nature. The attire and hairstyles of husband and wife suggest their "natural" state. Both wear animal skins. Wáh-chee-te's hair hangs loosely to her shoulders, while her part is painted with vermilion. Clermont's head has been shaved with the exception of a strip of hair, or roach, decorated with horse hair dipped in vermilion. Each is only partly clothed. He sits bare-chested. She exposes her shoulders, while their child is nude. Civilized customs have not been introduced by

129. George Catlin, *Clermont, First Chief of the Tribe* (Osage), 1834, oil on canvas, 29 × 24 in. National Museum of American Art, Smithsonian Institution, Washington, D.C.; gift of Mrs. Joseph Harrison, Jr.

130. George Catlin, *Wáh-chee-te, Wife of Clermont, and Child* (Osage), 1834, oil on canvas, 29 × 24 in. National Museum of American Art, Smithsonian Institution, Washington, D.C.; gift of Mrs. Joseph Harrison, Jr.

barber or dressmaker. Yet neither is the couple uncivilized. Clermont may wear leggings and hold a war club fringed with scalp locks, but his war trophies, brass armlet, and wampum earrings are as decorative as they are menacing. His club is not held aggressively but is cradled in his arms. His threat as warrior is further diminished by his passive seated pose and by the peace medal hung around his neck. Presumably obtained as gifts from the United States government, these medals symbolize white curtailment of Indian power. Wáh-chee-te has been similarly, if more lightly, touched by civilization. Although still "primitive," her demeanor is gentle. Also, her portrait touches on one of the few points of approval accorded to Indians by whites. As Robert Beverly wrote in 1705 in his *History and Present State of Virginia:* "Children are not reckon'd a Charge among them, but rather Riches."[13]

The Swiss artist Karl Bodmer accompanied Prince Maximilian zu Wied, a German naturalist, up and down the Missouri River in 1833 and 1834. Bodmer's background was different from Catlin's and his hand more deft, but their attitudes toward Indian life had much in common. Two Bodmer portraits, *Pioch-Kiäiu (Distant Bear), Piegan Blackfeet Man,* 1833, and *Leader of the Mandan Buffalo Bull Society,* 1834, combine features of the enlightened and romantic savage [131–32]. Pioch-Kiäiu is dramatically portrayed in profile, his face colored with blue earth and vermilion. His hair, fashioned in a frontal topknot, indicates his status as a tribal medicine man. According to Maximilian's journal, members of the buffalo clan wore

the skin of the upper part of the head, the mane of the buffalo, with its horns, on their heads; but two select individuals, the bravest of all, who thenceforward never dare to fly from the enemy, wear a perfect imitation of the buffalo's head, with the horns, which they set on their heads, and in which there

are holes left for the eyes, which are surrounded with an iron or tin ring.[14]

Both men portrayed by Bodmer occupy important positions in their tribes, and our appreciation of them is meant to rest in part on their status and achievement. Yet to nineteenth-century viewers they remained, as Maximilian noted, "people of the first man." Their appearance might have been intriguing, but animal skins, masks, and earth dyes—evidence of superstition—were essentially unacceptable. A medicine man was still a heathen and a hunter, even if the "bravest of all," making all too clear the Indians' tie to the chase rather than to the plow.

Scenes of Indian life from the 1830s through the 1850s also suggest that the intellectual concept of the Noble Savage still influenced painters of the American West. Typical of paintings from the 1830s, which frequently presented Indians at one with nature in a sweeping panorama, are Miller's *Surround of Buffalo by Indians,* circa 1848–58, and Catlin's *Bird's-eye View of the Mandan Village,* 1837–39 [133–34].[15] A spacious landscape, lit by a golden sky encompassing Indians and buffalo below, evokes an earthly paradise in Miller's painting. To the left, an Indian woman sits mounted on an elaborately caparisoned horse. In the distance, Indian hunters ride to entrap the buffalo herd, a scene Miller described in romantic hyperbole: "The activity, native grace, and self-possession of the Indians, the intelligence of their well-trained horses, and the thousands of Buffalo moving in every direction over the broad and vast prairies, form a most extraordinary and unparalleled scene."[16] In such statements (and paintings) Miller conjures "savages," whose grace and freedom (reason and intuition) put them in tune with nature. But by the mid-1850s others were ready to offer a conflicting view. A traveler in the

131. Karl Bodmer, *Pioch-Kiäiu (Distant Bear), Piegan Blackfeet Man*, 1833, watercolor on paper, 12⅜ × 10⅛ in. Joslyn Art Museum, Omaha; gift of Enron Art Foundation.

132. Karl Bodmer, *Leader of the Mandan Buffalo Bull Society*, 1834, watercolor and pencil on paper, 16¹⁵⁄₁₆ × 11⅝ in. Joslyn Art Museum, Omaha; gift of Enron Art Foundation.

Southwest, who might have witnessed a similar scene, wrote:

As horsemen they are unrivaled; they sit very ungracefully, lolling about as they ride, as if drunk or too indolent to sit up; but when roused to action, their energy is fearful. Their hideous yells—in making which they pass the hand rapidly over the mouth—and diabolical attire, are as appalling as the suddenness and fierceness of the attack. There is really nothing in them to command our admiration.[17]

Scenes of village life could also be viewed with an ambivalence reflecting cultural stereotypes. In *Mandan Village* [134] earthen huts set amid a verdant landscape shelter "stern warriors" and "wooing lovers" (as Catlin described them). Yet Indians at leisure, whether stern or amorous or asleep on lodge rooftops, might also be scorned by a culture that valued industriousness. The "Bible-toting mountain man" Jedediah Smith, encountering a Sioux camp that must have appeared as inviting as Catlin had found the Mandan village, commented in his journal that the scene would "almost persuade a man to renounce the world, take the lodge and live the careless, Lazy life of an indian."[18] It is well to remember that one person's Noble Savage was hopelessly indolent to another, and that white audiences probably viewed paintings such as *Mandan Village* with mixed reactions. Indians might not suffer from the ills of progress and civilization, but neither did they exhibit the virtues admired by white society.[19]

John Mix Stanley spent more than ten years traveling the West from Oklahoma to California and Texas to Oregon. The field sketches and Indian artifacts collected on his travels were later used in his studio to create "actual" paintings of Indian life. But these now appear to draw more from popular stereotypes than from his experiences. *Barter for a Bride,*

painted in Washington, D.C., sometime between 1854 and 1863, is a prime example [135]. Sitting astride a beautiful horse with arched neck and flowing mane, a young (Blackfoot?) Indian presents himself to the father of the intended. The elder wears a feather headdress, and both are clothed in buckskin decorated with quillwork and scalp locks. The prospective bride, in unadorned golden-colored buckskin, lies on her stomach in the grass and gazes at her suitor. Behind her, grouped in a monumental pyramid that predicts a stable, continuous life cycle, are various members of her family. From the spacious landscape at right four mounted figures proceed toward the central group. Two horses drag travois presumably bearing gifts for the father of the bride. The benign landscape promises that the gifts will be plentiful.

Although Indian marriages depended everywhere on economic considerations, there was much diversity in marriage customs among North American tribes.[20] For some the presentation of gifts to the bride's parents, the apparent subject of Stanley's painting, legitimized a marriage. But titillation was equally part of Stanley's image. The provocative young woman reveals her availability rather than her chasteness. She exemplifies an aspect of Indian life described by Prince Maximilian: "Prudery is not a virtue of the Indian women; they have often two, three, or more lovers: infidelity is not often punished."[21] The ceremony uniting man and woman was conspicuously pagan—material goods were exchanged for sexual possession. Such a "barter" may have intrigued contemporary whites, but it was not a practice openly endorsed.

In *Lacrosse Playing among the Sioux Indians,* 1851, Seth Eastman suggests the curiosity easterners exhibited in other Indian customs [136]. Games of chance and dexterity were common to all North American tribes. They appear to

133. Alfred Jacob Miller, *Surround of Buffalo by Indians,* circa 1848–58, oil on canvas, 30⅜ × 44⅛ in. Buffalo Bill Historical Center, Cody, Wyoming; gift of William D. Weiss.

have been "played ceremonially, as pleasing to the gods, with the object of securing fertility, causing rain, giving and prolonging life, expelling demons, or curing sickness."[22] Additionally games provided diversion as a chance to display physical prowess and to gamble.[23] To the winners (and those who bet on the winning team) went prizes of horses, guns, blankets, and beads. As one observer of a game among the Chippewa observed in 1860, "Hundreds of players assemble, and the wares and goods offered as prizes often reach a value of a thousand dollars and more."[24]

It is doubtful that white viewers knew of the ceremonial value of Indian games. The Eastman painting suggests that the contest might have held more appeal for both its comic and heroic athletics. One player attacks an opponent with a stick, while others lurch forward awkwardly, even crawling on the ground to reach the ball. Elsewhere skilled players wearing togalike garments race forward like Greek gods at play. Surely the natural setting, its rugged features and atmospheric highlights echoing the action in the foreground, might be considered a wilderness Olympus. Eastern viewers were probably also intrigued by an activity—competitive games—that suggested a similarity between the two races. Whatever the parallels, however, the exoticism (and violence) of Indian customs always remained to underline racial differences.

Indian "Massacres" and White "Battles"

Beginning in the 1840s paintings representing a more or less positive view of Indian life were challenged by two other subject categories. These were scenes of Indian-white conflict and, to a lesser extent, images of "doomed" Indians. Patronage no doubt broadened at this point. Bodmer, Catlin, and Miller painted for a limited clientele—the government, selected scientists and adventurers, and, later in their careers, a few easterners and European aristocrats. Revealing a more aggressive attitude toward westward expansion, the taste of the next generation was generally guided by the American Art-Union and popular prints made after conflict paintings. The source of this attitude was the political and social climate of the Jacksonian era.

President Andrew Jackson, in office from 1829 to 1837, argued pragmatically in his second annual address to Congress for the

134. George Catlin, *Bird's-eye View of the Mandan Village, Eighteen Hundred Miles above Saint Louis*, 1837–39, oil on canvas, 24⅛ × 29 in. National Museum of American Art, Smithsonian Institution, Washington, D.C.; gift of Mrs. Joseph Harrison, Jr.

geographical separation of Indians and whites, which he described as beneficial to both:

> The consequences of a speedy removal will be important to the United States, to individual States, and to the Indians themselves. The pecuniary advantages which it promises to the Government are the least of its recommendations. . . . It will separate the Indians from immediate contact with settlements of whites; free them from the power of the States; enable them to pursue happiness in their own way and under their own rude institutions; will retard the progress of decay, which is lessening their numbers.[25]

Typifying Jacksonian Indian policy, these self-serving, widely shared sentiments had already caused passage of the Indian Removal Act in 1830. This legislation provided Jackson with the authority to remove Indians from lands between the Great Lakes and Gulf of Mexico, which were desirable to land speculators, farmers, railroad magnates, bankers, and entrepreneurs of every stripe. Consequently sixty thousand Indians from tribes including the Cherokee, Chickasaw, Choctaw, Creek, and Seminole were removed from traditional lands

135. John Mix Stanley, *Barter for a Bride,* circa 1854–63, oil on canvas, 40 × 63 in. Diplomatic Reception Rooms, Department of State, Washington, D.C.; gift of the Morris and Gwendolyn Cafritz Foundation.

136. Seth Eastman, *Lacrosse Playing among the Sioux Indians*, 1851, oil on canvas, 28³/₁₆ × 40¾ in. The Corcoran Gallery of Art, Washington, D.C.; gift of William Wilson Corcoran.

to Indian territory west of the Mississippi.

Subsequent to Indian removal, Senator Thomas Hart Benton of Missouri and like-minded expansionists urged the country to explore and settle the vast territories of the West. Their desires were finally satisfied when the Northwest was secured in 1846 and the Southwest in 1848, new territories that established the continental boundaries for the nation. Now the dreams of expansion could be met. Opening western land to white settlement, however, ensured Indian-white conflict, since overland trails carried increasing numbers of emigrants through or to lands occupied by indigenous and newly removed Indian tribes. In 1790 the American population of 3.9 million lived

within fifty miles of the Atlantic Ocean; by the next half-century 4.5 million Americans had crossed the Appalachians.[26] The presumed necessity of this kind of rapid expansion thrust on Americans (and American artists) the need to resolve racial encounters precipitated by the appropriation of Indian lands. In effect, three different strategies emerged, one without an artistic counterpart (in itself revealing) and two that spawned new iconographies.

Indian removal was a singularly brutal and dramatic moment in the history of the United States, yet no hint of it ever appeared on canvas. Instead artists turned to conflict scenes in which Indians were cast as villains who prevented a peaceful appropriation of western lands. Such scenes gradually made obsolete the group of images first discussed in this chapter, which were often pejorative but not provocative. Conflict iconography (in both painting and literature) was a manufactured response to Indian hating, which gained renewed energy as settlers encroached on Indian land. The third strategy resolved the issue in another way by presenting Indians as doomed relics of the past. After more or less lamenting their fate, paintings in this group concede that the Indians' only recourse was to deliver their lands to a superior white race.

In the context of Indian removal and westward expansion Indians changed from denizens of the wilderness to barbaric savages. As historian Francis Jennings observes in *The Invasion of America* (1975): "Myth contrasts civilized war with savage war by accepting the former as a rational, honorable, and often progressive activity while attributing to the latter the qualities of irrationality, ferocity, and unredeemed retrogression. Savagery implies unchecked and perpetual violence."[27] Indians in battle were consistently viewed as barbarians who staged massacres while whites courageously defended themselves. The perception becomes apparent when following Stanley's account of white deaths at Indian hands. Traveling in the Northwest in the mid-1840s, Stanley narrowly avoided an encounter with a party of Cayuse who had just killed missionaries Marcus and Narcissa Whitman. Subsequently Stanley wrote to relatives and friends in Oregon and back east to tell them of the ordeal.[28] The accounts are strikingly different. His letters to local missionaries Cushing Eels and Elkanah Walker explained that it was commonly believed that the Cayuse had killed the Whitmans because they felt that Dr. Whitman was poisoning them. Cayuse children were dying in number during a measles epidemic, but white children were not. To test the doctor the Cayuse sent to him

for treatment one healthy and two sick men. When all three died, the Indians' suspicions were confirmed.

To his relatives in the East, Stanley wrote carefully organized, detailed descriptions of the massacre. These letters gave no hint that the Cayuse had reason, justifiable or not, to attack the Whitmans. For Stanley, the whites' behavior was by definition "rational," the Indians' was by the same ethnocentric nineteenth-century view "irrational."

Typical of early conflict paintings, which often feature a female victim (see note 5), is *The Murder of David Tally [Tully] and Family by the Sissatoons, a Sioux Tribe,* circa 1823–30, by the Swiss émigré Peter Rindisbacher [137]. On the right, David Tully fights for his life against three Indian warriors who brandish war clubs and tomahawk. Tully's own gun is presumably empty, since he uses it simply as a club. In the foreground, the most feared atrocity against white settlers transpires. A white women with three children, one apparently

137. Peter Rindisbacher, *The Murder of David Tally [Tully] and Family by the Sissatoons, a Sioux Tribe,* circa 1823–30, watercolor on paper, 6½ × 11 in. West Point Museum Collections, United States Military Academy, New York.

138. George Caleb Bingham, *Captured by Indians,* 1848, oil on canvas, 25 × 30 in. The Saint Louis Art Museum; bequest of Arthur C. Hoskins.

torn away from her breast, is assaulted by three Indians. The woman is sheltered by a frail tent that offers no defense against the arsenal of weapons raised against her. The final, dreadful outcome of the encounter is preordained, along with the unprovoked savagery of the Indians and innocence of their victims.

George Caleb Bingham's painting *Captured by Indians,* 1848, portrays in another guise the feared encounter between Indian men and white women, between savagery and civiliza-

tion [138]. A women sits in the dark of night with a child so innocent that sleep is possible despite the present danger. An Indian blanket draped over her torso, her dark hair falling to her shoulders, her face half in shadow, the danger of her participation in the tribal customs of her captors is already present as is her salvation. The light from the fire falls most directly on her, its radiance presumably divine. She sits with her eyes raised in prayer. As she is aware of the heavens, the warriors who surround her

139. John Mix Stanley, *Osage Scalp Dance*, 1845, oil on canvas, 40¾ × 60½ in. National Museum of American Art, Smithsonian Institution, Washington, D.C.; gift of the Misses Henry.

know only of the earth. Two sleep with bowed heads, one looks into the dark forest, where, according to conventions of the day, he reigned with the beasts.

Stanley's statement regarding Indian savagery is more complicated than that of Rindisbacher or Bingham. At the center of *Osage Scalp Dance*, 1845, kneels a white woman clutching to her side a partially naked child [139]. She raises her right arm to ward off a threatened death blow from one of the sixteen muscular warriors who surround her. Brandishing spears, bows, and war clubs, the warriors wear only loincloths and leggings. While the seminudity of the child suggests his vulnerability, that of the warriors indicates their brutality.

The drama of the painting rests with the struggle between the forces of civilization and those of savagery, between the forces of light and darkness, which Stanley so conspicuously indicates when he contrasts the fair skin of the heroine, who is highlighted and dressed in white, and the dark skin of the Indians who surround her. The presumed chief lifts his spear to prevent the raised war club from falling and killing the innocent victims. The rescue of the white woman and child, standard nineteenth-century symbols of civilization, indicates that barbarism has been arrested by the forces of reason. The Indian poised to deliver the death blow is the most menacing, both because of his gesture and suggestive fur breechcloth. In contrast, the Indian who moves to

140. Charles Deas, *The Death Struggle*, circa 1845, oil on canvas, 30 × 25 in. Shelburne Museum, Vermont.

protect the mother and child is the most civilized, not only because of his stance but because of the medal he wears around his neck. Alone among his fellow tribesmen, he has been visibly touched by white culture.

While their predicaments did not seem quite as keen to nineteenth-century audiences, white men were also frequently portrayed in mortal combat with Indians. One of the most tragic of these encounters was depicted sometime in the mid-1840s by Charles Deas in *The Death Struggle* [140]. An Indian and a white man, each with knife in hand, fall from a precipice to certain death in the chasm below. While the contrast of their dark and light mounts suggests the hackneyed symbolism of bad Indians and good whites, the message that Deas communicates is mixed. Neither will survive: the vines entangling the legs of their horses, like the twisted braid of the men's arms, symbolize their intertwined fate. The blood that is about to be spilled is portended by the red shirt of the trapper and red wound on the shoulder of the Indian's mount. The sky threatens, the tree the white man futilely clutches is dead, and vultures wait below. The beaver still caught in its trap stretches across the front of both men—an image boding disaster for each side of Indian-white strife.[29]

Conflict scenes presume the innocence of whites, who usually are represented as victims, not aggressors. Typical of this more common image is Arthur F. Tait's *Prairie Hunter, "One Rubbed Out!"* 1852 [141]. Clad in buckskin tunic and leggings, a trapper races for his life before a party of Indians, one of whom he has just "rubbed out." Outnumbered, with no place to take refuge, his rifle, perhaps out of ammunition, held downward, his fate appears sealed. In an earlier day, however, independent trappers and those associated with fur companies lived and hunted alongside Indians. Indeed Indians were major suppliers of pelts to the fur companies. An instruction issued by James Knight, governor-in-chief of Hudson's Bay Company, suggests, albeit in paternalistic tones, the basic intention to maintain good relations with Indians. "Treat them civilly," he advised, "not Useing to much familiarity with them for that will make them prove Saucy & impudent but carry your Self wth Gravity and Solidity."[30]

But the fur trade had actually been in decline for twenty years by the time Tait painted *The Prairie Hunter*. The artist views nostalgically a figure that popular writers and printmakers had elevated to a new pantheon of frontier heroes.[31] That he was portrayed in the 1850s at the mercy of "savage" Indians had less

141. Arthur F. Tait, *The Prairie Hunter, "One Rubbed Out!"* 1852, oil on canvas, 14 × 20 in. Gene Autry Western Heritage Museum, Los Angeles.

142. Carl Wimar, *The Attack on an Emigrant Train,* 1856, oil on canvas, 55⅛ × 79⅛ in. The University of Michigan Museum of Art, Ann Arbor; bequest of Henry C. Lewis.

143. Theodor Kaufmann, *Westward the Star of Empire,* 1867, oil on canvas, 35½ × 55½ in. The Saint Louis Mercantile Library Association.

to do with history than with increasing demands to remove Indians from the pathway of settlement.

One of the most common subjects found in paintings of the American West at midcentury was the pioneer caravan under Indian attack. So popular was it, in fact, that Carl Wimar painted *The Attack on an Emigrant Train,* 1856, while studying in Düsseldorf (where high drama was the prevailing style) and brought it home to sell [142].[32] Intersecting diagonals formally announce the raging conflict between white settlers and Indians. Inside the lead wagon the wounded are tended to, while the able-bodied fire from behind, beside, and inside the wagon. Their shots have successfully hit two Indian assailants. Although the wagon train has been halted by the fierce

assault, the battle is no more than a temporary setback to westward travel. A careful count suggests that the intrepid settlers are holding their own. And behind the lead wagon, stretching along the receding diagonal, are three more wagons and inevitably behind these, yet more settlers on the move.

If Indians are a menace in the Wimar painting, they are portrayed as demonic beasts crawling on their bellies in *Westward the Star of Empire,* painted by Theodor Kaufmann [143]. Railroad building proceeding across the northern plains in 1867 (the year the painting was completed) provoked Sioux and Cheyenne attacks against construction crews, which delayed but did not prevent completion of the first transcontinental railroad in 1869. Thus the Indians in this painting attack one of the

144. Tompkins H. Matteson, *The Last of the Race,* 1847, oil on canvas, 39¾ × 50¹⁄₁₆ in. The New-York Historical Society, New York; gift of Edwin W. Orvis on behalf of his family, 1931.

preeminent symbols of American progress and westward expansion. As the light of civilization approaches, the forces of evil skulk in the dark, carrying out their devilish plans to derail the approaching train and, by extension, the progress of white civilization.

American Expansion, Indian "Doom"

During the same period that paintings of Indian-white conflict appeared with such frequency so did those of another major theme,

the doomed Indian. The belief that Indians would succumb to the forces of civilization reaches back to the seventeenth century, but by the nineteenth century what had been expressed as sentiment began to look like fact. Thomas Nuttall, for example, a Philadelphia scientist investigating Indians along the Ohio, Mississippi, and Arkansas rivers, apologized in 1819 for writing a popular rather than a scientific account of his trip. Nevertheless, he felt compelled to call attention to the plight of the "unfortunate aborigines, who are so rapidly dwindling into oblivion."[33] In literature William Cullen Bryant wrote a number of poems between 1815 and 1831 with Indians as the central characters. Almost all concern death, as their titles suggest: "An Indian at the Burial-Place of His Fathers," "Indian Girl's Lament," and the "The Disinterred Warrior," the last concluding: "A noble race! but they are gone."[34] The characterization of Indians as doomed also appeared in popular art. In 1839 the prolific Lydia Sigourney, "sweet singer of Hartford," penned "Our Aborigines," which begins:

> I heard the forests as they cried
> > Unto the valleys green,
> Where is the red-browed hunter race,
> > who loved our leafy screen?
> Who humbled 'mid these dewy glades
> The reindeer's antlered crown,
> > Or, soaring at his highest noon,
> Struck the strong eagle down.[35]

Literary references to the doomed Indian continued through the nineteenth century and after, coinciding with an increased need to resolve Indian–white conflict. The first related images appeared in the 1840s. Then, during the 1850s and early 1860s, the subject was frequently depicted in paintings, prints, and sculptures. The popularity of the image subsequently declined in the late 1860s and 1870s, perhaps because during those years the Plains Wars reached a frantic pitch and no artist could afford to lament the passing of the Indian. After the wars were over, or at least under control, the image reemerged.

One of the first paintings featuring the doomed Indian, Tompkins H. Matteson's *Last of the Race,* 1847, typifies images with similar titles that followed over the next decades [144]. A tribal elder, surrounded by his family, stands at land's end, contemplating the ominous procession of clouds on the horizon. Generations of Indian life end here, the painting implies. The ocean is an abyss at the family's feet, the setting sun parallels their waning life and power. The mood is contemplative and melancholy. The young male on the right sits with bowed head, while the woman resting near him angrily stares back toward the ground already traveled. A dog looks up at its master, as if to ask "what next?" Aware of sentiment in the East for pictures that constructed a romantic fade-out of Indian life, the American Art-Union offered to its subscribers prints of *Last of the Race* for distribution in 1847.

The Dying Tecumseh, a monumental sculpture completed by Ferdinand Pettrich in 1856, represents a Shawnee Indian who fought with the British in the War of 1812 [145]. He died at the Battle of the Thames, the American victory signaling the end of combined British and Indian resistance in the Old Northwest, the region around the Great Lakes and between the Ohio and Mississippi rivers. Significantly Pettrich carved this sculpture while living in Washington, D.C., where he actively sought, but never received, government patronage. By the 1850s Tecumseh probably symbolized Indian opposition to westward expansion as effectively as had any Indian in United States history. The Shawnee chief had organized a formidable Indian confederacy in the Old Northwest between 1805 and his death eight years later. He urged local tribes to resist white purchase of Indian land and to continue communal ownership of property—ideas that made him an Indian nationalist and leader of enduring fame. Even whites recognized his greatness, but his death, tragic as they made it out to be, signaled the inevitability of white advance. Pettrich's marble, which creates for Tecumseh the role of a dying Roman general, passes judgment on all Indian "heroes" who died in battle against whites. Their courage and skill, Pettrich maintains, were devoted to the wrong cause. Their deaths argued not for Indian rights but for the triumph of expansionism.

Valentine Walter Bromley painted *Crow Indian Burial,* one of the most arresting images of the doomed Indian, in 1876, the year Custer was defeated at the Little Bighorn [146].[36] Unlike many other images of Indian grave sites, this painting does not attempt to document a burial custom. Death as an element of melodramatic narrative is the subject. The wrapped body of the deceased rests on a tree branch in the upper-right corner of the painting. When compared to the grisly scene at the center of the composition, the human seems the easier death. A cadaverlike horse, using its last energy, strains at its lead to drink from a nearby stream. Either the horse will choke itself or die of thirst, a grim metaphor for the plight of western tribes. Bromley reinforces the symbolism with his representation in the background of an Indian village silhouetted against a lurid sunset. The body of the deceased points directly toward the village, indicating that not a single Indian has been buried but a whole tribe, a whole race.

The material for this painting was supposedly collected by Bromley, an English painter, during a six-month expedition through Colorado, Montana, and Wyoming territories in 1874. The trip had been financed by Windham Thomas Wyndham-Quin, fourth earl of Dunraven, an Irish adventurer wealthy enough to satisfy his desire to hunt in far-off places. Traveling with physician, cook, steward, and artist, Windham perceived the West as a rosy place for future investment. The earl and his company owned land in Estes Park, Colorado, where they planned to establish a hunting lodge, game preserve, and cattle ranch. For Bromley's patron, then, the paintings must have served a dual purpose: they lament the past and the demise of the Indian, but they simultaneously acknowledge that barbaric customs must give way to a more "productive" use of the land.

The spirit of expansion, which thrived during the mid-nineteenth century, again seized the country between 1890 and 1914. This time the nation looked beyond its borders, annexing Puerto Rico, the Philippines, Guam, the Hawaiian Islands, and the Isthmus of Panama. Indians no longer threatened American expansion

145. Ferdinand Pettrich, *The Dying Tecumseh,* 1856, marble, length 77¼ in. National Museum of American Art, Smithsonian Institution, Washington, D.C.

146. Valentine Walter Bromley, *Crow Indian Burial*, 1876, oil on canvas, 42 × 70 in. Gordon Fraser, Minneapolis.

as they had at midcentury; since the ending of the Plains Wars in 1890 Indians had been contained on reservations or allotted lands. Nostalgia now took a different turn, pitting Indians against the modern world.

Henry Farny conveyed this message more effectively than any other artist of the turn of the century. His major work in this genre, *The Song of the Talking Wire*, 1904, was reportedly conceived by Farny in 1881, when he visited Fort Yates in Dakota Territory on the Missouri River [147]. The artist apparently observed an Indian named Long Day listening at a telegraph pole so that he could tell fellow Indians that he

had heard spirit voices over the wires, thus proving his ability to become a medicine man.[37] Long Day uses the tools of civilization to assist in the continuity of his own culture. But Farny turns the scene around to illustrate the Indian listening at the telegraph pole, as if for his own demise.

The telegraph wires symbolize white progress, which dispossesses Indians of their culture. Leaning against a telegraph pole, the lone Indian is surrounded by death—the buffalo skull and barren, snow-covered landscape. He carries the white man's gun yet clings to his own traditions, wearing moccasins and buf-

147. Henry Farny, *The Song of the Talking Wire,* 1904, oil on canvas, 22 1/16 × 40 in. The Taft Museum, Cincinnati; bequest of Mr. and Mrs. Charles Phelps Taft.

falo hide and living by the hunt, as suggested by the dead deer hanging from his saddle.[38] His inability to change will finally defeat him. Certainly this had been the opinion of Henry Rowe Schoolcraft, one of the nineteenth-century's leading anthropologists a generation earlier: "He [the Indian] evinces little care for the present and makes only slight use of the experience of the past. Taught from early infancy to revere the traditions and institutions of his fathers, he is satisfied of their value, and dreads the anger of the Great Spirit, if he departs from their teachings."[39]

Farny again represented doomed Indians in *Morning of a New Day,* 1907 [148]. The "new day" belongs to the distant train progressing over tracks that trespass through the wilderness. In contrast, Farny's Indians labor through the wintery landscape, dragging their goods on travois. Women with children on their backs

and the elderly are not mounted but trudge through the snow. The Indians are pushed to the margin of the picture, the two leading figures already cut off by the frame. Not only do figures travel in the opposite direction but a chasm separates them from the train, from the white world of progress. A final clue to the meaning of the picture is the angle of light that broadens as it falls across the landscape, illuminating the path of the train but throwing into shadow the dispirited procession of Indians.

At the turn of the twentieth century elaborate international expositions—grand entertainments as well as advertisements of the country's developing industrialism—were organized to celebrate American culture. Painters and sculptors often contributed to these expositions images of the West that served as allegorical reminders of the nation's frontier past. James Earle Fraser modeled *End of the Trail* in the

1890s and enlarged it to monumental size for display at the Panama-Pacific Exposition of 1915 in San Francisco [149]. The exposition marked the completion of the Panama Canal and a watershed in California history, separating the state's pioneer past from its future as a center for Pacific commerce. Fraser's sculpture is, in effect, a bow to the modern world. The profile of the despondent Indian and his tired horse describes a series of downward arcs that eloquently reinforce the mood of the piece. A symbolic wind whips the pony's tail and bends the rider's back. Body drained of energy, the Indian slumps lifelessly, his spear, once raised in war and the hunt, hangs downward, as if about to slip to the ground. Even the land beneath horse and man has been shrunk to provide but precarious footing. This particular formulation of the ill-fated Indian has projected a powerful stereotype through the twentieth century. It can be seen today on belt buckles, in advertisements and commercial prints, and, in perhaps its most ironical manifestation, on signs designating retirement communities.

White philanthropists held but one hope for the supposedly doomed Indian and that was acculturation (or assimilation, as it was called). It was presumed that to survive, the subordinate Indian culture must adopt the beliefs and habits of the dominant white culture. President

148. Henry Farny, *Morning of a New Day,* 1907, oil on canvas, 22 × 32 in. National Cowboy Hall of Fame Collection, Oklahoma City.

Thomas Jefferson spoke to such a belief when in 1803 he wrote to Creek agent Colonel Benjamin Hawkins:

In truth, the ultimate point of rest and happiness for them is to let our settlements and theirs meet and blend together, to intermix, and become one people. Incorporating themselves with us as citizens of the United States, this is what the natural progress of things will, of course, bring on, and it will be better to promote than to retard it.[40]

The acculturation movement sputtered along until the latter third of the nineteenth century, when a spirited alliance of government and religion attempted to enforce the so-called civilizing process. Christian philanthropists inside and outside government wished to lead Indian-white relations away from the sword and toward the Bible. Such tactics were initiated with President Ulysses S. Grant's Indian "peace policy." In his first annual message to Congress in 1869, Grant sought to reverse the policy based on war and removal: "A system which looks to the extinction of race is too horrible for a nation to adopt without entailing upon itself the wrath of all Christendom and engendering in the citizen a disregard for human life."[41] Grant also specified that religious leaders, rather than political appointees or military personnel, would now administer Indian policy. But the system that Grant had in mind was still essentially paternalistic. Referring to the model of the Society of Friends among the Indians, he wrote, "I have attempted a new policy toward these wards of the nation (they can not be regarded in any other light than as wards), with fair results so far as tried."[42]

The next step in the acculturation process, the passage of the General Allotment (Dawes) Act in 1887, again raised hopes, for few comprehended how devastating the results would be. Well-meaning philanthropic organizations

149. James Earle Fraser, *End of the Trail*, circa 1894, bronze, height 44 in. Thomas Gilcrease Institute of American History and Art, Tulsa.

insisted on the overthrow of tribalism and communal organization.[43] As a result, reservations were broken up into 160-acre homesteads and distributed to individual families of each tribe. Indians became subject to white law, and Indian children were required to attend English-speaking schools provided by the government.[44] The philanthropic organizations "acted on the assumption that inside every Indian was a white American citizen and property holder waiting to be set free; the job of reform was to crack the shell of traditional tribal life and thus free the individual."[45]

One of few contemporary doubters of this scheme was Senator Henry Teller of Colorado. He and four delegates from the Cherokee and Choctaw tribes submitted to the Senate in 1881 a memorial that concluded: "This experiment has seductive allurements for visionary persons who have not carefully studied the subject, but is full of mischief for us."[46] Their conclusion was accurate: in 1887 Indians held 138 million acres; by 1934, when the Dawes Act was canceled, that number was reduced to 51 million acres.[47] And Indian culture suffered proportionately. Artist Ernest L. Blumenschein, in an 1899 issue of *Harper's Weekly,* sardonically portrays the future results of Grant's peace policy and the Dawes Act in *Wards of the Nation— Their First Vacation from School* [150]. White-sponsored schools, operating often at great distance from the reservations, had indeed separated Indians from their tribal heritage.

If acculturation came to an unhappy ending, it nevertheless was an attractive concept for some nineteenth-century patrons. Several early images present intermarriage as a means of intermingling races, although these are mostly limited to liaisons between white fur traders or trappers and Indian women. These relationships were commonly recognized as expedient, either because Indian women were the only women available or because they provided

a useful link with their tribes. At one of the annual rendezvous of the fur traders, a notoriously bawdy and drunken event, a reluctant participant and lay missionary, William H. Gray, observed: "Today I was told . . . that Indian women are a lawful commerce among the men that resort to these mountains, . . . thus setting at defiance every principle of right, justice and humanity, and law of God and man."[48]

The Trapper's Bride, 1850, by Miller, may, in fact, be a chaste rendering of contemporary reports describing Indian women as "lawful commerce" among fur trappers [151]. In Miller's words, "the scene represents a Trapper taking a wife, or purchasing one. . . . He is seated with his friend to the left of the sketch, his hand extended to his promised wife, supported by her father and accompanied by a chief, who holds the calumet, an article indispensable in all grand ceremonies."⁴⁹ The trapper wears garments made from animal hides, which are cut with an eastern flair. Adorned with beads, feathers, and bear-claw necklace, the chief wears more "primitive" dress. He sits astride a horse, which to nine-teenth-century viewers might have seemed no more tamed than its owner. The Indian woman occupies a position between the two males, between white and Indian cultures. She appears shy but not precisely demure; Miller describes her as "pensive" and "dreamy."⁵⁰ She stands barefoot, literally in touch with na-ture, dressed in yellow buckskin, which fairly glows with warmth. Other than her hand, the part of her anatomy closest to the trapper is her pelvis. She represents, in other words, a male fantasy, an encounter with the exotic other, the sort of liaison a white Victorian male might contemplate as a means of escaping a confining moral and social environment. Per-haps as proof of this appeal, *The Trapper's Bride* was Miller's best-selling image.⁵¹

The Trapper's Bride broached the sugges-tion of union, not only between races but be-tween nature and civilization. The large tepee in the background defines the apex of a triangle embracing savage life, while the smaller trian-gle on the left, which includes the groom, a colleague, and an Indian with a peace pipe, represents the ameliorating effect of civiliza-tion, a subtheme of most pictures illustrated in this chapter.

Charles Deas also painted the union of a white man and an Indian woman in *The Voya-geurs,* 1845 [152]. The voyageur was a French-Canadian or half-blood trapper of French de-scent who often intermarried with Indians. "Half-bloods" were sometimes judged to em-body the worst traits of both races, but more often they were viewed ambivalently.⁵² Alex-ander Ross, who lived on the frontier for more

151. Alfred Jacob Miller, *The Trapper's Bride,* 1850, oil on canvas, 30 × 25 in. Joslyn Art Museum, Omaha.

than fifty years, married an Indian woman, and raised half-blood children, wrote in 1855:

Half-breeds, or as they are more generally styled, brulés, from the peculiar colour of their skin, being of a swarthy hue, as if sunburnt, as they grow up resemble, almost in every respect, the pure Indian. With this difference that they are more designing, more daring, and more dissolute. . . . They are by far the fittest persons for the Indian countries, the best calculated by nature for going among Indians. . . . They are vigorous, brave; and while they possess the shrewdness and sagacity of the whites, they inherit the agility and expertness of the savage.[53]

Deas's painting follows the Ross interpretation of half-blood character. The family consists of parents and children, who range in age from infancy to young adulthood. Their ages alone

152. Charles Deas, *The Voyageurs,* 1845, oil on canvas, 31½ × 36 in. Rokeby Collection; on loan to the Metropolitan Museum of Art, New York.

suggest the longevity of the union, which appears harmonious. The father and eldest daughter paddle the canoe, while the eldest son spears fish. The mother tends to the youngest, while another child ladles water from the stream. The family appears to have met the basic needs of companionship and sustenance, right down to the coffeepot attached to their covered cargo.

The canoe and stream, along with the family, are the principal metaphors in the picture. The canoe represents the family's domestic headquarters. The ripples around the snag in the current suggest that the canoe is proceeding upstream, deeper into the wilderness, into a gathering storm that drives ducks back down the river. The half-breed family, the agent of civilization, is establishing on the frontier a new but precarious foothold, presided over by a ménage that eastern viewers, uneasy about interbreeding, could only accept at long distance as a necessary consequence of expansion.[54]

The White Man's Indian

The treaty existed as a form of negotiation with the Indians until the early 1870s, when Congress ceased to consider tribes as independent nations. When treaties were in use, they presumably assured the rights of both Indians and whites. But Henry Schoolcraft's advice in 1849 to an Indian commissioner suggests otherwise:

An Indian council is a test of diplomacy. The Indians are so *fickle,* that they will change their minds twice a day. It requires some of the qualities of Job to get along with them, and their friends, the half-breeds. But perseverance in right views, will ultimately prevail. They have, after all, very little confidence in themselves, and a great deal in the United States.[55]

The belief that Indians were unequal partners to be led in the "right" direction is confirmed in a popular painting of the mid-nineteenth century entitled the *Treaty Makers* [153]. Negotiations appear to turn on the presentation of liquor to the chief, who seems the most gullible. The presumed inequality between negotiators is shown in more elaborate fashion by California artist Charles Nahl.

Nahl painted the astonishing *Treaty with the Shoshone Indians in 1866* at the request of Caleb Lyon, both governor and superintendent of Indian affairs in Idaho [154]. Lyon had mediated a peace settlement with the western Shoshone and white settlers. The negotiations led to Indian cession of lands in southern Idaho in exchange for a reservation on the Bruneau River. The treaty was never ratified by Congress, but Lyon, who had moved to California

153. Unidentified artist, *Treaty Makers,* mid-nineteenth century, oil on canvas, 27½ × 40½ in. National Museum of the American Indian, Smithsonian Institution, New York; Heye Foundation.

154. Charles Nahl, *Treaty with the Shoshone Indians in 1866, South Idaho Treaty*, 1866, oil on canvas, 27 × 37 in. Thomas Gilcrease Institute of American History and Art, Tulsa.

several months after the negotiations, commissioned Nahl to commemorate the event.[56]

Treaty with the Shoshone Indians was probably painted in the artist's San Francisco studio. In an effort to create an aura of authenticity Nahl drew on various sources. Photographs in common circulation provided models for the woman seated with two prairie dogs in the center foreground and for the man who stands with his hand on his hip to the left of the treaty table.[57] Nahl also included Indian artifacts, each accurate in themselves but not commonly used by the Shoshone. The woman standing along the left edge of the picture is dressed in a fiber-and-feather skirt of California origin; the Indian standing beside the minister wears a Northwest Coast woven cap; and three Pima baskets appear in the lower-right corner.[58]

Nahl's attempt to enhance the authority of the painting with anthropological details is continued in the formal strategy he adopts to represent whites and Indians. In the center of *Treaty with the Shoshone Indians* stands Dr. Hiram Hamilton, a minister, and Governor Lyon. The reverend and the governor, the latter patriotically dressed in red, white, and blue, are woodenly erect representatives of government authority. A military regiment, arranged in tight rows in the background, mimes the posture of the white officials. Between the two white men stands the treaty table, fancifully decorated with an American flag and a spray of peacock feathers. Below the table lies a mound of gifts for the Indians, including trade blankets, beads, peacock feathers, and copper and brass pots. A few of these pledges of good faith already appear on their recipients, since to the right of Lyon are presumably tribal leaders smoking a pipe of European origin and wearing a calico trade coat.

Once specific anthropological items are identified, the Shoshone who fill the foreground represent little more than popular stereotypes of western Indians. Nahl presents a naive, unruly, and licentious group. Indeed, as many interpreted the state of savagery, the Indians appear to represent the childhood of humanity. Surely Horace Greeley concurred when he wrote in 1859: "The Indians are children. Their arts, wars, treaties, alliances, habitations, crafts, properties, commerce, comforts, all belong to the very lowest and rudest ages of human existence."[59] If the Shoshone understood the consequences of the treaty, it is not apparent in Nahl's presentation. Whites and Indians hardly look at one another, each occupying a separate world.

Animals, both dead and alive, are scattered throughout the crowd of Indians. The mix of skins—raccoon, fox, and cougar—is a reminder of the barbaric yet exotic state of the tribe. The live animals—pairs of fawns, prairie dogs, prairie hens, and cubs—suggest fertility and represent gifts to the white negotiators. Adding to the "primitive" quality of the scene, bare-breasted women are conspicuous in the lower-left corner of the painting, two with children and one confronting the spectator in a bold, suggestive manner.

Nahl distinguishes between civilized and

155. Tompkins H. Matteson, *The Meeting of Hetty and Hist*, 1857, oil on canvas, 24 × 18 in. Gordon Fraser, Minneapolis. (Detail illustrated on p. 148.)

156. John Mix Stanley, *Eleanora C. Ross,* 1844, oil on canvas, 39¾ × 31½ in. Thomas Gilcrease Institute of American History and Art, Tulsa.

uncivilized peoples to imply the rightness of the treaty just concluded, which supposedly gives to whites land they know how to develop and takes from Indians resources they cannot use productively. The sentiments expressed in 1817 by President James Monroe in his first message to Congress continued to affect Americans long after Monroe's time: "The earth was given to mankind to support the greatest number of which it is capable, and no tribe or people have a right to withhold from the wants of others more than is necessary for their own support and comfort."[60]

Perhaps the single most crucial issue of acculturation was the Indians' acceptance of Christianity. No Indian pleased white Americans more than one who had been baptized (and presumably benefited from Christian teachings). Although actual conversions were rarely depicted, the subject was addressed by Matteson in a painting of 1857 entitled *The Meeting of Hetty and Hist* [155]. The subject is drawn from James Fenimore Cooper's *Deerslayer,* first published in 1841.[61] Hetty is a feeble-minded but devout young woman who faces the forest alone to rescue her father from captivity among the Huron. With only intuition to guide her and innocence to shield her from danger, she prepares to use the Bible to persuade the Huron to release her father. Hist, a Delaware Indian girl whom Hetty meets in the forest, acts as interpreter.

In representing Hetty and Hist, Matteson suggests, as had Cooper, the kinship of the two women, who felt as sisters despite their dissimilar backgrounds. Hetty turns to the Bible for guidance, while Hist relies on nature. Matteson represents Hetty with the facial expression and upturned gaze of a seventeenth-century saint, while Hist becomes an Indian princess with a halo of nature behind her. A spiritual bond unites the two women, enforced by striking color harmonies and the line that gently circumscribes their shoulders, heads, and extended arms. In the end, artist and writer arrive at a solution for racial coexistence that would have appealed to readers of Cooper's novels, if not to federal officials like Caleb Lyon.

Eleanora C. Ross, a Cherokee girl painted in 1844 by Stanley, descended from a tribe that by the early nineteenth century had absorbed more of white culture than any other [156]. The Cherokee had developed an alphabet and written language, acquired a sizable population of half-bloods, undertaken an agricultural economy, and adopted concepts of property similar to those of the white culture, becoming owners of plantations, mills, and trading establishments.[62] Eleanora's father, John Ross, a noted opponent of Indian removal, had adopted many white customs and encouraged education in the tribe. Indeed it is within the context of the continual drive led by missionaries and the government to educate native Americans that Eleanora must be seen.

From the colonial period and the Henrico College venture in Virginia of 1616–24, Indian education was understood to mean fluency in English.[63] A writer in the Northern Methodist Annual Report for 1851 described why this skill was important to the so-called civilizing process: "With the English language, the Indian will acquire the elements of English literature, and the forms of thought, and the feelings which it represents, both social and religious. We doubt whether the Indians will ever be raised to a good state of civilization and religion, without the use of the English language."[64] Not only could the English language be used to introduce Indians to white thoughts and feelings, but the schools where English was taught could be used to separate Indians from tribal culture.

Seated in a landscape perhaps alluding to her Indian heritage, Eleanora is a picture of genteel accomplishment. Her soft pink dress chastely covers her young body, her hair is neatly combed and contained in plaits. She poses with a pencil in hand and a book open to an ideal landscape drawing. Her image is constructed to convince whites of her capacity to absorb the gentle arts of reading, writing, and drawing. Eleanora's portrait also represents a gender stereotype, more fully revealed in *Sacramento Indian with Dogs,* 1867, which rehabilitates a male Indian for white consumption [157].

Sacramento Indian with Dogs, a stunning image of assimilation by Nahl, portrays Wahla, a former chief of the Yubu, a northern California tribe.[65] Wahla was the protégé of Milton S. Latham, a California governor who had risen to prominence arguing a proslavery stand for his adopted state (he was a native of Louisiana).[66] Latham's support of slavery, however, did not prevent him from adopting an Indian and providing him with an education. Wahla's rewards for having undergone the civilizing process were a short haircut, a suit, and a job as Latham's coachman. The Nahl portrait, however, attempts to give Wahla a grander status. Based on a century-old tradition of depicting gentry in parklike settings, this painting suggests that Wahla has overcome his "Indianness" and made his way in white society as a responsible citizen.

And yet Wahla's trim appearance makes one uneasy. He is too neat, too fixed, too conspicuously part of a contrived environment. For all the artist's effort (and that of Latham, who commissioned the portrait) to demonstrate Wahla's new status, one senses that it is hollow. Wahla is still just a servant—one among many domestic animals owned by Latham. Surely this is a portrait of a "white" Indian painted to naturalize a ritual similar to the one enacted the first day pupils arrived at Indian boarding school. The following descrip-

157. Charles Nahl, *Sacramento Indian with Dogs*, 1867, oil on canvas, 42¹/₁₆ × 49¼ in. The Fine Arts Museum of San Francisco; gift of Mrs. Milton S. Latham.

tion was written by a Quaker teacher in the 1850s:

The service to a new pupil was to trim his hair closely; then with soap and water, to give him or her the first lesson in godliness, which was a good scrubbing . . . and then he was furnished with a suit of new clothes, and taught how to put them on and off. They all emerged from this ordeal as shy as a peacock, just plucked. A new English name finished the preparation for the alphabet and the English language.[67]

Like the new pupils in boarding school, Wahla is made to assume a veneer of white cultural attributes, one that puts at ease politicians like Latham. Wahla has been removed from the wilderness and placed in circumstances that ac-

knowledge acculturation. But his lacquerlike perfection and the fact that the portrait has apparently never been identified by the sitter's name indicates just how far Wahla had advanced.

William Fuller, who painted *Crow Creek Agency, Dakota Territory* in 1884, represents the goal of assimilation urged by government policy and philanthropic belief [158]. Fuller, who worked at Crow Creek Agency, was a carpenter with considerable artistic talent.[68] Painting in a naive style, he constructed this spacious domestic landscape to accommodate both whites and Indians. Fields are laid out in an orderly fashion, neat white homes dot the landscape, a church stands in the middle of the composition, and the smoke of steamboat

158. William Fuller, *Crow Creek Agency, Dakota Territory,* 1884, oil on canvas, 24⅝ × 51¾ in. Amon Carter Museum, Fort Worth, Texas; in memory of René d'Harnoncourt, trustee, 1961–68.

159. Alexander Pope, *Weapons of War,* 1900, oil on canvas, 54 × 42½ in. Buffalo Bill Historical Center, Cody, Wyoming.

stacks suggests the material progress of white civilization. Tepees and Indians in traditional dress still survive but on the outskirts of town. The grid pattern imposed by white notions of order suggests that the two Indians in the left foreground wearing suits will become the norm rather than the exception. Indeed the well-dressed white man who stands near them seems to encourage the acceptance of domestic life-styles forged by an agricultural economy and symbolized by the nearby sparkling wagon.[69] The activity depicted on the agency grounds provides a white model for Indian life—a model hauntingly close to one proposed by Thomas Jefferson in 1802, when urging a group of Miami, Potawatomi, and Wea to accept the benefits of white civilization:

We shall with great pleasure see your people become disposed to cultivate the earth, to raise herds of useful animals and to spin and weave, for their food and clothing. These resources are certain, they will never disappoint you, while those of hunting may fail, and expose your women and children to the miseries of hunger and cold. We will with pleasure furnish you with implements for the most necessary arts, and with persons who may instruct [you on] how to make and use them.[70]

Many Indians resisted the path that led to the farm, refusing to submit to white education and religion as well as an agricultural economy. While the voice of Indian resistance often comes to us through the pen of white interpreters, it is a voice that argues for the survival of Indian culture. In 1744 Virginia delegates meeting in Lancaster County with representatives of the Six Nations suggested that Indian youths might attend the College of William and Mary. An Onondaga chief responded:

Several of our young People were formerly brought up at the College of the Northern Provinces; they were instructed in all your sciences; but, when they came back to us, they were bad runners, ignorant of every means of living in the Woods, unable to bear either Cold or Hunger, neither how to build a Cabin, take a Deer, or kill an enemy, spoke our language imperfectly, were therefore neither fit for hunters, Warriors, nor Counsellors.[71]

Indians refused not just education and the Bible but the field and plow as well. According to a Wyandot Indian, the Bible "had a great many things that did not suit a people that hunted, but those who worked the earth, as its figures [of speech] were suited to them and not us. When it speaks of plowing and sowing, and reaping, the whites understand these things, and the language suits them. But what does an Indian know of this?"[72]

Real Indians never inhabited the paintings of white artists. Paintings in which Indians were represented were created to embody whites' attitudes about nature, the right of conquest, and the priorities of civilization. To whites, Indians at odds with Anglo-Saxon culture, refusing to abandon tribal custom and become "productive" citizens, were either primitive, savage, or doomed. Over the nineteenth century Indians had been reduced to a few stereotypes or worse, as Alexander Pope suggests in *Weapons of War,* 1900 [159]. In this image Indian culture no longer possesses even the myth of corporeal presence but has been reduced to an aesthetic arrangement of bric-a-brac devoid of function, impoverished of meaning, and displayed against yet another grid of white construction.

Notes

I am indebted to the Office of Professional Development, Northern Arizona University, Flagstaff, for research support toward completion of this essay.

1. Quoted in John F. McDermott, "The Art of Seth Eastman," in *Smithsonian Report for 1960* (Washington, D.C.: Smithsonian Institution, 1961), 584.

2. "The Pappoose," *Harper's Weekly* 18 (October 24, 1874): 880.

3. Limerick, *Legacy of Conquest*, 190.

4. Quoted in Saum, *Fur Trader and the Indian*, xi.

5. A few major examples are earlier, like John Vanderlyn's *Death of Jane McCrea*, 1804 (Wadsworth Atheneum, Hartford), as well as a number of popular images.

6. Material drawn from Berkhofer, *White Man's Indian*, 72–80.

7. Quoted ibid., 77.

8. Cosentino, *King*, 169, no. 333

9. Quoted in James D. Horan, *The McKenney-Hall Portrait Gallery of American Indians* (New York: Crown, 1972), 296.

10. Ibid.

11. Cosentino, *King*, 63.

12. Quoted ibid., 66.

13. Quoted in Szasz, *Indian Education*, 8

14. Quoted in Thomas and Ronnefeldt, *People of the First Man*, 245.

15. *Surround of Buffalo by Indians* is a later version of a scene Alfred Jacob Miller first conceived in the 1830s.

16. Quoted in Michael Bell, introduction to *Braves and Buffalo: Plains Indian Life in 1837* (Toronto: University of Toronto Press, 1973), 160.

17. J.D.B.S., "Wanderings in the Southwest," *Crayon*, 3, pt. 2 (February 1856): 40.

18. Quoted in Saum, *Fur Trader and Indian*, 95.

19. However George Catlin might criticize civilization and admire Indian life, his distance from primitive culture is suggested by the use of words such as "curious" and "strange" to describe the Mandan village. As Patricia Limerick has written, Catlin "enjoyed denouncing the vices of 'civilization,' but he was fully loyal to its virtues" (Limerick, *Legacy of Conquest*, 185).

20. Frederick W. Hodge, *Handbook of the American Indians North of Mexico* (Washington, D.C.: Smithsonian Institution, Bureau of Ethnology, 1907), 1:808.

21. Quoted in Thomas and Ronnefeldt, *People of the First Man*, 242.

22. Culin, "Games of North American Indians," 34.

23. Ibid., 563. Lacrosse was a product of native American institutions; it was so-named by the French because of its three-foot-long racket resembling a bishop's crozier (Edward J. Nygren and Peter C. Marzio, eds., *Of Time and Place: American Figurative Art from the Corcoran Gallery* [Washington, D.C.: Smithsonian Institution Traveling Exhibition Service, 1981], 34).

24. Quoted in Culin, "Games of North American Indians," 566.

25. Israel, *State of the Union Messages* 1:334.

26. Rogin, *Fathers and Children*, 3–4.

27. Jennings, *Invasion of America* (1975 ed.), 146.

28. John Mix Stanley to Cushing Eels and Elkanah Walker, December 1, 1847, Fort Walla Walla, December 31, 1847, Fort Walla Walla, and February 24, 1848, Oregon City, Beinecke Rare Book and Manuscript Library, Yale University, New Haven. Also, Stanley to an unidentified person, January 8, 1848, Fort Vancouver, Stanley to Salma and Lucius Stanley, probably Canandaigua, New York, March 7, 1848, and undated and unidentified newspaper clippings in Stanley's scrapbook, 1843–72, 17 and 22 respectively, private collection.

29. Despite the tragic implication of the subject, by the 1840s the trapper must have become an expendable frontier hero, whose demise was an inevitable consequence of more permanent (and more civilized) white settlement. That probably made the painting less objectionable to easterners like George W. Austin, a noted collector and treasurer of the American Art-Union, who purchased *The Death Struggle* from the Art-Union in 1845 (see Amon Carter Museum, *American Frontier Life*, 65).

30. Quoted in Saum, *Fur Trader and Indian*, 5

31. Illustrations, engravings, and chromolithographs after western paintings by Charles Deas, William Ranney, and Arthur F. Tait were widely known in the 1850s (see Amon Carter Museum, *American Frontier Life*, 51–77, 79–107, 109–29).

32. While in Düsseldorf, Carl Wimar gleaned

frontier "experience" from a number of sources. *Attack of an Emigrant Train* was apparently inspired by an episode in *Impressions de voyages et aventures dans le Mexique, la Haute Californie, et les régions de l'or* (1851) by the French author Gabriel Ferry (see Rathbone, *Wimar*, 15–16).

33. Thomas Nuttall, *A Journal of Travels into the Arkansas Territory* (1821; Ann Arbor, Mich.: University Microfilms, 1966), vi.

34. *The Poetical Works of William Cullen Bryant* (1903; New York: Appleton-Century, 1935), 107.

35. *Wisconsin Enquirer,* June 15, 1839, 1.

36. Perhaps because the painting was commissioned by an English lord, it expresses sympathy for Indians at a time when Americans in general felt little.

37. Carter, *Farny,* 33. Carter cites an article of 1910 ("Studio Impressions of Farny," *Cincinnati Times-Star,* April 2, 1910, 6) to suggest that Farny observed Long Day while working at Standing Rock Agency in 1884. The article is inaccurate on two counts. Farny visited Standing Rock Agency in 1881, not 1884, and he was there to visit, not work (see Appleton and Bartalini, *Farny,* 11–12, 22).

38. Farny inadvertently cloaked the Indian in a robe worn by females to celebrate puberty rites (Hassrick, *Way West,* 197). Faulty anthropology, however, does not lessen the impact of the robe, which in this case is worn by the Indian solely as an emblem of tribal culture.

39. Henry Rowe Schoolcraft, *History of the Indian Tribes of the United States* (Philadelphia: Lippincott, 1857), 6:561.

40. Quoted in Drinnon, *Facing West,* 83.

41. Israel, *State of the Union Messages* 2:1199–1200.

42. Ibid. 2:1199.

43. The ground for this act was laid in the early 1880s by various philanthropic associations formed with the intention of aiding the Indians. These groups included the Boston Indian Citizenship Committee, Indian Rights Association, Women's National Indian Association, and, most influential, Friends of the Indians.

44. Prucha, *Indians in American Society,* 23.

45. Limerick, *Legacy of Conquest,* 196.

46. "Senate Debate on Bill to Provide Lands in Severalty, January 20, 1881," in Wilcomb E. Washburn, comp., *The American Indian and the United States:*

A Documentary History (New York: Random House, 1973), 3:1695.

47. Limerick, *Legacy of Conquest,* 198.

48. Quoted in Tyler, *Miller,* 31.

49. Quoted in Glanz, *How the West Was Drawn,* 37.

50. Tyler, *Miller,* 43

51. Ibid., 57.

52. William J. Scheick, *The Half-Blood: A Cultural Symbol in Nineteenth-Century American Fiction* (Lexington: University Press of Kentucky, 1979), 3.

53. Quoted ibid., 3.

54. Saum, *Fur Trader and Indian,* 84.

55. Quoted in Satz, *Indian Policy,* 98.

56. "Caleb Lyon's Bruneau Treaty, April 12, 1866," *Idaho Yesterdays* 13 (Spring 1969): 17–19, 32+. Appreciation is extended to Joan Carpenter, curator of exhibitions, Thomas Gilcrease Institute of American History and Art, for searching the Gilcrease files for information.

57. Appreciation is extended to Paula Fleming, National Anthropological Archives, Smithsonian Institution, for identifying photograph sources.

58. Appreciation is extended to William C. Sturtevant, William L. Merrill, and John C. Ewers, National Museum of Natural History, Smithsonian Institution, for information regarding the Indian tribes portrayed in *Treaty with the Shoshone Indians.*

59. Quoted in Rogin, *Fathers and Children,* 117.

60. Israel, *State of the Union Messages* 1:152.

61. Groeschel, "Matteson," 61.

62. Satz, *Indian Policy,* 2.

63. The substantial contributions of English royalty, pious gentry and merchants, and the Virginia Company toward the founding of Henrico College indicated a secure future for the education of Indians. The Indian wars in 1622 and transfer of the Virginia colony to the British crown led, however, to the demise of Henrico College in 1624 (see Szasz, *Indian Education,* 54, 58, 60–62). Jennings (*Invasion of America* [1975 ed.], 54) doubts that the college was built or that "a single Indian was ever proselyted through its agency."

64. Quoted in Berkhofer, *Salvation and the Savage,* 33.

65. For information regarding *Sacramento Indian with Dogs,* see Stevens, *Nahl,* 136.

66. *Dictionary of American Biography* 11:13.

67. Quoted in Berkhofer, *Salvation and the Savage,* 36.

68. *Amon Carter Museum of Western Art: Catalogue of the Collection, 1972* (Fort Worth, Tex.: Amon Carter Museum of Western Art, 1973), 30, no. 53.

69. Fuller obligingly numbered and identified on the back of the canvas the principal figures in *Crow Creek Agency*. The two "civilized" Indians are Drifting Goose, a Catholic convert, and Wizi, a mediator of disputes between Indians and whites (see Hassrick, *Way West,* 189).

70. Quoted in Prucha, *Indians in American Society,* 12.

71. Quoted in Sheehan, *Seeds of Extinction* (1973 ed.), 32–33.

72. Quoted in Berkhofer, *Salvation and the Savage,* 108.

4

Settlement and Development

Claiming the West

ELIZABETH JOHNS

Moving into and onto new land was no simple matter, and artists who represented the process conveyed—and also hid—much of this complexity. Paintings of discovery, nature, Indians, and the early trappers and first emigrant wagons were constructions of retrospective justification. That is, artists presented early explorers as having come to the continent with high moral purpose, nature as being ready for Americans' wise use, Indians as appropriately yielding to whites, and scouts and pioneer families as only the first in a long line of intrepid pioneers. They painted these images about actions that had actually been carried out with varied, even conflicting motives. But from the 1830s to the 1850s, when so many of these pictures were created, many Americans claimed that it was the citizenship's very responsibility to fan out across the continent. Artists embodied these convictions in images that promoted, justified, and celebrated moving west.[1]

Artists representing the next part of westward expansion—the actual claiming of the land through settlement and economic development—followed a slightly different agenda. Some featured citizens themselves or the work of their hands and brains. While many pictures of discovery and nature asserted that the enterprise of appropriation was deeply spiritual, images of settlement and economic development embodied claims about social relationships. Modifying the excitement with which westward moving citizens contemplated a fresh start were assumptions and anxieties about social class, economic success, and the primacy of the individual. These convictions and worries guided them in building homes and establishing communities, working the land and extracting its resources, and setting up political and legal institutions. The few citizens who were wealthy worried that the huge tide of ambitious, raucous, and ignorant seekers of fortune would swamp the ship of economic and political order, and the many who were not prosperous feared that they would lose out to those with economic and social power.

Such tensions determined much of the tone of settlement pictures. The viewers for whom the artists made the images seem to have had the largest voice in settlement and development, and many were proud of having achieved this power "by their own bootstraps." Whether they could have specified it as such or not, they depended on paintings to vouch for their own worth and the importance of their activity. These images idealized their success, subordinated material that contradicted it, and set apart the accomplished viewers from those who were not.

We cannot always be sure at just what point in their ventures citizens commissioned such pictures or were receptive to an energetic painter who proposed them. At least three functions in most images, however, are striking. The paintings claimed that the most important westerners and the fruits of their labor had social respectability by eastern standards. Second, they asserted that western exploitation was accomplished through impressive technology and hard work, also highly approvable by eastern standards. And, finally, artists demonstrated that social classes and behavior in the West that were obviously not "genteel" or even respectable were kept in their place. Either such manifestations of a Wild West were controlled by citizens who knew the proprieties or were more subtly subordinated as a kind of tourist attraction. Because the images were made for the more prominent westerners and thus by implication for distant easterners whose standards were a model, they projected both self-promotion and reassurance—the ideology of the newly successful. It is true that printmakers and photographers were occasionally critical of western development; the print especially was the vehicle of amusement and caricature. In contrast, what is most apparent in paintings—representations in which the image maker traditionally exalted the ideals

sanctioning human activity—was a self-satisfaction that hovered between boastfulness and amazement.

Claiming Political and Legal Power

Whereas the first and longest-enduring motivation that impelled Americans westward was their individual drive for economic success, an issue they had to struggle with collectively was the establishment of political life. Very few homesteaders lived in isolation for long, and the growth of settlements into communities meant that politics soon became important. Back east, the democratic configuration of this activity was of consuming importance in the vocal ideology justifying westward growth. Supporting this expansion in the 1840s was the conviction expressed in sermons, political speeches, and newspaper editorials that democracy, as planted on the western part of the continent by the United States, was what the western lands deserved, what the world needed, and what God wanted. It was already clear by the 1840s that what men described as broadly based suffrage (its exclusion of women and African-Americans seemed natural to them) had its disadvantages, not the least of which were that political parties and clever leaders could manipulate the less intelligent voters. But many Americans, particularly Democrats who identified their party as that "of the people," argued that the common man had a purity, wit, and self-interest in what was right far beyond what the elite expected. For many, the very political process itself—campaigning for office, voting, and incorporating the results of the election into public life—demonstrated the common sense of "ordinary" voters and the unusual resilience of democracy. No better cauldron existed for the testing of this confidence than western areas settled by a broad cross-section. Whereas the East and South were dominated by established political interests, the newly settled West—at least as many westerners liked to believe—was still fluid and open, an arena in which the give-and-take of political argument was most prominently reflected in election results.

Thus it is not surprising that the major pictures about the political process were produced in an early western state by a native western artist. Missouri, the first state to be formed west of the Mississippi River and home of painter George Caleb Bingham, was the area perhaps longest identified with the West.[2] A major location for the "jumping off" of expeditions, commercial ventures, and settlement in the Far West, Missouri was where the forces of western freedom and commercial and political responsibilities were synthesized very early. Although when it was admitted to statehood in 1821, Missouri contained areas so wild that even Daniel Boone found there the solitude he craved, by 1850, when Bingham painted his election scenes, the state was overwhelmingly agricultural. It was a region of many communities, ranging from a store at a crossroads to the substantial old city of Saint Louis. The Democratic party had long dominated the state, although the Whigs began to make gains in the 1840s, and Senator Thomas Hart Benton had been a powerful voice in national political debate since Missouri's admission to the Union. There were plenty of Missourians of wealth and family who, as would be expected, dominated aspects of local political, economic, and social life, but Bingham chose to explore in his pictures the implications of a large, relatively undifferentiated electorate—that is, a substantially middle- and lower-class sovereignty—engaged in the process of political choice.

The position that Bingham brought to this enterprise, one that he initiated himself, was that of an urbane westerner. He had grown up on Missouri farms, gone to the East Coast to study and then paint portraits in Washington, D.C., and returned to Missouri to make his living as a portraitist. He found his patronage in small communities as well as in Saint Louis and traveled frequently to paint sitters in Mississippi and Kentucky. An artist at home with a wide variety of individuals, Bingham seems to have been working for several audiences: for Missourians and other westerners along the Mississippi and Ohio rivers, who were hopeful about their communities, and for New Yorkers and other viewers on the East Coast, who wanted images that would confirm their own varied opinions of westerners, opinions that ranged from critical to amused, from enthusiastic to simply tolerant.

Bingham shared the western city dwellers' broad vision of the West as an area where a variety of human enterprises and types could flourish. They saw politics on their frontier as lively, occasionally chicanerous but on the whole no different from that in the East and on occasion better. In their inclusive vision of the citizenry Bingham and other Missourians accepted self-made merchants, colorful boatmen, ambitious politicians, well-heeled bankers, and stolid farmers as part of a political and economic process that would somehow function almost reliably despite lapses, even manipulation.

Thus in his images Bingham's vision of American politics is rich and forgiving. Passionately devoted to politics, Bingham developed a group of pictures on electioneering and voting that put the process in a heartily varied light. An early theme he probed was that of the political candidate making his pitch to a small audience. His *Canvassing for a Vote*, 1851–52, set in front of a rural tavern, shows an eager speaker leaning forward in his chair to persuade his listeners of an important point

160. George Caleb Bingham,
Canvassing for a Vote, 1851–52,
oil on canvas, 25⅛ × 30³⁄₁₆
in. The Nelson-Atkins Mu-
seum of Art, Kansas City,
Missouri (Nelson Fund).

[160]. The speaker gestures confidently, his pitch at the moment aimed at the well-dressed citizen opposite him who seems ready to go along with the argument. Between these two is a third listener, a fat man smoking a pipe who grins knowingly, as though he has heard it all before. These three, dressed in topcoats and vests and wearing ties and shirts, share roughly the same social class, or perhaps it is that the skeptic and politician aim to associate them-selves with the powerful–looking citizen in the foreground, who asserts his importance with a carefully honed walking stick. His face lined and his top hat somewhat battered, the politi-cian seems to be one of the group of "new men," ambitious to achieve a modicum of power. Behind this foreground group, standing and leaning forward, is a man clearly of lower social status: he may be the tavern keeper. Wearing a long apron over clothing that in-cludes neither tie nor coat, he strains to keep up with the sophistication of the argument. A

man behind him dressed in black with a soft hat pulled down over his head turns his back on the scene, peering instead through the tavern window. He may represent the nameless unwashed who are uninterested in politics. Bingham's scene of the prominent and subtle differences in the sovereignty is presided over by the national symbol of the eagle on the tavern sign. A pentimento in the middle right of the image suggests that he had originally planned a considerably longer extent of village buildings; the format he settled on, however, much more vividly suggests the rural anchoring of political activity. To emphasize the itin-

erant nature of politicking, Bingham included the politician's saddlebag at his side, and we see his horse standing behind him. Providing contrapuntal metaphors are the dog on the left who sleeps through the politician's pitch, the rear end of the horse placed behind the earnest speaker, and the beautifully blue sky that arches over the scene as though to purify and endorse the activity below.[3]

With *The County Election*, 1852, Bingham turned his attention from campaigning to voting, and for this he created a substantial cast of characters [161]. Once again the location is a small town, and again a western tolerance of

161. George Caleb Bingham, *The County Election*, 1852, oil on canvas, 38 × 52 in. Boatmen's National Bank, Saint Louis.

diversity, human frailty, and exuberance ra-diates from the image. Across the painting a rich assortment of male humanity (all white) lines up to cast their votes to a judge and clerk who are installed on the porch of an official–looking building. On one pillar is a banner that can be read as celebratory or ironical—"The Will of the People, the Supreme Law." The clothing, postures, body types, and facial fea-tures of the figures in the crowd clue the viewer to the social variety in this constitu-ency. There seem to be merchants, farmers, la-borers, and hangers-on in addition to ambi-tious politicians urging their cause on voters right up to the ballot box. According to popu-lar phrenological principles, the wide foreheads of some men testify to intelligence and the wide mouths and heavy chins of others indicate a fondness for the sensual pleasures. The few drunks represent the bought votes that were a fact of life in the politics of mass democracy and the two boys in the foreground, the prom-ise of posterity. Once again Bingham encour-aged viewers to temper both their idealism and their reservations about the political process. In this picture he counterbalances the jolly toper in the left foreground and drunken celebrant on the right with an orderly sweep of town and church architecture in the background and a glorious blue sky that forms a canopy over the gathering.[4]

Bingham turned next to the other major events in the election process—campaigning before a large crowd and gathering to hear the election results. In *Stump Speaking*, 1853–54, as he had done in the earlier pictures, Bingham made his viewer very much aware of the social strata in the western scene but at the same time gathered his subjects together into the common enterprise of making political decisions [162]. Most of the men listening to the energetic poli-tician who stands over them at the stump on the left are of the "humbler orders," dressed

casually, without ties, vests, or in some in-stances even coats, and wearing hats that have seen much use. Their faces project interest or dullness or confusion. Others in the crowd ap-pear more substantial, with top hats, velvet-collared coats, ties, and demeanors reflecting their standing in the community. They listen to the speech with considerably sharper alert-ness. The implications for the sovereignty in Bingham's social inventory are that the citi-zenry can somehow manage with extremes. The politician appeals to voters who are, on the one hand, as uncomprehending as the man standing in the foreground dressed in dark clothing and leaning on a stick and, on the other hand, as self-assured as the man immacu-lately attired in the light-colored suit and top hat who has seated himself in the most promi-nent position in the audience. Bingham's own attitude toward this motley crew was benign. He reported during the painting process, "The gathering of the sovereigns is much larger than I had counted upon. A new head is continually popping up [in the painting] and demanding a place in the crowd, and as I am a thorough democrat, it gives me pleasure to accommodate them all."[5] After *Stump Speaking* he went on to paint the logical successor to *The County Election*—a scene he called *The Verdict of the People*, 1854–55, in which the results of an election are announced [163]. In this picture, too, the town provides an orderly backdrop and the clear sky a kind of blessing for the hurly-burly of reaction, calculation, and ex-change taking place in the town square. An of-ficial has just read the vote tally and the citi-zens are engaged in a spectrum of reactions, from swirling their hats in exaltation to sol-emnly paying off bets. An American flag waves over the scene. Once again, although the sovereignty is large, comprising varied classes, Bingham is concerned almost exclu-sively with white males. A black man assumes

162. George Caleb Bingham, *Stump Speaking*, 1853–54, oil on canvas, 42½ × 58 in. Boatmen's National Bank, Saint Louis.

a menial role in the foreground; and (white) women appear only on the hotel balcony in the extreme right, relegated to positions as onlookers.

What Bingham's political friend and patron James Rollins, also of Missouri, enthusiastically wrote about *The County Election* he might well have claimed about all three works: "It is a *National* painting, for it presents just such a scene, as you would meet with on the Aroostock in Maine, or in the City of New York, or on the Rio Grande in Texas, on an election day." Rollins enumerated the social types with particular delight: "[Bingham] has left nothing *out,* the courtier, the politician, the labourer, the sturdy farmer, the *bully* at the poles, the beerseller, the *bruised* pugilist, and even the boys playing 'mumble the peg' are all distinctly recognized in the group . . . [as] a delineation of character it is superb." Rollins went on to identify the foundation of Bingham's conception. "The elective franchise is the very corner stone, upon which rests our governmental superstructure and as illustrative of our fine institutions, the power and influence which the ballot box exerts over our happiness as a people, the subject of this painting was most happily chosen, and executed with won-

163. George Caleb Bingham, *The Verdict of the People*, 1854–55, oil on canvas, 46 × 65 in. Boatmen's National Bank, Saint Louis.

derful skill by its gifted author."[6]

Such cheerful assessment of democracy's functioning amid citizens high and low, all on the lookout for their own interest, was not only peculiarly western but even there, subject to alteration. Bingham himself became temporarily disenchanted about political parties, writing to his friend Rollins in 1853 that not until the present system had been broken up would the United States "have a revival of the good old times, when honesty and capacity, rather than party servility, will be the qualifications for office."[7]

When painters took up the courtroom trial to explore legal relationships among the citizenry, they conveyed something of this pessimism. In the legal aspects of public life there was much less ambiguity about democracy. American law followed an English model, which saw every man as equal before the law (and whenever possible judged by his peers) but also every law court as necessarily run by the elite of the community who had the education and wisdom necessary for the responsibility. The conflict in the young United States between a franchise in which each male citizen had the vote and a legal system in which the dominant had the power was not always clearcut. In fact, as the law was implemented in newly settled areas there was a great similarity between the lawyer and small-town justice, who trained themselves at the expense of the ignorant (and not always adequately), and the striving politician, who mastered the art of rhetoric to catapult himself into the state legislature. In both situations large numbers of the humbler orders took what their more ambitious fellow citizens imposed on them. They voted for the politician who most cleverly appealed to their self-interest, and in the courts they were subject to the authority of those in charge, whether or not this power was exercised appropriately.

Having invested much of his energies in interpreting the political process, Bingham did not paint a courtroom scene until 1874. But back on the East Coast, upstate New Yorker Tompkins H. Matteson painted *Justice's Court in the Backwoods* for the American Art-Union exhibition in New York in 1850 [164]. The scene reveals at once Matteson's cynicism. The justice is a shoemaker-tavern keeper who has propped up his feet; the prosecutor is a dandy who asserts his case with a verve suggesting that his argument is all noise and no substance; the other members of the cast of characters, including the plaintiff on the right and defendant on the far left (being comforted by a woman), look benighted, dull, curious, and not the least bit amazed. Only one person in the picture seems to know something about the law: he conspicuously shows a text, no doubt a law book, to the self-satisfied judge.

164. Tompkins H. Matteson, *Justice's Court in the Backwoods,* 1850, oil on canvas, 31¾ × 44 in. New York State Historical Association, Cooperstown.

Two years later in Missouri, William Josiah Brickey painted a considerably more orderly legal hearing. While Matteson had condemned backwoods court proceedings, Brickey presented the workings of justice in an established urban area in *Missouri Courtroom, 1852* [165]. Social and legal hierarchies organize the composition. A dignified judge in black, with pointed collar, is elevated behind a desk, before which other well-dressed court officials perform their roles with ease. In extreme distress, in contrast, is the disheveled defendant, to whom the apparently well-heeled witness points in testimony to the judge. In the far right, behind the rail separating not only the lawyers' area from that of the audience but the dominant members of the community from the masses, a number of casually and even sloppily dressed men stand to look on. This separation into classes is continued across the back of the painting; there behind a tall picket rail, effectively a fence, is the docket and in it wait several dismal defendants, a woman among them. Out the courthouse windows behind them are

165. William Josiah Brickey, *Missouri Courtroom,* 1852, oil on canvas, 29⅛ × 36 in. National Museum of American Art, Smithsonian Institution, Washington, D.C.

the three- and four-story buildings of a busy commercial center. In this stacked house of privilege the ignorant seem to have a bleak chance indeed.

Whether Brickey was sympathetic to those in his painting who are down on their luck is not clear, but by 1874 Bingham seems to have found the ignorant citizen more amusing than defensible, appropriate for a painting at the expense of those on the bottom of society. Bingham constructed *The Puzzled Witness* so that the viewer looks directly at the raised dais of the judge's bench [166]. Everyone in the painting—most very comfortable looking—is seated, except the puzzled witness, who, clothed in the common garb of a farmer, scratches his head in confusion. He is the focus of the image. All look on his consternation with interest. The man immediately behind the questioning attorney leans forward tensely as though his case depends on this witness's dubious ability to get things straight; a young man on the right stares with open-mouthed amazement; and even the dog seems to wait for the witness's testimony.

Both courtroom scenes characterize the

166. George Caleb Bingham, *The Puzzled Witness,* 1874, oil on canvas, 23 × 28 in. Kennedy Galleries, Inc., New York.

humbler citizen as not just ordinary but in his ignorance as incapable and even potentially harmful to the "solid" members of the community. As the Far West was settled across the latter years of the century, writers and storytellers constructed entertaining tales about the law, specifically the justice, in frontier areas. This lore shaped the myth of the West that many easterners found increasingly congenial: that westerners were virtually lawless. Derived from a few sensational occurrences—from exaggerated reports of the settlers themselves, whose generalizations were fed by their own anxieties, and by reports of eastern travelers who went west for tourist experiences—stories about town shoot-outs and vigilante hangings achieved an independent life.[8] The reasons for their popularity back east were complex. Surely it is significant that the stereotypes developed after a substantial number of citizens had made the West a location of tremendous economic and political power that challenged the hegemony of the East. These stories conveyed to listeners already tense about their own stake in the country a point of view enabling them to condescend to their political competitors. Another factor, which seems contradictory, may have been even more important. In an era of rapid urban and industrial development in the East and of the channeling of social structures from the small to the corporate across the nation, the fantasy of a lawless or at least unstructured West sustained many easterners' perhaps unconscious wish that there was some place left where individualism was untrammeled.

Frontier justice or no, constructions from late in the century accusing western citizens of being trigger-happy in matters of justice and politics are best evaluated in the context of the considerably more generous assessments of western give-and-take presented by Bingham in the 1850s.

Claiming Homes and Communities

One of the earliest activities of those who moved west was to mark the new territory as their own by building a home. For serious-minded emigrants, the first temporary shelters—dugouts on the prairie, tents in mining camps, log cabins in the mountains, and hastily erected frame houses in small communities— were not meant to indicate their probity or social aspirations. Rather it was the permanent home that distinguished the solid citizen, setting apart the responsible entrepreneur who lived an orderly life from the adventurer who drifted from one flash in the pan to another. In representations of homes, artists conveyed the distinctions of social class, work ethic, and economic attainment with which viewers and patrons interpreted their own position in the West.

One of the earliest of such images was made by Bingham some time before 1845. *Family Life on the Frontier* presents the ideal genteel family [167]. In the early evening, family members carry out functions appropriate to their gender: the mother nurses the baby while the daughters set the table for the evening meal; the well-dressed father sits in the foreground, absorbed in his study of a book that is perhaps the Bible; and the young boys of the family play in front of the fire. Only the frontier cabin marks the scene as different from any representation of the proper middle-class life of an eastern, urban family.

As Bingham apparently did not exhibit the picture, we can only guess that his intended audience, if eastern, would have needed the assurance that the western-moving enterprise was so exemplary, and, if western, would have appreciated this flattering reading of their domestic respectability. Some five years later, when he painted *The Squatters,* Bingham presented an assessment of westward-moving settlers that

167. George Caleb Bingham, *Family Life on the Frontier,* before 1845, oil on canvas, 24¼ × 30 in. Private collection.

is nearer what many eastern audiences expected to be shown.

In *The Squatters* Bingham pictures two generations of temporary settlers looking dreamily toward the viewer [168]. The vast distance on the right seems to beckon the settlers as well as the speculation of the viewer further into the wilderness. Although established citizens often referred to them with disdain because they simply squatted on land and then moved on rather than buying and farming it, squatters performed an essential function in the settlement of the West by very virtue of their restlessness. This urge to move on was commended by Senator Benton and many others as essential for the settlement of the great continent. In Bingham's picture, however, such dreamy aspirations to keep going are

projected only by the men in the image: the lone woman is bent over the washtub. She is the one person in the family who performs any labor at all, in fact. Whether Bingham recognized his ideology or not, he constructed the female domain in the westward movement as task-oriented and supportive, the male role as ruminative and decisive. He sent the painting to New York, where he knew his audience would have a wide range of opinion on the matter—not only of the place of women on the frontier but of the fiber of the squatter class. He left the issue of character tacit: his settlers are certainly not middle-class, but they project an openness that in the eyes of many redeemed the squatters' failure to settle down.

James Henry Beard's *Westward Ho!* circa 1850, is another matter [169]. Beard painted this work as part of a series he projected, "Poor White Folks," and he presented his westward-moving subjects as anything but sympathetic. The father, just having returned from a hunting trip with his young son, looks exhausted by the experience. His lethargy is a curious reaction to the fine deer and smaller animals that he has brought back. The wife is hopeless looking, and even the children and dog seem to be waiting for things to pick up. Their lean-to shelter verges on collapse. Beard, who had grown up in the orderly communities of Ohio, may well have been appealing to a vast eastern constituency who worried that the West was filling up with the uneducated and unambitious. These emigrant types, as far as northeastern viewers were concerned, may have approximated the poorer settlers of the Carolinas who moved into Alabama, Mississippi, and Arkansas in the 1820s and 1830s and quickly became known as "backwoodsmen" and "crackers."

Bingham's *Family Life on the Frontier* and *The Squatters* and Beard's *Westward Ho!*—images that are respectively flattering, ambiguous,

168. George Caleb Bingham, *The Squatters,* 1850, oil on canvas, 23⅛ × 28¼ in. Museum of Fine Arts, Boston; bequest of Henry L. Shattuck in memory of the late Ralph W. Gray.

and critical of western emigration—comprised "reports" to comfortable eastern audiences about the domestic arrangements of the middle to lower orders who were moving west. Another group of pictures was made for more selective viewers: the successful who had moved west themselves. These paintings represented the carefully established good and elevated life. Such an image is Bingham's *"Forest Hill,"* which the artist painted for Thomas Withers Nelson during an extended visit in 1877 [170].

The spacious "estate-scape" portrays a comfortable, respectable way of life, one that would be impressive by eastern standards (and indeed might look eastern, except for the presence of cattle in the yard). The imposing Georgian-style house with its grand two-story portico is sheltered by huge, old trees, as though the grouping has been a part of the natural landscape for generations. The Missouri River flows in the background. Three children of the family, the African-American nurse who cared for them, and the carriage of the doctor who delivered the fourth child appear in the foreground.[9] The painting is thus a memento of a particular moment in the history of the family (the birth of the last child), a statement about Nelson's architectural and real property, and a tribute to the enduring (and eastern-patterned) gentility of the family's way of life.

Such an inventory and tribute seem also to have been part of the commission given to Joseph Lee in his painting *Residence of Captain Thomas W. Badger,* circa 1871 [171]. This

image too is a veritable paean to a comfortable and fashionable homestead, and it contributes to a sequence of increasing prosperity. Positioned in a light-filled landscape, under a cloudy sky, the Victorian-Gothic house has a veranda across the entire front and gabled roofs on all sides. The architectural style might have seemed somewhat old-fashioned on the East Coast by this time, but like the Georgian house of Bingham's patron in Missouri, it represents the utmost in middle-class respectability. The scene contains evidence of the transportation

169. James Henry Beard, *Westward Ho!* circa 1850, oil on canvas, 62 × 79 in. DePauw University Permanent Art Collection, Indiana.

that was bringing commerce and wealth to
Oakland, an area across the bay from San
Francisco—train, steamboat and sailboats
in the bay, and, just behind the trees near the
home, the mast of a sailing ship that alludes to
Badger's own maritime career. The few figures
in the picture may be family members, but
they are incidental to the claims for wealth and
careful development made by the architecture,
features such as the windmill, water tower, and
large barn. A picket fence demarcates the house
from the surrounding territory and adds the
finishing touch to a scene of prosperity and
self-satisfaction.

The most "genteel" of these three claims
for wealthy western homesteads is a picture by
Ernest Narjot, *Under the Redwoods, Spout*

170. George Caleb Bingham,
*"Forest Hill": The Nelson
Homestead, Boonville, Missouri,*
1877, oil on canvas, 22 × 27
in. Anna Birch Stephens Family, Davis, California.

171. Joseph Lee, *Residence of
Captain Thomas W. Badger,
Brooklyn, from the Northwest,*
circa 1871, oil on canvas, 26¼
× 42 in. The Oakland Mu-
seum, California; gift of the
Oakland Society of Pioneers.
(Detail illustrated on p. 190.)

172. Ernest Narjot, *Under the
Redwoods, Spout Farm,* 1873,
oil on canvas, 30 × 25 in.
The Elisabeth Waldo-Dentzel
Collection, Northridge,
California.

Farm, 1873 [172]. Born in Saint-Malo, France,
Narjot was one of the international fortune-
hunters attracted to California by the discovery
of gold. After sixteen years of prospecting, he
settled down in San Francisco to take up a career as a painter. He enjoyed patronage from
the well-to-do of the Bay Area, including such
prominent men as Leland Stanford. The individuals in *Under the Redwoods* are obviously of
the leisured classes. Narjot, however, did not
inventory the homestead of his patron (whose
identity is not known)—as had Bingham and
Lee in making pictures for their clients—but
made a more subtle assessment of their wealth.
He depicted a lovely picnic grove, in which an
assortment of seriously conversing men and
three women enjoy themselves.[10] On the one
hand, the picture is a kind of conversation
piece, a format popular in the eighteenth century, and, on the other, a picnic scene, fashionable in nineteenth-century painting. This
picnic, however, elevates talking above eating,
and thus Narjot's picture makes a most flattering assertion: that his patrons and their friends
had created an intellectual salon in the West.

   Although many citizens back east thought
of the move west as highly individualistic, it
was the establishment of communities that sustained new arrivals, developed the exchange of
goods and services necessary for growth and
prosperity, and in turn encouraged more immigration. Just what type of community was
being organized was a matter of pride to founders and settlers. Tent- and shantytowns were
associated with arrivals who had rushed in to
make money quickly rather than settle down as
responsible citizens. In contrast, towns planned
from the beginning on orderly plats derived
from careful eastern models projected responsibility and moral development. Just as painters
constructed the shades of difference in their
representations of the individuals and families
who moved west, so they interpreted the fla-

vor of communities, attentive to the assumptions of their residents and other viewers.

Two pictures of differing settlements, one Anglo-American and the other Spanish, illustrate these rhetorical purposes very clearly. John Mix Stanley's *Oregon City on the Willamette River,* 1850–52, conveys the paradisiacal nature of settlement by citizens who carried with them Anglo-Saxon (and thus Protestant) traditions of order, hard work, and entrepre-

neurial energy [173]. To many back east, the Oregon Territory seemed impossibly inaccessible and distant, its potential new Eden, with plentiful water and wholesome climate, little more than a pipe dream. Yet by 1844 the Oregon Trail, which led from Independence, Missouri, across the high plains and through the treacherous Rocky Mountains into the Willamette Valley, was virtually jammed with citizens moving westward. Struck by the phe-

173. John Mix Stanley, *Oregon City on the Willamette River,* 1850–52, oil on canvas, 26½ × 40 in. Amon Carter Museum, Fort Worth, Texas.

174. Lorenzo Loraine, *Oregon City,* 1857, albumen print, 9½ × 13 in. Oregon Historical Society, Portland (21079).

nomenon of the thousands of families who undertook the journey, Horace Greeley emphasized the dedication and courage that the dream elicited from settlers: "Why do they brave the desert, the wilderness, the savage, the snowy precipices of the Rocky Mountains, the weary summer march, the storm-drenched bivouac, and the gnawings of hunger?"[11]

Painter Stanley effectively showed why in his depiction of the Oregon interior only a few years after it was settled. With the ideal virtues of northeastern know-how, culture, and business acumen, settlers braved the hazards to establish communities. At least this was how many interpreted their adventure to themselves and others. Stanley's painting shows an orderly, planned settlement, whereas a photograph of the town by Lorenzo Loraine a few years later reveals a veritable jumble of buildings [174]. In Stanley's landscape, which looks toward the falls on the Willamette River, two Indians occupy the high left foreground. Their presence reminded viewers that Indians had merely roamed across the land rather than developing and using it wisely and that their displacement by whites was therefore justified. Into the depth of the picture run the streets of Oregon City, lined with precise wood-frame structures. These models of neatness include businesses, barns and markets, residences, and perhaps hotels. At the far end of the street is a prominent church. Stanley painted this vision with a predominantly cool palette, using fresh greens and blues and grays to describe the clear, temperate climate of the valley. Neat rows of trees and shrubs enhance the effect of the white-washed buildings in proclaiming a settlement already civilized. Fully one-half of the painting is sky, alluding subtly to the claims of many that Oregon was "God's country," where settlers with towns and farming on their mind were of the highest moral fiber.

In strong contrast is Worthington Whit-

tredge's painting *Santa Fe,* 1866 [175]. The Spanish West was a matter of curiosity to northeasterners. The land ceded to the United States by Mexico presented an otherness in the terrain itself as well as in the cultural traditions of the Indians, the Spanish, and the Mexicans who had settled there. On a variety of expeditions eastern travelers charted the territory for military use, railroad development, or scientific information. Whittredge went as a "sight-seer" and landscapist. His depiction of Santa Fe constructs the old city as horizontal, laid out in rectangular segments now startlingly empty; the colors are those of the earth, the air virtually vibrating with dry heat. The Catholic church is the largest and most prominent structure in the oil sketch (the finished painting for which Whittredge made this sketch is now unlocated). In the right foreground are several Indians or perhaps Mexicans dressed in shawls, clearly identifying the landscape for the eastern viewer as that of an alien and primitive people. Whittredge placed the horizon high in the landscape, as though the earthiness of Santa Fe, its strangeness by northeastern standards, was remote from a transcendent, divine order.

If settlements in Oregon and the South-

west were distinct, those in California were both curious and archetypal. To most citizens in the United States, in fact, the spectacular development of California during the 1850s was the very reference point of what moving west could mean for individuals as well as groups.[12] The discovery of gold in 1848 identified California as the place where citizens could strike it rich, if not literally, then perhaps figuratively. California was where people went to recover from bad circumstances, to start over. California was where dreams came true and where, if one were lucky, they came true quickly.

The chaos near Sutter's Creek after the discovery of gold was a source of astonishment to all who experienced it. Photographs in 1849 of San Francisco, the nearest port, show the harbor jammed with hundreds of ships that had been sailed around the horn of South America. Full of would-be prospectors, they were abandoned, even by their captains, as passengers rushed for the hills. Citizens in the inland town of Sacramento, accessible by river from San Francisco and only a few miles from

the gold mines, struggled to meet the economic opportunities of outfitting, feeding, and entertaining the hordes of prospectors who passed through the town and at the same time attempted to maintain a semblance of order. Other river towns, too, such as Stockton, were torn between opportunity and stability. W. H. Creasy's watercolor of Stockton in October 1849, made in the first year of the California gold rush, captures something of this dilemma [176]. From an imaginary vantage point on the San Joaquin River, one looks onto what comprises Stockton at this point: a jumble of tents, ship masts, boats made into dwellings covered by canvas, barrels strewn about after hasty unloading, and ox-drawn wagons ready for departure to the mining camps.

Sometimes it was best simply to deny the disorder. Thus when George Tirrell put brush to easel in Sacramento a few years later, he constructed a scene of beatific calm. His *View of Sacramento*, circa 1855–60, effectively separates Sacramento as a civic enterprise from the economic and social chaos in all directions

175. Worthington Whittredge, *Santa Fe*, 1866, oil on canvas, 8 × 23⅛ in. Yale University Art Gallery, New Haven; gift from the estate of William W. Farnam, B.A. 1866, M.A. 1869, to the Peabody Museum of Natural History.

around it [177]. Painted perhaps for a local booster, Tirrell's view looks toward Sacramento from across the river, from which point the city hall and waterworks on the left assert the orderly civic and economic planning of the community. Tied at a city wharf, visible precisely between two prominent dark smokestacks on foreground ships, is the steamer *Antelope,* built in New York in 1847 and converted to a riverboat after service on the East Coast and between San Francisco and Panama. In the peaceful river are various other craft—a rowboat, barge (likely to be transporting vegetables and grain to the city from the upriver ranches), and several large houseboats. Tirrell was quite an enthusiast for the wonders of California development. In 1860 he had constructed what he claimed to be "the longest panorama ever painted," covering 25,300

square feet of canvas, that enabled his viewers to tour California from the coastal towns of Monterey and San Francisco inland to Yosemite. The panorama is now lost, but such an expansive, idealizing vision informs *View of Sacramento.*[13] The painting is constructed with four basic tones: aqua, coral, white, and gray. The buildings in the background and every detail of the rivercraft are conveyed with straight, clear lines that present a community in control. Tirrell's Sacramento is pristine, orderly, and civilized.

A decade later boosters in San Francisco had come to terms with the fact that their city derived its very success from the constant flux. Arriving newcomers from the eastern United States as well as Europe and Asia increased the opportunities for those with good business sense. Successful individuals who had been in California since the gold rush had by the late 1860s formed a sizable group of civic boosters and art patrons. This clientele, who had made their money as merchants and investors, saw the very bustle participated in by groups of all social classes as part and parcel of their enterprise. William Hahn's sweeping *Market Scene, Sansome Street, San Francisco,* 1872, caught up this activity with a rich variety [178]. Trained in Dresden and Düsseldorf, Germany, before coming to the United States in the early 1870s, Hahn presented his prosperous audience with evidence that economic exchange was booming. In his picture truck farmers, who grew vegetables and fruit across and south of the bay, have brought their produce to the city, stopping their wagons and setting up displays on the sides of the street. The shoppers are stylishly dressed city women, at least one of whom has brought her children. A panoply of social classes appears in the image. On the far right are Chinese truck farmers; on the far left is an African-American woman. In the right foreground are street urchins who snitch from

176. W. H. Creasy, *Stockton, October, 1849,* 1849, watercolor on paper, 17½ × 20¾ in. The Haggin Museum, Stockton, California.

the display, and gathered here and there on the right side of the picture are groups of working men. In population, at least, this is a representative gathering, excluding, of course, the bankers and investors who bought the pictures. Evidence of booming trade lines the street. Stores boast signs announcing "Seedsman," "Produce," and "Drugs," and in the right distance two pitchers on top of a building advertise a crockery firm. Also on the street are print shops, the newspaper office of the *California Republican,* bakeries, and a bar. A circus billboard on the building at the left subtly en-

riches the viewer's appreciation of the hustling going on here.

Hahn's ability to capture this wide variety of economic and social mingling made him extremely popular with the new merchant class. Working from precisely the opposite impulse of exclusivity that organized pictures of patrons' homes, artists making images of businesses and of the commercial district within which the enterprises of the city founders flourished emphasized inclusiveness. In *Sacramento Railroad Station,* 1874, Hahn focused on a wealthy family meeting an arriving young

177. George Tirrell, *View of Sacramento, California, from the Sacramento River,* circa 1855–60, oil on canvas, 27 × 47¾ in. Museum of Fine Arts, Boston; gift of Maxim Karolik to the M. and M. Karolik Collection of American Paintings, 1815–1865.

178. William Hahn, *Market Scene, Sansome Street, San Francisco,* 1872, oil on canvas, 60 × 96 in. Crocker Art Museum, Sacramento.

179. William Hahn, *Sacramento Railroad Station,* 1874, oil on canvas mounted on board, 53¾ × 87¾ in. The Fine Art Museums of San Francisco; gift of M. H. de Young Endowment Fund.

woman but placed vignettes of the considerably less privileged conspicuously to the right and left of the prosperous group [179]. Enclosing and rising above the scene are monuments of entrepreneurial progress: the engine on the left, impressively belching steam; three- and four-story buildings in the background; and the railroad itself, the terminus of the great Central Pacific Railroad.

Laying Connections: Images of Transport by Water and Rail

East-West connections sprang first from the gifts of geography and only later from technical ingenuity. The first mode of connection between East and West was the vast network of rivers that drained the continent. Even after Americans had devised roads and coaches to ride on them and then railroads and elaborate engines to pull cars loaded with goods, water vehicles continued to be the cheapest, most dependable means of transportation. Scouts and trappers penetrated the wilderness on rivers; early settlers floated their household goods downstream and later sent their agricultural and other products to market by the same means; and cities—like Saint Louis, Sacramento, and Stockton—sprang up on rivers that in turn became even more important conduits for the commerce then spreading across the continent. Even though financiers, investors, and other enthusiasts boasted about canals, toll pikes, and railroads, it was the river, long a favorite ingredient in the landscape tradition, that attracted the major attention of artists.

180. Unidentified artist, *Rafting Downstream,* circa 1840–50, oil on canvas, 17¾ × 22⅞ in. Indiana University Art Museum, Bloomington.

At the same time their images celebrated the development and romance brought to the expanding nation by rivers, artists also carefully inventoried just what social group was implicated in each type of use. For instance, in an unidentified artist's *Rafting Downstream,* circa 1840–50, the center of attention is the makeshift raft in the foreground, on which a motley crew variously lounge and enjoy themselves [180]. Flatboatmen enjoyed none too happy a reputation, being accused by traveling easterners of scandalous behavior on shore and laziness on the job. On the far shore are other evidences of rural, "unambitious" classes: a country cabin with smoke blowing out its chimney and a man fishing as he sits on a log. Coming up the river, toward the viewer, however, is an impressive steamboat, denizen of a more ambitious social order. Its double smoke-

stacks puff, signaling that the boilers are in full operation. In the distance are several more steamboats, the wave of the future, and mediating the distinction between old and new, two men row a small boat between the raft and the near side-wheeler. A figure on the bank in the right foreground waves a long stick, hailing the steamboat and perhaps serving as the artist's device to ensure that the viewer grasps the full implications of the juxtaposition. It was a coming together not only of transportation new and old but of types of citizens.

A closer examination of the social class that would eventually be forced off the river was carried out by Bingham in *Watching the Cargo,* 1849 [181]. This image suggests the underside of the progress hailed in *Rafting Downstream.* In *Watching the Cargo* a disabled steamer tilts in the middle ground. Its freight has been off-loaded onto a sand bar, where several riverboatmen protect it from thieves. An irony in the picture is that riverboatmen, associated with the old ways, are here deflecting the disadvantages of progress. The youngest of the three blows on driftwood to start a fire; the other two look directly at the viewer, inviting their appraisal. These are the hazards of river travel, and these are the men, themselves none too respectable looking, who stand guard against the worst excesses of their western associates. Bingham gauged well his New York audience's fascination with such ambiguous aspects of western settlement: the American Art-Union, which had bought his earlier images of riverboatmen, snapped up this one, too.

Few relatives of the men represented in either of these pictures would have been found in the cabin pictured in the watercolor *Interior of the Steamboat "Princess,"* 1861, by Marie-Adrien Persac [182]. The sumptuously appointed interior, typically reserved for the most privileged passengers, was the only space in

181. George Caleb Bingham, *Watching the Cargo,* 1849, oil on canvas, 26 × 36 in. The State Historical Society of Missouri, Columbia.

which women mixed socially with men. Such luxury would also have been part of the *Antelope,* the steamship painted by Tirrell at its new home on the Sacramento River [see 177]. The cabin of the *Princess* has Gothic tracery across its ceiling, a clerestory effect in the stained glass of the two upper galleries, and a series of paired lancet windows down the side walls. A long table in the middle seems absolutely laden with food, its diners attended by servants every few feet. Persac, a cartographer, pasted cut-out figures onto the watercolor, giving the rendering a surprising and lively three-dimensionality.[14] Steamboat meals typically included as many as five or six meats, other courses, and

desserts. Mark Twain was astounded by the appointments of such craft:

[The steamboat] was as clean and as dainty as a drawing-room; when I looked down her long, gilded saloon, it was like gazing through a splendid tunnel; she had a oil-picture, by some gifted sign-painter, on every stateroom door; she glittered with no end of prism-fringed chandeliers; the clerks office was elegant, the bar was marvelous, and the bar-keeper had been barbered and upholstered at incredible cost. . . . This was unutterable pomp.[15]

But pomp in appointments was part of the easterners' energetic providing of equipment for their westward counterparts as well as the western citizens' insistence on eastern standards of luxury. Few paintings show this reciprocation more clearly than John Burgum's literal *An Express Freight Shipment of Thirty Coaches,* circa 1868 [183]. Across the canvas from left to right are exactly thirty coaches on flatbed railroad cars, the bright red of each carriage body gleaming with newness. A sign proclaiming the shipment stands in the foreground as though it were part of the landscape; a man just behind it points to the trainload with pride, his female companion standing fully erect in appropriate awe. Behind the train the simple New England village of Concord testi-

fies to the source of the technical capacity that made this contribution to western development. As a painter of landscapes on coach doors, Burgum had for years been in the employ of the coach company.[16]

The Concord stagecoach had dominated eastern transportation during the era before the Civil War and was to prevail in the West after the war. Created in the late 1820s by the firm Abbott, Downing, the Concord owed its success to its resilience and strength: hung on leather braces, it could bounce over even the roughest terrain without breaking.[17] Just as important in settling the West as eastern techno-

182. Marie-Adrien Persac, *Interior of the Steamboat "Princess,"* 1861, gouache on paper, 17 × 22¹⁵⁄₁₆ in. Anglo-American Art Museum, Louisiana State University, Baton Rouge; gift of Mrs. Mamie Persac Lusk.

logical capacity was eastern commercial and business sense. The Wells Fargo & Company had been organized in New York in 1852 to operate an express service combining banking with the transport of messages, money, and mail for the expanding western market. By the late 1860s, when Burgum celebrated Abbot, Downing's fulfillment of its order of stage-coaches, Wells Fargo had built a virtual empire in the West.[18] As the company developed express lines in Colorado, Arizona, and Idaho, it ordered Concord coaches to be shipped by rail to Omaha, from which they would fan out to service the territory. The coaches were in for heavy duty: in 1867 the time required for the trip between Sacramento and Omaha on the Great Overland Mail route was fifteen days, the fare three hundred dollars.[19]

No other artifact was so clear a symbol of progress as the stagecoach, at least for a while. The *Denver Rocky Mountain News* was happy to report:

Wells, Fargo & Co. have lately added one more emblem to civilization to their stage and express business in Colorado. It is an express delivery wagon, of the style and pattern used in the eastern cities. The wagon is from the shop of Abbott, Downing & Co., Concord, New Hampshire, and is an excellent piece of workmanship. The harness and horse are in keeping with the wagon, both excellent specimens. Who says Colorado is not advancing in the belongings of civilization?[20]

Ironically the very means of transport of the stagecoaches in Burgum's picture in 1868—the railroad—was ultimately to spell the demise not only of the stagecoach but of the Wells, Fargo express service as well.

Claiming the Treasures of the Earth

The development of transportation was the province of relatively few entrepreneurial investors, but mining was another story.[21] The search for gold was an opportunity and a challenge few could resist. It required, many thought, little more than ambition, courage, and luck—all qualities that most felt were their particular province. The announcement of the discovery of gold in California in January 1848 at Sutter's Mill on the American River initiated a virtual flood of new arrivals. Would-be prospectors rushed in from San Francisco and Monterey, then from San Diego and Oregon, and then, as the word flew across the hemisphere, from the Hawaiian Islands, Mexico, Peru, and Chile; they came by steamer, sailing ship, and overland trail. By May a San Francisco newspaper was decrying, "The whole country, from San Francisco to Los Angeles, and from the sea shore to the base of the Sierra Nevadas, resounds with the sordid cry of '*gold,* GOLD, *GOLD!*' while the field is left half planted."[22] Within one year almost one hundred thousand had arrived with high hopes, skewing the state's population to a proportion of 90 percent male.[23]

It was impossible to pick up a newspaper almost anywhere in the United States without seeing headlines and columns on every page devoted to news from the gold diggings. Citizens on the East Coast and in the Midwest variously dreamed, schemed, and abandoned their jobs to go to California in the hope—usually to prove illusory—of striking it rich. Caricatures, like Currier and Ives's *Independent Gold Hunter on His Way to California,* 1850, laughed at the impractical optimism of the nation's new universal man—the gold seeker [184].

The New York painter William Sidney Mount, who had been depicting American farmers as slightly ludicrous for two decades, had his say on the western fever, too. Like Currier's, his point of view was that of the skeptical easterner. In *California News,* 1850, first exhibited as "News from the Gold Dig-

183. John Burgum, *An Express Freight Shipment of Thirty Coaches, April 15, 1868,* circa 1868, oil on canvas, 20 × 40 in. New Hampshire Historical Society, Concord.

184. Nathaniel Currier and James Ives, *The Independent Gold Hunter on His Way to California,* 1850, lithograph, 12⅜ × 8¼ in. Denver Public Library Western History Collection.

gins," Mount presented a gathering on the front porch of a rural post office reacting to material that a man in the foreground is reading from the *New York Daily Tribune* [185]. On the table at which he and another man sit is a prominent note commanding, "CALIFORNIA emigrants, look here!!!" The people on the porch represent a varied lot. At the center of the composition is a young boy, struck with wonder at the news, and behind him a well-dressed man of substance who appears to comment knowingly on the situation. To the left are a young man and woman, the man gesturing toward the newspaper and the woman raising her arms in a gesture combining delight, wishfulness, and feminine passivity. On the right are two characters who will not partake of the benefits of the gold rush: an old man who leans on his cane with wistful regret and a young black man who looks on with interest but turns away from the gathering as though constrained to stop his dreaming. On the wall are notices of ship sailings, the favored passage to California for men who were traveling light (in other words, those heading west simply to "make their pile" and return); on the far left is a sign announcing the sale of a farm and on the far right an advertisement for outfits for gold diggers. The man seated at the right of the table has what seems to be a sailing ticket in his pocket, and thus the partially visible chair across the table from him may be inviting potential "California emigrants" to step up to the table, where a pen, book, and blotter await, and book their passage. Two details complete Mount's representation. Over the post office door is a picture of pigs at a trough. And, as one reviewer noted gleefully, Mount steeped the image in a tonality resembling the gold dust that was on everyone's mind.

Mount did not go to California, but many artists did. Typically they did not take up their paintbrush until their luck as prospectors had run out. When they did begin to make pictures, humor about the experience stood ready to serve them, but they were also so invested in the expertise of mining that they often took great pains to convey its procedures. Charles Nahl, trained in Germany, was one such artist. After his prospecting turned to naught, Nahl moved to Sacramento and then to San Francisco, where he made comic vignettes of miners for periodicals. Many of his other engraved images, however, conveyed information about the mining process for an audience, some of them back east, who were eager to talk expertly about placers, lodes, and sluice boxes.[24] Nahl's painting *Miners in the Sierras,* 1851–52, which he created with Frederick A. Wenderoth, for patron August Heilbron in Sacramento, takes mining very seriously [186]. Its colors suggest the climatic conditions that were friendly to mining outdoors and its large scale, the grandeur of the natural setting. These almost heroic-looking miners are working a pla-

cer, a deposit of gold found loose in sandbars or gravel banks (as distinct from gold deposited in sold form as veins in rocks), and have moved one step beyond simple panning. They have constructed a long tom, a sluice with cleats across the bottom to catch the heavier gold as the gravel and sand are washed out of the narrow box. They have diverted the stream, damming it up with earth and rocks, and are digging deposits from the potentially rich bed and putting them into the tom. To

185. William Sidney Mount, *California News,* 1850, oil on canvas, 21½ × 20¼ in. The Museums at Stony Brook, New York; gift of Mr. and Mrs. Ward Melville, 1955.

carry out such a process miners typically had to wait until June or July, when the rivers had receded from the spring vigor. Then they worked at a temporary dam for weeks, hoping that once it was complete they could strip the river bottom of its gold before the return of the rains. A procedure often undertaken by large companies, it is carried out in this picture by four miners who have tackled a small stream. A cabin in the background suggests that they live nearby, where they could guard their stake, and clothes on the line and smoke in the chimney imply that a woman is on the scene or at least someone who is meeting their domestic needs. The miners themselves are long-haired and bearded (the young man at the near end of the sluice, however, is beardless) and wear high boots, shirts and pants that have seen hard service, and old hats. In this regard Nahl met the expectations of virtually any viewer who had heard about miners. This was the appearance associated with these men, as–

186. Charles Nahl with Frederick A. Wenderoth, *Miners in the Sierras,* 1851–52, oil on canvas, 54¼ × 67 in. National Museum of American Art, Smithsonian Institution, Washington, D.C.; gift from Fred Heilbron Collection.

sessed as admirably sensible by some and as a curiosity by others.

Whereas Nahl's picture shows miners as Anglo-Saxon, working their claim with diligence and a kind of cooperative individualism, a substantial mining population in California was from other heritages. One of the most notable was the Spanish—from Mexico, Peru, and Chile. Painters represented this group as anything but enterprising and independent. Rather than portraying them directly as lazy, however, artists assumed the viewpoint of tourists and emphasized the local color of the miners' customs. Alexander Edouart's *Blessing of the Enrequita Mine, New Almaden*, 1860, is an excellent example [187]. The New Almaden mines, south of San Francisco Bay, not far from San Jose (and named after a quicksilver mine in Almadén, Spain), extracted quicksilver, or mercury, which was used in gold washing.[25] Worked by Mexicans, the mines at New Almaden were a favorite tourist stop from 1850 on; two round-trip coach lines were made daily from nearby San Jose.[26] The Enrequita mine in particular had begun continuous mining of quicksilver in 1859, its product in increasing demand by miners who had already harvested the most accessible gold in the placer deposits.

Edouart pictured an activity that had become an annual tourist attraction: the blessing of the mine by the Catholic curate from San Jose. The miners, all Roman Catholic, had made the first cavity in the mine into a chapel dedicated to the Virgin of Guadalupe; there they prayed and sang Ave Marias on their way to and from work. Each year the shrine, the miners, and their enterprise received a ritual blessing.

Edouart's painting takes the viewpoint of the tourist: some figures bow their knees in religious devotion and others, gaily dressed spectators in the foreground, simply observe the activities. With the onlookers mediating our perception of the scene, the pious, even superstitious miners become the other. One who had enjoyed the ceremony reported,

On the morning of the day set apart for this ceremony (which took place on the Feastday of San Antonio, the patron saint of the mine) . . . the Mexican and Chilean señors and señoras began to flock into the little village at the foot of the canyon, from all the surrounding country, in anticipation of a general holiday, at an early hour. The Catholic curate arrived in procession, performed mass, and formally blessed the mine and all who worked in it, during which service a band of musicians was playing a number of airs. At the close, fire-crackers and the boom of a gun cut in the ground, announced the conclusion of the ceremony on the outside; when they all repaired to the inside, where the Father proceeded to sprinkle holy water, and to bless it. Afterward, the more than two hundred participants and guests went to the residence of the proprietor, a Mr. Laurencel, where on tables under overarching sycamore trees they feasted and drank. The upper classes were entertained inside the home. Then [outside] there was music, dancing, and demonstrations of horsemanship.[27]

Edouart's painting formed the basis for an engraving illustrating the popular travel book *Scenes of Wonder and Curiosity in California* (1876).

Just as Whittredge's landscape painting of Santa Fe [see 175] conveys his attitude toward Indian and Mexican cultures as alien, so paintings in California of those of such heritages were typically condescending and form part of a group in which we can assess the Edouart. For instance, in Nahl's *Sunday Morning in the Mines*, 1872, three miners who seem to be Anglo-Saxon are studying the scriptures and one serious-looking young man inside the cottage is writing; all the others, who seem to be of Mexican descent, are fully devoting themselves to roughhousing and pleasure [188]. Another image by Nahl is close to the tourist-

187. Alexander Edouart,
*Blessing of the Enrequita Mine,
New Almaden, California,*
1860, oil on canvas mounted
on fiberboard, 29½ × 47½
in. Bancroft Library, University of California, Berkeley;
The Robert B. Honeyman,
Jr., Collection.

188. Charles Nahl, *Sunday
Morning in the Mines,* 1872, oil
on canvas, 72 × 108 in.
Crocker Art Museum,
Sacramento.

attraction motif put forward by Edouart. In
Nahl's *Sunday Morning in Monterey,* 1874, two
Mexican horsemen perform tricks to impress
an audience of loafers [189]. Circling the performance, some on their way to a bull fight in
the upper part of the painting, are dark, stereo-
typically suspect types: a flirting man and
woman; a dark woman making tortillas behind
whom is a dark-skinned man lounging; a ton-
sured friar or monk buying from the tortilla
vendor, who wears a low-cut blouse. In the
left foreground two men on horseback assess
the scene; wearing Mexican clothing, they
nonetheless seem to be tourists in this scene of
joyful profligacy and irresponsibility.

This condescension toward Mexicans and

South Americans is quite clear in the judgment by one commentator on the mines, who, after reporting the typical pay of the miners, told an eastern readership,

These wages seem to be very just and liberal, yet, such is [the workers'] improvidence, that no matter how much they earn, the miners are not one *peso* better off at the end of the month than they were at its beginning. . . . [Mexicans] are, perhaps, the most impracticable people in the world, going on as their fathers did before them, firmly believing in the axiom, that "sufficient unto the day is the evil thereof."[28]

For the most part, mining was pictured as an individual enterprise. Yet mining on its most productive scale was the work of entrepreneurs who organized human and material resources into companies. The painting *Mining in the Boise Basin in the Early Seventies,* circa 1870–80, conveys the hierarchical, carefully organized nature of large-scale mining [190]. Gold was found in the Boise Basin of Idaho in 1862, and during the first two years of its exploitation the population reached its height. As soon as the more obvious placer gold was exhausted, mining groups stepped in to undertake a more arduous kind of exploitation: hydraulic mining.[29] This process involved washing away the gravel deposits on the mountainsides to carry the gold-laden dirt down to where it could be shoveled and run through sluices. The water aimed at the deposits had to be under very high pressure. This was achieved by building flumes through which water would be conducted to the top of a high hill, lead pipes through which it would fall under tremendous pressure, and hoses through which the pressurized water would be aimed at the deposits. This type of mining was expensive and required a large amount of water, a steep slope, and a trained and coordinated labor force.

As we see in Mrs. Jonas W. Brown's *Mining in the Boise Basin,* this mining operation was impressive as evidence of technological progress but hardly pretty. On this site it created a huge canyon amid a light green landscape with gentle hills. The labor and class relationships in Brown's picture of the Boise Basin mark this type of mining as quite different from that of the small community of miners in Nahl's *Miners in the Sierras* [see 186]. First, the labor is not manual but mechanical and a large investment in equipment is required in getting the water to the top of the slope in hoses. Second, distinct classes of people are involved in the enterprise. Men identically dressed in light-colored raincoats and hats are in the gulch working the hoses. There is none of the individuality in attire and function that prevails in the Nahl picture. And three men in suits stand on the top of the ridge in supervisory capacities. They are doing nothing but

189. Charles Nahl, *Sunday Morning in Monterey,* 1874, oil on canvas, 71 × 112 in. The Santa Barbara Museum of Art, California; gift of Mrs. Silsby M. Spalding.

looking on. As though to emphasize their privileged position, two women stand nearby, making social pleasure out of observing the complex operation.

Just how exploitative this mining was, of both worker and land, is revealed in a travel article that appeared in *Beadle's Monthly* in August 1866. Describing the power of the water played against the walls of the canyon, the traveler wrote:

It would knock down a brick building as if it were a child's cob-house. At ten feet from the nozzle it would cut through a man like a cannon-ball. At forty feet it would crush him to jelly. Directed against the side of a hill, it sends clouds of earth and boulders flying in every direction, bores into the compact gravel like a huge augur, and penetrates the narrowest crevices of rocks, loosening and bringing down fragments like sugar-hogsheads. At the bottom, laborers stand in water up to the thighs, clearing away the debris, which the stream washes, rocks and all, into the flume. . . . Sometimes the undermined hills cave in, and bury the laborers. While working, they glance up uneasily at the melting hill, which, any instant, may fall upon them. Three of these streams will cut down and wash away a section of hill twenty feet long, twenty wide and two hundred high, in twelve hours.[30]

Citizens who lived in mining towns, whether near company operations or individual stakes, and eastern travelers who visited these communities assessed them in various ways. Amid mining's heyday writers from the east tended to romanticize it. Mark Twain in *Roughing It* (1872) treated the mining camp as exuberant, chicanerous, and dubious but altogether healthy. Testimony from some who lived in the mining towns was not sanguine, such as the warning of Emily Meredith in 1863 about her experience in two Montana mining camps: "I never would advise anyone to come to a new mining country because there is a great deal of risk and a great deal to endure."[31] Yet other eastern travelers thought sure they

190. Mrs. Jonas W. Brown,
Mining in the Boise Basin in the Early Seventies, circa 1870–80, oil on canvas, 27 × 21 in. Idaho State Historical Society, Boise.

found evidence of gentility. Sara Lippincott, for instance, who wrote as Grace Greenwood, visited several mining towns in Colorado and reported:

Young as it is,—scarcely a year old,—there are evidences here of prevailing ideas of comfort and taste. . . . That evening we sat down to supper with a goodly company of "honest miners" men in rough clothes and heavy boots, with hard hands and with faces well bronzed, but strong, earnest, intelligent. It was to me a communion with the bravest humanity of the age,—the vanguard of civilization and honorable enterprise.[32]

Such commentary, many felt, was a kind of whistling in the dark. For although mining was a means toward wealth and evidence of the power of technical know-how and persistence to lead one to a new life, the exploitation of mineral wealth was usually associated with instability. The population who sought riches typically rushed in and established themselves during the first months after the discovery of gold, stayed while the mining was good, and then left. As one New England woman who lived in the Feather River mines, north of Sacramento, in 1851–52 observed, "Our countrymen are the most discontented of mortals. They are always longing for 'big strikes.' If a 'claim' is paying them a steady income, by which, if they pleased, they could lay up more in a month than they could accumulate in a year at home, still, they are dissatisfied, and, in most cases, will wander off in search of better 'diggings.' "[33] Towns often survived for less than six years, some only for one year. A writer noted ruefully in 1863 about the fate of Scotts Bar, California: "But the placers are mostly worked out, the population has started after new mines and fresh excitements, over half the houses are empty, four-fifths of the population gone, business has decayed, and the

town is dilapidated."[34] The quick playing out of the gold resulted also in the gambling of the fortunes of a community and of the merchants, tradespeople, doctors, teachers, and investors who had staked themselves on it.

Sometimes, however, mining towns attracted lumbering, trade, manufacturing, and agriculture, all of which survived long after the gold fever had died down. Many a farmer had earlier been a miner. Some mining communities were successful in attracting a railroad, and this meant that after the railroad had been used to carry gold back to depositories and bring in equipment and supplies, it was utilized to connect the new enterprises of the town with regions elsewhere.

Claiming the Fruit of the Earth

Whereas mining was arguably a get-rich-quick investment, settlers who took up agriculture felt themselves to be carrying out the fundamental task of Americans—to make the nation a garden. Much of the early rhetoric about the West, in fact, proclaimed it would become a rural paradise that would extend the agrarian society of the East. While many citizens headed west in search of immediate wealth in the form of minerals and others went as merchants and tradespeople to exploit the commercial potential of the West, most permanent settlers went as farmers. In nearly simultaneous waves of farming settlement during the 1850s and 1860s, arrivals learned to work the plains of Kansas and Nebraska while their counterparts who had journeyed to Oregon and California were adapting to the requirements and possibilities of agriculture there. Representations of farming and of emigrants who bound their lives to the soil assert that commitment, pride, and even grandeur are intimately involved in the agricultural process.

Olof Krans's *Sowing Grain at Bishop Hill,* circa 1896, pays tribute to the simplest and most time-honored activity in making the earth fruitful—that of preparing the ground and sowing grain [191]. Bishop Hill colony in Illinois was established by Swedish Lutherans in 1846. Over a nine-year period about fifteen hundred Erik Janssonists, a sect seeking religious freedom, came to the community by way of Buffalo and the Great Lakes, walking on foot from Chicago.[35] Krans records the planting season, conveying the community's devotion to an ordered, simple life. Across the background, just in front of the horizon line, seven farmers guide plows pulled by two-mule teams. In the foreground three men sow seed on prepared ground. The painting may be a kind of portrait of the entire working community, or it may simply celebrate with these few figures the sect's devotion to communal labor. A curious aspect of the work is the woman in the right foreground, who, with a long stick in her right hand, seems to be present in a supervisory capacity, or perhaps she looks out at the viewer to vouch for the authenticity of the scene.

As agriculture was the basic livelihood of utopian communities and group settlements, so it was also the first resource of most individuals who moved west. To homestead was to farm. The successful weathering of several seasons of farming—especially in environments so totally different from any that the pioneers had previously experienced—was cause for rejoicing. Sallie Cover, who settled in Garfield County, Nebraska, in the 1880s, seems to have done just that in painting the sod house and farm of her neighbor in *Homestead of Ellsworth L. Ball,* circa 1880–90 [192].

The Balls had apparently recently finished a new sod house. Citizens moving west in the 1850s began to outdistance the forest with the settlement of the Kansas-Nebraska territory. Without timber to construct wood houses, they used what was available—sod and grass. Typically they first made structures dug out of the hillside in which they would live and keep their livestock and equipment. The walls away from the hill were constructed of blocks of sod and the roof from poles, brush, grass, and a final layer of dirt. Later, when prosperity began to set in, they would construct a separate sod house, typically sixteen feet wide and twenty feet long, containing two rooms and a fireplace in the middle.[36] The roof would be finished with blocks of sod, laid grass side down, and it was not long before wild grass and flowers bloomed from the roof. Despite their inconveniences—they were dark, close, and particularly messy and uncomfortable when it rained—sod houses were warm in the

191. Olof Krans, *Sowing Grain at Bishop Hill,* circa 1896, oil on canvas, 35 × 47 in. Bishop Hill State Historic Site, Historic Preservation Agency, Illinois.

winter and safe from fire and wind. These
were no small advantages. Moreover, as one
pioneer claimed proudly, they were "made
without mortar, square, plumb, or
greenbacks."[37]

Cover's painting represents an ideal stage
in the lives of her neighbors. She seems to
have been a self-taught artist, employing in this
picture the sense of color and design that she
might have brought to needlework. She placed
each occupant of her neighbors' household in a
proprietary position. Mrs. Ball sits near her
front door with a baby in her lap and a very
young child at her side. Behind her are the
neatly curtained windows of her house and in
front are orderly rows of trees and flowers that
proclaim her as a genteel person who cherishes
beauty. Indeed she has made the dessert
bloom. While Mrs. Ball is the domestic half of
the partnership, her husband manages the animals, mechanical conveniences, and farming.
He stands in the middle depth of the right side
of the picture with a two-horse team and red
buggy. Behind him is a long sod shed and behind that is a very large field in which at least
two grains are being grown. Haycocks over to
the right testify to a successful harvest. Two
other figures people the landscape, suggesting
that the Balls' homestead is an enterprise of no
small scale. Just how selective and flattering
Cover's image is can be noted by comparing it
with the photograph by Solomon Butcher,
John Curry Sod House near West Union, circa
1886 [193]. Butcher depicts the Currys' pride
in possessing a number of objects that make
life more comfortable—such products of eastern manufacturing as factory-produced furniture, metal birdcage, and sewing machine.
Cover, in comparison, was discreet about the
Balls' possessions but flattering about the order
and scope of their homestead.

Few contrasts were more dramatic than
that between the individual homesteads in the

Midwest and the large holdings in the Far
West. California agriculture was distinctive for
being, with the arrival of Anglo settlers, highly
mechanized. With the coming of huge numbers
of people during the gold rush and then in the
1860s with the decline of mining, agriculture
became a mainstay, with wheat and barley the
primary crops.[38] California's climate and topography presented conditions ideal for agricultural production. The first area of large-scale
farming was in northern California because of
the proximity of water transportation for ex-
port, but the availability of railroad transportation in the 1860s led to large-scale farming
throughout the state.

Artists who represented California agriculture seem to have made the images primarily

192. Sallie Cover, *Homestead
of Ellsworth L. Ball,* circa
1880–90, oil on canvas, 19½
× 23 in. Nebraska State Historical Society, Lincoln.

for local audiences. They caught a number of currents. One was the reliance of most large-scale agriculturalists on immigrant labor. Thomas Hill's *Irrigating at Strawberry Farm,* circa 1865, for example, shows Chinese workers in a strawberry field under the supervision of an overseer [194]. While the image conveys the stratification of labor, it also vouches for the place that Chinese immigrants had carved out for themselves very quickly after first coming to California after the discovery of gold. Many who headed from San Francisco for the mine fields took up occupations other than mining (as laundrymen, laborers, cooks, barbers, and servants); others thereafter were employed as laborers in the building of railroads; from about 1865 large numbers began to work in agriculture as well as in manufacturing, milling, and sea industries. In the San Francisco

193. Solomon Butcher, *John Curry Sod House near West Union, Custer County, Nebraska,* circa 1886, print from glass-plate negative, 6½ × 8½ in. Nebraska State Historical Society, Lincoln.

area many became expert truck gardeners, raising their produce often on leased lands and marketing it to urban clients.[39] In the mid-1860s landholders facilitated the move of Chinese agricultural workers into the cultivation of strawberries as sharecroppers. Extremely labor-intensive, strawberry farming required one worker for every two acres of vines and during picking season the average-size fifteen-acre farm needed forty-five workers.[40] The laborers in Hill's picture may well be collective owners of their enterprise, as are the vegetable vendors depicted in Hahn's San Francisco *Market Scene* [see 178].

Hill achieved a reputation as an agricultural landscapist, and one can see why landowners appreciated him. In *Irrigating at Strawberry Farm* the specific circumstances of the commission and thus of the location have been lost, although the mountains in the background are clearly the foothills near the coast. Hill's picture compliments the landowner in several regards. The estate just beyond the clump of trees is regal, embodying Spanish style. The canal irrigating the fields is also used for pleasure, as one sees by the family grouping and small gazebolike shelter in the left middle ground. Attired in his impressive best, the head of the enterprise supervises closely his crew of five; only he is turned toward us and we see the laborers from the back. Thus the viewpoint, as of most pictures of this type, is that of the entrepreneur who has made it.

Whereas strawberry cultivation takes place on a small scale, the procedure under way in Andrew Putnam Hill's *George W. Hoag's Record Wheat Harvest,* 1876, is a monument to agriculture as spectacle [195]. Agricultural practices in large land holdings in California represented the latest achievements in the United States. Bonanza farming of wheat was an impressive union of mechanization, entrepreneurship, and ambition. Transportation of wheat down the

194. Thomas Hill, *Irrigating at Strawberry Farm,* circa 1865, oil on board, 12½ × 19 in. Bancroft Library, University of California, Berkeley; The Robert B. Honeyman, Jr., Collection.

Sacramento River enabled farmers to ship it all over the world, and there was a ready market for it in an era when grain crops elsewhere were failing.

Originally from New York, George Hoag was one of several farmer-machinists who schemed and tinkered to increase agricultural productivity. He set up shop on acreage he had leased from Dr. Hugh J. Glenn, the major landholder in Colusa County, northwest of Sacramento, where he had as many as fifty machinists working at seven forges to keep harvesters, mowers, and steam engines working at top speed.[41] During 1874 he devised the monster thresher called the Monitor that became one of the most famous of all the California in-ventions: it incorporated three threshers bolted together with a feeder attached; the thirty-five-foot long, thirteen-foot high separator was painted red. In August 1874 the Monitor set a world record, sacking 5,779 bushels of wheat in twelve hours. The attending crew consisted of fifty-six men (including Chinese, who per-formed the manual labor of bagging the wheat and carrying away the chaff), ninety-six horses and mules, and numerous other machines and wagons.

The next year Hoag commissioned the painter Andrew Hill to memorialize the record. Hill spent July 1875 making sketches of the harvest currently underway. In paying tribute to the bonanza harvest Hill attempted to pic-

195. Andrew Putnam Hill, *George W. Hoag's Record Wheat Harvest,* 1876, oil on canvas, 34 × 48 in. Donald F. Houghton, Saint Helena, California.

196. After Andrew Putnam Hill, *George Hoag's Steam Threshing Outfit and Crew Setting New One-day World's Record,* 1878, lithograph, 26 × 34⅞ in. F. Hal Higgins Library of Agricultural Technology, University of California, Davis.

ture as much of the enterprise as possible. That the fundamental achievement is Hoag's, however, is not in doubt: the red Monitor has the position of honor in the middle ground of the painting, but in the foreground, clearly claiming pride of invention, is George Hoag, driving a black buggy pulled by an impressive team of trotting horses. This vision of California agriculture as a technological triumph was lithographed and in turn incorporated in 1878 into a persuasive advertisement for agricultural warehouses [196].[42]

In contrast to Hill's construction, William Hahn, in *Harvest Time,* 1875, presented a considerably more relaxed, traditional scene [197]. The territory depicted is also in the Sacramento Valley. On the left, a thresher is powered by teams of horses and mules, and on the right, a separator, also driven by horsepower, is fed loads of grain brought in from the fields. The earthen red separator provides the major color element in an image dominated by dry, golden browns. On the far right, sacks of grain await shipment downriver or possibly by rail to world markets. The pictures by Hill and Hahn emphasize the distinct difference between the frenetic, production-line character of harvesting Hoag's bonanza crop and the more humanly paced enterprise in *Harvest Time*. In Hill's image, wagons full of grain encircle the scene and presumably continue beyond the picture to the right; in Hahn's canvas only two old-fashioned wagons stand by. Contributing to the calm of Hahn's picture is the presence of three children on the right, who, along with their dog, have made the occasion festive and family-oriented.

Hill, who worked in his early years as a carriage painter, pursued a career as a landscapist in both New England and California, riding the crest as well as the trough of the market for landscapes. During the 1870s he was enormously successful in California, until patrons lost interest in local scenes and began to collect

197. William Hahn, *Harvest Time,* 1875, oil on canvas, 36 × 70 in. The Fine Arts Museums of San Francisco; gift of Mrs. Harold R. McKinnon and Mrs. Harry L. Brown.

198. Thomas Hill, *California,* 1879, oil on canvas, 42 × 70¼ in. Alice and Paul Elcano, Reno, Nevada.

works from Europe. Hill's large painting *California,* 1879, completed when patronage was waning, highlights another aspect of the state's prosperity—cattle ranching [198]. In this view, spread out across a low foreground, beyond which foothills and then mountains rise in the distance, Hill depicts a Mexican horseman tending cattle. The picture is dominated by the browns and golds of California's inland valleys. Although the raising of cattle had been pursued by Mexican rancheros before California entered the Union, Anglo businessmen transformed the industry with the importation of American cattle and techniques for raising them on the Great Plains. Hill's painting combines the old and new: the cattle are the fat

American breeds of the period after the 1850s, but the vast area across which they graze suggests a land that will always remain open. Hahn's canvas conveys a spaciousness and a leisure in the pursuit of work that is absent in his pictures of city life.

The story these pictures tell is that of the winners in the West. From Missouri to Nebraska to California, with activities from electioneering to mining to farming, artists showed diverse viewers that the social world of the West was full of promise. There the disciplined settler flourished, gentility went hand-in-hand with technical expertise, and, above all, energy and hard work were rewarded.

Notes

1. For studies of the ideology of western expansion, see Limerick, *Legacy of Conquest;* Slotkin, *Fatal Environment*; and idem, *Regeneration through Violence*. I have also drawn with some modification on Earl Pomeroy, "Toward a Reorientation of Western History: Continuity and Environment," *Mississippi Valley Historical Review* 41, no. 4 (March 1955): 579–600. Pomeroy proposed an alternative to the frontier thesis of 1893 by Frederick Jackson Turner, which analyzed the western environment as producing a new type of character. For a case study, see R. A. Burchell, "The Character and Function of a Pioneer Elite: Rural California, 1848–1880," *Journal of American Studies* 15, no. 3 (December 1981): 377–90. For surveys of paintings of the West, see Amon Carter Museum, *American Frontier Life;* Glanz, *How the West Was Drawn;* Goetzmann and Goetzmann, *West of the Imagination;* and Hills, *American Frontier*.

2. On Missouri, see Duane Meyer, *The Heritage of Missouri: A History* (Saint Louis: State Publishing, 1973); and Paul C. Nagel, *Missouri: A Bicentennial History* (New York: Norton, 1977). On George Caleb Bingham, see Bloch, *Bingham Catalogue Raisonné;* and McDermott, *Bingham*. In addition, see Tyler, "Bingham," 25–49.

3. Bingham had earlier made two images like this one; this painting seems to have been the source of a lithograph by Claude Regnier, published by M. Knoedler in New York in 1853. Earlier versions are *Country Politician*, 1849 (The Fine Arts Museums of San Francisco), and *Listening to the Wilmot Proviso* (unlocated). See Bloch, *Bingham Catalogue Raisonné*, nos. 198 and 180, respectively.

4. When Bingham painted a second version of the scene in order to have an image for the engraver as well as one with which to recruit subscriptions, he omitted a figure on the courthouse steps who tosses a coin. This activity perhaps too strongly tilted the viewers' disposition to disapprove of democratic politics as irrational.

5. Bingham to C. B. Rollins, November 7, 1853, in Rollins, "Letters of George Caleb Bingham to James S. Rollins," 17.

6. Rollins to A. Warner, Columbia, Missouri, January 11, 1852 (quoted in Tyler, "Bingham," 38).

7. Bingham to Rollins, November 23, 1853, in Rollins, "Letters of George Caleb Bingham to James S. Rollins," 169.

8. See Wayne Gard, *Frontier Justice* (Norman: University of Oklahoma Press, 1949); and Philip Jordan, *Frontier Law and Order: Ten Essays* (Lincoln: University of Nebraska Press, 1970).

9. Bloch, *Bingham Catalogue Raisonné*, 240.

10. Until recently it was believed that the picture had been commissioned by Leland Stanford and that included in the scene are such luminous friends as the philosopher Josiah Royce, naturalist John Muir, geologist Joseph LeConte, and writer Charles Warren Stoddard (Hough, *California's Western Heritage,* 56).

11. Quoted in Joseph Schafer, *The Social History of American Agriculture* (New York: Macmillan, 1936), 3.

12. On California, see David Lavender, *California: A Bicentennial History* (New York: Norton, 1976); and Starr, *Americans and the California Dream*.

13. Museum of Fine Arts, *Frontier America: The Far West* (Boston, 1975), 126.

14. Tyler, *Visions of America,* 201.

15. Mark Twain, *Life on the Mississippi* (1883) (quoted in Tyler, *Visions of America,* 105).

16. Hassrick, *Way West,* 100.

17. Oliver W. Holmes and Peter T. Rohrbach, *Stagecoach East: Stagecoach Days in the East from the Colonial Period to the Civil War* (Washington, D.C.: Smithsonian Institution Press, 1983).

18. John Theobald and Lillian Theobald, *Wells Fargo in Arizona Territory* (Tempe: Arizona Historical Foundation, 1978), 3.

19. Advertisement in W. Turrentine Jackson, *Wells Fargo & Co. in Idaho Territory* (Boise: Idaho State Historical Society, 1984), 20.

20. *Denver Rocky Mountain News,* June 1, 1867 (quoted in W. Turrentine Jackson, *Wells Fargo in Colorado Territory* [Denver: Colorado Historical Society, 1982], 34).

21. On mining, see Paul, *California Gold;* idem, *Mining Frontiers;* Rohe, "Western Mining Town"; Duane A. Smith, *Rocky Mountain Mining Camps: The Urban Frontier* (Bloomington: Indiana University Press, 1967).

22. *California Star* (San Francisco), May 20, 1848

(quoted in Paul, *Mining Frontiers,* 13–14).

23. Population figures quoted in Paul, *Mining Frontiers,* 15–17.

24. The lithography firm of Anthony and Baker published a number of wood engravings from Charles Nahl's drawings; for examples, see ibid., illustrations following 108.

25. Quicksilver amalgamated with gold, excluding foreign matter; the subsequent vaporizing of the mercury in a retort would result in pure gold.

26. Henry Winfred Splitter, "Quicksilver at New Almaden," *Pacific Historical Review* 26, no. 1 (February 1957): 33–50.

27. Reported as the correspondence from "a friend" in Hutchings, *Scenes of Wonder and Curiosity in California,* 198–202.

28. Ibid., 197.

29. By 1870 Chinese immigrants were the major group involved in placer mining, the highest percentage among miners in any part of the country (see Paul, *Mining Frontiers,* 138–44).

30. Albert D. Richardson, "Nevada and California," *Beadle's Monthly* 2, no. 7 (August 1866): 101–15.

31. Quoted in Duane Allan Smith, "Mining Camps: Myth vs. Reality," *Colorado Magazine* 44, no. 2 (1967): 108.

32. Grace Greenwood [Sara Lippincott], *New Life in New Lands* (New York: Ford, 1873), 80–81.

33. Quoted in Paul, *Mining Frontiers,* 27.

34. Quoted in Rohe, "Western Mining Town," 114.

35. Eric Norelius, *The Pioneer Swedish Settlements and Swedish Lutheran Churches in America, 1845–1860,* trans. Conrad Bergendoff (Rock Island, Ill.: Augustana Historical Society, 1984), 11–13.

36. Everett Dick, *The Sod-House Frontier, 1854–1890* (New York: Appleton, 1937), 113.

37. Ibid., 114.

38. Ellen Liebman, *California Farmland: A History of Large Agricultural Landholdings* (Totowa, N.J.: Rowman & Allanheld, 1983), 16.

39. Chan, *This Bitter-sweet Soil,* 124–31; and Donald J. Pisani, *From the Family Farm to Agribusiness: The Irrigation Crusade in California and the West, 1850–1931* (Berkeley: University of California Press, 1984).

40. Chan, *This Bitter-sweet Soil,* 129.

41. Richard Steven Street, "Mystery Achievement," *California Farmer* (February 1, 1987): 8.

42. Reproduced in Hassrick, *Way West,* fig. 146. A report of the painting and a review of the harvest appeared in *Wagon Wheels: Colusa County Historical Society* 1, no. 2 (August 1951): 1.

5

"The Kiss of Enterprise"

The Western Landscape as Symbol and Resource

NANCY K. ANDERSON

In the summer of 1870 American landscape painter Sanford R. Gifford, in company with fellow artists Worthington Whittredge and John F. Kensett, traveled to the Colorado Rockies aboard the recently completed transcontinental railroad.[1] Both Whittredge and Kensett had ventured west on earlier journeys, but for Gifford the 1870 trip was a first. An accomplished landscape painter in search of new subject matter, Gifford had come west to "mine" the landscape as surely as any argonaut who came looking for California gold. For Gifford and other landscape painters who came west on trails blazed by forty-niners, the western landscape was a natural resource, a raw material, that could be used to construct seductively beautiful works of art that reflected in both direct and subtle ways, the material and spiritual needs of the culture that gave them birth.

Gifford and his companions arrived in Denver early in August 1870. Their timing was fortuitous, for in Denver Gifford met F. V. Hayden, director of the United States Geo-logical Survey. In Hayden the twin enthusiasms of the age of exploration were united. A serious and exacting scientist, Hayden was also an unabashed believer in the beneficial effects of progress. A man of enormous energy, Hayden had begun "surveying" the West before the government gave the activity official bureaucratic sanction. As early as 1862 he declared that his ambition was to lead a government-sponsored geological survey that would "lay before the public such full, accurate, and reliable information . . . as will bring from the older states the capital, skill, and enterprise necessary to develop the great natural resources of the country."[2] When the geologist and artist met in Denver, Hayden was about to depart for Wyoming Territory to lead a survey party on just such a mission and he invited Gifford to join the group as his guest. Recognizing a golden opportunity, Gifford quickly accepted Hayden's offer. Within days the two men had arrived at the survey party's base camp near Cheyenne. There Gifford met another member of the team, William H. Jackson, a professional photographer, whom Hayden had persuaded to join the survey with a promise of remarkable scenery and free board. Finding they shared interests in both photography and painting, Gifford and Jackson quickly struck up a friendship.

On August 7, 1870, despite a "cold sleety rain," the survey party broke camp.[3] Two days later Jackson took the photograph that serves as the point of departure for the discussion that follows. Seated before castellated buttes near Chugwater Creek in southeastern Wyoming, Gifford, his color box on his lap, is at work on an oil sketch of the landscape before him [199–200]. Jackson's photograph, a sophisticated work of art in its own right, documents the first step in the process whereby the raw material, the western landscape, was

199. William H. Jackson, *Castellated Rocks on the Chugwater, S. R. Gifford, Artist,* 1870, albumen print, 5 × 7¼ in. International Museum of Photography at George Eastman House, Rochester, New York.

200. Sanford R. Gifford, *Valley of the Chugwater, Wyoming Territory,* 1870, oil on canvas, 7¾ × 12⅞ in. Amon Carter Museum, Fort Worth, Texas.

transformed into both a work of art that conveyed cultural messages and a commodity exchanged in a commercial market.

Years later Jackson turned the tables and had a similar record made of his own pursuit of the western landscape [201]. This self-conscious attempt to document the "truth" of the image secured in the field was carried to its limit when Christian Jorgensen, a California landscape painter, had himself photographed (in full western costume) painting a plein air

201. Unidentified photographer, *William H. Jackson Perched on Glacier Point, Composing a Panorama of the Yosemite Valley*, circa 1888, albumen print, 7³⁄₁₆ × 4¹⁄₈ in. Colorado Historical Society, Denver.

landscape while standing, with admirable aplomb, aboard a portable studio hitched to a team of horses [202].

Such insistent efforts by artists to document their confrontation with the western landscape represent thinly veiled attempts to promote their work as an accurate (that is, literal) transcription of the landscape. In fact, for artists like Gifford, the plein air sketch was simply the first step in a much longer process that was more often than not completed far from the western frontier.

In studios like those of Gifford's contemporaries Albert Bierstadt and Thomas Hill, artists who had traveled west combined and edited the field sketches, color studies, and photographs they had gathered, to produce paintings that in their constructed artifice carried cultural messages [203–4]. As unique and isolated objects, however, the finished paintings do not disclose the artist's compositional and editing decisions. We see only what is on the canvas, we do not see what has been excised, and conversely, we may not be conscious of what fabricated elements have been added.

To explore the range of meanings conveyed by western landscapes produced during the nineteenth century, four groups of images related to four different but representative western landscape subjects (Wyoming's Green River cliffs, the Colorado River and Grand Canyon, Donner Pass in the Sierra Nevada, and the big tree groves of California) have been selected as the focus of discussion. By juxtaposing drawings, sketches, photographs, popular illustrations, advertisements, and studio paintings that represent these subjects, some of the process whereby artists edited raw material and constructed western landscape paintings to convey certain messages becomes clear—as does the nature of the message.

Looking at nineteenth-century paintings

with twentieth-century eyes carries unavoidable risk, for the modern viewer is privy to history's judgment, while his nineteenth-century counterpart (both artist and viewer) was charting a new course on untrodden land. Thus many nineteenth-century landscape images, whether photographs, drawings, or illustrations, document practices modern viewers would characterize as exploitative, destructive, and appallingly shortsighted. As modern viewers, however, we must set aside our own concerns (particularly environmental concerns) and recall that following the Civil War, when capital and labor were freed from destructive conflict and redirected toward what was viewed as constructive growth, the American West functioned as both an iconic symbol of national identity and a resource to be used in transforming the nation from a wilderness republic into an industrial power.

This is not to say that thoughtful observers were unaware of the price of progress. On

202. Unidentified photographer, *Christian Jorgensen in Yosemite,* circa 1905, albumen print, 4 × 5 in. Bancroft Library, University of California, Berkeley.

203. Charles Bierstadt, *Interior of Malkasten,* 1866–71, stereograph. Mrs. Orville DeForest Edwards, Dobbs Ferry, New York.

204. Unidentified photographer, *Interior of Thomas Hill's Studio in Yosemite,* after 1886, sepia-toned silver gelatin print, 4¼ × 7 in. The Oakland Museum, California; gift of Cherene Holsinger and James W. Cravagan III.

205. Unidentified photographer, *"The Domes of Yosemite" in the Rotunda of the Lockwood Mansion,* circa 1870, stereograph. Lockwood-Mathews Mansion Museum, Norwalk, Connecticut.

206. Carleton E. Watkins, *Thomas Hill's Paintings in Lick House, San Francisco,* circa 1870, albumen print, 2⅞ × 4⅝ in. William L. Schaeffer, Chester, Connecticut.

the contrary, numerous travelers (including artists) who ventured west during the second half of the nineteenth century commented on "denuded" mountains and ravaged forests; others deplored the effects of mining. As early as 1858, for example, one visitor to California expressed dismay at the devastating effects of hydraulic mining: "The result is a most horrid desolation, of which every line of natural beauty is gone forever. If some camp of demons had been pitched for a year, tearing the earth by their fury, and converting it to the model of their own bad thought, they could hardly make it look worse."[4]

These were not, however, the scenes that appeared in nineteenth-century western landscape paintings. The destruction that progress often left in its wake was rarely addressed overtly in studio paintings. Skillfully crafted and consciously composed for a market interested in the West (often as an investment), most western landscapes carried a conciliatory message implying that the natural and technological sublime were compatible, that the wilderness landscape Americans had used to define themselves and their nation since the seventeenth century could endure as a cultural icon while being converted to economic use.[5]

Such carefully composed messages were frequently directed at particular audiences, for landscape paintings were commercial as well as aesthetic objects. Thus Legrand Lockwood, a wealthy New York financier, who paid Bierstadt fifteen thousand dollars for *The Domes of the Yosemite,* which he installed in his home, and James Lick, who commissioned a series of California landscapes from Thomas Hill for his luxury hotel in San Francisco, saw in western landscapes images that complemented their entrepreneurial drive [205–6].[6] Heavily invested in the development of western resources, such patrons were the principal buyers of large panoramic landscapes that celebrated the grandeur

(and potential) of the land that for them had literally become El Dorado.

Others, lacking the resources of Lockwood or Lick and unable to buy original paintings, were nevertheless induced by the heroic western landscapes of artists like Bierstadt and Thomas Moran to travel great distances to see the mountains and canyons that had inspired the paintings. The tourists that figure so prominently in William Hahn's *Yosemite Valley from Glacier Point,* 1874, and Oscar Berninghaus's *Showery Day, Grand Canyon,* 1915, testify to the power of the images through which such natural wonders were initially introduced to

eastern audiences and to the commercial bonanza the West represented when transformed into a tourist mecca [207–8].

Like the miners, loggers, farmers, and ranchers who traveled cross-country to capitalize on the material resources of the American West, artists like Gifford, Bierstadt, and Moran, journeyed west to mine the landscape for the raw materials from which they fashioned studio paintings. The photographs, lithographs, engravings, illustrations, and advertisements discussed here document the awesome scenic grandeur and enormous economic potential of the West as well as the technological

207. William Hahn, *Yosemite Valley from Glacier Point,* 1874, oil on canvas, 27¼ × 46¼ in. California Historical Society, San Francisco.

208. Oscar Berninghaus, *A Showery Day, Grand Canyon*, 1915, oil on canvas, 30 × 40 in. The Santa Fe Collection of Southwestern Art, Chicago. (Detail illustrated on p. 236.)

achievements of man as he set about conquering the land and converting its riches to his own use. The juxtaposition of these widely varied images allows us to witness some of the editing that took place as artists composed images to meet certain cultural needs and convey particular messages. Minimizing the conflict between the spectacular natural beauty of the land (by midcentury an indelible part of America's self-definition) and the inevitable changes that accompanied the conversion of minerals, forests, and water, the conciliatory message of many studio paintings was that the natural and technological sublime were compatible, that

the West could endure as both a symbol and resource.

Green River, Wyoming

In July 1868, in an area where fur trappers once held their annual rendezvous and Captain Benjamin Bonneville built his first fort, the modern age, in the form of the Union Pacific Railroad, arrived on the banks of the Green River in Wyoming Territory.[7] In a heated race with their Central Pacific counterparts, the construction crews of the Union Pacific were laying between one and three miles of track daily across the Wyoming plains. Leapfrogging from one supply terminus to the next, engineering and construction crews had successively passed through Cheyenne, Laramie, and Benton on their way to Green River. For two decades before the arrival of the railroad, emigrants following the Oregon Trail to the Promised Land had exercised caution in fording the Green River. High water and a fickle current had been known to upturn even a heavily loaded wagon. The men of the Union Pacific, however, were about to take the threat out of the Green River with elevated steel rails. Conquest was at hand; the road to the future would be smooth and fast.

Knowing that progress in laying the rails would be delayed by the necessity of bridging the Green River, speculators had arrived early to lay out a town near the banks of the river. Within eight weeks, two thousand people had arrived hoping to profit from the needs of the construction crews. Traveling with the men of the Union Pacific was Andrew Joseph Russell, a professional photographer who had taken on the task of documenting the progress of the railroad. In 1869 fifty of Russell's photographs were published under the title *The Great West Illustrated*. One of these, *Temporary and Permanent Bridges and Citadel Rock, Green River,* 1868, records the inevitable encounter between the natural and technological sublime in the American West [209].

Russell's photograph clearly celebrates the triumph of technology and human will over a hostile environment. At the far right, the temporary wooden trestle, which allowed the Union Pacific to continue its race to Promontory, Utah, supports crew members and a smoking engine. Near the center of the photograph, additional crew members pose atop stone battlements built to support the more permanent bridge. In the distance, towering

above all, is Citadel Rock, one of the distinctive sandstone buttes through which the Green River carved its path. With an artist's eye, Russell selected his view so that the magnificent rocky tower shaped by the forces of nature is juxtaposed with the man-made structures (the water tower and stone bridge supports), which mimic its form. Acknowledging both the technological triumph of the railroad and the scenic grandeur of the Green River landscape, Russell's photograph records change and progress. As a mediating or conciliatory image, the photograph also suggests that the natural and technological sublime could coexist, that the landscape that had long claimed mythic status in the American imagination was not compromised by the tracks and trestles of the future's messenger.

The domestic changes the railroad brought were seen in a wholly positive light by Eli Sheldon Glover, who produced the view of Green River City, published by the Chicago Lithographic Company sometime after the Union Pacific and Central Pacific railroads were joined at Promontory on May 10, 1869 [210]. Looming above the burgeoning city, as it did in Russell's photograph, is Citadel Rock. At the far left is the completed bridge, which was under construction when Russell took his photograph. The very image of prosperity, Green River City could boast, according to the caption provided by the lithographer, "a School House and Church, several Stores, a First-Class Hotel, and a Brewery." While the castellated buttes surrounding the city speak of the sublimity of the western landscape, schoolhouses, churches, and pleasure boats on the river suggest that the domestication of Green River has begun in earnest. The railroad, economic lifeblood of the community, is firmly established with a major switching yard visible near the riverbank. Two trains, one heading east and the other west, steam off at opposite

209. Andrew Joseph Russell, *Temporary and Permanent Bridges and Citadel Rock, Green River,* 1868, albumen print, 8⅝ × 11½ in. Yale Collection of Western Americana, Beinecke Rare Book and Manuscript Library, New Haven.

210. Eli Sheldon Glover, *View of Green River, Wyoming Territory (Looking North),* circa 1869, tinted lithograph (hand-colored), 15½ × 21⅛ in. New York Public Library, Print Collection, The Miriam and Ira D. Wallach Division of Art, Prints, and Photographs, Astor, Lenox, and Tilden Foundations.

ends of town. A promotional image, the lithograph carries the additional claim that Green River City is located at "the center of the most picturesque portion of the country through which the Union Pacific Railroad passes." Potential travelers are advised that "beautiful Rocky Mountain Specimens of all kinds can be procured" in Green River City. With the advent of the railroad the Green River landscape became quite literally a commodity available for purchase.

In 1871, two years after the transcontinental railroad had been completed and well after Green River City had claimed its place on the map, Thomas Moran journeyed west for the first time. About to join Hayden's expedition to Yellowstone, Moran traveled by rail as far as Green River. Stepping off the train, he found himself standing before a landscape unlike any other. The striated sandstone cliffs with their yellow, orange, red, and lavender bands were ideally suited to a painter who found his inspiration in the color of J. M. W. Turner. Like Yellowstone and the Grand Canyon, Green River was a subject Moran would return to repeatedly over a period of forty years.

Unlike the images produced by Russell and Glover, Moran's Green River paintings did not overtly applaud the technological achievement of the railroad or the advent of civilization in the Far West. Instead Moran focused almost exclusively on the sublimity of the landscape, editing out nearly every reference to change instigated by man.

By 1871, when Moran arrived in Green River City, civilization had taken root, but even in his earliest drawings his attention was drawn to the striated cliffs sculpted by the ancient forces of wind and water. A small watercolor inscribed "First sketch made in the West at Green River, Wyoming 1871" contains only the broadest notation of the landscape's pri-

First sketch made in the West at Green River, Wyoming 1871

211. Thomas Moran, *First Sketch Made in the West at Green River, Wyoming 1871*, 1871, watercolor on paper, 3½ × 7¼ in. Thomas Gilcrease Institute of American History and Art, Tulsa.

212. Thomas Moran, *Cliffs, Green River, Utah*, 1872, watercolor on paper, 6³⁄₁₆ × 11¹¹⁄₁₆ in. Museum of Fine Arts, Boston; M. and M. Karolik Collection.

213. Unidentified photographer, *Green River, Wyoming*, circa 1876. Sweetwater County Historical Museum, Green River, Wyoming.

mary features: the sandstone cliffs, languid river, and sparse trees [211]. There is no sign of human life and not the slightest hint that a hotel and brewery are already in operation a short distance away. What is evident, however, is Moran's early fascination with the colors of the Green River landscape. Although measuring only about four by eight inches, Moran's watercolor sketch is filled with the silver, lavender, and pink that later became far more intense when translated to oil.

The following year Moran returned west to complete a commission for illustrations to be published in *Picturesque America* (1872–74). Once again he traveled to Green River and again he completed a watercolor sketch duplicating the point of view of his earlier study [212]. Larger by several inches (6³⁄₁₆ × 11¹¹⁄₁₆ in.), the second sketch includes far more geologic detail and, in the far distance, a diminutive train. An acknowledgment of recent change, the train is, however, so small it is barely visible. For Moran, neither the railroad nor the burgeoning town that had sprung to life beside the railroad tracks threatened the vast and awesome grandeur of the landscape, for in his art he was free to edit and invent,

preserving on canvas the mythic landscape endowed by history with symbolic as well as economic value [213].

Excised from Moran's Green River landscapes are the bridge celebrated in Jackson's photograph, the tall smokestack that rose in challenge to Castle Butte, and all buildings, whether schoolhouse, hotel, or brewery [214]. Added to the landscapes are bands of exotically clad Indians moving diagonally through the foreground toward camps on the distant horizon [215]. Far from anthropological specimens, however, Moran's Indians inhabit a dreamscape. As he reworked the Green River imagery over a period of years, Moran continued to paint the shimmering landscape of El Dorado as if nothing had changed.

The evolution of Moran's Green River imagery came to full fruition in *Green River Cliffs, Wyoming*, 1881 [216]. When juxtaposed with the artist's first sketch of the Green River landscape, completed a decade earlier, *Green River Cliffs, Wyoming* demonstrates the extent of Moran's studio manipulation. The sandstone buttes have grown in stature, dramatic plays of light and shadow direct the viewer's eye toward the setting sun, and a reconfigured foreground becomes a stage for an Indian caravan winding its way toward a distant village. An ambitious reworking of a landscape he had first sketched a decade earlier, *Green River Cliffs, Wyoming* offers insistent assurance that the ancient grandeur that had inspired the earliest chroniclers of the West remained intact.[8]

Such paintings struck a popular chord and numbered among the artist's most commercially successful works. True testament to the marketability of the subject came in 1881, when a chromolithograph after one of Moran's Green River paintings was published by Prang and Company [217]. Banking on the popular appeal of the image to sell large runs of lithographs, Prang invested commercially in Mor-

214. William H. Jackson, *Green River Butte,* circa 1870, contact print from glass-plate negative, 18 × 22 in. Colorado Historical Society, Denver.

Colorado River and Grand Canyon

In the spring of 1871, three years after Russell photographed the crews of the Union Pacific Railroad constructing a permanent bridge across Wyoming's Green River, John Wesley an's carefully composed assurance that the grandeur of the West had not been compromised by the advent of technological progress.

Powell and the men who would accompany him on his second descent of the Colorado River pushed a flatcar to the east end of the then completed Green River Bridge and unloaded the three handcrafted boats that would carry them on their journey downriver. Built to Powell's specifications in Chicago, the boats had been shipped by rail to Green River City, where Powell, who had become a folk hero after his harrowing descent of the Colorado in 1869, waited to launch a second expedition.[9]

215. Thomas Moran, *Cliffs of the Upper Colorado River, Wyoming Territory*, 1882, oil on canvas, 16 × 24 in. National Museum of American Art, Smithsonian Institution, Washington, D.C.; Ranger Fund.

Although he had done well just to survive the earlier descent, Powell was eager to undertake a second, for he had seen enough of the stratified walls through which the Colorado River carved its path to know he had discovered a geologist's dream. The corrosive action of the river had exposed thousands of years of geologic history.

E. O. Beaman, a professional photographer, was one of ten men Powell selected to accompany him on the expedition. In a clever bit of self-promotion, Beaman placed his camera (its hood displays his name) near the bow of one of the expedition vessels on the day of departure, May 22, 1871 [218]. Chronicler of the first part of the voyage, Beaman took approximately 350 photographs along the expedition route. Beaman's camera (dubbed "the terror of the party"), glass plates, chemicals, and darkroom tent were frequently hauled up rocky cliffs at considerable risk in an attempt

to secure documentary photographs.[10] Once on site, the tent was raised and the glass plates were prepared, exposed, developed, washed, and finally stored in a protective container for transport back to the boat. The process was difficult and tedious, but Powell, who had seen photographs and drawings produced on earlier surveys, understood well the value of a visual record. Powell was, however, ill-served by Beaman, who not only left the expedition early (it is not clear whether he deserted or was fired) but attempted to beat Powell into print with his own illustrated account of the expedition.

Powell was much better served by Thomas Moran. Although not a member of Powell's expedition party, Moran came west to see the Grand Canyon in 1873 (after the descent had been completed) at Powell's invitation. Two years earlier Moran had journeyed west to join Hayden's expedition to Yellow-

216. Thomas Moran, *Green River Cliffs, Wyoming,* 1881, oil on canvas, 25 × 62¼ in. Spring Creek Art Foundation, Inc., Dedham, Massachusetts.

217. After Thomas Moran, *Cliffs of the Upper Colorado River, Wyoming Territory,* 1881, chromolithograph, 12³⁄₁₆ × 7¹⁄₁₆ in. Amon Carter Museum, Fort Worth, Texas.

218. E. O. Beaman, *Before the Start at Green River City, Wyoming,* 1871, albumen print, 4¹⁄₄ × 7¹⁄₄ in. Library of Congress, Washington, D.C.

stone. Fascinated by the colors and canyons of what some had called "Coulter's Hell," Moran returned east and composed a seven-by-twelve-foot painting, *The Grand Canyon of the Yellowstone* [see 41], which so captivated members of Congress that they appropriated ten thousand dollars for its purchase. Aside from establishing Moran's reputation, the picture had done much to aid Hayden in his efforts to secure continued funding for his survey expeditions.[11]

Following that early triumph, Moran began to entertain the notion of painting a pendant for the Yellowstone picture. After listening to Powell describe the Grand Canyon, he rightly suspected that he might find in the canyons of the Colorado River a subject equal in stature to Yellowstone. Powell invited Moran to join him in the Southwest as early as the spring of 1872, but Moran was unable to accept the offer until the summer of the following year.

Early in August 1873, accompanied by John Hillers, who had assumed the role of photographer during the second part of Powell's river expedition, Moran stood above the Grand Canyon for the first time. He later described the moment in a letter to his wife, "On reaching the brink the whole gorge for miles lay beneath us and it was by far the most awfully grand and impressive scene that I have ever yet seen."[12] Moran spent two days sketching near the rim of the canyon at Toroweap. Intrigued by the colors and configuration of the river and its canyons, Moran quickly made preliminary pencil sketches. Elegant in their spare line and brevity, the sketches are dotted with color notes. One such study [219] bears the inscription:

The general color of the Canon is a light Indian red. The upper surfaces gray intermixed with red & going to a yellowish red at the bottom of the Canon. The near rocks of the foreground are a flesh color with gray surfaces & man holes w/ water pockets. Where water lines enter the Canon they are generally white from lime water from the levels above.

Later, with Powell serving as his guide, Moran stood above the canyon (on a plateau the expedition leader had named for himself), gazing out from the spot Powell felt was "the greatest point of view in the Grand Canyon."[13] Moran had found the source for a landscape that could hold its own with his earlier Yellowstone panorama.

While Moran and Powell stood above the canyon a loud, violent thunderstorm swept above them. Sheets of rain dropped from roiling thunderclouds, and as the rain struck the sunbaked canyon walls a heavy, hot mist rose from the rock. Moran later cast the thunderstorm as chief protagonist in *The Chasm of the Colorado*, 1873–74, the seven-by-twelve-foot painting he began shortly after his return east [220]. *The Chasm of the Colorado* is a painting rich in meaning and intricately tied to the thesis of Powell's thoughtful and progressive publication, *Report on the Lands of the Arid Region of the United States* (1878).[14]

Powell's report was the culmination of years spent in the field as a practicing geologist. Although hailed as the Conqueror of the Colorado, Powell had actually done far more than simply ride the white water. He had measured, mapped, and studied the Colorado in an attempt to decipher the geologic textbook the river had laid bare. Among the conclusions he reached was one that challenged the boosters who promoted rapid settlement of the Southwest despite the severe limitations imposed by climate and geography. Powell declared that the low level of rainfall in the Southwest required cooperative land and water management. He understood that the usual system of distributing land for settlement (often 160 acres

marked off on a grid) was not suitable for an area where the single most important resource was water. Powell's topographical studies along the course of the Colorado River taught him that water was both a destructive and redemptive force. The same river that carved a channel through rock, that ate away at the earth's surface leaving enormous chasms, also brought life. Although Moran's enormous painting of the Grand Canyon exalts (in the tradition of nineteenth-century American landscape art) the sheer grandeur of the land itself, *The Chasm of the Colorado* also reflects Moran's understanding of Powell's thesis, for the active components in the picture are water and light, elements that sustain life. The storm and river threaten and nourish simultaneously.

Despite Moran's declaration that he had found the subject for his picture while standing above the canyon at Powell's Plateau, *The*

219. Thomas Moran, *Foot of Toroweap*, 1873, pencil on paper, 10^{13}/$_{16}$ × 14^{15}/$_{16}$ in. Jefferson National Expansion Memorial, National Park Service, Saint Louis.

220. Thomas Moran, *The Chasm of the Colorado*, 1873–74, oil on canvas, 84⅜ × 144¾ in. United States Department of the Interior, Office of the Secretary, Washington, D.C.; on loan to the National Museum of American Art.

Chasm of the Colorado is a composite, a painting constructed from sketches, photographs, and recollections, rather than a strict topographical view. Powell recognized Moran's method and applauded the results, describing the painting as "a most composite picture; a picture of many pictures."[15]

Because of their close association during the early stages of the painting's conception, Moran must have been particularly pleased when Powell praised the picture for its truth, "Mr. Moran has represented the depths and magnitudes and distances and forms and color

and clouds with the greatest fidelity. But his picture not only tells the truth . . . it displays the beauty of the truth."[16] The "truth" Moran's painting told was not universally admired. Although not attacked by critics, *The Chasm of the Colorado* did not enjoy the same enthusiastic reception *The Grand Canyon of the Yellowstone* had received. Nearly every reviewer expressed some reservation about the picture. Clarence Cook, writing in 1874 for the *Atlantic Monthly*, spoke for many when he described the picture as "wanting almost entirely in the beauty" that had distinguished Moran's earlier Yellowstone

221. Timothy O'Sullivan, *Green River Cañon, Junction of Yampah at Green River*, 1872, albumen print, 7¾ × 11 in. American Geographical Society Collection of the Golda Meir Library of the University of Wisconsin, Milwaukee.

painting.[17] Such remarks, however, did not dampen the enthusiasm of Congress. In June 1874 Moran exhibited the painting at the Corcoran Gallery of Art in Washington, D.C.; the following month Congress appropriated ten thousand dollars to purchase the picture. Although clearly a landscape celebrating a uniquely American scene, the painting also made a subtle argument for a cautious and rational approach to the development of the Southwest, an idea Powell championed with little success.

Moran's Green River, Yellowstone, and Grand Canyon landscapes brought the artist substantial financial and professional rewards. They also brought him contracts with railroad companies anxious to promote travel by advertising the scenic wonders that could be seen en route. The most profitable of Moran's corporate relationships was undoubtedly that with the Atchison, Topeka, and Santa Fe Railway, which began late in the 1870s but came to fruition in 1901, when the line was extended to the Grand Canyon.[18] In a cooperative arrangement involving the exchange of pictures for travel and lodging, Moran's paintings of the canyon were placed in parlor cars, hotels, and corporate offices. More important, however, were

222. Timothy O'Sullivan, *Cañon of the Colorado River, near Mouth of San Juan River, Arizona,* 1873, albumen print, 8⅛ × 10³⁄₁₆ in. Boston Public Library, Print Department.

the images that appeared in guidebooks, on posters and calendars, and as chromolithographs. These were distributed widely during various promotional campaigns for the railroad, but they also served to promote the work of Moran. Neither the artist nor the picture-buying public seemed to tire of his Grand Canyon paintings. Following the completion of the railroad spur to the canyon in 1901, Moran returned to the area annually until his death in 1926. During that period he produced hundreds of Grand Canyon paintings for a market that owed at least part of its strength to the tireless promotional efforts of the Atchison, Topeka, and Santa Fe.

Perhaps no other artist matched Moran's success in marketing the Grand Canyon, but the geologic textbook Powell had discovered in the canyons of the Colorado attracted other survey parties and offered numerous artists and photographers the opportunity to document and interpret a landscape unique in its beauty and contribution to science. Among the most talented of those who came to glimpse geologic time, to measure, map, observe, and photograph were Timothy O'Sullivan and William Henry Holmes.

Employed at various times by geologists Clarence King and George Wheeler, O'Sullivan produced a number of extraordinary photographs along the Colorado River. His feel for the panoramic view that contained passages of startling detail is most clearly evident in a photograph taken along the Green River, the upper tributary of the Colorado [221]. In O'Sullivan's image huge swaths of striated stone are upended as if twisted and spun with a giant spatula. Barely dusted with soil and scrub foliage, the rocky cliffs testify to the convulsive birth of the river basin.

In a second image of the Colorado River Canyon, taken near the mouth of the San Juan River in Arizona [222], O'Sullivan placed his camera above the chasm in a position echoing the point of view Moran offered in *The Chasm of the Colorado*. Standing on the rim, looking down into a maze of canyons, O'Sullivan captured the counterpoint of light and shade that defines the massive stone walls blocking clear passage to the river at the center of the image. In the foreground at the right, O'Sullivan found a slight section of delicately layered rock exposed by wind and rain. Silhouetted against the deep shadow of a canyon wall, the sharp brittle layers are stacked in a vertical timeline.

O'Sullivan's beautifully composed photographs are a fitting reminder that many of the images secured on government-sponsored expeditions were so stunning in their documentation that aspirants for government funding, including Hayden, King, Wheeler, and Powell, recognized their promotional value and capitalized on their power of persuasion. Landscape photographs taken on government expeditions regularly found their way to Capitol Hill just as discussions regarding future appropriations came to the floor.

In addition to photographers, nearly every survey party that traveled west in the 1870s and 1880s included at least one topographical artist. Of these perhaps none was more talented than William Henry Holmes [223]. Beginning in 1872 and continuing through the

223. William Henry Holmes, *William Henry Holmes and George B. Chittenden Measuring a High Mountain Station,* 1874, watercolor on paper, 9⅛ × 6½ in. National Museum of American Art/National Portrait Gallery Library, Smithsonian Institution, Washington, D.C.

decade, Holmes was closely associated with Hayden. In 1872 Holmes was a member of Hayden's Yellowstone expedition, and the following year he accompanied Hayden on a reconnaissance mission to the canyons of the Colorado. Four years later much of his work was published in Hayden's *Atlas of Colorado*. In 1881 Holmes returned to the Grand Canyon in company with Major Clarence E. Dutton, who was charged with continuing the geologic studies begun by Powell a decade earlier. On this trip Holmes completed the preliminary drawings [224] for the extraordinary illustrations that accompanied Dutton's classic study, *Tertiary History of the Grand Cañon District* (1882). Panoramic in scope, Holmes's illustrations

224. William Henry Holmes, *The Grand Cañon from Toroweap Cone, Looking East,* 1881, pencil on paper, 12⅞ × 19⅛ in. United States Geological Survey, Field Records Library, Denver.

225. William Henry Holmes, *The Grand Cañon at the Foot of the Toroweap—Looking East.* From Dutton, *Tertiary History of the Grand Cañon District* (1882). Smithsonian Institution Libraries, Washington, D.C.

raised topographical drawing to an art form.

One of Holmes's illustrations, *The Grand Cañon at the Foot of the Toroweap—Looking East* [225], offers a view not far from the spot where Moran first looked down into the depths of the chasm. No one, however, would confuse Holmes's drawing with a work by Moran. Crisp and linear, Holmes's view unites the precision of science with the poetry of art.

During the 1880s and early 1890s, while others carried on the work he had begun in the canyons of the Colorado River, Powell continued to write, lecture, and exhort in an attempt to persuade lawmakers to face the reality of the southwestern climate and plan accordingly. Powell offered a blueprint for the rational management of "arid land" that advocated the division of the Southwest into water districts to be

administered by groups empowered to allocate water for the good of the greatest number. It was a revolutionary idea that flew in the face of promoters who preached the redemption of the West through irrigation. In 1893, at the second International Irrigation Congress in Los Angeles, Powell stood before the assembled dreamers and stated in blunt terms that there was not enough water to "redeem" more than 12 percent of the Southwest regardless of the number of ditches and dams built.[19] It was not a message they wished to hear. Recently described as "a model of ecological realism in an unsympathetic age of unbounded expectations," Powell's proposal was ignored.[20] Instead the boomers set out to conquer the Southwest through irrigation, and control of the Colorado River was key to any plan promising to turn the desert into a garden.

Shortly after the turn of the century two entrepreneurial engineers built a canal that channeled Colorado River water to a southern California desert known as the Salton Sink. Renamed, with ironic appropriateness, Imperial Valley, the area quickly became one of the richest agricultural regions in the country.[21] The early canal proved unsatisfactory, however, and shortly after the desert had been turned into a garden, calls for greater control over the water source were heard. The result was Hoover Dam. Proposed in 1904 and completed in 1936, the dam was an engineering marvel that altered forever the Colorado River and the land it drained [226–27].

In 1893, when he spoke before the International Irrigation Congress, Powell issued a stern warning: "I tell you gentlemen you are piling up a heritage of conflict and litigation over the water rights for there is not sufficient water to supply the land."[22] Time has proven Powell correct, for the Colorado River has inspired more litigation than any other river in the country. The continued court battles stem

from the fact that in the American West water is the most valuable resource. Thus ironically the landscapes that carry the Colorado River story to its conclusion are those appearing on fruit crates shipped from southern California orchards. Employing a method not unlike that used by Moran, the commercial artists who created the crate labels composed images that transmitted messages about the lifeblood of the West, water. In *Splendid,* circa 1935, an idyllic

226. Spence Air Photos, *Hoover Dam,* 1937, 4⅝ × 6⅝ in. Library of Congress, Washington, D.C.

227. Spence Air Photos, *Hoover Dam and Lake Mead,* 1936, 4⅝ × 6⅝ in. Library of Congress, Washington, D.C.

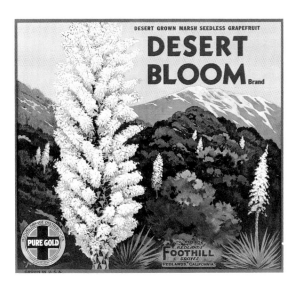

228. Unidentified artist, *Splendid,* circa 1935, chromolithograph, 8¾ × 10¼ in. The Oakland Museum, History Department, California.

229. Unidentified artist, *Desert Bloom,* circa 1938, chromolithograph, 10 × 10¼ in. The Oakland Museum, History Department, California.

scene of agricultural paradise recedes behind a cascade of brightly colored lemons [228]. As Kevin Starr notes in *Inventing the Dream* (1985) California recreated itself between 1880 and 1920, turning deserts into winter gardens with borrowed water.[23] Colorado River water sustained the regimented rows of citrus trees that transformed the mythical land of milk and honey into a marketable reality.

Desert Bloom, circa 1938, a second example of California's commercial landscape, promotes desert-grown grapefruit and bears in the lower-left corner the trademark of the Mutual Orange Distributors [229]. In bold letters at the center of the insignia are the words "Pure Gold." Although the history of the Far West is punctuated with numerous "rushes" for gold and silver, the real gold of the West was liquid and in short supply. Well before the end of the first decade of the twentieth century the white water Powell had ridden through geologic time had been tamed. The dreamscapes promoted on fruit crates were advertisements for an invented land sustained by water diverted from the Colorado River.

Donner Pass

In April 1868, just months before the construction crews of the Union Pacific reached the Green River in Wyoming on their way to Promontory, their counterparts from the Central Pacific celebrated the successful passage of the first train over the most daunting obstacle in the path of the transcontinental railroad, the Sierra Nevada. From the outset, the planners and funders of the railroad enterprise had recognized the severity of the test posed by the mountains, for the allocation of $16,000 per mile jumped to $48,000 for rails laid through mountainous regions.[24] Even this added provision, however, did not cover the expense incurred in blasting the rails through the granite wall of the Sierra Nevada. Nine tunnels were eventually bored through the Sierra; the summit mile alone was estimated to have cost $350,000.[25]

Progress was also hampered by heavy snow in the High Sierra. The winter of 1866–67, when construction crews were attempting to reach the summit, was one of the severest on record. Work continued despite hazardous conditions, but construction engineers recognized that even during winters far less harsh, cumulative snowfall would prevent trains from passing over the Sierra. To counter this threat engineers proposed building snowsheds over the most vulnerable stretches of track, thus allowing trains to pass through what effectively became snow tunnels.

Newspaper reporters, alert to the adventure inherent in a tale of men against nature, kept their readers informed regarding the battle being waged between the railroad crews and Sierra snow. Thus it was common knowledge that the original snowsheds were a total failure. Poorly designed, they plummeted down a mountainside during the first heavy snowfall. When a later design met with greater success, construction forged ahead. Eventually thirty-seven miles of snowsheds were built at a cost of more than two million dollars. By the fall of 1869, when the sheds were finished, sixty-five million board feet of timber had been consumed in their construction.[26]

The festivities accompanying the completion of the sheds were recorded with naive charm in a painting by Joseph H. Becker, a staff artist for *Leslie's Illustrated Weekly Newspaper* who traveled west aboard the first cross-Rockies Pullman train in 1869 [230]. During a six-week stay in California, Becker made a number of studies of the Chinese workers who formed the backbone of the labor force that built the Central Pacific Railroad and the snowsheds. In Becker's painting they may be seen cheering the safe passage of a train through the sheds that were quickly touted as an engineering marvel and described at length in California guidebooks.

Public interest in the conquest of the Sierra was also spurred by the fact that the mountain pass through which the railroad made its way carried the name of the Donner party, the ill-fated group of emigrants that became trapped in the High Sierra by early snow during the winter of 1846–47.[27] Their tale of starvation and cannibalism had become the best known of many stories chronicling the dark side of the journey to the Promised Land.

The Donner tragedy resulted from a combination of bad advice, inexperienced leadership, delayed travel, and early snow. The construction of the snowsheds represented, therefore, a special kind of triumph, for it was snow that killed some members of the Donner party and drove others to eat the flesh of their companions in order to survive. Like the crews of the Union Pacific who had taken the danger out of crossing the Green River, the men of the Central Pacific, with their tunnels and snowsheds, robbed the Sierra Nevada range of much of its destructive power. In a confrontation pitting nature against technological ingenuity, the Central Pacific claimed victory. As might be expected, numerous travel writers, photographers, and artists made their way to the site of such a triumph. Among the most important of these was Bierstadt, who produced a major painting of the Sierra summit near Donner Lake early in the 1870s [231].

Bierstadt traveled to California for the first time in 1863, six years before the completion of the transcontinental railroad. Journeying overland by stagecoach, he crossed the Sierra on precipitous mountain roads. Eight years later he returned to California aboard the recently completed transcontinental railroad.[28] Within days of his arrival in San Francisco, however, he retraced his steps, heading for Donner Pass in company with Collis P. Huntington, vice president of the Central Pacific Railroad.

Although he eventually became one of the "Big Four" railroad barons, Huntington arrived in California inauspiciously.[29] Like thousands of others, he came west with the forty-

230. Joseph H. Becker, *Snow Sheds on the Central Pacific Railroad in the Sierra Nevada Mountains, May 1869,* circa 1869, oil on canvas, 19 × 26 in. Thomas Gilcrease Institute of American History and Art, Tulsa.

niners, but after one day in the gold fields he concluded that his fortune lay elsewhere. Returning to Sacramento, he opened a hardware store catering to the needs of miners and prospered. Eventually Huntington and his partner in hardware, Mark Hopkins, joined dry-goods merchant Charles Crocker and grocer Leland Stanford to form the partnership that succeeded in launching the Central Pacific Railroad.

By 1871, when he joined Huntington in San Francisco, Bierstadt had made a name for himself painting large, panoramic views of the western landscape. Huntington, who had undoubtedly seen some of these works, commis-

sioned Bierstadt to produce a painting of the area near Donner Pass, where the railroad had faced its greatest challenge. Late in July, Huntington traveled to the site with the artist to select the point of view from which he wanted the picture painted. After this initial trip Bierstadt returned to the site several times to complete the sketches he needed to compose the six-by-ten-foot canvas.

As was his practice, Bierstadt allowed reporters to visit his studio and comment on works in progress. Thus a writer preparing a profile of the artist for *Scribner's* in March 1872 described the unfinished painting and reported

that in making studies of the early morning sun above Donner Lake, "Bierstadt rose morning after morning at four o'clock, until he had secured the desired effect of light and shade and color."[30] Subsequent reports kept the public informed of Bierstadt's progress so that by January 1873, when the painting was exhibited for the first time (in San Francisco), hundreds of people turned out to see what they had been reading about for months. Among the most perceptive of the California observers was the

critic for the *Overland Monthly* who described the point of view as several hundred feet above the Central Pacific Railroad, at the summit of the Sierra:

This point was chosen at the instance of the gentleman for whom the picture was painted, because right here were overcome the greatest physical difficulties in the construction of the road, while the immediate vicinity was the scene of the most pathetic tragedy in the experience of our pioneer immigration, for it was on the shore of Donner Lake that

231. Albert Bierstadt, *Donner Lake from the Summit,* 1873, oil on canvas, 72 × 120 in. New-York Historical Society, New York.

the Donner party were caught in the winter snows, and suffered horrors worse than the death which overtook so many of them. The two associations of the spot are, therefore, sharply and suggestively antithetical: so much slowness and hardship in the early days, so much rapidity and ease now; great physical obstacles overcome by a triumph of well-directed science and mechanics.[31]

More than twenty years before Bierstadt and Huntington made their pilgrimage, the Sierra summit had figured prominently in William S. Jewett's early painting *The Promised Land—The Grayson Family* [see 83]. Described as having "just emerged from the wilderness," Andrew Jackson Grayson and his family look down from the summit of the Sierra Nevada "upon the promised land lying in its still beauty like the sleeping Princess of the story, waiting but the kiss of Enterprise to spring into energetic life. There below them is not only the field for industry and enterprise, but a panorama of natural charms destined to inspire poets, to glow on the canvas of painters, and to take on the magic of human association and tradition."[32] By the time Bierstadt began his painting of Donner Lake, enterprise had embraced not only California's sleeping valleys but also her granite peaks.

Although commissioned by one of the leading railroad promoters of the age, Bierstadt's painting does not include a single railroad car. At first glance, in fact, *Donner Lake from the Summit* appears to be another of the artist's panoramic views of spectacular western scenery. In the far-right corner, however, are snowsheds, those man-made structures that allowed the railroad, the mechanical harbinger of the modern age, to speed to the Pacific Coast despite snow drifts as high as sixty feet. Contemporary photographs by Russell and Carleton E. Watkins confirm the topographical accuracy of the view as do Bierstadt's own preliminary sketches of the site, including *View of Donner Lake, California,* 1871/72, which focuses on the precariously perched snowsheds [232–33]. In the final painting, however, the sheds are but a tiny thread strung along the rugged flank of a mountain peak. Ethereal Donner Lake, cast in the golden glow of the rising sun, is the center of attention.

The absence of overt references to the railroad was applauded by several San Francisco critics. A writer for the *Evening Bulletin,* for example, commented:

The railroad, with its enveloping snow-shed, is indicated plainly enough without any obtrusion of its ugliness, the puff of blue smoke that the train left as it plunged into a short tunnel suggesting with a touch of beauty all that is not seen. It is wonderful to think that a railroad was ever laid along the face of this forbidding cliff.[33]

Another critic, for the *Overland Monthly,* wrote, "Through a tunnel in this rocky battlement the cars pass; but the hard fact of the railroad is only hinted by a puff of smoke, and by an unobtrusive sketch of the line of snowsheds."[34]

Bierstadt's solution to the problem posed by the "hard fact of the railroad" was masterful, for he managed to celebrate both the natural sublimity of the western landscape and the technological sublimity of the railroad. By allowing only snowsheds in his painting Bierstadt focused not on the railroad itself (by 1871 the railroad was old news) but on the physical objects that continued to speak of the struggle and ultimate triumph associated with the construction of the railroad through the Sierra Nevada. Bierstadt's subtle reference to the railroad was a powerful endorsement of the transcontinental enterprise, for if the artist's evidence was to be believed, the beauty of the Sierra had not been compromised by the arrival of the railroad. The message was clear: it was possible to build a railroad without destroying the scenic

quality of the landscape through which it passed.

By design *Donner Lake from the Summit* served as a splendid promotional tool for the transcontinental railroad. All the alpine scenery Bierstadt included in his composition was by implication available for viewing by passengers traveling west in the deep-pile comfort of Pullman Palace cars. Before being added to Huntington's private collection (where it was undoubtedly seen by numerous investors in the West), the painting was placed on exhibition in several cities, where it functioned as an effective advertisement for the scenic rewards awaiting those who traveled to the Pacific by rail.

Donner Lake from the Summit drew so much attention in the press (particularly in San Francisco) that inevitably other artists were drawn to the site. Among them was William Keith, who responded to the beauty of the Sierra with a looser stroke and brighter palette in *Donner Lake,* circa 1878–79 [234]. Remarkable for its radiance, Keith's view is one of many paintings spawned by Bierstadt's example. By the end of the 1870s Donner Pass

had become so inextricably linked with the triumph of the railroad that even without the tangible evidence of the snowsheds the association was clear.

When Bierstadt traveled to the Pacific Coast for the first time in 1863, he was accompanied by Fitz Hugh Ludlow, a talented member of New York's literary set. Following their return east, Ludlow reported on the overland journey in a series of articles published in the *Atlantic Monthly*. In one of these, "Through Tickets to the Pacific," Ludlow described the railroad as the "greatest popular enterprise in the world" and went on to exclaim in language worthy of a publicity agent, "Our foremost scientific men, for the sake of the great national enterprise, have taken their lives in their hands, going out to meet peril and privation with the cheerful constancy of apostles and martyrs."[35] Ludlow's celebratory point of view regarding the construction of the railroad was one that those who directed the enterprise wisely chose to exploit. Both the Union Pacific and Central Pacific had in their employ professional photographers assigned to document the construction of the railroad.

From 1864 to 1869 Alfred A. Hart was employed as official photographer for the Central Pacific, documenting in hundreds of photographs the labored progress of the construction crews battling the Sierra Nevada. In Hart's photographs the snowsheds (barely visible in Bierstadt's painting) take on the grandeur of a cathedral under construction. In one example, notable as much for its formal as its documentary quality, crew members pose in front of a snowshed only partly completed [235]. Testifying to the massive amount of timber required to build the snow tunnels, Hart's photograph ironically juxtaposes the support structure of a shed with living examples of the fir and pine trees that were destroyed in huge numbers to build the snowsheds.

In another remarkable photograph Hart re-
versed the direction of his lens and placed his
camera inside one of the sheds [236]. Parallel
rails lead from the sheltered passage of the
snowshed into a landscape that quickly dissolves into light. No more fitting image could
be offered by the company that advertised a
safe and scenic journey to the promise that was
California.

The same snowsheds present in Bierstadt's
panoramic painting and Hart's photographs
were translated into yet another medium for
purposes of promotion. Two views, one from
the interior showing the timbered structure,
and a second, an aerial view presenting a
succession of sheds winding around the edge of
a mountain, were used as poster illustrations
by the Central and Union Pacific Railroad to
promote the "Great American Overland
Route" [237]. The sheds (called "snow galleries") were also illustrated in numerous editions
of George Crofutt's popular guidebook, *New
Overland Tourist and Pacific Coast Guide* (1878–
79), which described in some detail the sights
along the routes of various rail lines [238]. In a
passage applauding the technological achievement of the snowsheds while reassuring travelers of their safety, Crofutt noted, "The mighty
avalanches which sweep down the mountain
sides in spring, bearing everything before
them, pass over the sloping roofs of the sheds
and plunge into the chasms below, while beneath the rushing mass the cars glide smoothly
along, the passengers hardly knowing but that
they are in the midst of an enormous tunnel."[36] Aside from celebrating the conquest of
nature, the strategy of turning the snowsheds
into an attraction rivaling the alpine scenery of
the Sierra may have been a ploy intended to
counter the unfortunate fact that while the
snowsheds allowed the train to pass over Donner Pass despite deep snow they obscured
much of the view just as the train passed

234. William Keith, *Donner Lake,* circa 1878–79, oil on canvas, 24 × 14¾ in. Hearst Art Gallery, Saint Mary's College of California, Moraga.

235. Alfred A. Hart, *Snow Cover near the Summit,* circa 1866–69, stereograph. California State Railroad Museum, Sacramento.

236. Alfred A. Hart, *Snow Sheds at Emigrant Gap,* circa 1866–69, stereograph. Bancroft Library, University of California, Berkeley.

237. Unidentified artist, *Central and Union Pacific Railroad Line.* From *Keepsakes* 7 (1869). California State Railroad Museum, Sacramento.

through the most spectacular scenery on the route. Complaints became so frequent that during the summer the side paneling on some sheds was removed to restore the view.

An early twentieth-century photograph by an unidentified photographer suggests that efforts to promote the snowsheds as attractions rivaling the spectacle of Sierra scenery met with some success. Simply titled *Etta at Opening of Snowsheds,* the image shows a young woman outfitted in a traveling costume, standing on the railroad tracks before one of the

Central Pacific snowsheds [239]. The technological conquest of the Sierra (as represented by
the iron rails and snowsheds) has displaced the
landscape as the subject of a tourist view.

Big Tree Groves, California

In 1852 Augustus T. Dowd, an employee of
the Union Water Company in Murphy, California (one of the hastily built camps that dotted the Sierra foothills), wounded a bear on a
hunting expedition.[37] Trailing his prey for the
final kill, Dowd found himself in unfamiliar
territory, standing beneath the largest trees he
had ever seen. Abandoning the bear, he hurried
back to camp with news of his discovery. His
companions greeted the tale with universal
disbelief. So incredulous were his compatriots
that not a single volunteer would return with
him to confirm his discovery. A patient man,
however, Dowd devised a plan to redeem his
honest name. Several days later, when most
had forgotten his story, Dowd went hunting
again. He returned to camp claiming he had
killed a grizzly so large he needed help bringing it back. Lured to the big trees by a lie,
Dowd's companions readily acknowledged,
when standing beneath the giant sequoia, the
truth of his "big tree yarn."

Word of the mammoth trees spread
quickly and soon the opportunists arrived.
Among them was George Gale, who singled
out the finest tree in the grove (Mother of the
Forest) and set about stripping off the bark to a
height of more than one hundred feet. Believing he had a curiosity to rival any in P. T.
Barnum's museum, he shipped the bark east,
reassembled the pieces, and put the hollow
trunk on exhibition. The scheme proved a total
failure, however, when visitors refused to believe such a large tree actually existed and
branded the whole spectacle a humbug.

238. Unidentified artist, *Summit Sierra Nevadas, Donner
Lake, Snow Sheds and Tun-
nels.* From Crofutt, *Crofutt's
New Overland Tourist and Pacific Coast Guide* (1878–79), 1:
fig. 14. Library of Congress,
Washington, D.C.

239. Unidentified photographer, *Etta at Opening of Snowsheds,* circa 1905, cyanotype,
2½ × 3⅞ in. California State
Railroad Museum, Sacramento.

Tourists who later visited the grove deplored Gale's act and came to refer to the desecrated tree as the Saint Sebastian of the Forest (steel spikes had been driven into the trunk as the bark was removed). A reporter for *Harper's Weekly* called the act "vandalism," a crime carried out "with as much neatness and industry as a troop of jackals would display in cleaning the bones of a dead lion."[38] Literally flayed, the Mother of the Forest lived only a few years before falling a martyr.

The tree was still standing, however, when William W. Lapham opened a hotel, the Mammoth Tree Cottage, near the grove. Quick to recognize a tourist opportunity when

he saw one, Lapham was also a skilled publicist. Thus his hotel occupies the central position in the collection of big tree views produced by Thomas A. Ayres for a lithograph printed in 1855 [240]. The Mother of the Forest appears at the left, complete with scaffolding. Beneath it, in the lower left, is the Big Tree Stump, which resulted from the felling of one of the largest of the mammoth trees by some of the opportunists *Harper's* described as "jackals." The tree was cut down less than a year after Dowd's discovery and made news when it was reported that because of the great size of the trunk, all traditional methods of felling trees had proven ineffectual. Undeterred,

240. Thomas A. Ayres, *The Mammoth Tree Grove, Calaveras County*, 1855, tinted lithograph, 17⅜ × 25¹³/₁₆ in. New York Public Library, Print Collection, The Miriam and Ira D. Wallach Division of Art, Prints, and Photographs, Astor, Lenox, and Tilden Foundations.

however, the five men who undertook the task spent more than three weeks boring pump augers into the trunk [241]. Even when the trunk and the stump had been severed, the tree remained upright. Wedges were then pounded into the gash and the tree that had survived for more than two thousand years fell.

James Mason Hutchings, publisher of *California Magazine,* later reported that the stump was smoothed and used as a dance floor [242]. During one fourth of July celebration thirty-two people "were engaged in dancing four sets of cotillions at one time, without suffering any inconvenience whatever."[39] Commenting on the fate of the fallen tree, Hutchings wrote:

In our estimation it was a sacrilegious act; although it is possible that the exhibition of its bark among the unbelievers of the eastern part of our continent, and of Europe, may have convinced all the "Thomases" living, that we have great facts in California that must be believed, sooner or later. This is the only paliating consideration with us in this act of desecration.[40]

After a brief and disappointing career as a forty-niner, Hutchings became one of California's most successful promoters. Leader of the first tourist party to enter Yosemite Valley, he mounted a tireless campaign to draw attention (and tourists) to the "great facts" in California, including the big trees.

Increased tourism was clearly the reason for Ayres's lithograph as well. In addition to the Mother of the Forest and the Big Tree Stump, Ayres included vignettes of the Father of the Forest (a tree that had fallen without human intervention), the Three Graces, and the Pioneer's Cabin and Miner's Cabin (two trees with trunks hollowed out by fire) as well as a descriptive paragraph detailing the amenities of the hotel, including a claim that the rates were reasonable, "it being the aim of the proprietor to make the Grove a fashionable and popular

AUGUR-HOLES THROUGH THE ORIGINAL BIG TREE (SHOWING HOW IT WAS FELLED).

241. Unidentified artist, *Boring Pump Augers.* From *Scribner's Monthly* 3 (January 1872): 263. National Museum of American Art/National Portrait Gallery Library, Smithsonian Institution, Washington, D.C.

242. Charles C. Curtis, *Quadrille on Redwood Stump, Tulare County,* circa 1895, albumen print, 5¼ × 8¾ in. Bancroft Library, University of California, Berkeley.

place of resort." Few natural wonders on the North American continent were turned to the use of commerce and tourism as rapidly as the big trees of California.

In 1857, five years after Dowd discovered the Calaveras Grove of big trees, Galen Clark, a sickly New Englander who had come to Yosemite to get well or die, discovered a second grove of mammoth trees not far from Yosemite Valley.[41] Spurning suggestions that he attach his own name to the grove, Clark chose instead to call the trees "Mariposa," using the Spanish word for the butterflies so common to the area. Once he had regained his health, Clark built a cabin near the trees and not far from one of the major routes into Yosemite Valley. The cabin soon became a popular way station and Clark found himself host to a number of distinguished guests including Carleton E. Watkins, a young San Francisco photographer who made his first trip to Yosemite and the Mariposa Grove in 1861.

When he stopped at Clark's cabin, Watkins had with him a custom-made camera capable of accommodating eighteen-by-twelve-inch glass plates as well as a smaller stereo camera. During the course of his visit to Yosemite, Watkins made thirty mammoth and one hundred stereographic negatives of big trees near the valley. Among these are two "portraits" of Grizzly Giant, the largest and oldest tree in the Mariposa Grove [243–44]. Estimated to be between twenty-five hundred and three thousand years old, the massive tree rises more than two hundred feet and measures more than thirty-one feet across at the base. The first large limb (ninety-five feet above the ground) measures six feet in diameter. Watkins attempted to convey the enormous scale of the tree by including in his photograph several figures posed at the base. Reduced to the size of pygmies, these men are barely visible. The strength of Watkins's image comes less from

its reference to the measure of man than from the extraordinary silhouette of knotted and twisted branches towering above the neighboring trees.

In December 1862 a number of Watkins's mammoth-plate views of Yosemite and the Mariposa trees were exhibited at Goupil's Gallery in New York. Among those who responded enthusiastically were Bierstadt and Ludlow, whose spring plans included a trip west but who may not have intended to journey as far as California—until they saw Watkins's photographs.[42]

Bierstadt and Ludlow arrived in San Francisco in July 1863 and within two weeks were on their way to Yosemite. In *Heart of the Continent* (1870), the published account of their journey, Ludlow reported on their visit to the Mariposa trees. Like most other travelers, Ludlow despaired of conveying the size of the trees and later declared that he found no one in the East who believed "the literal truth which travellers have to tell about these marvelous giants."[43] He also wrote that although Bierstadt and the other artists traveling with their party made studies of the trees, they faced a nearly impossible task:

Of course our artists neither made nor expected to make anything like a realizing picture of the groves. The marvelous of size does not go into gilt frames. You paint a Big Tree, and it only looks like a common tree in a cramped coffin. To be sure, you can put a live figure against the butt for comparison; but, unless you take a canvas of the size of Haydon's your picture is quite as likely to resemble Homunculus against an average timber tree as a large man against *Sequoia gigantea*. What our artists did was to get a capital transcript of the Big Trees' color,—a beautifully bright cinnamon-brown, which gives peculiar gayety to the forest, making sunshine in the shady place.[44]

Despite Ludlow's discouraging remarks about the difficulty of doing justice to the big

trees on canvas, Bierstadt produced several paintings of the mammoth trees. One of these, *Giant Redwood Trees of California*, 1874, may have begun with sketches made on site, but in Bierstadt's studio a transformation took place [245]. Capitalizing on the public's fascination with both the size and age of the giant sequoias, Bierstadt invented an Indian idyll that harkens back to the beginnings of life on the North American continent. By the time Bierstadt painted his big tree pictures (c. 1873–78) tourists rather than Indians would have been camping beneath the mammoth trees then believed to be the oldest living things on earth.[45]

By carefully manipulating light and shade,

Bierstadt directed the viewer's attention to the cavernous opening at the base of the largest tree. Inside the dark, cavelike passage an Indian camp is visible. The ancient and powerful tree shelters America's primeval race.

In July 1864, one year after Bierstadt and Ludlow arrived in California, President Abraham Lincoln signed the bill setting aside Yosemite Valley and the Mariposa Grove as a protected park to be administered by the state of California. Thus the big trees in the Mariposa Grove were spared from the "desecration" that had taken place in the Calaveras Grove. Other giant sequoia stands, however, were not similarly protected. The shrill sound

243. Carleton E. Watkins, *Grizzly Giant,* 1863, albumen print, 20¼ × 14³⁄₁₆ in. Print Department, Boston Public Library.

244. Carleton E. Watkins, *Section of Grizzly Giant,* 1861, albumen print, 15¾ × 20½ in. Private collection.

245. Albert Bierstadt, *Giant Redwood Trees of California*, 1874, oil on canvas, 52½ × 43 in. The Berkshire Museum, Pittsfield, Massachusetts; gift of Zenas Crane.

of the saw was heard even in the vicinity of Yosemite, for in *Heart of the Continent* Ludlow noted that twelve miles into the fifty-mile ride to Yosemite from Mariposa they found themselves at "one of those inevitable steam sawmills with which a Yankee always cuts his first swath into the tall grass of Barbarism."[46] Ludlow's observation is a fitting reminder that at the same moment tourists were traveling great distances to see the giant trees, others were intent on turning them into shingles and grape stakes. Contemporary references to the big trees frequently contain what appear today to be contradictory elements: astonished praise for a wondrous work of nature coupled with precise calculations regarding the number of board feet each tree would yield.

Because of their size, the California redwoods challenged the logging industry in nearly every respect. New saws, on a scale previously unknown, were required, and a steam-powered engine (nicknamed a "donkey") was invented to assist in the movement of logs from the forest to the head of a skid road, where bull teams could take over the transport. The contest between man and tree was rarely the subject of painting, but numerous photographs document what was viewed by many at the time as another display of man's ingenuity in turning natural resources to his own use.

Among the most striking of these images is A. W. Ericson's photograph of a twelve-foot saw [246]. At the left, on top of a stump, a logger stands holding the enormous saw; to the right lies the evidence of his industry and perseverance. In the foreground, a large pile of splintered wood testifies to the waste that was part of every logging operation. Clearly intended to celebrate the conquest of nature, the photograph betrays a naive confidence in unlimited supply. The process is carried one step further in another photograph documenting the use of steam-powered donkeys to pull huge

pieces of tree trunks to the rail line for transport on flat cars [247]. In another celebratory photograph Ericson records the final stage in the conversion process [248]. More than twenty huge pieces of redwood (each filling an entire flatcar) are shown en route to a saw mill. Only slightly diminished in size as they recede into space, the enormous redwood sections suggest an endless supply of a convertible resource.

As late as 1893, when the World's Columbian Exposition was held in Chicago, the enormous size of the big trees was still a matter of curiosity and skepticism. To counter disbelief (and promote tourism and national pride), the federal government selected a three-hundred-foot sequoia standing outside the protective boundary of the newly created Sequoia National Park to cut down and display (in part) in Chicago. Ironically the tree had been named in honor of General John Willcock Noble, secretary of the interior and a supporter of forest preservation. A photograph by Charles C. Curtis records the dismantling of the General Noble Tree [249]. Like Etta before the snowsheds, three women pose beside the fallen tree amid the rigging required for the dismembering. Although many big trees had been set aside for protection in the thirty years that separated Dowd's discovery of the Calaveras Grove in 1852 and the exhibition of pieces of the General Noble at the World's Columbian Exposition in 1893, the destruction, for promotional purposes, of a tree that had survived an estimated twenty-five hundred years was an activity endorsed by the government. Duplicating the behavior of private citizens, the federal government cast a protective arm around several groves of giant sequoia (their use as tourist attractions having been demonstrated) at the same time it endorsed the destruction of other trees for displays in road shows and fairs. When the supply of big trees was perceived as

246. A. W. Ericson, *Twelve-foot Saw for a Twelve-day Job,* 1892–93, photograph. Peter E. Palmquist, Arcata, California.

247. A. W. Ericson, *Humboldt County (California Lumbering),* 1892–93, photograph. Wells Fargo Bank, San Francisco.

248. A. W. Ericson, *In the Redwoods: Logging at Freshwater, Humboldt County,* 1892–93, albumen print, 7¾ × 9⅝ in. Peter E. Palmquist, Arcata, California.

249. Charles C. Curtis, *Dismantling of the General Noble Redwood Tree*, 1892, albumen print, 7¾ × 9⅝ in. Peter E. Palmquist, Arcata, California.

unlimited, all uses were sanctioned.

In what appear to be contradictory responses, some observers saw America's past in the big trees, others saw its future. The astonishing age of the sequoias prompted rejoicing for those who looked on the trees as America's antiquity. In 1859, for example, journalist Horace Greeley, stopped at the Mariposa Grove on a hurried visit to Yosemite Valley. As countless tourists would do after him and perhaps in response to the same feelings of disbelief, Greeley gathered detailed and precise measurements of the huge redwoods. Having convinced himself firsthand that the reported size of the trees was not exaggerated, he went on to express wonder by speculating on their age: "That they were of very substantial size when David danced before the ark, when Solomon laid the foundation of the Temple, when Theseus ruled in Athens, when Aeneas fled from the burning wreck of vanquished Troy, when Sesostris led the victorious Egyptians into the heart of Asia, I have no doubt."[47]

Also fascinated by the age of the trees was Thomas Starr King, the charismatic San Francisco preacher who wrote a series of letters published by the *Boston Evening Transcript* in

1861 praising California scenery. King marveled that one tree "was a giant in the time of the first Crusade" and antedated "the foundation stone of the oldest Gothic spire in Europe."[48]

In 1869 Charles Carleton Coffin, reporting on a round-the-world journey, placed the big trees in a period before history. "These are the survivors of an almost extinct flora,—of the period of mastodons, megatheriums, and of bullfrogs weighing a ton. They seem to be out of place in the flora and fauna of these times, and more in keeping with the extinct monsters of those primeval years."[49]

While Greeley, King, Coffin, and many others marveled at the timelessness of the trees, others looked at the giant sequoia and saw America's future—in board feet. A steady stream of reports, some issued by the government, entertained the reading public with statistics as astonishing as the age of the trees. The largest of the trees, the General Sherman (now protected in Sequoia National Park), for example, was estimated to weigh fourteen hundred tons and contain six hundred thousand board feet—enough to build forty five-room houses.

The disparity represented by these opposing points of view would suggest that a strict division separated them. In fact, the opposite was true. The deep ambivalence regarding the preservation of what was seen as America's antiquity and the conversion of a natural resource into a commodity that spoke of the future was so pervasive that both points of view were frequently expressed by a single writer, often within the same article. In *Picturesque America,* for example, James Smillie described the special character of the Mariposa redwoods and in the same breath commented, "A mill, at this place, saws them into lumber."[50]

Perhaps the most striking example of the accommodation forged between seemingly contradictory viewpoints is evident in Edgar Cherry's *Redwood and Lumbering in California Forests* (1844). A folio volume illustrated with photographs, Cherry's book was designed to promote products made from northern California redwoods. Although he wrote at length about the superiority of redwood (little shrinkage and warping, natural resistance to fire and rot, color and texture suitable for cabinetry, etc.) and gave numerous reasons for harvesting the trees, he also commented:

Almost the first thought passing one's mind, as he enters a virgin forest of redwoods, is one of pity that such a wonderful creation of nature should be subject to the greed of man for gold. The same feelings of awe pervade one's being upon his first introduction to this apparently exhaustless army of giants, that impress the beholder of Niagara, Yosemite, and the near relations of the redwoods—the Big Trees of Calaveras and Merced.[51]

Cherry's comment about the "apparently exhaustless" supply of redwoods lies at the heart of the accommodation that produced a publication promoting the use of redwood products while lamenting the destruction of the trees. Conservation was not an issue if the supply was seen as unlimited.

Although Bierstadt and several other artists used the big trees as a subject for major paintings, the artist who became most closely associated with the giant sequoias was Thomas Hill. English by birth, Hill grew up in Taunton, Massachusetts. In 1861 he moved to San Francisco, hoping California's climate would restore his health. Two years after his arrival, Hill visited Yosemite for the first time. Almost immediately he began producing the Yosemite views with which he became inextricably linked. In 1883 he built a studio in Yosemite near the Wawona Hotel and the Mariposa Grove of big trees [250]. Quite literally on the tourist trail, Hill responded to the demand for

250. Unidentified photographer, *Thomas Hill's Studio in Yosemite,* after 1886, silver gelatin print, 5 × 4 in. The Oakland Museum, California; gift of Cherene Holsinger and James W. Cravagan III.

Yosemite views (including the big trees) by producing hundreds of paintings. Among these were a number of the Wawona Tree, a giant sequoia through which a tunnel had been cut in 1881. The tree is the subject of an enormous canvas (99¾ × 30 in.), which shows Indians riding through the passage toward a slain deer in the foreground [251]. In a composition echoing Watkins's photograph of Grizzly Giant [see 243], Hill attempted to convey the grandeur of the tree by displaying its full height. The image carries, however, an ironic message. The tunnel that had been cut through the tree was an enormously successful tourist gimmick that drew an increasing number of visitors each year, but Hill does not place tourists in his painting. Instead he substituted a vignette from America's primitive past. Hill juxtaposed the most "commercial" of the big trees with figures suggesting that nothing had changed.

251. Thomas Hill, *Indians in the Wawona Tunnel Tree,* 1892, oil on canvas, 99¾ × 30 in. The Yosemite Museum, National Park Service, California.

The Wawona Tree appears as one of the principal elements in Hill's update [252] of Ayres's earlier big tree composite [see 240]. Once again at the center of the image is a hotel, this time the Wawona. The original building was completed in 1879 but proved so popular with tourists that additional accommodations were added. In Hill's painting vignettes of two of Yosemite's most famous views flank the central hotel panel. Serving as backdrop are the lower portions of two enormous trees, the Wawona on the right and Grizzly Giant on the left. In front of all is a panel advertising the wealth of game available for hunters and fishermen.

By the turn of the century the Wawona Tree had become so well known as a novelty that it was frequently used in advertising. The Southern Pacific Railroad, for example, used the tree on both the front and back covers of a brochure promoting travel to California and as the central image of an advertisement that read "California: The Home of the Big Tree" [253–54]. Juxtaposed with the Flatiron Building in New York, the Wawona towers over the new skyscraper. Although promoting the natural wonders of California (and travel to see them), the final line of the accompanying text reads: "Cut into one-inch boards it would entirely sheath the building on all sides."

The question about the proper use of the big trees—whether they were to be preserved and protected as resources for the travel industry or cut down and turned into shingles, fence posts, and grape stakes—took an ironic turn when Hill painted portraits of the Wawona and Grizzly Giant on redwood panels [255–56]. In a final twist of fate the image and object had become one. In the most literal sense the subject of the painting had been consumed in the production of the image.

252. Thomas Hill, *Big Tree—Mariposa Station,* circa 1886, oil on board, 22 × 27 in. Dr. and Mrs. Oscar Lemer, Dale City, California.

253. Unidentified artist, *Big Trees, California*. From a Southern Pacific brochure (1901): front and back cover. Bruce Heard, Arlington, Virginia.

254. Unidentified artist, *California: The Home of the Big Tree*. From *Country Life in America* 6 (April 1904): 551. Library of Congress, Washington, D.C.

255. Thomas Hill, *The Wawona,* circa 1890, oil on panel, 44 × 10 in. Bancroft Library, University of California, Berkeley; gift of Warren R. Howell.

256. Thomas Hill, *The Grizzly,* circa 1890, oil on panel, 44 × 10 in. Bancroft Library, University of California, Berkeley; gift of Warren R. Howell.

Vast in its measure and varied in its character, the American West assumed metaphorical status as the physical confirmation of divine favor and future promise, well before the earliest survey parties returned with reports of staggering material resources. As a land of awesome beauty, the West had become an inextricable part of the nation's definition of itself long before the conclusion of the Civil War allowed the forces of labor and capital to turn their attention to the development of the economic gold mine that lay west of the Mississippi. Development brought change, however, and change brought conflict.

Many of the images discussed here celebrate both the bounty of the West and man's ingenuity in converting that bounty to his own use. By any measure the completion of the transcontinental railroad, for example, was an achievement worthy of acclaim. Numerous photographs, lithographs, popular illustrations, and advertisements record America's pride in what was seen as a technological triumph. But the railroad also brought change to much of the western landscape. Reluctant to give up the spectacular vistas that had already entered the nation's mythology, Americans took comfort from the constructed artifice of studio paintings that offered assurance that the West could endure as both iconic symbol and economic resource. Carefully composed and skillfully executed, such paintings minimized the conflict that accompanied development by suggesting that the natural sublimity of the land and the technological achievements of man could harmoniously coexist.

Notes

1. For information regarding Sanford R. Gifford's trip west in 1870, see Weiss, *Poetic Landscapes,* 130–33; and Nancy Dustin Wall Moure, "Five Eastern Artists Out West," *American Art Journal* (November 1973): 15–31.

2. Quoted in Hales, *Jackson and the American Landscape,* 68.

3. Ibid., 72.

4. Horace Bushnell, "California: Its Characteristics and Prospects," *New Englander* 16 (February 1858): 158–59.

5. Leo Marx, *The Machine in the Garden* (1964; New York: Oxford University Press, 1980), 194.

6. For an account of Legrand Lockwood's commission of *The Domes of the Yosemite,* see Gordon Hendricks, "Bierstadt's *The Domes of the Yosemite,*" *American Art Journal* 3 (Fall 1971): 23–31. For the placement of paintings by Thomas Hill in the Lick House, see Arkelian, *Hill,* 14.

7. For a comprehensive account of the building of the Union Pacific Railroad, see Robert G. Athearn, *Union Pacific Country* (1971; Lincoln: University of Nebraska Press, 1976).

8. Although the provenance of *Green River Cliffs, Wyoming* remains unclear, another of Moran's large Green River pictures, *The Mirage,* 1879 (Stark Museum of Art, Orange, Texas), was owned by Reginald Vanderbilt, grandson of Cornelius and son of William Henry Vanderbilt, one of the chief railroad financiers of his day.

9. For detailed accounts of John Wesley Powell's expeditions, see his *Canyons of the Colorado* (1895), reprinted as *The Exploration of the Colorado River and Its Canyons* (New York: Dover, 1961); Frederick S. Dellenbaugh, *A Canyon Voyage: The Narrative of the Second Powell Expedition down the Green Colorado River* (1908; New Haven: Yale University Press, 1962); Goetzmann, *Exploration and Empire;* and Stegner, *Beyond the Hundredth Meridian.*

10. David Lavender, *Colorado River Country* (1982; Albuquerque: University of New Mexico Press, 1988), 120.

11. See Kinsey, "Moran and the Surveying of the West," 89–160.

12. *Home-Thoughts, from Afar: Letters of Thomas Moran to Mary Nimmo Moran* (East Hampton, N.Y.: East Hampton Free Library, 1967), 39.

13. Quoted in Wilkins, *Moran,* 86.

14. See Kinsey, "Moran and the Surveying of the West," 241–316.

15. Quoted in Wilkins, *Moran,* 92.

16. Quoted ibid.

17. Quoted ibid., 93.

18. See Kinsey, "Moran and the Surveying of the West," 316–48.

19. Worster, *Rivers of Empire,* 132.

20. Ibid., 133.

21. For an account of the development of Imperial Valley, see Carey McWilliams, *California: The Great Exception* (1949; Santa Barbara, Calif.: Peregrine Smith, 1976), 293–316.

22. Quoted in Worster, *Rivers of Empire,* 132.

23. Kevin Starr, *Inventing the Dream: California through the Progressive Era* (New York: Oxford University Press, 1985), 134.

24. Lucius Beebe, *The Central Pacific and the Southern Pacific Railroads* (Berkeley, Calif.: Howell-North, 1963), 20.

25. Richardson, *Beyond the Mississippi,* 464–65.

26. Keith Wheeler, *The Railroaders* (New York: Time-Life, 1973), 106.

27. For a full account of the Donner party disaster, see George R. Stewart, *Ordeal by Hunger: The Story of the Donner Party* (New York: Holt, 1936).

28. According to the *Daily Alta,* July 21, 1871, Albert Bierstadt arrived in San Francisco on July 20, 1871.

29. For Collis P. Huntington's role in the railroad enterprise, see Oscar Lewis, *The Big Four: The Story of Huntington, Stanford, Hopkins, and Crocker, and of the Building of the Central Pacific* (New York: Knopf, 1938).

30. D. O. C. Townley, "Albert Bierstadt, N.A.," *Scribner's Monthly* 3 (March 1872): 608.

31. "Two California Landscapes," *Overland Monthly* 10 (March 1873): 286.

32. Benjamin Parke Avery, "Art Beginnings on the Pacific," *Overland Monthly* 1 (July 1868): 30–31.

33. *San Francisco Evening Bulletin,* January 11, 1873.

34. *Overland Monthly* 10 (March 1873): 287.

35. Fitz Hugh Ludlow, "Through Tickets to the

Pacific," *Atlantic Monthly* 14 (November 1864): 604.

36. Crofutt, *Crofutt's New Overland Tourist and Pacific Coast Guide,* 183.

37. Augustus T. Dowd's discovery was described in "The Mammoth Trees of California," *Hutchings' California Magazine* 3 (March 1859). The article was later reprinted in Hutchings, *Scenes of Wonder and Curiosity in California,* 205–17.

38. "The Big Trees of California," *Harper's Weekly* 2 (June 5, 1858): 357.

39. Hutchings, *Scenes of Wonder and Curiosity in California,* 210.

40. Ibid., 211.

41. For a detailed account of Galen Clark's long association with Yosemite Valley, see Shirley Sargent, *Galen Clark: Yosemite Guardian* (Yosemite, Calif.: Flying Spur Press, 1981).

42. According to Fitz Hugh Ludlow (*Heart of the Continent,* 412), Bierstadt examined Carleton E. Watkins's photographs in New York and San Francisco before traveling to Yosemite himself in 1863.

43. Ibid., 422.

44. Ibid., 424.

45. *Redwood Trees of California* was part of the original bequest to the Berkshire Museum in 1903 from its founder, Zenas Marshall Crane, a prosperous mill owner and paper manufacturer. Crane & Co., Inc., continues to produce the paper used by the federal government for the printing of currency.

46. Ibid., 420.

47. Horace Greeley, *An Overland Journey from New York to San Francisco in the Summer of 1859* (1860; New York: Knopf, 1964), 264.

48. Thomas Starr King, "A Vacation among the Sierras," *Boston Evening Transcript,* January 12, 1861.

49. Charles Carleton Coffin, *Our New Way Round the World* (1869; Boston: Estes & Lauriat, 1884), 480.

50. James Smillie, "The Yosemite," in *Picturesque America* (New York: Appleton, 1872–74), 1:470.

51. Peter E. Palmquist, *Redwood and Lumbering in California Forests: A Reconstruction of the Original Edgar Cherry Edition* [1844] (San Francisco: Book Club of California, 1983), 51.

6

"Doing the 'Old America' "

The Image of the American West, 1880–1920

ALEX NEMEROV

I sometimes feel that I am trying to do the impossible in my pictures in not having a chance to work direct but as there are no people such as I paint it's "studio" or nothing.

FREDERIC REMINGTON, 1908

No one and nothing lives *a story.*

HAYDEN WHITE, 1975

On January 6, 1909, John J. Clinton, the chief of police in Abilene, Texas, wrote to Frederic Remington about the painter's *Fight for the Water Hole,* 1903 [257]. Looking at a reproduction of it, Clinton had been uncannily reminded of a similar fight in which he had once participated. The painting was "so realistic," Clinton wrote, believing himself to be one of the depicted men, "that I feel sure some one of the Defenders described it to you." He closed by asking Remington to forward the name and address of the "Defender" on whose story the painter had allegedly based his view.[1]

There is no record of Remington's reply, if any, to Clinton's letter, but he probably felt that the police chief had taken his painting too literally. On the occasion of another such speculation about his picture's "truth," he wrote in his diary: "Jack English and some well bred boys called and they take my pictures for veritable happenings and speculate on what will happen next to the puppets so ardorous are

257. Frederic Remington,
Fight for the Water Hole, 1903,
oil on canvas, 27¼ × 40 in.
The Museum of Fine Arts,
Houston; The Hogg Brothers
Collection, gift of Miss Ima
Hogg.

boys' imaginations."[2] In his western paintings Remington envisioned a more complex project than the kind of simple reflection in which Clinton thought he saw himself.

A letter from Remington to fellow western painter Carl Rungius begins to suggest this larger purpose. "We fellows who are doing the 'Old America' which is so fast passing," he wrote, "will have an audiance in posterity whether we do at present or not."[3] Like many people living in the turn-of-the-century industrialized East, Remington was obsessed with the difference between his own modern era, with its sprawling cities, rumbling machinery, and foreign immigrants, and an idealized, sentimentalized "Old America" left in its wake.[4] It was from this obsession, virtually the central drama in Remington's life, that his vision of the West emerged. In the age of the automobile, what could more poignantly express the disappearance of the old ways, the sentimentalized obsolescence of a traditional America, than Remington's *Old Stagecoach of the Plains,* 1901 [258]?

As a nostalgic icon, moreover, such an image took its place not only among other western scenes but among a variety of antimodern themes. In his *Church at Old Lyme, Connecticut,* 1905, for example, Childe Hassam represents his subject in terms similar to Remington's, reducing the past to a single potent image [259]. In each painting this past becomes figuratively difficult to reach. For Hassam, the past exists coincidentally with its commemoration. It can be known only through monuments or markers such as the church or the painting itself. For Remington, at least in this painting, a past exists outside representation but only faintly. The stagecoach is evanescent, not easily discernible from its own shadows or from the night whose westerly descent it follows. In Remington's painting the stars and lanterns guide not only the stagecoach but our

interpretation: the past flickers.

Yet the idea that Remington's paintings are realistic, that they are magical windows onto their depicted worlds, is as old as the paintings themselves. The principal thing to which the paintings refer, according to this view, is the reality they describe. If Remington painted a stagecoach descending into darkness, and if this stagecoach calls to mind an Apollonian chariot come to earth, he did so because stagecoaches actually did go down hills at night. If he painted a water-hole fight in which spectral shadows and even the sand itself seem to darken, cover, and literally bury the water hole's occupants, it is because such things actually happened. The tautology here—that such paintings are the only evidence of the reality they are said to depict—goes unnoticed. Wrote Theodore Roosevelt, whose *The Winning of the West* (1904 ed.) featured *Fight for the Water Hole* as the frontispiece for volume 4: "The soldier, the cow-boy and rancher, the Indian, the horses and cattle of the plains, will live in [Remington's] pictures and bronzes, I verily believe, for all time."[5]

It is this idea—that the paintings of Henry Farny, Remington, Charles Russell, Charles Schreyvogel, and other turn-of-the-century artists provide us with a documentary or immediate view of the "Old West"—that this chapter will dispute. As an alternative, I will propose that the iconography of cowboys and Indians that arose so vigorously around the turn of the century is best understood in relation to the urban, industrial culture in which this iconography was produced. In other words, what I am concerned with here is this urban, industrial culture as *mediation*. I want to show how this culture embodied a set of attitudes that intruded on and indeed determined the historical subject matter of artists such as Remington.

I take this approach not to call Remington a "bad" historian; in fact, in several respects he seems to have been quite a good one. I take it instead to demonstrate in his work and in that of his contemporaries the subjectivity that is common to all history. This in itself is a rather unremarkable point, but the realistic power so often assigned to these pictures, their continuing existence as a kind of history immediate in which the presence of the historian is effaced, will perhaps warrant my line of investigation. So too might the fact that the works of art themselves display the artists' awareness, conscious or unconscious, of their history's subjectivity. If this chapter demonstrates the fabrication of the turn-of-the-century view of the Old West, it will not undertake this demonstration in the simple sense in which any history can be shown to be fabricated. It will do so instead in an attempt to illustrate that an awareness of this subjectivity, of the fabrication of "objective" history, was part of the artists' own outlook as they made their pictures. It will do so assuming that evidence of this awareness has been effaced by subsequent discussions that have made the pictures' realism or style the end point of analysis.

This study is then an attempt to restore a lost historical context to the works. Investigating this context—asking what it might mean that Remington and others painted their cowboys and Indians in an era of telephones, phonographs, automobiles, and airplanes—will entail two kinds of analysis of the paintings' claims to document the past.

The first will involve the extent to which these works escape the concerns of their own time. In other words, do *Fight for the Water Hole* and other last-stand scenes come across less as documents of the old-time plains than as allegorical expressions of the urban, industrialized world, circa 1900—a world of strikes and proposed anti-immigration legislation? Do the era's depictions of Indians express the artists' sympathy for Indian cultures or do they instead

258. Frederic Remington,
*The Old Stagecoach of the
Plains,* 1901, oil on canvas,
40¼ × 27¼ in. Amon Carter
Museum, Fort Worth, Texas.

259. Childe Hassam, *Church
at Old Lyme, Connecticut,* 1905,
oil on canvas, 36 × 32 in.
Albright-Knox Art Gallery,
Buffalo; Albert H. Tracy
Fund, 1909.

communicate an urban culture's desperate
search for authenticity, for lost origins, a
search that damagingly equated Indian and
other non-white cultures with a lower or previous state of evolution?

The second kind of analysis will examine
something I have already mentioned. If the
night in *The Old Stagecoach of the Plains* com-
plicates our view to the past, literally making
this past difficult to see, and if further it in-
vokes a series of metaphors involving the passing of time, to what extent do other western
paintings acknowledge, via similar formal
means, the logical problems involved in recording a traditional America "which is so fast
passing"? So often considered to be bombastic,
almost thoughtless illustrations of the American past—as if their creators nonchalantly believed that this past could be resurrected with

nothing more than technical facility, a few Indian artifacts, and a copy of Francis Parkman—
the works of Remington and his contemporaries, I believe, express the painters' sublimated
acknowledgment of the difficulties involved in
making history in a time so self-consciously
dislocated from the historical era they sought
to represent.

Order, Scatter, Deny:
Constructing a Real West

Yet any analysis of the image of the West must
begin with the base of its ideological power: its
accreted claims to realism. People from Remington's time to our own have taken his paintings and those of his contemporaries as the
facts about the American West. How has this
occurred?

The paintings themselves provide an important though limited explanation. If the
works of Remington, for example, evoke the
past in subtle and problematic ways—and if
viewers such as John J. Clinton missed these
implications, seeing these works as little more
than accomplished illustrations of this past—it
is nevertheless true that Remington practiced a
kind of documentary approach to his western
subjects. In this respect he was typical of turn-
of-the-century western artists. From his various homes in and around New York, he made
many trips west, where he met cowboys, soldiers, and Indians. He collected a staggering
number of western artifacts, including toma-
hawks, rifles, and still-sharp swords, to place
in the hands of his models and thus ensure the
historical accuracy of his paintings. He wrote
to historical societies for information about
prospective subjects.[6] And he did not hesitate
to condemn other artists for their ignorance of
the Old West. After the American expatriate

Frederick MacMonnies received a commission for a public monument in Denver (a commission that Remington himself wanted), Remington wrote in his diary, "MacMonnies in the country and I expect he will want some more information for his Denver monument but I guess he'll have to go it alone. I haven't accumulated all my knowledge of these matters to glorify a[n] . . . artist who knows no more of our West than a Turk." He called Schreyvogel's *Custer's Demand,* 1903 (Thomas Gilcrease Institute of American History and Art, Tulsa), "half-baked" and "unhistorical." In particular, looking at Schreyvogel's painting, he found fault with the accuracy of the cartridge belts, warbonnets, saddlebags, the shade of the soldiers' trousers, and even the length of the horses' hair. Having begun his career as a magazine illustrator, Remington never lost interest in the most minute facts of western life.[7]

Fight for the Water Hole exemplifies this interest. In the picture's foreground two cowboys virtually offer their carefully rendered armaments for our inspection. As in the hands of the foremost cowboy, the rifle is caressed, venerated, held out to us as something of a true relic [260]. Like such a relic, it has the power to testify to the reality of the historical world of which it is a fragment.[8] In Remington's painting the illusionistic weight of this rifle, its very palpability, ensures the historical authenticity of the entire scene. As certainly as the rifle exists so does the entire episode.

The scattered shells perform a similar function. Lying randomly on the sand, they echo the supine position of the water hole's defenders and the haphazard deployment of their distant assailants. As such they assert the random, unstaged character of the action; they claim that the event and the people within it have not been subject to the controlling hand of an outsider, an artistic creator, who would organize or arrange the randomness. Instead

everything has happened away from such artifice. Things have fallen where they may.

The ability thus to deny its own making is crucial to the realism not only of *Fight for the Water Hole* but of many other turn-of-the-century images of the American West. It is also crucial to the ideology of these images, for when an image loses the time and place in which it was made—when it loses the sense *that* it was made at all—it becomes reified, or mistaken for what it represents. The image of the West becomes the West. As such, it gains the power of common sense or what is "natural" about its object.[9]

Yet one painting, one bunch of spent bullets, cannot alone effect this transformation. Nor can one artist. The realistic power of western images and of the ideology that stood

260. Frederic Remington,
Fight for the Water Hole (detail).

to gain from what was defined as real came primarily through neither their accurate detail nor naturalistic style but through their coherence into an expansive discourse of the West. The most significant display of this discourse, in turn, was the archival collection.[10] Several paintings of the American West conjured more powerfully than any single image the realism of their object. Here were many images of the same place, the same theme: proof in numbers.

The representation of the West in New York, where many turn-of-the-century western artists made or sold their work, exemplifies how this realism worked. Visitors to Remington's 1909 exhibition at Knoedler's Gallery, for example, would have seen seventeen western subjects, paintings with titles such as *Buffalo Runners—Big Horn Basin, The Lost Warrior, The Sun Dance,* and *The War Bridle.* From previous trips to Knoedler's and other galleries these visitors might also have recalled western paintings by Irving Couse, Remington, Russell, and others. After visiting the gallery they might have gone to the Metropolitan Museum of Art, where four Remington bronzes—*The Bronco Buster, The Cheyenne, The Mountain Man,* and *The Old Dragoons of 1850*—were in the collection.[11] From there they could have gone to a bookseller and selected from a myriad of western fictions. Works by Emerson Hough, Frank Norris, Owen Wister, and Remington himself, among others, were all available. They might also have attended a performance of Buffalo Bill's Wild West Show, where they would have seen reenactments of stagecoach robberies, last stands, Indian war dances, and other "typical" western subjects. Taken together, these representations defined something called the Old West. Their pervasiveness alone vouched for the existence of such a place. Numerous representations of last-stand fights by different writers and artists suggested not only that such fights regularly took

place (how could so many people be wrong?); more crucially, these paintings and stories suggested that they occurred in virtually the exact terms in which they were represented [261–65]. Each image featured heroic whites desperately fighting larger numbers of Indian adversaries. Taken together, the sameness of these images—the appearance of identical last stands in different media in the work of different artists and writers—testified to the truth of such an event as a last stand. It is primarily in terms of such collections, then, that the powerful realism of paintings such as *Fight for the Water Hole* must be understood.

The image of the cowboy-and-Indian West, in turn, was only one such discourse to emerge around the turn of the century. Indeed, although the need to arrange and classify information is probably universal—every culture creates systems for understanding the world—we owe to this particular time an unparalleled faith in that particular discursive form, the archival collection, as a means to achieving this understanding. To the same culture that produced the collected image of the Wild West, we owe the large-scale development of museums, academic disciplines such as history and art history, archival libraries, and other taxonomic systems bent on defining in an absolute way their objects of study.[12] These systems instituted a view—for example, that Rembrandt was a great painter—whose status as contingent opinion was erased by the sheer prevalence with which it was announced: ten books claiming that Rembrandt was a great painter established this point of view as fact. In this way the books, the opinions, lost the evidence that they ever were made. The reality of Rembrandt's greatness, just like the authenticity of the last stand, was literally not to be debated. It was common knowledge.

The point is worth stressing. At the time in which the image of the Wild West appeared,

261. Frederic Remington,
The Last Stand, 1890, oil on
canvas, 64 × 47 in. Woolaroc
Museum, Bartlesville,
Oklahoma.

262. Charles Russell, *Caught
in the Circle,* 1903, oil on canvas, 24 × 36 in. National
Cowboy Hall of Fame Collection, Oklahoma City; Albert
K. Mitchell Collection.

263. Frederic Remington, *Rounded-Up,* 1901, oil on canvas, 25 × 48 in. Sid Richardson Collection of Western Art, Fort Worth, Texas.

264. Henry Farny, *Rounded-Up, by God,* 1906, oil on canvas, 39½ × 19½ in. American Heritage Center, University of Wyoming, Laramie.

the archival collection—the vast body of information about a single object of study—had become accepted as a vital access to the reality of this object. Through the collection, through its expansive claim to know its object, people in Remington's time came to understand what was real. Before they ever set foot in Knoedler's Gallery, then, our visitors' expectations would have been thoroughly conditioned.

This raises another important issue: the extent to which these collections could mutually reinforce each other's factual authority. As I mentioned, four Remington bronzes were in the collection of the Metropolitan Museum during his lifetime. At the Metropolitan the claim of these pieces to represent the real West was reinforced by the museum's claim to represent the real history of art. That Remington occasionally went to the Metropolitan to study historical artifacts—no doubt believing in the accuracy with which they represented the past—amplifies this point. For the correctness of his art, he relied on the museum's claims to a similar accuracy.[13] Several of his sculptures then took their place in the very galleries in which he had studied, there to be copied in their turn.

From a recognition of this incestuousness among images can come a critique of the realism of Remington's era. For we begin to see that the different terms in a collection—whether they are paintings, books, or other artifacts—refer not so much to a common reality, to a real object existing or once existing in the world, as to the rest of the collection of which they are part. In the example of the many paintings of the last stand, the similarity between the different representations derives not so much from any actual last stands to which they might refer as from the fact that these images, directly or indirectly, rely on each other to comprehend their object. It is through other images that each picture comes

to define the real. However much *Fight for the Water Hole* may have reminded Clinton of an actual experience, Remington's painting relied on the image of the last stand as its point of reference.

Of course, this reliance on other images extended far beyond the immediate group of last-stand paintings themselves. Western artists from Remington's time inevitably recycled their subjects from the work of their predecessors. For his *Discovery of San Francisco Bay,* 1896 [266], for example, William Keith relied on a conventional imagery of glorious discovery that had been in place a full fifty years in American painting, going back to pictures such as John Vanderlyn's *Landing of Columbus* [see 55]. Before they ever went west, in fact, Remington and other artists had virtually completed

265. N. C. Wyeth, *Fight on the Plains,* 1916, oil on canvas, 32 x 40 in. Mr. and Mrs. Andrew Wyeth Collection.

their frontier iconographies. As a teenage student at Highland Military Academy in Worcester, Massachusetts, Remington made sketches that adumbrate, sometimes remarkably closely, his later subjects.[14] As early as 1881, when he was twenty, he enthusiastically appreciated the work of the French military painter Alphonse-Marie de Neuville.[15] As a boy in New York, George de Forest Brush had seen George Catlin's Indian Gallery and actually met Catlin.[16] When Farny was twelve, a full twenty-two years before he first went west, he made sketches of frontier warfare, replete with howling Indians and trappers in buckskin.[17]

The pages of the young Farny's sketchbook, with their hodgepodge of subjects, summarize the point. On several of these pages, such as the one identified as *Daniel Boone at the Age of Fourteen,* circa 1859, partially drawn an-

tique busts hover over the western action [267]. On one level these busts reflect nothing more than Farny's youthful interest in different artistic models; on another, however, they figuratively depict the ubiquity of other art in the making of the real. This other art, as it were, hangs in the air of a realistic picture as an elemental force from which other images must be derived. This other art inspires from above not only the young Daniel Boone but the figure for whom Boone is a thinly disguised substitute, young Farny himself. Holding his penlike gun, almost as if he has just completed drawing the mouth to his right, he stands tentatively to one side of the virtual diagram of artistic creation—image upon image upon image—he has just made (and that has just made him). The Indians at lower right take an even more uncomfortable view of the situation: they run away.

That the recognition of intertextuality might be traumatic, especially as it came to be applied to the project of knowing the past, is important to consider when discussing late nineteenth-century western art. I believe that at varying levels of sublimation each artist treated here acknowledged the problems of knowing a real past only through the example of other representations. For Farny, at either side of his picture, the recognition was cause for consideration and outright terror. In other artists it provoked similar reactions. For all of them, the recognition might partly have motivated their exacting, obsessive quest for the real. For example, the tight naturalism of Farny's paintings—their effacement of brushstroke, scrupulous detailing, and ostensible isolation from artistic precedents (few of his Indians seem derived from antique statuary)—might be seen as a repression of the fearsome knowledge conveyed by a drawing such as *Daniel Boone at the Age of Fourteen.*

This brings us back to the scattered bullets

266. William Keith, *The Discovery of San Francisco Bay,* 1896, oil on canvas, 40 × 51 in. The Elisabeth Waldo-Dentzel Collection, Northridge, California.

267. Henry Farny, *Daniel Boone at the Age of Fourteen*, circa 1859, pencil on paper, 7¼ × 9½ in. James E. Walter Collection, Toledo.

of *Fight for the Water Hole* [see 257], for the realistic strategies of other western painters can be considered as similar repressions. As we saw, the scattered shells created a notation of the real—a detail that in its very arbitrariness, in its difference from anything that might seem plotted, established the authenticity or unstaged quality of the scene. Such notations appear throughout turn-of-the-century western art. In addition to the random detail, Remington, Russell, and Schreyvogel favored images of violent death to mark the real [see 261–62, 277]. An implicit contrast to the era's sentimentalized painting and literature (art for art's sake, as it was called), the image of a dead man, his limbs

splayed in random final attitude, starkly bespoke a painter's disdain for artistic style of any kind. Such things—the blood, staring eyes, twisted limbs—could happen only in real life.

Combining the picture's space with that of the viewer comprised yet another marker for the real [see 257]. By representing figures staring and even shooting into the viewer's space, Remington and Schreyvogel in particular sought to incorporate the viewer into a depicted action and thus collapse the boundary between painted and real worlds.

Yet the same may be said about something like Bernini's *David*. The path of the rock, as David prepares to hurl it, will cross the viewer's space. The dynamic incorporation of the space of the viewer, in other words, is an artistic (and specifically baroque) convention. By the time Remington and his contemporaries employed it, the incorporation of the viewer's space was a well-traveled marker for the real. So too were images of violent death and of the random array of objects, or still life.

Each of these conventional markers for reality appears in the art of western painters; the crucial point, however, is that generally each does not, at least on a manifest level, appear as a convention. In these images there is little open self-reflection or acknowledgment of the history of art. Openly to make such an acknowledgment would be to admit the fictional quality of the paintings—to admit their correspondence not to the West but to other images, whether of Geronimo or Michelangelo, and such an admission, as the Indians in Farny's drawing show, might be cause for terror indeed. The exacting realism of western art, its apparently humorless attempt to merge with the real, can thus be seen as a repression of what each artist recognized. An image can know the real only through other images.

The Social Function of Western Art

It is difficult, then, to rely on the paintings of Remington and his contemporaries as documentary evidence. Too much artistic "noise" intrudes between the painters and their subjects; moreover, as the juvenile drawings of Farny and Remington reveal, the subjects themselves were derived from artistic conventions. Both artists knew Indians, that is to say images of Indians, before they even went west. In turn, the way in which these images came to be regarded as realistic had little to do with a real West. Instead it had to do with the powerful ability of images to make a coherent dis-

course that defined this real West as, among other things, the land of last stands.

Yet, if the image of the last stand did not represent an actual West, what did it represent? After the Battle of the Little Bighorn in 1876, according to historian Richard Slotkin, the last stand became a powerful metaphor in the industrialized eastern United States.[18] Discussing its regular inclusion in newspaper coverage of eastern events (strikes, for example), Slotkin has identified the last stand as an allegory of the plight of capitalism in an era of frequent conflict between labor and management. Simultaneously it could represent both the managerial elite's desperate situation and its potential for salvation in the form of a new kind of hero, a violent young aristocrat, of which Custer was the archetype. The example is part of Slotkin's larger thesis: that, as a code understood by most everyone, the image of the frontier came to have meaning in the industrialized East. Slotkin points out, for example, that it was not uncommon for newspapers to refer to laborers and immigrants as "savages" or "redskins." Nor was it uncharacteristic of Theodore Roosevelt to associate Indians with certain kinds of "unprogressive" whites, whom he called "the cumberers of the earth."[19] Given their well-established pejorative meanings, such definitions implied the barbarity of those whom they described. As such, the image of the frontier—that great space of right and wrong, of white and red—became a powerful tool by which the eastern environment could be defined.

The era's countless paintings of combat between cowboys and Indians or soldiers and Indians may be understood in these terms. The most telling comparison between images of the East and West is the similar ways in which western artists conceived these two ostensibly different topics. Both Remington's *Mounted Policemen Arresting Burglars Uptown in New York*

and Schreyvogel's *How Kola!* 1901, depict a
fallen adversary at the mercy of a mounted
man in uniform [268–69]. Although Schreyvogel's officer, at least, will spare his foe, each
picture unequivocally establishes in vertical
terms the superiority of the uniformed officer
and indeed of the "uniform" or normative values he represents: up versus down(trodden).[20]
Moreover, each artist represents this superiority as ineluctable. Schreyvogel does so in the
irresistible surge of his troopers from the direction of the mountain in the left background;
Remington in the sweeping, unbroken fence
lines that trail the path of thieves and officers.
Indians on the plains and thieves in Manhattan
are represented in similar ways. When we consider that Schreyvogel made his painting in
Hoboken, New Jersey, it becomes all the more
possible to read *How Kola!* in urban terms. As
a depiction of leniency toward a "friend" of
the law, the picture pronounces its faith in a
just legal system. Those who assist the law
will be remembered and spared. Those who vi-
olate it will be swiftly punished [270].

Remington, for his part, could see urban
situations specifically in frontier terms. Like
many who prided themselves on a supposedly
pure Anglo-Saxon lineage, he was traumatized
by the country's large-scale influx of foreign
immigrants. Blaming them for the country's
unprecedented labor problems, he advocated
violence, a manifestly frontier approach, as a
"solution." "You cant glorify a Jew—coin
'loving puds'—nasty humans," he wrote to his
friend Poultney Bigelow, the editor of *Outing*
magazine. "I've got some Winchesters and
when the massacreing begins which you speak
of, I can get my share of 'em and whats more I
will." He continued by excoriating "Jews—
inguns—chinamen—Italians—Huns, the rubish
of the earth I hate."[21]

Sent to Chicago by *Harper's Weekly* to
cover the Pullman Strike, Remington identified

the rebellious workers as a "malodorous crowd of anarchistic foreign trash" and praised the government soldiers brought in to maintain order.[22] For him, the two sides were clear-cut. "Pure and simple of speech," the soldiers were "honest, and no man can be one who can't pass the most rigid physical examination imaginable." Their presence alone keeps the "social scum from rising to the top." The strikers, "vicious wretch[es] with no blood circulating above [the] ears," will follow "readily any demagogue with revolutionary tendencies."

In *Giving the Butt,* one of the illustrations he made for his Pullman stories, Remington represents a violent method of strikebreaking [271]. In his mind, moreover, the violence contains its own justification not only in the squalid character of the strikers, with their decrepit clothing and grizzled features, but in

their "wildness" as well. Significantly, in an image otherwise given to a tight grid of verticals and horizontals, he portrays the hand of one striker flailing upward. In this gesture he finds a metaphor for the strikers' unruliness, their irrationality.

In *Mounted Policemen* [see 268] he employs a similar formal language to contrast social order and wildness. Whereas the arm of the standing thief flails in a way similar to that of the Pullman striker and the tangled limbs of the fallen thief become pejoratively equated with those of the animal above, the arms of the lead officer are wrapped tightly in front of his torso, making his upper body into a boxlike shape that identifies him with the fences and houses. Like them, he is a structure of authority.

The same formal relationships exist in Remington's images of the West. In *The Intruders,* 1900, for example, frontiersmen are depicted in a monumental pyramid, its solidity echoed by the stable forms of the men themselves [272]. Even the rifles, deployed on steady horizontals, connote the order or logic of their position. In contrast, when Remington depicted Indians in combat, it was often in the terms in which he had represented his laborers or thieves [273].

Similarly Charles Russell tended to portray warring Indians as ruthless, bloodthirsty mobs. In images such as *For Supremacy,* 1895, or *When Blackfeet and Sioux Meet,* 1908, he pictured Indian warfare as melee, a close-quarter combat in which bodies, weapons, and horses confusedly overlap [274–75]. His warring Indian was an amalgam of exaggerated or raucous gesture: mouth open, face contorted, body leaning elastically, weapon slung far back or overhead. Moreover, Russell thought of the Indian battle largely in terms of diagonals comprising a generally asymmetrical composition. The resulting lack of compositional stability thus became an analogue for the "imbalance" or unreasonableness of the Indian fight. It is not beside the point that Russell's sources for such pictures were the hunt scenes of Peter Paul Rubens. To convey the frenzy of a boar or lion with a spear in its flank, Rubens employed the whirling, tumultuous compositions that well suited Russell's need to show the "animal" quality of his Indians in combat.[23]

Such an assumption embodied the era's social Darwinism. In the Darwinian view of history the conquest of the frontier could be explained as only the latest in a centuries-old pattern of Anglo-Saxon victories. In *The Winning of the West,* for example, Theodore Roosevelt elaborately extended this pattern back to the German invasions of the late Roman Em-

271. Frederic Remington, *Giving the Butt*. From *Harper's Weekly* 38 (July 21, 1894): 680. Frederic Remington Art Museum, Ogdensburg, New York.

272. Frederic Remington, *The Intruders,* 1900, oil on canvas, 27 × 47 in. Private collection.

273. Frederic Remington, *Thrust His Lance through His Body*, 1889, oil on canvas, 28 × 19⅝ in. Indianapolis Museum of Art; gift of the Harrison Eiteljorg Gallery of Western Art.

pire.[24] Anglo-Saxon superiority could be explained in terms of a succession of frontiers, from the Black Forest to the Black Hills. In each, the figure of the lone hunter, epitomizing the best of the Anglo-Saxons, had proved the race's superiority through acts of violence to other cultures. These other cultures—Huns, Celts, Indians, and then (with immigration) still more Huns and Celts—were relatively interchangeable. What mattered was their capability in defeat to evince the powerful racial identity of their Anglo-Saxon foe. Through violence (or its representation) Anglo-Saxons could thus come to know the peculiar virtue of their race.

In this respect, if they relate to his police officer in Manhattan, Remington's frontiersmen also relate to the fearsomely stern nordic legions in an image such as N. C. Wyeth's *First Cargo*, 1910 [276]. In a ten-gallon hat or a ten-gallon helmet, the Anglo-Saxon literally identified with the race through a capacity for violence. The Norsemen might be in buckskin, the cowboys in armor, but it made little difference. Each stood for an identical racial virtue.[25]

Yet it might be objected that many western paintings, particularly those of last stands, hardly match the kind of unequivocal, wall-to-wall Anglo-Saxonism of *The First Cargo*. In Schreyvogel's *Defending the Stockade*, circa 1905, the flailing arms this time belong to the soldiers; falling down, bandaging their wounds, scorching their hands in desperate clasps of intruding rifles, they scurry to close the fort's gates to the enemy [277]. In Remington's *Dash for the Timber*, 1889, eight cowboys find themselves in an equally perilous situation [278]. Hurtling toward the viewer's space, they are pursued by a substantially larger band of Indians whose limitlessness or "hording" is suggested by the way it runs off the right side of the canvas. If each picture celebrates the heroism of its Anglo combatants, each also registers doubts about their survival.

In turn, given the ready interchangeability of images of East and West, city and frontier, these doubts may be related to concerns about another kind of survival: that of an Anglo-Saxon race in a world "overrun" with immigrants. Like the troopers in *Defending the Stockade*, Uncle Sam in *The High Tide of Immigration—A National Menace* tries to protect his borders from a foreign invasion that literally does not know or respect such a concept [279]. Like the Indians in *A Dash for the Timber*, the "riff raff immigration" extends beyond the picture's borders. Remington's painting and the *High Tide* cartoon thus underscore not only

274. Charles Russell, *For Supremacy*, 1895, oil on canvas, 23⅛ × 35 in. Amon Carter Museum, Fort Worth, Texas.

275. Charles Russell, *When Blackfeet and Sioux Meet*, 1908, oil on canvas, 20½ × 29⅞ in. Sid Richardson Collection of Western Art, Fort Worth, Texas.

276. N. C. Wyeth, *The First Cargo*, 1910, oil on canvas, 47 × 38 in. New York Public Library, The Central Children's Room, Donnell Library Center.

their sense of the immigrants' massive numbers but also the perceived disrespect for borders, troped in the picture's border itself, that has led them to immigrate in the first place. Of course, Schreyvogel's painting could relate to the image of immigration in more direct ways as well [280].

The point is not that artists such as Remington and Schreyvogel consciously matched their western subjects to social phenomena such as increased immigration. Their pictures were not deliberate allegories. On the contrary, if Schreyvogel made "closing the door" his central theme, he did so because the terms he possessed for representing the West emerged from a culture in which the idea of closing the door, of enacting anti-immigration legislation, was important. Faced with the challenge of

showing an intrusion, Schreyvogel made his picture in the terms in which his culture understood the word: as a forceful violation of racial and national borders. At work here then is a culturally specific definition, a definition that could organize any subject to which it was applied.[26] It is not beside the point that the theme of defending the fort, in the terms in which Schreyvogel represented it, began virtually with this image. To a culture obsessively concerned with protecting its borders, we owe the image of uniformed troopers defending an imperiled stockade.

The Indian captivity theme, on the other hand, is as old as white American culture itself, dating to the narrative of Mary Rowlandson, published in 1682, and before. Around 1900, however, it came to have specific meanings not unlike those of *Defending the Stockade* and other battle scenes. The escape or at least the possibility of escape had always been part of the captivity theme; without an escape, after all, captives could never tell their stories. In American painting even the most pessimistic depictions, such as George Caleb Bingham's *Captured by Indians* [see 138], held out the possibility of a nearby rescuer. In Remington's *Captured*, 1899, and Farny's *Captive*, 1885, however, we are given a glimpse of virtually hopeless situations [281–82]. In Remington's picture the distant lookout establishes rescue as a "remote" possibility, and in Farny's work the two distant hills at left, echoing the positions of captor and captive, underscore the monotony of the landscape, expressing spatially the similar monotony of the captive's torture.

On one level, like the objects cluttered around the fire in Remington's painting, these desperate situations suggest the real character of the action, its claim to be beyond the dramatic conventions that would organize a plot and make rescue a reasonable possibility. The skin of the captives, catching the viewer's eye

277. Charles Schreyvogel, *Defending the Stockade,* circa 1905, oil on canvas, 28 × 36 in. Gaylord Broadcasting Company Collection, Oklahoma City.

278. Frederic Remington, *A Dash for the Timber,* 1889, oil on canvas, 48¼ × 84⅛ in. Amon Carter Museum, Fort Worth, Texas.

279. Louis Dalrymple, *The High Tide of Immigration—A National Menace.* From *Judge* 45 (August 22, 1903): centerfold. Enoch Pratt Free Library, Baltimore.

immediately, is the most decisive trope for this stylistic nakedness.

Yet, on another level, Farny's captive bears a powerful relationship to other art, specifically to representations of Christ or more precisely Saint Peter on the cross. His skin is a clothing of sacrifice. It relates his suffering to a centuries-old rhetoric of noble victims and evil oppressors. As such, it conventionally views the whites of the Old West as heroic sacrifices to the modern day: they died so that the West could be settled. Yet it also conjures the idea of heroic sacrifice as it might relate directly to this modern era. For an Anglo culture struggling to comprehend numerous misfortunes, such an image could suggest a higher or sacrificial purpose to the suffering.

A stronger racial identity, forged through increased awareness of the "inferiority" of other cultures, might have been one such higher purpose. For if the paintings of Remington and Farny acknowledge a "danger to American ideas and institutions," they also dwell forcibly on the absolute difference between light and dark. In each painting the whiteness of the captive's flesh sharply separates him from his captors. In one of his careful details, the saddle pointing like a two-pronged stick at the captive and one of his captors, Remington underscores the concept of racial polarity that informs his picture. There is now no room, as there was in Bingham's painting, for a confusion of races, a darkness of white and whiteness of dark. Instead Remington's picture, working like Farny's to connect its captive with ancient concepts of heroic sacrifice, depends on its obsession with unmistakably different skins to express this heroism. The trooper's creamy flesh contrasts forcibly with the buffalo hide or skin worn by the adjacent Indian. Remington emphasizes this contrast by rhyming light- and dark-skinned horses behind the two figures. Associating the Indian with the buffalo skin and thus with the act of flaying, Remington not only implies what is in store for the trooper (the standing Indian holds a weapon partially concealed under his blanket), he also establishes a complex metaphor allowing him to judge both white "heroism" and Indian "savagery." As a Dionysian rite, flaying had long been associated with passion, frenzy, barbarousness—with qualities usually ascribed by western culture to any non-white others. Its association here with Indians is part of this tradition. Yet the act of being flayed had also come to stand for a kind of divine purification by which a person's outward body could be stripped away to reveal the "soul" beneath.[27] In the theme of flaying, with its ancient origins in the story of Apollo and Marsyas and the martyrdom of Saint Bartholomew, Remington compactly established

AN INTERESTING QUESTION

both the barbarousness of his Indians and the racial soul—the spirit revealed in suffering—of his white captive.

This racial identification became even starker in late nineteenth-century representations of female captives, where the possibility of miscegenation is repeatedly posed. In this respect little separates these works from the tradition of the captivity narrative. Since the time of Puritan culture, the question of race mixing had been an important theme. The obsessive development of the theme in paintings such as Irving Couse's *Captive,* 1892, however, relates these works to a dominant culture that had begun to hinge the future of "civilization" to the maintenance of racial separation [283]. "If the valuable elements in the Nordic race mix with inferior strains or die out through race suicide," wrote Professor Henry Fairfield Osborn, summarizing a prevalent view, "then the citadel of civilization will fall for mere lack of defenders."[28]

280. E. M. Ashe, *An Interesting Question.* From *Life* 21 (June 22, 1893): 398–99. John and Selma Appel, East Lansing, Michigan.

281. Frederic Remington, *Captured,* 1899, oil on canvas, 27 × 40⅛ in. Sid Richardson Collection of Western Art, Fort Worth, Texas.

282. Henry Farny, *The Captive,* 1885, gouache on paper, 22⅝₁₆ × 40¹⁄₁₆ in. Cincinnati Art Museum; gift of Mrs. Benjamin E. Tate and Julius Fleischmann in memory of their father, Julius Fleischmann.

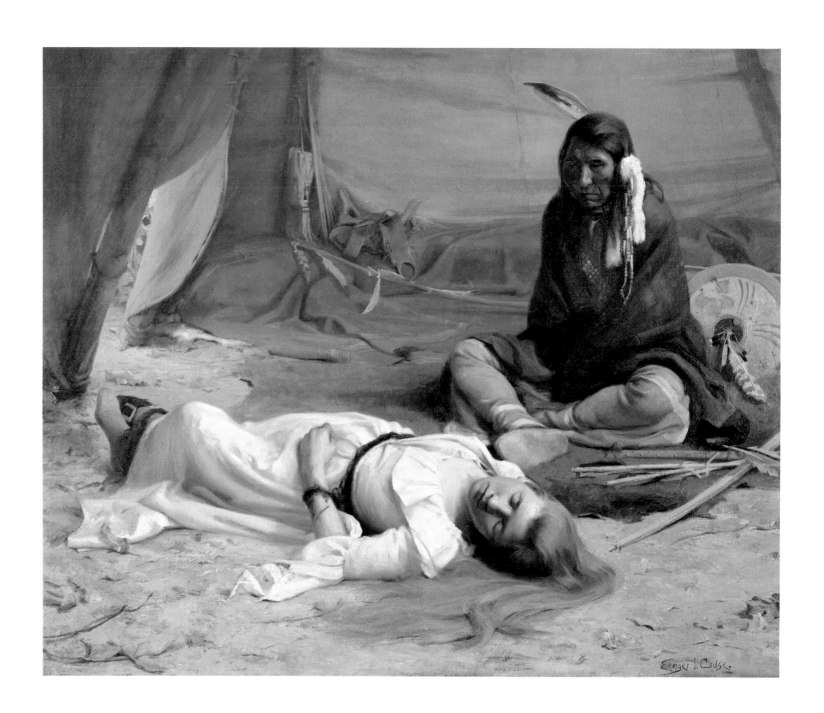

283. Irving Couse, *The Captive,* 1892, oil on canvas, 50 × 60 in. Association Administrators and Consultants, Inc., Irvine, California.

Depicting the seventeen-year-old Lorinda Bewly as captive of the Cayuse chief Five Crows, Couse's lurid treatment of a historical event (set in 1847) unconsciously expresses his culture's fears of miscegenation. This is evident first in the network of intimations that thinly repress an actual sexual encounter. Bewly's skewed and foreshortened body, recalling the martyr's pose of Farny's captive, suggests as much as the blood on her wrist a violent physical confrontation with Five Crows. The array of phallic objects pointing in her direction, together with the tepee's open entry, further imply a sexual encounter, as does the picture's one instance of cross-cultural "touching"—the nudging, in two dimensions, of Five Crows's right foot against Bewly's body.

Yet, at odds with its violent racial drama, the picture develops another, quieter erotic relationship. If Bewly's body is skewed and foreshortened, cut and cut-off, it is at the same time almost gently displayed for the viewer. Against the logic of the narrative, Bewly's figure is oriented more to the picture plane than to her Indian captor. It is the viewer who sees her face, hair, and covering gesture. Through the fiction of the scene, what is denied to Five Crows becomes available to the (white) audience who would see Couse's painting.

This second, erotic relationship establishes another kind of identification at work in Couse's picture. If the viewer was able to define himself racially against the Indian, he was also able to define himself sexually against the figure of Bewly. If Five Crows is objectified as an "Indian"—proverbially violent and inscrutable—in a similar way Bewly is reduced drastically to a set of traditional and pejorative definitions of "woman": recumbent, helpless, unaware. In this sense ostensible polarities (Indian and woman) exist as similarly marginalized others—each objectified or captured by the artist.

Couse's picture comes from a culture fascinated with capturing Indians. This captivation could be actual, as in the relegation of numerous tribes to reservations or in the pursuit of a famous adversary. (On his first *Harper's Weekly* traveling assignment, Remington accompanied an expedition to capture Geronimo.)[29] It could be "scientific," as in the widespread anthropological confiscation of tribal artifacts or exhumation of tribal burial grounds.[30] And this captivation could also be artistic. Following the prototype of Catlin and other earlier "Indian gallery" creators, numerous photographers and painters amassed huge archives of Indian images at this time.

Edward Sheriff Curtis's *Book of North American Indians* (1907–30) is the most well known of these archives. By 1930, when the last of his project's twenty volumes was published, Curtis had taken more than forty thousand photographs over several decades of fieldwork. Among the work of painters, the Indian portraits of Elbridge Burbank were the most extensive. His project began in 1897, when his uncle, the wealthy entrepreneur Edward Everett Ayer, commissioned a portrait of Geronimo, who had by then been captured and confined to a reservation at Fort Sill, Oklahoma Territory.[31] After that, Burbank began painting or drawing the likenesses of as many Indians, from as many different tribes, as he possibly could. The result was more than twelve hundred such images by 1914 [284–89]. Many of these were purchased by Ayer and donated to the Newberry Library in Chicago as a study resource (Burbank's portrait of his patron reveals Ayer's interest in Indian cultures [290]).

"The vast ethnological value" of these portraits, according to one contemporary writer, lay in their claim to preserve on canvas a record of the "authentic" Indian. Burbank "fully appreciates that it is now or never," continues the writer, (for)

ONE STAR
BRULE SIOUX
ROSEBUD S DAK
1903

NE-J-SO-NE
YUMA

PAH-LAH-WOOL-EY
HOPI

CHIEF YELLOW HAMMER
MODOC

KO-PE-LEY
MOQUI

284. Elbridge Burbank, *One-Star, Brulé Sioux*, 1903, oil on canvas, 13 × 9⅛ in. National Museum of American Art, Smithsonian Institution, Washington, D.C.; bequest of Victor J. Evans.

285. Elbridge Burbank, *Ne-I-So-Meh, Yuma*, 1904, oil on canvas, 13 × 9⅛ in. National Museum of American Art, Smithsonian Institution, Washington, D.C.; bequest of Victor J. Evans.

286. Elbridge Burbank, *Pah-Lah-Wool-Ey, Hopi*, 1904, oil on canvas, 13 × 9 in. National Museum of American Art, Smithsonian Institution, Washington, D.C.; bequest of Victor J. Evans.

287. Elbridge Burbank, *Chief Yellow Hammer, Modoc*, 1901, oil on canvas, 13 × 9 in. Thomas Gilcrease Institute of American History and Art, Tulsa.

288. Elbridge Burbank, *Ko-Pe-Ley, Moqui*, 1897, oil on canvas, 13 × 9 in. Thomas Gilcrease Institute of American History and Art, Tulsa.

289. Elbridge Burbank, *Kla-Aughts, Yuma*, 1904, oil on canvas, 11 × 9 in. Thomas Gilcrease Institute of American History and Art, Tulsa.

the store coat is replacing the one of buckskin, the dances, the ceremonies, are rapidly disappearing; the chief, the hunter, the warrior, and the medicine-man are almost extinct; the hoe takes the place of the spear; the Indian's civilization is going and with it all that makes him unique among men.[32]

"Real" Indians, like the Old West, were "rapidly disappearing." It consequently became important to make an accurate record or archive of all tribal cultures. Ostensibly these accurate records did "justice" to Indians, treating them not as stereotypes but "exactly as [they] look."[33] Yet what these images preserved was not Indians so much as that for which Indians had become a metaphor: the past. In a self-consciously bureaucratized, enervated culture, images of Indians became the very incarnation of that idealized place Remington called the "Old America." Works such as N. C. Wyeth's *Invocation to the Buffalo Herds*, 1910, Hermon Atkins MacNeil's *Chief of the Multnomah Tribe*, 1907, and Alexander Phimister Proctor's *War Chief*, 1898, came to represent the set of mythic American values—pride, defiance, freedom—in whose name actual Indian cultures had been decimated [291–93].

As heroic-scale sculpture, moreover, many of these works took their places in American parks and expositions. A photograph of Cyrus Dallin's *Protest of the Sioux*, taken at the Saint Louis World's Fair of 1904, summarizes both the scale of such monuments and metaphorically the "little man," the consummate bureaucrat, whose vigor the monuments were supposed to restore [294]. Indeed the little man's complacent function here—he is nothing more or less than "scale"—is an apt register of the very enervation that popularized the image of the hollering heroic Indian.

As a marker for an idealized past, the image of an Indian was in one sense interchangeable with other antimodern representations. Like images of medieval culture, colonial

America, or the Old West in general, it appealingly suggested a proverbially simpler time.[34] Although Farny's *Happy Days of Long Ago*, 1912, differs markedly from Willard Metcalf's *In the North Country*, 1923, each picture idealizes a small, "old-time" community in harmony with the natural environment [295–96]. Many other western scenes, such as Jules Tavernier's *Indian Village at Acoma*, 1879, can be read as similar idealizations of the preindustrial community [297].

In other Farny paintings, moreover, it is not white explorers and soldiers but the railroad that augurs the end of the "happy days." The train in *Morning of a New Day* announces the modern age's actual and spiritual mechanization [see 148]. The Indians, on the other hand, conventionally represent a traditional, older way of life. For both Farny and Russell, the historical story of industry's appearance on the frontier—trains, wagons, and steamboats eyed warily by Indians, whose point of view each painter repeatedly adopts—expressed their own apprehensions about the modern industrial age. What was "doomed" in such pictures was not only Indians but the Old America.

In another sense, however, these Indian images must be read apart from other nostalgic themes. They differ because they alone helped sanction the decimation they represented. By equating Indian cultures with the past they implicitly accepted a theory of social evolution that posited the disappearance of "primitive" peoples before the inexorable advance of "civilization." Indians or at least "authentic" Indians had no existence in the present.

In this conception, according to the anthropologist Johannes Fabian, history is represented as a "temporal slope": a gradually ascending timeline, ending in the present day, on which the evolutionary development of various human cultures is plotted.[35] To western civilization, at the peak of this slope, is granted the

privileged position of looking down on "earlier" cultures.

At the turn of the century this privileged position, in turn, informed attitudes toward Indians that indeed existed in the western present. Rather than people whose cultures (like all cultures) were constantly developing, adapting to changing historical circumstances, these Indians were regarded as remnants from a stopped or dead culture of the past. As such, although they lived in the present, they belonged to a "primitive" era that did not, nor could not, comprehend the technological and intellectual achievements of this present.

If they themselves could not understand, however, the point was precisely that Indians could be understood by whites. According to Fabian, the idea of the temporal slope has been crucial to virtually all discourse that (literally) examines another culture. As a visual model, it has represented the fact that it is the distance between cultures that allows for objectivity.

290. Elbridge Burbank, *Edward Everett Ayer,* 1897, oil on canvas, 25 × 32 in. The Newberry Library, Chicago.

291. N. C. Wyeth, *Invocation to the Buffalo Herds,* 1910, oil on canvas, 35½ × 25½ in. Private collection.

292. Hermon Atkins Mac-Neil, *A Chief of the Multnomah Tribe,* 1907, bronze, height 32 in. Thomas Gilcrease Institute of American History and Art, Tulsa.

293. Alexander Phimister Proctor, *War Chief,* 1898, bronze, height 40⅛ in. Thomas Gilcrease Institute of American History and Art, Tulsa.

294. Unidentified photographer, *"Protest of the Sioux"* by *Cyrus Dallin at the Louisiana Purchase Exposition of 1904 in Saint Louis,* 1904. Missouri Historical Society, Saint Louis.

295. Henry Farny, *The Happy Days of Long Ago*, 1912, oil on canvas, 33 1/16 × 22 3/4 in. Private collection.

296. Willard Metcalf, *In the North County,* 1923, oil on canvas, 39⅞ × 45 in. The Metropolitan Museum of Art, New York; George A. Hearn Fund, 1924.

297. Jules Tavernier, *Indian Village at Acoma,* 1879, oil on canvas, 64 × 29½ in. The Anschutz Collection, Denver.

The idea of temporal distancing, Fabian argues, has thus been indispensable in western attempts to know other cultures. Without such distance, in conventional anthropological thinking, the object of study would literally be too close to be objectively understood.

The way in which artists such as Farny made their paintings exemplifies this temporal distancing. For such paintings do not show the artist's actual studio confrontation with an Indian model. Instead they represent a finished product, like *Happy Days of Long Ago,* in which this confrontation—occurring in the coincident time of painter and model—is transferred or distanced into the past-tense world of the painting. In this way, through depiction on canvas, the Indian model is taken from the present, from a coeval relationship with the painter—no temporal slopes but two people in the same room—and inserted into the distant past-tense realm in which he can be apprehended as earlier and hence inferior.[36]

Yet the two realms, studio and painting, cannot be divided absolutely. In their ability to equate Indians with the past, images such as *Happy Days of Long Ago* informed attitudes toward Indians existing in the western present. With this point in mind, we can better understand the situation of *Ogallala Fire*, Farny's primary model [298]. Ogallala Fire was the janitor for the Cincinnati Art Club, a position far removed from the heroic roles in which Farny cast him in his paintings. "The hand that erstwhile wielded the tomahawk and scalping knife," wrote Farny, "now handles the broom and dustpan."[37]

In one sense the discrepancy is chilling. In Farny's portrait of Ogallala Fire the thorough transformation from janitor to warrior, from present to past, eerily suggests the artist's need to distance his subject from the modern day. Ogallala Fire cannot be "understood" as someone walking around the same room with the artist. Yet in another sense no discrepancy is involved; as janitor or warrior, Ogallala Fire is demeaningly confined. Only the props placed in his hands or on his head are different. Moreover, for Farny, Ogallala Fire's depiction as warrior might well have helped explain his role as janitor. As a member of a "vanishing" race, he can be expected to do no more than handle "the broom and dustpan."

Like the Indian portraits of Burbank, Bert Phillips, and Joseph Sharp, Farny's *Ogallala Fire* employs a close-up, bust-length format in which the sitter is seen against a bare background. This format implies the immediacy of the image, as if there were no time for props, poses, or the other baggage of the *portrait d'ap-*

298. Henry Farny, *Ogallala Fire,* 1902, oil on panel, 12 × 16 in. Richard and Mary Bowman Collection, Denver.

parat. Farny's painting, like those of Burbank, is thus meant to appear outside the domain of artistic convention. It strives for a kind of documentary realism.

In addition to this effect, the bust- and half-length formats of Burbank's portraits imply the urgency of his undertaking [see 284–89]. His goal was to render as many Indian likenesses as possible before his subjects "disappeared."[38] This simplified style thus suggests the lack of time dictating Burbank's project in the first place. In the depiction of a "vanishing" race there literally was not enough time to make complicated, full–length portraits.

The format also indicates Burbank's pri-

mary area of interest: the face. This is particularly evident in his red-chalk drawings, in which sitters are sometimes reduced to little more than disembodied heads floating on the page [299–300]. In the face would be contained the information subsequent generations would need to study a vanished culture.

For many of his sitters, moreover, Burbank made both front and profile views of his subjects. The resemblance to mug shots may not be accidental; at the 1893 World's Columbian Exposition in Chicago, where Burbank lived, an exhibit featured Alphonse Bertillon's newly developed criminal-classification system.[39] Whether or not Burbank saw the ex-

299. Elbridge Burbank, *Kis-To, Pima,* 1905, red chalk on paper, 15 × 10 in. The Newberry Library, Chicago.

300. Elbridge Burbank, *Mah-Sin-Dah, Digger,* 1906, red chalk on paper, 15 × 10 in. The Newberry Library, Chicago.

hibit, his Indian portraits employ the same means to define their subjects. An image or two images, carefully made, would allow subsequent viewers to objectify an absent person as a certain type—in the case of Burbank's portraits, as an "Indian."

In the logic of the collection, however, it is not actual Indians but the portraits themselves that define an "Indian." Across virtually all his portraits Burbank employs the same means—"authentic" clothing and weapons, somber faces, formal poses—to help his viewers gain a coherent definition of "Indian." Indians were understood in the way in which they were systematically represented in the collection. And with a tomblike name and date identifying each likeness, this systematic representation focused on an idea of Indians' inevitable disappearance.

Yet, like Farny's Ogallala Fire, Burbank's Indian subjects were living in the modern day. To document Indian cultures Burbank had to suppress evidence of his sitters' contemporary lives. So that his Indian chiefs could appear in "true war regalia," he outfitted some of them in costumes borrowed from the collection of an Indian named Yellow Bird. Because many of these subjects could not be counted on to possess war paint, he always carried extra paints "such as the Indians used." Although it could not be discovered in the portrait itself, a Crow chief named Pretty Eagle posed for Burbank amid "the silk and satin sofa pillows" of a frontier living room [301]. A Navajo owned a Dodge automobile. A Mohave chief made money selling bows and arrows to train passengers. A whole tribe, the Warner Ranch Indians, lived in a government-constructed village.[40] Like other Indian painters of the time, Burbank rarely indicated these changed circumstances. Only in images such as Paul Frenzeny's *Big Medicine Man,* 1882, or Remington's *Method of Sketching at San Carlos* [302–3], do

301. Elbridge Burbank, *Chief Pretty Eagle, Crow,* 1897, oil on canvas, 13 × 10 in. Thomas Gilcrease Institute of American History and Art, Tulsa.

we see evidence of the sort of mediations omitted in portraits such as Burbank's.

"I am calling the hand that is in your hat."

Burbank's omissions begin to suggest the modern-day intrusions faced by every western painter at the time. Recounting an attempt to sketch Pikes Peak in 1911, Schreyvogel wrote to his wife: "I started [a sketch] with Pike's Peak in the back ground and it looked fine. I was there at 7:30 A.M. Then the smelters started in and the black smoke just covered the whole valley so that I couldn't see a thing and had to stop."[41] Back east, where he made many of his paintings on the roof of his apart-

THE 'BIG MEDICINE MAN'

302. Paul Frenzeny, *The Big Medicine Man*, 1882, pencil, watercolor, and gouache on paper, 12½ × 18⅝ in. Museum of Fine Arts, Boston; gift of Maxim Karolik.

303. Frederic Remington, *Method of Sketching at San Carlos*. From *Century Magazine* 38 (July 1889): 398. Buffalo Bill Historical Center, Cody, Wyoming.

ment building in Hoboken, Schreyvogel's models were Grant Bloodgood, the neighborhood handyman, and Storie Schultze, the teenage son of a local champagne salesman [see 44].[42] Like other artists, Brush found an Indian model at a Madison Square Garden appearance of Buffalo Bill's Wild West Show.[43] For his *Moose Chase* [see 308], Brush eventually abandoned attempts to sketch a live model in the heavily hunted forests of Quebec, where he was living at the time; ultimately he found the moose of the final painting in a local traveling circus.[44] For action-packed pictures such as *Cavalry Charge on the Southern Plains in 1860*, 1907, Remington posed his models on a saddle display in his yard in New Rochelle, New York [304–5]. He studied buffalo in the Bronx Zoo and in his diary lamented the modernity of an Indian model: " 'Kinrade' my indian came to pose. Says he is a Sac and Fox—he had a good figure but don't know how to put on a G string and is innocent of indian business. He acts tongue bred and dresses 'western' actor fashion."[45]

Each of these scenarios suggests an acute tension between the finished realism of western paintings and the actual circumstances in which they were made.[46] The point, however, is not that these artists openly thought of their methods as false ways of recording the Old West; on the contrary, both the artists and their audiences unself-consciously regarded studio work and poses as the necessary means to accurate or realistic representations of the past. Yet, in retrospect, these examples suggest the hopeless separation of western artists from the era they sought to document. And this sense of separation intrudes on the final paintings themselves, for in sublimated ways within these works western artists acknowledge their inability to recover a real past.

This sublimated acknowledgment focuses on the idea of mediation. It concentrates on

304. Frederic Remington, *Cavalry Charge on the Southern Plains in 1860*, 1907, oil on canvas, 30⅛ × 51⅛ in. The Metropolitan Museum of Art, New York; gift of several gentlemen, 1911.

what comes between artist and historical subject, on what makes a picture inherently incapable of providing a permanent record of the past. Western paintings reveal their obsession with at least three such mediations. One is other art. A second is the passing of time. A third is the act of painting itself. In western art made around the turn of the century, each of these mediations comes to represent an unavoidable obstacle to a realistic retrieval of the past.

As a result, it is possible to say that there are at least two competing subjects at work in western paintings from this time: a historical subject, powerfully retrieved through a realistic style, and then a metahistorical subject, which focuses on one or more of the mediations mentioned and thus questions this act of historical retrieval.

In N. C. Wyeth's *Wild Bill Hickok at Cards* [306], for example, this second or metahistorical subject is the mediation of other art. As might befit an image made in 1916, ten years after Wyeth had last visited the West, the picture refers more to the history of art than to a real West. It bears a compositional and thematic resemblance to Supper at Emmaus scenes, such as Caravaggio's version in the National Gallery, London [307].[47] Not only does the long-haired Hickok assume the role of Christ, he also enacts a drama that, like the one at Emmaus, centers around the revelation of information. Whereas Christ reveals his identity to the two disciples, with a similar gesture Hickok reveals the cheating of his fellow cardplayer. Reliance on baroque prototypes was not uncommon among western painters; the difference is that Wyeth does not attempt to

305. Attributed to Frederic Remington, *Model Posed on a Saddle Display,* before 1900, albumen print. Frederic Remington Art Museum, Odgensburg, New York.

deny or hide his artistic source. On the contrary, in the poster on the wall he plainly announces the fictive space in which his western action occurs.[48]

Moreover, Wyeth transforms the picture's drama—Hickok's line, "I am calling the hand that is in your hat"—into a commentary on the perils of this openly reflexive picture-making. Near the center of his picture Wyeth displays the cheating gambler's revealed "hands," both his actual left hand and, on the table, his hand of cards. On one level, the hands forcefully express the end of the gam-

bler's fraud. On another, however, the gambler's hands represent the revelation of still another hand: that of the artist. In a picture so willing to acknowledge its fiction, it is the artist's hand or style that becomes visible. In this sense the artist and the cheating gambler are related. Like this gambler, the artist conceals extra hands—the influences of other artists—that make their way, usually imperceptibly, into his realistic pictures.

When these extra hands are discovered, however, when the artist's claims of realism are seen to rest on nothing more than the influence of other images, people do not take kindly to the revelation. This much Wyeth tells us in the figure of Wild Bill Hickok, who points a gun at the faceless gambler whose features, were he to turn around, might be those of Wyeth himself. In the punning world of *Wild Bill Hickok at Cards,* however, it is the artist who gets the last laugh, for Hickok's gun, like Hickok himself and the rest of the scene, has literally been "drawn": in this painting nothing exists outside representation. The closed door further announces that the action takes place in its own separate world, shut off from the real. Moreover, if the door did open onto the next room, one would more likely interrupt Caravaggio's *Supper at Emmaus* than the real counterparts of Hickok and his fellow gamblers.

George de Forest Brush also self-consciously relied on the history of art in making his western paintings. If, however, Wyeth underscored his painting's fiction through references to other art, delighting in the disconsonance between the Supper at Emmaus and a frontier card game, Brush used the same kinds of old master paintings to hit on what he considered to be eternal truths. In "this commercial age," as he called his own era, Brush believed that the works of the old masters could keep both artist and viewer in touch with time-

306. N. C. Wyeth, *Wild Bill Hickok at Cards,* 1916, oil on canvas, 32 × 40 in. William D. Weiss Collection, Jackson Hole, Wyoming.

307. Michelangelo Merisi da Caravaggio, *Supper at Emmaus,* circa 1600, oil on canvas, 55½ × 77¼ in. National Gallery, London.

less values.[49] "In our times," he wrote to a friend, "all old ideas are changing rapidly so that we come to doubt whether there is anything permanent, but there is the unchangeable in art."[50]

For Brush, American Indians also represented the unchangeable. Conventionally aligning Indians with the past, Brush wrote, "There are more superb and symmetrical men among [Indian populations] than I have ever seen elsewhere, their beardless faces reminding me always of the antique. . . . Their constant light exercise, frequent steam-baths, and freedom from overwork develop the body in a manner only equaled, I must believe, by the Greek."[51] To underscore the Indians' status as representatives of an unchanging past, Brush depicted Indian cultures in poses and compositions borrowed from the modern world's other "unchangeable," the art of the old masters. In *The Moose Chase,* 1888 [308], for example, the spear-bearing Indian recalls a figure such as Raphael's *Saint Michael,* 1518 [309]. *Study of Indian for "The Moose Chase,"* circa 1888, in which an almost saintly glow emanates from a more anglicized Indian than the one of the finished painting, emphasizes Brush's desire to connect Indians with his definition of eternal values [310].

In the wake of such a comparison, however, the ability of a painting such as *The Moose Chase* to point beyond itself may be questioned in two ways. First, given its open interest in other images, it cannot necessarily be relied on as a document of an Indian culture. It does not point to the real, in the sense in which the real may be equated with a painter's interest in historical accuracy. This much Brush freely acknowledged. "In choosing Indians as subjects for art," he wrote, "I do not paint from the historian's or the antiquary's point of view. . . . I hesitate to attempt to add any interest to my pictures by supplying his-

torical facts. If I were required to resort to this in order to bring out the poetry, I would drop the subject at once."[52] Second, the clear relation between Brush's Indian and an old master prototype such as the *Saint Michael* reveals that the higher meaning to which *The Moose Chase* points, the set of eternal values it is meant to summon, resides only in another image. Brush's picture does not refer to the unchangeable but to his idea of the unchangeable—to his own system for timelessness—represented here by the art of Raphael. Despite Brush's interest in eternal values, the relation between *The Moose Chase* and Raphael's *Saint Michael* is thus no less disconsonant, no less artificial, than Wyeth's good-humored relation between a frontier card game and the biblical Supper at Emmaus. Only Brush's rhetoric makes it different.

If Brush still believed in art's ability to transcend a "commercial age," some of his works nevertheless reveal his uncertainty about possibilities for this transcendence. In *The Picture Writer's Story,* circa 1884, for example, he questions his art's ability to point not only to a real world but to a set of eternal values as well [311]. The basis of this questioning is the relationship between Brush's figures and their inspiration, Michelangelo.

The painting depicts an Indian artist explaining a work of art to two male viewers. A third observer, a woman, stands in the background at right. The figure of the artist is modeled, in reverse, on Michelangelo's Libyan Sibyl for the Sistine Chapel ceiling; and the reclining viewer is modeled, also in reverse, on the figure of Adam in the Sistine Creation of Man. As much as they recall the figures of Michelangelo, however, Brush's Indians just as forcefully proclaim their difference from such prototypes. This is particularly true of Brush's Adam, who conspicuously withholds the arm through which, in Michelangelo's painting, he

308. George de Forest Brush,
The Moose Chase, 1888, oil on
canvas, 37⅝ × 57⅜ in. Na-
tional Museum of American
Art, Smithsonian Institution,
Washington, D.C.; gift of
William T. Evans.

309. Raphael, *Saint Michael*, 1518, oil on canvas (transferred from panel), 105½ × 63 in. Musée du Louvre, Paris.

310. George de Forest Brush, *Study of Indian for "The Moose Chase,"* circa 1888, charcoal and chalk on paper, 20½ × 12½ in. Private collection.

had been brought to life.

Through such differences Brush's painting plays itself despairingly against Michelangelo's hubristic idea of creation. If, in the Creation of Man, the divine act is in some sense an allegory of Michelangelo's own formidable ability to bring things to life, Brush's picture can substitute only a torpid Adam, unable even to lift his arm, and a ghostly "hand," comprising the lower-right edge of the artist's hide, that unsuccessfully attempts to animate him.[53] As an

allegory of the painting's inability to create the real or bring its figures to life, this detail implicates Brush's paintings in the enervated modern age he often condemned.

It also suggests that, for Brush, the history of art contributed to this enervation, not so much helping him find the eternal as standing in his way. For, in *The Picture Writer's Story,* the torpor comes about because a previous artist, Michelangelo, has already established a direct relationship with the eternal. Metaphysically Brush posits an idealized time in which artists such as Michelangelo could know the world and the eternal without recourse to other images. Subsequent images, such as those of Brush's own time, could only copy the originals of these old masters. It was no longer possible to have an unmediated relationship with eternal values because of the inherited images of these eternal values. It is this consignment to mediation, this resentment of the priority of other images, that informs the torpor of Brush's picture.

The absolute contrast to Brush's self-consciousness, apparently, is the art of Charles Russell. If Brush's Adam is aligned with the dead birds at his side, incapable of animation, Russell's paintings confidently announce their ability to perform just this kind of creative act. The emblem for this transformative power is the buffalo skull that appears as part of every Russell signature. It marks not only the realism of Russell's historical scenes—they once existed as surely as the skull proves the existence of the buffalo—but also the paintings' ability to restore this real West to our modern-day vision. For, through the emblem of the skull, each Russell painting plays its naturalism against the viewer's awareness that such scenes no longer exist.

Russell's cowboy persona enhanced his claim to represent the real West. Unlike every other western painter considered in this chapter, Russell spent virtually his entire life in the West. He painted most of his western scenes in Montana, where he lived from 1880 until his death in 1926. Before he began to paint full-time, moreover, he had worked eleven years as a ranch hand on the Montana prairies. Whereas his eastern counterparts were "western fakers," as writer Emerson Hough described the "Lyme School of Western Artists," Russell himself was, according to his own description, a "Cowboy Artist."[54]

To take Russell at his word, however, is to miss the extensive stylistic influences at work in his paintings. As art historian Brian W. Dippie has shown, the work of Théodore Géricault, Maxfield Parrish, and Remington, among others, informed Russell's vision of the West.[55] For all his professed distaste for "teckneque," Russell adopted the work of other painters in as sophisticated a manner as Brush or Wyeth.[56] In turn, these borrowings led him to the kinds of reflexive questions characteristic of the work of these other artists.

Carson's Men, 1913, for example, contains powerful metaphors that run counter to its claims for a straightforward realism [312]. Specifically these metaphors concern the Crucifixion. Placed above a pair of Golgothian skulls (the one of Russell's signature and the other of a buffalo carcass), Carson and his companions are arranged in cruciform shapes that suggest Christ and the two thieves on their crosses. In particular this is true of Carson, the figure in

311. George de Forest Brush, *The Picture Writer's Story,* circa 1884, oil on canvas, 24 × 36 in. Canajoharie Library and Art Gallery, New York.

312. Charles Russell, *Carson's Men,* 1913, oil on canvas, 24 × 35½ in. Thomas Gilcrease Institute of American History and Art, Tulsa.

the middle. The line of his erect body is continued by the stiff front left leg of his horse and then crossed by his musket, making a shape echoed in the cruciform figure on the musket's stock. The man at right is also crossed by a musket; and, although the man at left also bears a horizontally disposed musket, it is his partly extended right arm that establishes his cruciform shape.

Other details—the halolike hats, the twilight sky that recalls the time of day of the Deposition, and above all the remarkably symmetrical arrangement of Carson and the two men, with the centralized Carson higher against the sky and closer to the viewer—intensify the picture's allusions to the Crucifixion. The canvas thus plays both on Carson's first name, *Christ*opher (identifying him here more with Christ than the Christ-bearing saint), and on his just completed action of crossing the river, to represent the early western explorer as messianic victim.

Given that Russell made his painting in 1913, it is possible that Carson is conceived here as a sacrifice to the present in which the picture was made: to the era of progress partly enabled by his exploration of the land. From Russell's twentieth-century vantage, the act of discovery had settled the country, initiating its transformation from skeletal wasteland to a place of potentially limitless industrial and agricultural fecundity, but it had also determined the discoverers' fate. With no more land to discover, the need no longer existed for explorers such as Carson. Their very skill in exploring the land had hastened their obsolescence. Hence the Progressive era's conventional understanding of such figures as sacrifices to the present.

In his references to a Christian theme Russell thus employs a rhetoric of timelessness to announce the continued pertinence of the Old West. In this respect he is like Brush. Historical change is arrested by reference to an eternal concept. Yet, in the prominence of the animal carcass, Russell poses an alternative: history is nothing more than inexorable decay, a ruin testifying to the past's intractable *im*pertinence to the present. Here, in romantic language, Russell's picture registers his culture's sense of separation from the Old America. If the buffalo's bones affirm the past's existence, they also affirm its irrevocable loss. In a modern culture careering forward, the bones offer one view of all that remains of the American past.

Within itself, then, *Carson's Men* represents history as both a meaningful and meaningless sacrifice. If Russell ultimately favors the former, reserving for Carson and his men the most prominent role, he proclaims his own powers of representation to be the crucial difference between a usable and a dead past. Whereas the animal died unrecorded, Carson's sacrifice is represented by Russell. In keeping with the picture's metaphors it is this representation that allows Carson's cross into the present. Without the powers of the image, Russell claims, the heroism of the Old West, even Carson himself, would be nothing but a useless ruin. Russell is aware that the past lives only in its representation.

Accordingly, the picture comments on its own representational powers. Placing his signature in the undergrowth at lower left, Russell announces his presence "in the brush" that has brought Carson to life. In the way in which parts of this brush overlap the pristine surface of the water at the picture's left edge, *Carson's Men* enacts the process of applying paint or brushstrokes to a bare canvas. The animal carcass further analogizes this bare canvas, suggesting (like the signature skull) the beginnings or understructure of a painting whose fruition is the detailed figures of Carson and his men.

If *Carson's Men* posits representation as the sole means by which we know the past, it does not however acknowledge how this past can be represented. Through its signature skull the painting insists that it represents a real West. Yet its references to the Crucifixion reveal that it is only in terms of other images that this real West can be known. The disingenuity of *Carson's Men* and indeed of Russell's cowboy-artist persona resides in this unwillingness to acknowledge artistic influence. His paintings claim to depict a real West, yet they rely surreptitiously on other images for this reality.

If Russell rejected the idea that history is a ruin, seeing representation as the means by which the past could be revived, Remington more acutely questioned his paintings' ability to restore the past to modern-day perception. Ultimately, at sublimated levels, he acknowledged that both the passing of time and then the act of painting itself hopelessly compromised his pictures' claims to historical realism.

In part Remington's obsession with time may have been prompted by his situation in and around New York, the environs where he lived and worked from 1885 until his death in 1909. Even as he escaped this urban environment, retreating to various rural and wilderness locales whose relatively primitive conditions he explicitly equated with the past, Remington remained very much a part of his modern era. He rode in automobiles. He talked on the telephone. He listened to music on the phonograph. Occasionally the era's rapid technological progress drew uneasy acknowledgment: "Peary discovered North Pole. A ship crossed the ocean in 4 days and machines fly," he wrote in his diary.[57] But more often this

progress led him to sentimentalize a traditional American past left in its wake. He quotes a poem in his diary:

> *Thou art a creature of the Present Age*
> *Thy past is an obliterated page;*
> *The rest that follows may not see the more,*
> *Make best of what is worst and do not rage.*[58]

In his *Fight for the Water Hole,* the picture whose realism so impressed John J. Clinton, Remington unconsciously expressed his interest in the passing of time, acknowledging thereby the historical distance that could question such realism [see 257].

The subject of *Fight for the Water Hole,* represented in temporal terms, is the last stand of five outnumbered cowboys. The shadows, diminishing water, and spent bullets register almost cinematically the lapsing of time as the cowboys fight. With the passing moments, their situation becomes increasingly perilous.

Yet the picture's interest in time extends far beyond its manifest narrative. Shadows, for instance, represent not only the fading day but the passing of the cowboys themselves. For example, the creeping shadows that continue the hidden lower body of the most prominent cowboy imply his gradual transformation into shade. The hidden lower body, in turn, suggests the idea of burial—a concept reinforced by the cowboy in the right foreground and quite explicitly in the cowboy at far left, whose legs have all but disappeared in the sand. And then there is the gaping hole itself.

The burying sand suggests the sand of the hourglass, the proverbial sands of time. The unbroken line of distant mountains paradoxically resembles water or waves, a conventional figure for time's inexorable passing. Finally the water hole itself bears an irresistible relation to a clock, replete with the eleven, twelve, two, five, and six o'clock positions marked and the two most prominent guns suggesting hour, minute, or second hands in motion. As in combat terminology, the field of battle is transformed into a huge timepiece, with enemies said to be at points on the clock; except, for Remington, this terminology expresses not only the positions of the combatants but the expiration of time as they fight.

The time that passes so relentlessly in *Fight for the Water Hole* refers not just to the cowboys but to the historical era they represent. Each is doomed. Moreover, the picture acknowledges that this doom—this extinction of an older way of life—makes the past difficult, perhaps impossible, to represent. For all its believable recovery of the past, Remington's painting posits its own temporal distance from the Old West as a crucial problem for its realism. The passing of time is a dilemma not only for the cowboys but for the painter himself.

The shadows express this dilemma. As flat representational surfaces, they relate to the surface of the painting itself. It is thus possible to see the shadows as metaphors of the painting's ability or inability to depict its subject. As the shadows of the foremost cowboy's gun are to the gun itself, so Remington's painting considers itself to the Old West. As flat surfaces, moreover, the shadows are matched by the water of the water hole. It too is a flat surface inadequate to the purpose of realistic representation. This water appears to reflect the mountains in the distance, which can be read here as figures for the historical distance. What this water actually reflects, however, are only the heads and pointed ears of the nearby horses. Like the painting itself, the water shows the distance only through illusion.

If Remington came unconsciously to see the passage of time as a problem to his pic-

tures' realism, he also saw the very process of painting—the act of applying pigments to a flat surface—as perhaps the most fundamental obstacle to a realistic retrieval of the past. He arrived at this self-consciousness through his interest in impressionism and its tentative, proto-modernist willingness to acknowledge the representational limitations of paintings—to admit their existence as two-dimensional surfaces inherently incapable of the kind of realism they had been supposed to bring off ever since, and some time before, Alberti's pronouncement about a window onto the world.

Remington's nocturnes exemplify his proto-modernist sensibility. In paintings such as *Apache Scouts Listening,* 1908, *Shotgun Hospitality,* 1908, and *In from the Night Herd,* 1908, the historical subjects become "hidden" by the painterly night [313–15]. The past becomes literally difficult to see. Our hindered perception, moreover, is reciprocated by the confusion of the figures. Their strained attempts to observe enact the uncertainty of artist and viewer.

As a temporal metaphor, the night becomes a kind of evident mediation, a representation of the modernity separating Remington and his historical subjects. It is almost as if the modern-day ruptures in Remington's history have evanesced into the dark air intruding between the artist and the past. The night becomes a metaphorical boundary between the present-tense world of the artist and the past-tense world of the painting.

Further, thinking of Remington the proto-modernist, I believe there is a sense in which this night actually corresponds to the picture plane, as if Remington had not only painted *on* the picture plane but had also painted *the picture plane itself,* in this way unconsciously representing the very surface of the canvas as the boundary between his world and the historical world he portrayed. The act of painting is represented as inherently unable to provide a win-

313. Frederic Remington,
Apache Scouts Listening, 1908,
oil on canvas, 27 × 40 in.
The Alan and Cindy Horn
Collection, Los Angeles.

314. Frederic Remington,
Shotgun Hospitality, 1908, oil
on canvas, 27 × 40 in. Hood
Museum of Art. Dartmouth
College, Hanover, New
Hampshire; gift of Judge Hor-
ace Russell, class of 1865.

315. Frederic Remington, *In from the Night Herd,* 1908, oil on canvas, 27 × 40 in. National Cowboy Hall of Fame Collection, Oklahoma City; Albert K. Mitchell Collection.

dowlike view of the past. The canvas itself, opaque and here (for good measure) represented as opaque, will always intrude. The painting indeed covers, as would a shroud, the Old West.

Yet Remington wanted to cover the West in the reportorial sense as well. His acknowledgment of his medium's inherent inadequacy for this task was not made without considerable anxiety. In *Fired On,* 1907, for example, the painting's flatness is denied by the first object we see: the powerfully modeled white horse that in a truly baroque way seems to jut out at us, as if it protruded from the picture plane [316]. In this way it confirms for us, and Rem-

ington, the illusionistic power of his painting.

Then again, a closer look at the horse reveals Remington's acknowledgment of surface. The rump, although it is still a rump, is also a rich slather of impasto. The neck is a thinner swirl of paint in which a raised horizontal weave in the canvas prominently appears [317]. This horse is very clearly made of paint and canvas.[59]

That this is a fearful recognition for Remington is suggested by the white horse itself. Although the horse does not literally see itself in the water, in a figurative sense it does. It is terrified of the splashes of water that formally echo its own tail. These splashes of water, in

316. Frederic Remington,
Fired On, 1907, oil on canvas,
27⅛ × 40 in. National Museum of American Art,
Smithsonian Institution,
Washington, D.C.; gift of
William T. Evans.

317. Frederic Remington,
Fired On (detail).

turn, occurring on the flat surface of the water, suggest paint applied to the surface of the canvas itself, much like the paint Remington applied for the horse's tail. The white horse's fear and that of Remington as well arise from the recognition that the horse's body—its historical haunch, bone, and mane—is nothing more than paint and canvas.[60]

This fear applies to the other figures as well. Coming to the water's edge, they have literally reached a surface they cannot cross. The inviolable boundary of the water's surface analogizes the surface of the painting itself as another boundary that cannot be crossed. Expressing as well the picture's lateral boundaries, the water's edge is also a representation within the painting of the limits posed by the frame itself.

Perhaps only the protruding white horse and strange figure in the background, whose head and arm conspicuously transgress the boundary of hill against sky, challenge the picture's despairing recognition of its own literal limitations. The figure with his arm raised suggests that the artist conceives this challenge as both exhilarating (the primal yell) and painful (the unavoidable sense we get of the figure's mutilation, damage, or torture in attempting to move from one realm to another). The figure is thus paradigmatic of the conflict—a desire to refer beyond the boundaries of the painting that is continually questioned or denied—that underlies much of Remington's art.

Remington's more straightforwardly impressionistic paintings also acknowledge their surfaces as unavoidable obstacles to the recovery of the past. They also begin to play out the conclusion that must follow the acknowledgment of paint and canvas in the making of history, the recognition of perhaps the most powerful mediation of all, that of the painter, not only in front of the historical picture but within it as well.

In *Radisson and Groseilliers,* 1905, for example, our attention is repeatedly called to the painting's flatness [318]. Interrupting the historical illusion, various artistic tricks distinguish Remington's painting from similar but less self-conscious turn-of-the century images of exploration, such as Henry Farny's *As It Was in the Beginning,* 1905 [319]. Among the last two Indians in Radisson's canoe, the overlap of arm and leg, as if the rear Indian's foot were grasping the oar, suggests Remington's willingness to acknowledge the picture's two-dimensional limits. The flattening reeds in the foreground, stretching up and overlapping the canoe, also damage the painting's ability to suggest three dimensions. These reeds become difficult to distinguish from the paint of which they are made, appearing indeed as so much inchoate pigment applied onto the already completed picture.

This last detail suggests that as in his nocturnes Remington is interested here in the covering power of the painting's surface. In *Radisson and Grosseilliers* the water lilies most powerfully express this interest. If they float on the water, their blankness—their status as flat dots—makes it possible to say that they also float on the canvas. Their blankness denies the illusionistic capacities of both surfaces. In this ability to float simultaneously on water and canvas the lilies more than any other detail discredit the picture's three-dimensional illusion, for they help us see that the two surfaces can in fact be read as coincident. The flatness of the one is the flatness of the other. They demonstrate that the water can be read not only as receding backward but as tilting up, paralleling the picture plane.

Here Remington makes a narcissistic connection between the reflective capabilities of water and his painting. If the water lilies interrupt our vision of the past, they also create another kind of illusion, one that relates the sur-

318. Frederic Remington,
Radisson and Groseilliers, 1905,
oil on canvas, 17 × 29¾ in.
Buffalo Bill Historical Center,
Cody, Wyoming; gift of Mrs.
Karl Frank. (Detail illustrated
on p. 284.)

319. Henry Farny, *As It Was in the Beginning*, 1905, oil on canvas, 40 × 22 in. Dr. and Mrs. Thornton I. Boileau Collection, Birmingham, Michigan.

320. Unidentified photographer, *Frederic Remington Canoeing on the Saint Lawrence River*, circa 1900–1908, albumen print, 2¾ × 4½ in. Frederic Remington Art Museum, Ogdensburg, New York.

321. Frederic Remington, *Radisson and Groseilliers* (detail). From *Collier's Weekly* 36 (January 13, 1906): 8. J. N. Bartfield Galleries, New York.

face of the painting, as it tilts up before its maker, to the surface of water. They help identify the waterlike ability of Remington's painting metaphorically to reflect the space in front of it, the space of the painter at the easel, making the history.

To say that Remington saw himself in his paintings would not be a novel idea. In many of his works heroic soldiers and cowboys exist as surrogates for Remington himself.[61] In *Radisson and Groseilliers,* however, this reflection is particularly acute.

The painting represents the explorers in their journey down the Saint Lawrence in 1659. Remington made the painting in 1905, when he owned a summer home, "Ingleneuk," in the Thousand Islands region of the same river. During these summers one of his favorite pastimes was canoeing [320]. It is, however, the coincidence between the names *Remington* and *Radisson,* a coincidence that exceeds mere phonetic similarity, that best demonstrates the historical narcissism of Remington's painting.

The canoe is not the picture's only water- (or canvas-) borne horizontal. It is matched in relative deployment on the canvas by Remington's signature itself [321]. The two are parallel. Still more tellingly, the canoe corresponds in many particulars to the shape of Remington's signature. Its prow roughly duplicates the distinctive F; its stern matches the last n; and, finally, occurring appropriately enough at the midpoint of the canoe, Radisson's striking R shape matches the R in *Remington.*[62]

This identification between signature and canoe, between the world of the painter and the world of the past, metaphorically expresses the ultimately personal nature of Remington's historical vision. It registers his sublimated recognition that Radisson, as a historical entity, cannot ever be separated from Remington, his artistic creator. History must always reflect its maker. It will show the person who made it, the artist at the easel.[63]

Within their realism, running counter to it, expressing the tension between objective history and its representation, between the final painting and the model on the saddle display, two other Remington paintings acknowledge this last inescapable mediation. In the suggestively titled *With the Eye of the Mind,* 1908, three Indians attempt to identify the anthropomorphic shape of a distant cloud [322]. This cloud might represent the past itself, its evanescence or literal cloudiness in Remington's era. In this sense, thinking back to the rifle and its shadow in *Fight for the Water Hole,* the Indian's copying gesture might register the painting's own inadequacies in the copying of a too distant past.

But the cloud might also represent the imagination of the Indian, relating to him as a speech balloon might to a cartoon figure. This would be consonant with the picture's title, which seems to imply that history (the distance) is made or conjured within the mind of its creator.

The second painting is *Fight for the Water Hole.* I return to it because earlier one of its most conspicuous features escaped all but the slightest mention. This is the water hole itself. In one sense, its circular shape could affirm the picture's realism, serving as a vital statement of history as continuum, as circuit between present and past. Yet the water hole resembles less a circle than an eye. In this sense, it represents the transformative vision of the painter, his ability to perceive an object in the world (here the Old West) and interpret it. History thus occurs literally in the eye of the painter. This hypothesis matches the example of the rifle and its shadow; the real is altered in the act of perception, but it remains real nonetheless. Yet the shape of the water hole also suggests that history occurs in the mind of the painter, in the "I" of the mind, in the imagina-

tion, and that this process ultimately relies only on itself, on what it makes up, for its sense of the past.

The overdetermination of *Fight for the Water Hole,* with its disconsonant mix of powerful realism and an equally powerful metahistorical counter-realism, expresses the intellectual complexity of Remington's historical vision. It also begins, I hope, to take this vision out of the realm of the "permanent record" and make it an object of greater interpretive contention. Like the history he sought to record, Remington's own place in history cannot be reduced to a set of clear-cut narratives. If he could claim (in a letter to his friend Owen Wister) that "I am d— near eternal if people want to know about the past,"[64] he could also refer to his figures as "puppets" and write elsewhere in his diary, "I sometimes

322. Frederic Remington, *With the Eye of the Mind,* 1908, oil on canvas, 27 × 40 in. Thomas Gilcrease Institute of American History and Art, Tulsa.

feel that I am trying to do the impossible in my pictures in not having a chance to work direct but as there are no people such as I paint it's 'studio' or nothing." Ultimately Remington cannot be assigned one or the other position, neither wholly confident nor uncertain, and neither can his works. If then any kind of clarity obtains in the work of Remington and his contemporaries, it is the clarity of *Radisson and Groseilliers*—the clarity of an image that shows the artist and his historical subject, combined, indistinguishable, in the same boat.

Notes

1. John J. Clinton to Frederic Remington, January 6, 1909, Frederic Remington Papers, Archives of American Art, Smithsonian Institution, Washington, D.C., roll NOR-I. Remington's thoughts on the "impossible" are in Frederic Remington diary, January 15, 1908, Frederic Remington Art Museum, Ogdensburg, New York. Here and elsewhere I have retained Remington's original spelling and punctuation.

White's quotation is from Hayden White, "Historicism, History, and the Imagination," in *Tropics of Discourse: Essays in Cultural Criticism* (Baltimore: Johns Hopkins University Press, 1978), 112. On the relationship between history and the imagination, I have learned a great deal from White.

2. Remington diary, July 10, 1907.

3. Quoted in Dippie, *Remington and Russell,* 11.

4. For an in-depth analysis of this nostalgia, see Lears, *No Place of Grace.* I derive my use of the word *antimodern* from Lears.

5. Theodore Roosevelt, "An Appreciation of the Art of Frederic Remington," *Pearson's Magazine* 18 (October 1907): 394.

6. See, for example, the response of Reuben G. Thwaites, secretary and superintendent of the State Historical Society of Wisconsin, to Remington's request for information about Pierre La Vérendrye, the French explorer who became the subject of one of the Great Explorers paintings Remington made for *Collier's Weekly* in 1905–6 (Thwaites to Remington, March 15, 1905, Remington Papers, roll NOR-I).

7. Remington's opinion of Frederick MacMonnies is in Remington diary, April 17, 1908. See also Remington's diary entry for November 16, 1907. The monument in question, not completed until 1936, is Mac-Monnies's *Pioneer Monument to Kit Carson.* Remington's opinion of Charles Schreyvogel's *Custer's Demand* is in Horan, *Schreyvogel, 36.*

8. Roland Barthes "L'effet de réel," *Communications* 11 (1968): 84–89, and articles that use Barthes's formulation, such as Linda Nochlin, "The Imaginary Orient," *Art in America* 71 (May 1983): 119–31, 186–91.

9. See Barthes, *Mythologies.* Barthes writes, "Myth is constituted by the loss of the historical quality

of things: in it, things lose the memory that they once were made. . . . In passing from history to nature, myth acts economically: it abolishes the complexity of human acts, it gives them the simplicity of essences, it does away with all dialectics, with any going back beyond what is immediately visible, it organizes a world which is without contradictions because it is without depth, a world wide open and wallowing in the evident, it establishes a blissful clarity: things appear to mean something by themselves" (142–43). These quotations summarize what Barthes means when he calls myth "depoliticized speech."

10. My use of the word *discourse* is derived from Said, *Orientalism,* and then from Said's source, Michel Foucault, *The Archaeology of Knowledge and the Discourse on Language,* trans. A. M. Sheridan Smith (New York: Pantheon, 1972). For my understanding of the archive, as it came to be formulated in the late nineteenth century, I learned also from Sekula, "The Body and the Archive," 4–64.

11. Shapiro and Hassrick, *Remington,* 214.

12. For example, both the Metropolitan Museum of Art in New York and the Museum of Fine Arts in Boston were founded in 1870. The discipline of art history, as it developed at this time, sought to objectify the lives and artistic styles of various artists, affixing to each a set of seemingly immovable associations. Contemporary artists such as Remington were then judged according to these fixed definitions of artistic character and importance. See, for example, Royal Cortissoz, "The American Art of Frederic Remington," *Scribner's* 47 (February 1910): 181–95, in which Cortissoz refers with a kind of finality to beauty in the works of Ingres and Corot, love of form in Whistler, imagination in Millet, and excess of detail in Meissonier.

13. See, for example, Remington's wash drawing of military equipment, with the inscription "Metropolitan, August 1886" (Frederic Remington Art Museum).

14. See, for example, the drawings labeled "An Indian Campaign" in the sketchbook Remington kept at the Highland Military Academy in 1878, when he was seventeen.

15. See Samuels and Samuels, *Remington,* 37.

16. George de Forest Brush to Harold Bowditch, October 8, 1918, Nancy Douglas Bowditch Papers, Archives of American Art, roll 2828:1277.

17. Henry Farny sketchbook, Henry Francis Farny Papers, Archives of American Art, roll 1196:190–217.

18. Slotkin, *Fatal Environment.*

19. Idem, "Nostalgia and Progress."

20. Horan, *Schreyvogel,* 28.

21. Quoted in Samuels and Samuels, *Remington,* 177. Remington refers to Poultney Bigelow, "The Russian and His Jew," *Harper's Monthly* 88 (March 1894): 603–14. Remington made five illustrations for this article.

22. See Remington, "Chicago under the Mob" and "Chicago under the Law," *Harper's Weekly* 38 (July 21 and 28, 1894) (reprinted in Peggy Samuels and Harold Samuels, eds., *The Collected Writings of Frederic Remington* [Garden City, N.Y.: Doubleday, 1979], 152–59).

23. In *Looking at Russell,* Dippie relates one of Russell's Indian war scenes, *Duel to the Death,* circa 1891 (Amon Carter Museum, Fort Worth, Texas), to the work of several painters including Eugène Delacroix. The tradition, however, goes back through Delacroix to his source, paintings by Peter Paul Rubens such as the *Wild Boar Hunt,* circa 1615–16 (Musée des Beaux-Arts, Marseilles), and *Lion Hunt,* circa 1621 (Alte Pinakothek, Munich). Rubens's source, in turn, was the famous mural (now destroyed) by Leonardo da Vinci, *The Battle of Anghiari,* 1503–6 (see David Rosand, "Rubens's Munich *Lion Hunt:* Its Sources and Significance," *Art Bulletin* 51 [March 1969]: 29–40).

24. Slotkin, "Nostalgia and Progress," 621.

25. Remington makes the relationship between knight and cowboy explicit in the *Last Cavalier,* 1895 (private collection), an illustration he made for Owen Wister's article "The Evolution of the Cow-Puncher," *Harper's Monthly* 91 (September 1895): 602–17.

26. Donald Pease, "Melville and Cultural Persuasion," in Bercovitch and Jehlen, *Ideology and Classic American Literature,* 384–417. Pease uses the phrase "scene of cultural persuasion" to designate the Cold War discourse—our freedom against their totalitarianism—from which he believes the canonical interpretation of *Moby-Dick* was developed. Discussing "the postwar consensus on American literature as Cold War texts" that emerged after F. O. Matthiessen's *American Renaissance: Art and Expression in the Age of Emerson and*

Whitman (1941), Pease writes, "In totalizing the globe into a super opposition between the two superpowers—the free world supervised by the United States and the totalitarian countries under Soviet domination—the Cold War can recast all conflicts anyplace in the world in terms of this pervasive opposition." The Cold War scene, then, governed the views of *Moby-Dick*'s interpreters, who "converted Ahab into a figure whose totalitarian will opposed the freedom displayed in Ishmael's narrative formulations" (390–91). I have found Pease's model helpful in explaining how western paintings can be said to allegorize their era's dominant concepts, prominent among which was racial and national separatism. In the time of Schreyvogel and Remington, a "scene of cultural persuasion" was the opposition: white and dark, American and immigrant. In a manner similar to the way in which the Cold War ideology operated within the texts of Matthiessen and other critics, this racialized ideology made its way unconsciously into a painting such as Schreyvogel's as the very language the artist possessed for representing his subject.

27. For this interpretation of the symbolism of flaying, see Edgar Wind, *Pagan Mysteries in the Renaissance* (New Haven: Yale University Press, 1958), 142–46.

Remington repeatedly associated Indians with the act of flaying. See, for example, *The Sign of Ownership,* circa 1892 (unlocated), *Hungry Moon, 1906* (Thomas Gilcrease Institute of American History and Art, Tulsa), and *The Passion of Ah-we-ah,* 1899 (private collection). This last image is significant not only because it was made in 1899, when Remington painted *Captured,* but because it features a blanket-wrapped Indian figure standing in a pose similar to that of the central figure in the Sid Richardson painting. Each figure, moreover, stands this way as a prelude to furious action related to the act of flaying. The Indian in *Captured* is presumably ready to move forward to begin his prisoner's torture. Ah-we-ah, the Indian in *The Passion of Ah-we-ah,* is ready to move to the woman whose flaying of a moose has sexually excited him. In "The Story of the Dry Leaves" (*Harper's Monthly* 99 [June 1899]), the story that the painting illustrates, Remington writes: "Some little distance off stood the young man, leaning on his gun, and with his blanket drawn about him to his eyes.

He watched the girl while she worked, and his eyes dilated and opened wide under the impulse. The blood surged and bounded through his veins—he was hungry for her, like a famished tiger which stalks a gazelle." It is difficult to think of a more graphic example of Remington's belief that Indians were barbarous and sensual by nature and that these characteristics could be summarized by the act of flaying.

28. Henry Fairfield Osborn, introduction to Madison Grant, *The Passing of the Great Race; or, the Racial Basis of European History* (New York: Scribner's, 1916), xxxi.

29. See Samuels and Samuels, *Remington,* 67–80.

30. For an account of the vast numbers of Indian skeletons held in certain American natural history museums, see Douglas J. Preston, "Skeletons in Our Museums' Closets: Native Americans Want Their Ancestors' Bones Back," *Harper's Magazine* 278 (February 1989): 66–76.

31. Maxwell, "Burbank," 4.

32. Ibid., 6.

33. Ibid., 5.

34. For a comprehensive discussion of this nostalgia, see Lears, *No Place of Grace.*

35. Johannes Fabian, *Time and the Other: How Anthropology Makes Its Object* (New York: Columbia University Press, 1983).

36. Fabian identifies a crucial disjunction that characterizes anthropological practice: its requirement of fieldwork, which necessarily relies on the shared time of anthropologist and object of study, and then its subsequent requirement, in the anthropologist's act of writing, that this object be distanced. "On the one hand," writes Fabian, "we dogmatically insist that anthropology rests on ethnographic research involving personal, prolonged interaction with the Other. But then we pronounce upon the knowledge gained from such research a discourse which construes the Other in terms of distance, spatial and temporal" (ibid., xi).

37. Farny to Julius Fleischmann, mayor of Cincinnati, January 4, 1901 (reprinted in *Cincinnati Commercial Tribune,* January 8, 1901, Farny Papers, roll 1233:501–2).

38. The double meaning of "disappeared" is aptly expressed in Browne, "Burbank" 20. Browne writes, "[Burbank's] long training in painting heads has given

him a facility and an unfailing ability to catch a likeness at once. This is necessary in making Indian portraits from the difficulty of getting them to sit, and it is important to finish quickly *as there is no surety that they will hold out as long as the painter wishes*" (italics added). Indian models' impatience with posing, their inability to "hold out," becomes a trope for their perceived inability as a race to hold out or resist extinction.

39. Sekula, "The Body and the Archive," 26–27.

40. See Burbank, *Burbank among the Indians,* 131, 149–50, 148, 117, 109, respectively.

41. Charles Schreyvogel to Louise Schreyvogel, August 26, 1911, Carothers Collection, National Cowboy Hall of Fame, Oklahoma City.

42. Horan, *Schreyvogel,* 17.

43. Bowditch, *Brush,* 59.

44. Morgan, *Brush,* 72.

45. For Remington's trip to the Bronx Zoo, see Remington diary, September 16, 1907; for the story about the Indian model, see Remington diary, January 6, 1908.

46. An "acute tension between the finished realism of . . . paintings and the circumstances in which they were made" could certainly describe many works of art long before Remington's era. Artists have models, after all. What I am arguing, however, is that Remington's culture, the culture of Henry Adams's "Dynamo and the Virgin," found itself particularly estranged from an idealized past and that consequently this estrangement could not help but manifest itself in the very circumstances surrounding the construction of its historical representations. Here, however, it could be objected that most if not all cultures find themselves estranged from a proverbial better time. As Raymond Williams writes in *The Country and the City* (London: Chatto & Windus, 1973, 12), "nostalgia is universal and persistent." Williams points out, however, that each nostalgia is historically specific and thus requires analysis of its own particular characteristics. In keeping with Williams's formulation, here I want to analyze the historically specific codes governing turn-of-the-century representations of the Old America. I want to address the expressions of historical distance that are particular to Remington's era.

47. For pointing out the compositional similarity between N. C. Wyeth's painting and Caravaggio's

Supper at Emmaus, I am grateful to Melissa Webster, assistant curator, Whitney Gallery of Western Art, Buffalo Bill Historical Center.

Wyeth owned books on Rembrandt and Velázquez, both of whom made Supper at Emmaus scenes. Also he deeply respected the work of his acquaintance Gari Melchers, whose oeuvre included two Emmaus paintings.

48. As he grew increasingly dissatisfied with his status as an illustrator, Wyeth regarded both the conventions of illustration and the Old West itself—his first subject as an illustrator—as melodramatic. When he described the West as "theatrical" in an interview in 1921 (quoted in Duff, *Wyeth,* 17), it was only one time among many that he imputed this characteristic either to the West or to illustration.

49. Brush to Nancy Bowditch, undated, Bowditch Papers, roll 2826:664.

50. Brush to "Ed," undated, ibid., 761.

51. George de Forest Brush, "An Artist among the Indians," *Century* 30 (May 1885): 55.

52. Ibid., 57.

53. A second protruding tatter, occurring roughly two-thirds of the way up the hide's right edge, also acts as a pointing "hand."

54. Emerson Hough, "Wild West Faking," *Collier's Weekly* 42 (December 19, 1908): 18–19, 22. Hough's article contains a section entitled "The Sins of Frederic Remington." Wrote Remington in his diary (April 6, 1908), "met Emerson Hough and he has written an article for Collier's on *Western Faking*—in which I judge he gives me a roasting. That made me uncomfortable." See also Remington diary, December 19, 1908.

55. See Dippie, *Looking at Russell.*

56. The reference to "teck-neque" is quoted in Dippie, *Remington and Russell,* 15.

57. Remington diary, September 8, 1909.

58. Ibid., April 27, 1909.

59. It is often pointed out that, for the latter part of his career, Remington's paintings display an increasing tension between realistic subject matter and painterly execution. Although Remington claimed he stood "for the proposition of subjects," the evidence of this later work reveals his increasing fascination with paint itself. In examining how this tension is expressed in

Remington's subject matter, I have learned from Michael Fried's essay on Stephen Crane in Michael Fried, *Realism, Writing, Disfiguration: On Thomas Eakins and Stephen Crane* (Chicago: University of Chicago Press, 1987).

60. The splashes of water, though made by gunshots, constitute a more delicate fantasy of transgression, implying the movement of the horse's front hooves (the splashes of water they would have made) if the horse had crossed from land to water. My thanks to Jules Prown for this observation.

61. Remington explicitly identified with cowboys in his most elaborate self-portrait (*Self-Portrait on a Horse,* c. 1890 [Sid Richardson Collection of Western Art, Fort Worth, Texas]), in which he depicts himself not as an artist but as a cowboy in the West.

62. I have not reproduced the signature in the final painting but the one from the color illustration of *Radisson and Groseilliers* that appeared in the *Collier's Weekly* for January 13, 1906 [see 321]. There are too many doubts concerning the present signature on the painting itself. At some point a strip of canvas, including Remington's original signature, was cut from the bottom of the picture. The signature now on the painting was added subsequently, possibly by Remington himself (if he were responsible for cutting the canvas down, as perhaps he was, given his general dissatisfaction with the Great Explorers series, the rest of which he destroyed). This hypothesis, plausible enough, would make a reading based on the painting's signature

still possible. Yet, at some still later point, the middle portion of this second signature, specifically the letters *ic Reming,* was reconstructed by an unidentified restorer (see David C. Bauer to Dr. Sarah Boehme, undated, Buffalo Bill Historical Center files, Cody, Wyoming). The *Collier's* reproduction of Remington's original signature is consequently the most "primary" evidence available.

63. Some readers may think that I have made too tenuous a connection between the signature and the canoe. Yet, in the so-called initial pieces for several stories, precedents exist in Remington's art for representing a human figure explicitly in the shape of a letter of the alphabet [323]. Moreover, as an illustrator of stories, Remington spent much of his career doing precisely what I have claimed he has done in *Radisson and Groseilliers:* matching images with words. As an illustration of the painting's "story" or "writing"—the personalized history embodied in the words *Frederic Remington*—the signaturelike canoe thus operates in a manner similar to that of a great many other Remington illustrations. It differs in that the story it tells is what I have been calling the painting's second or metahistorical story, the story of the presence of the painter within and in front of his historical scene.

64. Remington to Owen Wister (quoted in Samuels and Samuels, *Remington,* 228).

323. Frederic Remington, *Untitled* ("Initial Piece"). From *Harper's Weekly* 42 (April 1898): 727. Buffalo Bill Historical Center, Cody, Wyoming.

HE Indian suns himself before the door of his tepee, dreaming of the past. For a long time now he has eaten of the white man's lotos—the bimonthly beef-issue. I looked on him and wondered at the new things. The buffalo, the war-path, all are gone. What of the cavalrymen

Artists' Biographies

JONI LOUISE KINSEY

The following biographies provide information on eighty-six artists whose work is illustrated in the preceding chapters. These biographies focus on the artists' experiences in the West from 1820 to 1920 or the influence of the West on their work.

"ANA" denotes the date of an artist's election as an associate member of the National Academy of Design, New York; "NA," election as a full member; and "HM," as an honorary member. "NSS" designates membership in the National Sculpture Society, New York.

Cross-references to artists whose biographies are included here appear in SMALL CAPS.

Ayres, Thomas Allmond
1816 New Jersey–1858 drowned at sea
Painter, illustrator

Joining the gold rush in 1849, Ayers sailed to California, where he spent his time well—although he did not find riches—sketching mining camp towns and Indian communities in northern California. In 1855 the San Francisco publisher James Mason Hutchings commis-

sioned him to produce the first paintings of Yosemite. In 1856 Ayers created a second Yosemite series, which he exhibited at the American Art-Union in New York. Many of his landscapes became part of a moving panorama, *Yosemite Valley and Falls,* 1857 (unlocated), painted with artist Thomas A. Smith. While in New York for the exhibition of the panorama, Ayers executed a series of California views for *Harper's,* and in 1858 the magazine sent him west. Enroute to San Francisco from San Pedro (near Los Angeles), his ship was lost at sea.

References
Nancy Anderson and Linda Ferber, *Albert Bierstadt: Art & Enterprise* (New York: Hudson Hills for the Brooklyn Museum, 1991); Hendricks, *Bierstadt.*

Beaman, Edward O.
Active 1860s–70s
Photographer

Relatively little is known about Beaman, apart from his one year in 1871 as photographer for John Wesley Powell's geological survey of the Colorado River. He apparently fought in the Civil War and worked as a professional photographer in western New York as well as in Illinois and Ohio. During his brief tenure with Powell, Beaman, using the cumbersome wet-plate method, produced more than 350 negatives of the arid lands and river systems of Arizona and Utah. These are among the first photographs of the region and were instrumental in disseminating accurate information about the area's character and appearance. Beaman's prints appeared in official exploration reports and were widely distributed as stereographs.

References

Current and Current, *Photography and the Old West,* 90–92; Darrah, "Beaman . . . Hillers," 491–503; Welling, *Photography in America,* 210, 215, 219, 222.

Beard, James Henry

1811 Buffalo–1893 Flushing, N.Y.
Painter; HM 1848, NA 1872

As an itinerant painter during the late 1820s, Beard worked in Pittsburgh, Cincinnati, and New Orleans. He eventually settled in Cincinnati in 1830 but continued to travel during the summer and for special commissions. He spent the year 1846–47 in New York, where he was involved in community art activities as a founding member of the Century Club. In 1873 he settled permanently in New York, joining his younger brother, artist William Holbrook Beard. In addition to James Beard's many genre paintings, his portraits of such notable Americans as John Quincy Adams, Henry Clay, Ulysses S. Grant, William Henry Harrison, and Zachary Taylor received much acclaim.

References

Barter and Springer, *Currents of Expansion,* 14, 63, 161; *The Golden Age: Cincinnati Painters of the Nineteenth Century Represented in the Cincinnati Art Museum* (Cincinnati: Cincinnati Art Museum, 1979), 35–37; S. Winifred Smith, "James Henry Beard," *Museum Echoes* 27 (April 1954): 27–30.

Becker, Joseph Hubert

1841 Pottsville, Pa.–1910 New York
Painter, illustrator

In 1859 Becker joined the staff of *Leslie's Illustrated Weekly Newspaper* as an errand boy. By 1863 he was a staff artist, following the Army of the Potomac during the Civil War. His only trip west began in October 1869 on a special Pullman train traveling the newly completed transcontinental line from Omaha to Sacramento in eighty-one hours. Becker stayed in California for six weeks, making sketches from which he composed paintings (*Snow Sheds on the Central Pacific Railroad* [230]) and illustrations. He returned east via Salt Lake City, where he recorded the surrounding landscape and scenes of Mormon life, and he may have passed through Denver. While working for *Leslie's* he made sketches of the Great Chicago Fire of 1871; he later became head of the newspaper's art department.

References

Paul A. Rossi and David C. Hunt, *The Art of the Old West* (New York: Knopf, 1971), 198, 317; Samuels and Samuels, *Biographical Encyclopedia,* 33–34; Taft, *Artists and Illustrators,* 89–93, 149, 153, 297 n. 28, 312–14, 337, 341.

Berninghaus, Oscar Edmund

1874 Saint Louis–1952 Taos, N.M.
Painter; ANA 1926

While working for various printers and lithography firms during the day, Berninghaus attended the Saint Louis School of Fine Arts at night. In 1899 the Denver and Rio Grande Railway sent him west to depict the scenery along its route. During this trip he visited Taos, New Mexico, the picturesque southwestern town that he was to be identified with for much of his career. Until he settled permanently in New Mexico in 1925, he worked as a commercial artist in Saint Louis during the winter and painted in his Taos studio during the summer. Berninghaus was a founding member of the Taos Society of Artists.

References

Eldredge, Schimmel, and Truettner, *Art in New Mexico,* 192; Gordon E. Sanders, *Oscar Berninghaus, Taos, New Mexico: Master Painter of American Indians of the Frontier West* (Taos, N.M.: Taos Heritage, 1985).

Bierstadt, Albert
1830 Solingen, Germany–1902 New York
Painter; NA 1860

Bierstadt and his family left Germany when he was two years old. With early ambitions to become a painter, he taught drawing in New Bedford, Massachusetts, then in 1853 returned to Germany, where he shared studio space in Düsseldorf with EMANUEL LEUTZE and WORTHINGTON WHITTREDGE. On his first trip to the West in 1859 Bierstadt traveled from Saint Joseph, Missouri, to the Wind River Mountains with Colonel Frederick W. Landers's Honey Road Survey. In 1860 he exhibited *Base of the Rocky Mountains* (unlocated) at the National Academy of Design. In 1863 he traveled to San Francisco and on to Yosemite. Highly regarded by local patrons and painters, his work commanded top prices. In 1871 he returned to California, where he stayed two years, painting views of the Sierra Nevada, including Yosemite. Through the mid-1880s he traveled in the West as well as to Nassau and Europe. His last trip west was in 1889. Changing tastes in the 1880s brought a decline in the popularity of his art, and he narrowly avoided bankruptcy in 1895.

References
Nancy Anderson and Linda Ferber, *Albert Bierstadt: Art & Enterprise* (New York: Hudson Hills for the Brooklyn Museum, 1991); Hendricks, *Bierstadt.*

Bierstadt, Charles
1819 Solingen, Germany–1903 Niagara Falls, N.Y.
Photographer

Brother of ALBERT BIERSTADT, Charles and a third brother, Edward, worked together for a time as wood workers in New Bedford, Massachusetts. While Albert was traveling in the West with the Landers expedition in 1859, a fire destroyed the family business. Upon Albert's return he moved to New York, and Charles and Edward worked together in New Bedford selling his western photographs. They ran their photography studio until 1866, when Edward turned to commercial printing. Charles moved permanently to Niagara Falls, where he specialized in views of the falls for the tourist trade. In 1870 he visited California and photographed Yosemite.

References
Hendricks, *Bierstadt,* 68, 93, 97, 112, 188, 196, 268; Taft, *Photography and the American Scene* (1964 ed.), 362–63, 502 n. 374; Welling, *Photography in America,* 139, 173, 241, 290.

Bingham, George Caleb
1811 Augusta County, Va.–1879 Kansas City, Mo.
Painter

Two passions—art and politics—dominated Bingham's life and career, and he was more successful at the former than the latter. In 1819 his family moved to Franklin, Missouri, on the Lewis and Clark Trail, were he grew up and became an itinerant preacher and portrait painter. In 1838, after studying briefly at the Pennsylvania Academy of the Fine Arts in Philadelphia, he exhibited *Western Boatmen Ashore* (unlocated) in New York at the Apollo Association, the forerunner of the American Art-Union. Through the latter organization Bingham sold numerous important pictures during the next decade. In 1846 Bingham, a passionate Whig, announced his candidacy for the state legislature. He lost in a bitterly contested race but ran again in 1848 and won. During the interim he painted *Stump Speaking* [162], the first of a series on the electoral process. Bingham's experiences in what he called "the mire of politics" undoubtedly colored his vigorous but incisive style.

References
Bloch, *Bingham: Evolution of an Artist;* McDermott, *Bingham;* Shapiro, *Bingham.*

Bodmer, Karl
1809 Zurich, Switzerland–1893 Barbizon, France
Painter, lithographer

Although Bodmer's American experiences comprised only a small part of his career, his images of the West are his crowning achievement. In search of an art market more favorable than that of his native Switzerland, Bodmer moved to Koblenz, Germany. While there he met Maximilian zu Wied, a naturalist who had toured Brazil in 1815 and was anxious to explore North America. During his travels with the prince in 1833–34 Bodmer sketched images for a published account of the journey. Bodmer's abilities transcended mere documentation. Not only did he make beautifully detailed drawings of artifacts and botanical and zoological specimens, but he also painted remarkable landscape views of the Missouri River Valley and portraits of the Blackfeet, Cree, Mandan, and Piegan.

References

John C. Ewers, "An Appreciation of Karl Bodmer's Pictures of Indians," in idem et al., *Views of a Vanishing Frontier* (Omaha: Joslyn Art Museum, 1984), 59–93; David C. Hunt, Marsha Gallagher, and William J. Orr, *Karl Bodmer's America* (Lincoln: University of Nebraska Press for Joslyn Art Museum, 1984); Reuben G. Thwaites, *Early Western Travels, 1748–1846* (Cleveland: Clark, 1904–7), 22–24.

Brickey, William Josiah

1826 Potosi, Mo.–1853 Saint Louis
Painter

Especially active in Missouri, Brickey began to paint when he was fourteen years old. During the 1840s he maintained a studio in Jefferson City, worked briefly in Union, and spent ten weeks at Arrow Rock in 1847 with GEORGE CALEB BINGHAM, copying the elder artist's paintings. Brickey later painted portraits and genre scenes in Boonville, Independence, and Lexington before moving to Saint Louis in 1850. There he and artist Alfred S. Waugh shared a studio, from which he continued his career as an itinerant painter. In 1853 Brickey left Saint Louis for Mississippi, intending, according to a newspaper account, to live in Jackson and depart from there for Europe. In fact, he went by boat to Natchez and finally on to New Orleans, where he contracted yellow fever and died at age twenty-seven.

References

Barter and Springer, *Currents of Expansion,* 80–81, 164; Raymond Luther Brickey, *The Brickey Heritage* (Radford Va.: Commonwealth Press, 1983), 103–4, 128–29; Taylor, *America as Art,* 85.

Bromley, Valentine Walter

1848 London–1877 London
Painter, draftsman

A well-regarded history and genre painter, Bromley exhibited regularly in London at the Royal Academy. His work appeared in various English periodicals, including *Fun, Illustrated London News,* and *Punch.* In 1874, at the invitation of the earl of Dunraven, Windham Thomas Wyndham-Quin, Bromley toured the West, preparing sketches of Indian subjects, wildlife, and scenery for the earl's book, *The Great Divide* (1876). Their route followed the Saint Lawrence River through the Great Lakes, to the Missouri River and then west before turning south to Estes Park, Colorado. In mid-August they traveled to Salt Lake City and then continued to Yellowstone. Only six of the twenty commissioned paintings of the expedition survive. In 1875–76 Bromley exhibited two major paintings of Indian subjects at the Royal Academy and western watercolors at the Royal Institute.

References

Paul Hogarth, "Indians at the Manor: Valentine Walter Bromley, 1874," in idem, *Artists on Horseback: The Old West in Illustrated Journalism, 1857–1900* (New York: Watson-Guptill, 1972), 111–30; Samuels and Samuels, *Biographical Encyclopedia,* 178; Richard T. York, "Valentine Walter Bromley (1848–1877)," *Southwest Art* 7 (August 1977): 22–27.

Brown, Margaretta (Maggie) Favorite

Also known as Mrs. John W. Brown; Mrs. Jonas
1818–1897 Boise, Idaho
Painter

Sometime during the mid-nineteenth century the artist moved to the West to join her married sister in northern California. In 1857 she married Jonas Brown in Yreka. In 1862 her husband left for the gold fields of Idaho, and Brown and her sister moved to Portland, Oregon, before joining him two years later. In 1882 she and her husband settled in Boise. Brown's somber palette and the condition of her murals for the Masonic Temple in Idaho City, painted in the mid-1860s, have prompted speculation about her technique. Some have suggested that she experimented with earth pigments, a process she may have learned from northern California Indians.

References

Doris Ostrander Dawdy, *Artists of the American West: A Biographical Dictionary* (Athens: Ohio University Press, 1985), 3:56–57; Utahna Hall, "Idaho City Artist: Maggie Brown," *Idaho World,* July 2, 1980, 1; Arthur Hart, "Idaho Yesterdays: Frontier Life Didn't Keep Artists from Seeking the Spirit of Idaho," *Daily Idaho Statesman,* June 5, 1978, 4A.

Brush, George de Forest

1855 Shelbyville, Tenn.–1941 Hanover, N.H.
Painter; ANA 1888, NA 1908

Brush studied in New York at the National Academy of Design and in Paris under Jean-Léon Gérôme, whose academic style became his model. In 1880 he traveled to the West with his brother. While living among the Arapaho, Crow, and Shoshone, he produced many images of Indian life for *Century* and *Harper's* magazines. Some of these were informal; others were more heroic and classical in style. Near the end of 1881 Brush returned east to teach at the Cooper-Union in New York. In 1886 he and a former student eloped to Canada, where they lived for nearly two years. Before returning to New York, they spent a summer camped in a tepee on Augustus Saint-Gaudens's New Hampshire farm. As his direct contact with native Americans lessened, Brush's paintings became more romanticized, and, perhaps due to his distress at their persecution, he stopped painting them. By the turn of the century his best-known canvases were portraits of women with children, conceived in the image of Renaissance madonnas.

References

C. Kurt Dewhurst, Betty MacDowell, and Marsha MacDowell, *Artists in Aprons: Folk Art by American Women* (New York: Dutton for Museum of American Folk Art, 1979), 101, 150–51, 159; George H. Meyer, *Folk Artists Biographical Index* (Detroit: Gale Research for Museum of American Folk Art, 1986), 56.

Burbank, Elbridge Ayer

1858 Harvard, Ill.–1949 San Francisco
Painter

As his first artistic commission, *Northwest Magazine* hired Burbank to depict the route completed in 1883 of the Northern Pacific Railway from Saint Paul to Puget Sound, Washington. In the late 1880s Burbank studied in Munich. After moving to Chicago in 1892, he began painting genre scenes and portraits, especially of African-Americans, some of which were distributed as chromolithographs. In 1895 he traveled with writer Hamlin Garland and sculptor HERMON ATKINS MACNEIL to the Hopi pueblos in Arizona. Burbank's uncle, Edward Everett Ayer, president of the Field Museum of Natural History in Chicago, subsequently commissioned his nephew to paint a series of portraits of native Americans. His first subject was Geronimo, painted from life at Fort Sill, Oklahoma. He then made likenesses of a variety of southwestern and Pacific Coast Indians, including Chief Joseph, Rain-in-the-Face, Red Cloud, and Sitting Bull. His work is often the only visual record of his sitters. Extremely prolific, Burbank made more than twelve hundred paintings of native Americans, representing over one hundred tribes.

References

Browne, "Burbank," 16–35; Burbank, *Burbank among the Indians;* Maxwell, "Burbank," 3–8.

Burgum, John

1826 Birmingham, England–1907 Concord, N.H.
Painter

In 1850 Burgum emigrated from England to Boston but soon moved to Concord, New Hampshire, to work for Abbot, Downing, a major manufacturer of stage coaches. Although he specialized in portraiture and decorative painting of carriages and signs, he also painted still lifes, seascapes, and animal scenes. In the 1860s he obtained several patents for his inventions of tools and gadgets. His *Express Freight Shipment of Thirty Coaches* [183] was painted from a photograph by Benjamin Carr.

References

Reggie Frost, "John Burgum, 1826–1907, and Edwin Burgum, 1858–1948: Coach Painters, Decorators, Artists, and Inventors," *Decorator* 37 (Spring 1983): 4–12; Hassrick, *Way West,* 110–11; Museums at Stony Brook, *Nineteenth-Century American Carriages: Their Manufacture, Decoration, and Use* (Stony Brook, N.Y., 1987), 52–59.

Catlin, George

1796 Wilkes-Barre, Pa.–1872 Jersey City
Painter; NA 1826

Catlin abandoned a law career to pursue his interests in art. In the early 1820s he achieved some success as a portrait miniaturist in Philadelphia. His real goal, however, was to depict American Indians and preserve their fast-disappearing culture. In 1830 he met explorer William Clark in Saint Louis and with him visited tribes living near the Mississippi River. In 1832 he traveled up the Missouri River to Fort Union, North Dakota. His portraits of the Mandans, with whom he stayed in 1832 before smallpox reduced the tribe in 1837, are today among his best-known works. By 1834, after crossing the southern plains to paint the Comanche, Catlin had visited more western tribes than had any other artist of his day. In 1841 he published his experiences and research in a two-volume work. His Indian Gallery (including artifacts and live Indian performers as well as nearly six hundred paintings) was exhibited throughout the East Coast and in Europe.

References

George Catlin, *Letters and Notes on the Manners, Customs, and Conditions of the North American Indians* (1841; New York: Dover, 1973); McCracken, *Catlin and the Frontier;* Truettner, *Catlin's Indian Gallery.*

Chapman, John Gadsby

1808 Alexandria, Va.–1889 Brooklyn
Painter, illustrator; HM 1832, NA 1836

Although he struggled financially during his lifetime, Chapman led a distinguished artistic career. He studied in Washington, D.C., under CHARLES BIRD KING and then in Philadelphia at the Pennsylvania Academy of the Fine Arts. In 1828 he traveled to Rome and Flor-

ence to continue his education. One of his European works was the first by an American to be engraved for distribution in Italy. In 1831 he returned to America, dividing his time between New York and Washington, exhibiting frequently, and gaining a reputation as a portrait painter. He also assumed a prominent role as a founding member of the Century Club in New York. Chapman is credited as the first popular book illustrator in America. He produced fourteen hundred wood engravings for Harper's *Illuminated Bible* (1843–46) and published *The American Drawing-Book,* which was reprinted several times from 1847 to 1858. His most notable achievements are his history paintings and portraits of famous American heroes. From 1848 to 1884 he lived in Europe. A visit to Mexico late in life suggests that he may have toured the West, and a recurring interest in Indian subjects is apparent in his work.

References

William Campbell, *John Gadsby Chapman: Painter and Illustrator* (Washington, D.C.: National Gallery of Art, 1962); Georgia Stamm Chamberlain, *Studies on J. G. Chapman, American Artist, 1808–1889* (Annandale, Va.: Turnpike, 1963); Cosentino and Glassie, *Capital Image,* 44–50, 255–56.

Church, Frederic Edwin

1826 Hartford–1900 New York
Painter; ANA 1848, NA 1849

Church and Thomas Cole, the two most esteemed painters of the Hudson River school, were associated from 1844 to 1846 as pupil and master. Church's early work, such as *The Hooker Company Journeying through the Wilderness* [79], continues an allegorical trend of growing importance in Cole's late work. By the 1850s, however, Church leaned toward a more objective rendition of landscape, particularly in his New England scenes. Church is also well known for his South American views, his hugely successful *Niagara,* 1857 (The Corcoran Gallery of Art, Washington, D.C.), exotic subjects such as *The Icebergs,* 1861 (Dallas Museum of Fine Arts), and views of the Middle East. His comprehensive landscapes incorporate extensive botanical, meteorological, and geological information as well as an almost unshakable faith in a deistic universe.

References

David Huntington, *The Landscapes of Frederic Edwin Church: Vision of an American Era* (New York: Braziller, 1966); Kelly, *Church;* Franklin Kelly and Gerald L. Carr, *The Early Landscapes of Frederic Edwin Church, 1845–1854* (Fort Worth: University of Texas Press, 1987).

Couse, Eanger Irving

1866 Saginaw, Mich.–1936 Albuquerque, N.M.
Painter; ANA 1902, NA 1911

In 1886, after attending classes at the Art Institute of Chicago and Art Students League in New York, Couse went to Europe, where he remained for nearly ten years. While in Paris he studied with the academic master Adolphe Bouguereau and exhibited frequently at the Salon. He first became interested in western subject matter after visiting his father-in-law's sheep ranch in Oregon. In 1902 artists Ernest Blumenschein and Joseph Henry Sharp invited him to Taos, New Mexico, where in 1909 he established a studio, dividing his time between the Southwest and New York. Couse concentrated primarily on monumental Indian subjects. When he died in 1936, he was among the best-known of the Taos school artists, having produced more than fifteen hundred oil paintings.

References

Eldredge, Schimmel, and Truettner, *Art in New Mexico,* 194–95; Virginia Couse Leavitt, "Eanger Irving Couse (1866–1936)," in J. Gray Sweeney, ed., *Artists of Michigan from the Nineteenth Century* (Muskeegon, Mich.: Muskeegon Museum of Art, 1987), 160–67; Nicholas Woloshuk, *E. Irving Couse* (Santa Fe, N.M.: Santa Fe Village Art Museum, 1976).

Cover, Sallie

Also known as Mrs. Ferdinand Cover
Active 1880s–90s Nebraska
Painter

Cover is known primarily for her oil painting *Homestead of Ellsworth L. Ball* [192]. She and her husband were early settlers of Nebraska in the 1880s, when the central prairies were first farmed by white homesteaders.

References

C. Kurt Dewhurst, Betty MacDowell, and Marsha MacDowell, *Artists in Aprons: Folk Art by American Women* (New York: Dutton for Museum of American Folk Art, 1979), 101, 150–51, 159; George H. Meyer, *Folk Artists Biographical Index* (Detroit: Gale Research for Museum of American Folk Art, 1986), 56.

Curtis, Charles C.

1862 Marshalltown, Iowa–1955 Pasadena, Calif.
Photographer

In 1881 Curtis joined the Kaweah Colony, a socialist community in central California. In 1884 he and a partner established a photography business in Hanford in the San Joaquin Valley. Curtis supplemented his earnings by working as an itinerant photographer in mining and logging towns. He is best known for his pictures of the cutting of the great redwoods in the 1890s. The huge trunk of the General Noble Tree, a giant sequoia, was sent to the 1893 World's Columbian Exposition in Chicago to convince easterners of the existence of such a species. Curtis photographed the tree's felling, cutting, transporting, and reconstruction as an attraction at the fair. He planned to recoup his investment by selling souvenir photographs of the tree to visitors but was prevented from doing so by fair officials.

References

Andrews, *Photographers of the Frontier West,* 113–17; Donald J. McGraw, "The 'Sequoiadendron Gigantium' Exhibit at the World's Columbian Exposition in Chicago, 1893," in Robert Linn, ed., *Proceedings of the First Conference on Scientific Research in the National Parks* (Washington, D.C.: National Park Service, 1979), 1:133–49; Harold Scott, "World's Fair Tree," *Tulare County Historical Bulletin* 6 (October 1950): 1–2.

Deas, Charles

1818 Philadelphia–1867 New York
Painter; ANA 1839

After an unsuccessful application to the United States Military Academy in West Point, New York, Deas decided to become an artist. GEORGE CATLIN's Indian Gallery, shown in New York in 1837–39, and the writings of James Fenimore Cooper and Washington Irving probably influenced Deas to travel west. In 1840 he left the east to live near Fort Crawford, Wisconsin. He then traveled north to Forts Winnebago and Snelling, Minnesota, to study the Sioux and Winnebago. During this trip he compiled studies for compositions that would occupy him for many years. By 1841 he had settled in Saint Louis, where he remained for two years, exhibiting at the Mechanics' Institute. In 1844 he traveled with Major Clifton Wharton's expedition to Pawnee settlements on the Platte River. Deas left Saint Louis in 1847, moving first to Newport, Rhode Island, and then to New York. In 1848 he suffered a nervous breakdown and was committed to Bloomington's Asylum for the Insane, where he died in 1867.

References

Carol Clark, "Charles Deas," in Amon Carter Museum, *American Frontier Life*, 57–77; Glanz, *How the West Was Drawn*, 44–50; John F. McDermott, "Charles Deas: Painter of the Frontier," *Art Quarterly* 13 (Autumn 1950): 293–311.

Eastman, Seth
1808 Brunswick, Maine–1875 Washington, D.C.
Painter; HM 1838

Combining a career in the military and the arts, Eastman was a professional soldier, whose primary duties included topographical drafting. From 1824 to 1829 he attended the United States Military Academy in West Point, New York, and was first posted to Fort Crawford, Wisconsin. He also served at Fort Snelling, Minnesota, and in Louisiana. In 1833–40, while teaching at West Point, he published a book on topographical drawing, studied oil painting under ROBERT WEIR, and exhibited at the National Academy of Design. Assigned again to the field, he sketched the Seminoles in Florida. In 1841 he returned to Fort Snelling, where he made many studies of local Indians. In 1848–49, after a brief stint in Texas, he was stationed in Washington, D.C., where he devoted himself to various art projects. He collaborated with his wife, the writer Mary Henderson Eastman, on several books on Indian subjects. He also illustrated more than 275 pages of Henry Schoolcraft's multivolume work on native Americans (1851–57). After retiring from the army in 1867, he remained in Washington. Among his last works was a series of frontier scenes for the House Committees on Indian Affairs and Military Affairs.

References

Lois Burkhalter, *A Seth Eastman Sketchbook 1848–1849* (Austin: University of Texas Press for McNay Art Institute, 1961); McDermott, *Eastman.*

Edouart, Alexander
1818 London–1892 Los Angeles
Painter, photographer

Edouart's father, Auguste Edouart, was an English silhouette artist who immigrated with his family to America in 1848. Alexander studied in Edinburgh, Scotland, and in Italy. By 1848 he was working in New York, exhibiting at the American Art-Union and National Academy of Design. As with many artists, Edouart followed the California gold rush, and in 1852 he made his home in San Francisco. He spent the year 1857 in Mendocino County and traveled to Europe in 1859. His oeuvre includes genre scenes, landscapes, magazine illustrations, photographs, and portraits. He turned to photography late in life; in 1889, at age seventy-one, he and his son established a photography studio in Los Angeles.

References

Baird, *Honeyman Collection*, 20; Groce and Wallace, *New-York Historical Society's Dictionary*, 206–7; Hughes, *Artists in California*, 143.

Ericson, Augustus William
1848 Örebro, Sweden–1927 Arcata, Calif.
Photographer

When he arrived in California in 1870, Ericson embarked on a varied career as a general-store clerk, printer, railroad hand, and redwood logger. In 1876 he and a partner opened a drug store. Ericson supplemented his income by operating a photography studio and the first library in the town of Arcata in Humboldt County. Ericson gradually compiled an impressive photographic collection of images of the logging industry and of the local Indians. His views of the everyday life and rituals of the Hupa and Yurok are important historical records of those cultures.

References

Andrews, *Photographers of the Frontier West,* 119–27; Peter Palmquist, *Fine California Views: The Photographs of A. W. Ericson* (Eureka: Interface California, 1975); Peter Palmquist and Lincoln Kilian, "A. W. Ericson," in *The Photographers of the Humboldt Bay Region* (Arcata, Calif.: Peter Palmquist, 1989).

Farny, Henry Francis
1847 Ribeauvillé, France–1916 Cincinnati
Painter, illustrator

In 1853 Farny and his family emigrated from France to Warren, Pennsylvania. They eventually moved to Cincinnati, where young Farny sold his first illustration to *Harper's* in 1865. He moved to New York in 1866 to work as an engraver and illustrator for the magazine, a relationship he maintained for nearly thirty years. Farny also aspired to be a painter and in 1867 left for Europe. While studying in Düsseldorf, he met ALBERT BIERSTADT who encouraged him and suggested that they travel to the Rocky Mountains together when they returned to America. Farny made his first trip to the West in 1881 and returned several times. In 1883 he accompanied financier Henry Villard and his party on an expedition to celebrate the completion of the Northern Pacific Railway from Saint Paul to Puget Sound, Washington. Farny completed many of his paintings after 1894, the date of his last trip west, from his vast collection of sketches and artifacts.

References

Appleton and Bartalini, *Farny;* Carter, *Farny;* Taft, *Artists and Illustrators of the Old West,* 177, 214, 217–25, 239, 244, 347, 367–71.

Fraser, James Earle
1876 Winona, Minn.–1953 Westport, Conn.
Sculptor; ANA 1912, NA 1917, NSS

Fraser is known for his portrait busts, public sculptures—including the 1935 pediment of the National Archives Building in Washington, D.C.—and medal-

lions—especially the 1913 buffalo nickel. As the son of a railroad employee working in Dakota Territory, he learned about western American culture at an early age. In 1896 he enrolled at the Ecole des Beaux-Arts in Paris and two years later became an assistant to Augustus Saint-Gaudens, the preeminent American sculptor of his time. Fraser's *End of the Trail* [149] was the most frequented exhibit at the Panama-Pacific Exposition of 1915 in San Francisco. In his obituary the *New York Times* judged it to be the best-known sculpture in America. Inspired by work he had seen at the 1893 World's Columbian Exposition in Chicago, the image of the defeated Indian on horseback was created when Fraser was only seventeen, and he devoted most of his life to reworking it.

References

Thomas Gilcrease Institute of History and Art, *James Earle Fraser: The American Heritage in Sculpture* (Tulsa, 1985); Kennedy Galleries, *James Earle Fraser: American Sculptor* (New York, 1969); Dean F. Krakel, *End of the Trail: The Odyssey of a Statue* (Norman: University of Oklahoma Press, 1973).

Frenzeny, Paul
1840 France–circa 1902 Honolulu
Draftsman

Frenzeny's experiences as a member of the French cavalry in Mexico are recorded in sketches that appeared in *Harper's Weekly* in 1868, shortly after his arrival in the United States. In 1873 the magazine commissioned Frenzeny and JULES TAVERNIER to illustrate scenes of the American West. The pair left New York by train and arrived in San Francisco in 1874, after accompanying an expedition led by General John E. Smith through Nebraska, Utah, and Wyoming. Working together, Frenzeny and Tavernier drew directly on wood blocks, which they shipped back east to be engraved and printed. Frenzeny may have been responsible for the foreground detail and Tavernier for the composition. In the late 1870s Frenzeny returned to New York, where he continued to submit illustrations to various magazines. In 1877 he may have traveled with Buffalo Bill's Wild West Show, perhaps to gather material for his illustrations of Harrison O'Reilly's *Fifty Years on the Trail: A True Story of Western Life* (1889).

References

Baird, *Honeyman Collection*, 26; Taft, *Artists and Illustrators of the Old West*, 115–16, 347; Trenton and Hassrick, *Rocky Mountains*, 245–47.

Fuller, William

Active 1860s–80s South Dakota
Painter

During the late 1860s Fuller worked on the Union Pacific Railroad as it progressed through Nebraska. He later took a job as a carpenter at Crow Creek Agency in Dakota Territory. Painting was a serious avocation for Fuller; for two months every other year he left his regular job to pursue his artistic interests. His *Crow Creek Agency* [158] is unusual for its notations on the back of the canvas identifying the Indians and buildings in the scene.

References

Jan M. Dykshorn, "William Fuller's Crow Creek and Lower Brulé Paintings," *South Dakota History* 6 (Fall 1976): 413; Peter H. Hassrick, "The American West Goes East," *American Art Review* 2 (March–April 1975): 63–78; idem, *Way West*, 188–89.

Gast, John

Active 1870s Brooklyn
Painter, lithographer

The publisher George Crofutt commissioned Gast to paint *American Progress* [122] from which was made a chromolithograph for subscribers to his travel guides. Apparently the two men worked together on the concept for *American Progress,* the single painting by which Gast is known. Much of the content and form belongs to Crofutt himself, who provided Gast with a list of elements to include. Crofutt published a wood engraving of Gast's image in his guidebooks to the American West. The 1878–79 edition of *Crofutt's New Overland Tourist and Pacific Coast Guide* notes that the reproduction was the author's own design and does not mention Gast.

References

Crofutt, *Crofutt's New Overland Tourist and Pacific Coast Guide;* Fifer, *American Progress*, 202–4.

Gifford, Sanford Robinson

1823 Greenfield, N.Y.–1880 New York
Painter; ANA 1851, NA 1854

A major Hudson River school painter with extensive European experience, Gifford traveled west several times. In 1870 he joined F. V. Hayden's geological survey to Wyoming, leaving his two artist-companions, John F. Kensett and WORTHINGTON WHITTREDGE, behind in Denver. Gifford produced only a few western landscape subjects (see his *Valley of the Chugwater* [200], which may be compared with a photograph by WILLIAM H. JACKSON of Gifford painting the scene [201]). Gifford journeyed to the Northwest Coast in 1874, visiting Oregon, Washington, British Columbia, and Alaska. Again he seems to have been more interested in the experience rather than in painting; only a few works have survived from this trip.

References

Nicolai Cikovsky, Jr., *Sanford Robinson Gifford (1823–1880)* (Austin: University of Texas Art Museum, 1970); Metropolitan Museum of Art, *Memorial Catalogue of the Paintings of Sanford Robinson Gifford, NA, with a Biography and Critical Essay by Prof. John F. Weir of the Yale School of Fine Arts* (1881; New York: Olana Gallery, 1974); Weiss, *Poetic Landscapes.*

Hahn, Carl William

1829 Ebersbach, Germany–1887 Dresden, Germany
Painter

Hahn began his study of art in Dresden and continued his education in Paris and Naples. In Düsseldorf he trained under EMANUEL LEUTZE and met many European artists working in America, including WILLIAM KEITH. Perhaps inspired by their example, he immigrated to America in 1871 and after living briefly in New York joined Keith in Boston. In 1872 the two artists left for San Francisco, where they shared a studio with THOMAS HILL and Virgil Williams. Hahn made numerous sketching trips to Placerville, the Russian River, and the Sierra Nevada as well as to Yosemite. His reputation rests on his genre paintings of the developing communities of California. In 1878 he moved to New York but continued to exhibit in San Francisco. After living briefly in London, he and his wife and young daughter moved to Dresden in 1885. They were planning to return to California when Hahn became ill and died.

References

Arkelian, *Hahn;* idem, *Kahn Collection,* 25; H. Armour Smith, *William Hahn: Painter of the American Scene* (Yonkers, N.Y.: Hudson River Museum, 1942).

Hart, Alfred A.
1816 Norwich, Conn.–1908 Alameda, Calif.
Painter, photographer

While in Hartford in 1848 Hart painted a panorama of John Bunyan's popular story *Pilgrim's Progress* and in 1852 exhibited a panorama of scenes from the New Testament. In 1862 he went to California and in 1870 photographed the route of the Central Pacific Railroad. Based in Sacramento, he produced around three hundred images of the company's operations as its principal photographer. During the 1860s–70s the New York photographic firm of E. and H. T. Anthony, capitalizing on the popularity of landscape views, sold prints by many artists, including those by Hart. Although he was primarily a landscapist, in 1875 he listed himself as a portraitist. Supported by his children, he spent his last years in poverty.

References

Ralph W. Andrews, *Picture Gallery Pioneers, 1850–1875* (Seattle: Superior, 1964), 50, 60–61, 113–15; Welling, *Photography in America,* 183, 185, 219, 222; Glen Gardner Willumson, "Alfred A. Hart: Photographer of the Transcontinental Railroad" (master's thesis, University of California, Davis, 1984).

Hill, Andrew Putnam
1853 Porter County, Ind.–1922 Pacific Grove, Calif.
Painter, photographer

Born to a family with colonial roots, Hill traveled to California via Panama in 1867. He settled first in San Jose, where he attended Santa Clara College Academy. With the career of an artist as his goal, he moved to San Francisco, where he studied under Louis Lussier and Virgil Tojetti, son of DOMENICO TOJETTI. Hill first specialized in portraiture, maintaining a studio with Lussier in Oakland in 1876–77 and then in San Jose in 1878–80, but he also painted landscapes and historical subjects. In 1892–95 Hill and artist Sidney Yard established a photography business focusing primarily on Santa Clara County subjects.

References

Caroline De Vries, *Grand and Ancient Forest: The Story of Andrew Putnam Hill* (Fresno, Calif.: Valley Publishers, 1978); Hassrick, *Way West,* 142–43; Richard Steven Street, "Mystery Achievement," *California Farmer* (February 1, 1987): 8–9, 12.

Hill, Thomas
1829 Birmingham, England–1908 Raymond, Calif.
Painter

Hill worked in Baltimore, Boston, and Philadelphia, where he attended the Pennsylvania Academy of the Fine Arts. In 1861 he moved to San Francisco and in 1862 made the first of many trips to Yosemite. Although during his lifetime Hill was known for his genre and still-life paintings, his reputation now rests primarily on his landscapes of Muir Glacier, the Rocky Mountains, the White Mountains, Yellowstone, and especially Yosemite. In 1866 he traveled to Paris, where he lived for less than a year before moving to Boston. In poor health during the early 1870s, Hill returned to California, where he settled permanently. In 1888 he was the first artist to set up a studio in Yosemite. He produced an inexhaustible supply of paintings (estimated to number more than five thousand canvases) of the park for the tourist trade. In 1887–91 he devoted himself to a massive picture, *The Driving of the Last Spike* (California State House, Sacramento), which celebrates the completion of the transcontinental railroad.

References

Arkelian, *Hill;* idem, *Kahn Collection,* 28–29; Miller, *California Landscape Painters around Keith and Hill.*

Hillers, John K.
1843 Hanover, Germany–1925 Washington, D.C.
Photographer

After serving the Union during the Civil War, Hillers remained in the army, stationed in the western garrisons, until 1870, when he resigned to accompany a sick brother to San Francisco. On his return east he stopped in Salt Lake City, where he found employment as a teamster. In 1871 geologist John Wesley Powell hired him as a general laborer and boatman to accompany Powell's second expedition through the Grand Canyon. The expedition photographer, E. O. BEAMAN, taught Hillers to operate the camera. Beaman left the party in 1872; when his replacement became sick, Hillers took over as official photographer. He remained with Powell until 1879, producing more than three thousand negatives of the Colorado River region and its Indian inhabitants. Many of his images are the first photographs of the Paiutes, Shoshone, and Utes as well as of the territory later named Zion National Park. His work appeared as stereographs and woodcut illustrations in popular magazines, including *Scribner's,* and from his photographs THOMAS MORAN obtained details for his paintings. After 1879 Hillers worked in Washington, D.C., for the Bureau of American Ethnology and United States Geological Survey, producing more than twenty thousand negatives.

References
Current and Current, *Photography and the Old West,* 88–103; Darrah, "Beaman . . . Hillers," 491–503; Don D. Fowler, *The Western Photographs of John K. Hillers: Myself in the Water* (Washington, D.C.: Smithsonian Institution Press, 1989).

Holmes, William Henry
1846 Cadiz, Ohio–1933 Royal Oak, Mich.
Painter, draftsman

Holmes led a remarkably varied life as an anthropologist, archaeologist, artist, draftsman, explorer, geologist, government official, and museum director. While studying under THEODOR KAUFMANN in 1871 in Washington, D.C., he met Fielding B. Meek of the Smithsonian Institution, who hired him to illustrate his pale-ontological reports. This was Holmes's first assignment requiring detailed drawings of fossils and other specimens. In 1872–79 he worked with geologist F. V. Hayden as a geologist-artist on Hayden's western surveys. Highlights of these years include travels to Yellowstone, discovery of the Mount of the Holy Cross and the Mesa Verde cliff dwellings in Colorado, and friendships with WILLIAM H. JACKSON and THOMAS MORAN. In 1880 Holmes worked with Major Clarence E. Dutton, preparing highly detailed topographical drawings of the Grand Canyon region for Dutton's *Tertiary History of the Grand Cañon District* (1882). Holmes later worked in the Field Museum of Natural History and taught anthropology at the University of Chicago. He then directed the Bureau of American Ethnography and National Gallery of Art (now National Museum of American Art) in Washington, D.C.

References
Cosentino and Glassie, *Capital Images,* 210, 214–18, 262–63; William E. Goetzmann, "Limner of Grandeur: William H. Holmes and the Grand Canyon," *American West* 15 (May–June 1978): 20–29; Nelson, "Holmes," 252–78.

Jackson, William Henry
1843 Keesville, N.Y.–1942 New York
Photographer

Jackson first worked in Troy, New York, retouching and hand-coloring portrait photographs. After serving the Union in the Civil War, he traveled west. In 1866 he opened a studio in Omaha, where he photographed the townspeople and local Indians. In 1869 the geologist F. V. Hayden invited him to join his survey of Wyoming as a photographer. While working as a member of Hayden's expedition party, he met SANFORD R. GIFFORD, WILLIAM HENRY HOLMES, and THOMAS MORAN, who influenced the development of his work. Jackson produced the first photographs of Yellowstone in 1871, Mount of the Holy Cross in 1873, and the Anasazi ruins of Colorado and Arizona in 1875. His views of Yellowstone, along with Moran's watercolors and sketches, were instrumental in convincing Congress to establish the region as the first national park. Jackson's landscapes appeared as stereographs and in government reports and popular magazines. In 1879, when Hayden's survey was concluded, Jackson established a studio in Denver and for the next decade worked on contract for the railroads. In 1894–95 *Harper's* sent him on a round-the-world photographic tour.

References

Hales, *Jackson and the American Landscape;* Beaumont Newhall and Diana E. Edkins, *William Henry Jackson* (Fort Worth, Tex.: Amon Carter Museum, 1974); *Time Exposure: The Autobiography of William Henry Jackson* (1940; Albuquerque: University of New Mexico Press, 1987).

Jewett, William Smith

1812 South Dover, N.Y.–1873 Springfield, Mass.
Painter; ANA 1845

Jewett studied at the National Academy of Design under Samuel F. B. Morse. By the mid-1830s he was a successful portrait painter, exhibiting regularly at the American Art-Union and National Academy. In 1849 he abandoned his New York clientele to become one of the many artists who sailed to California in search of gold rush patrons. Jewett worked prodigiously, painting several landscapes and portraits each week. He benefited financially not only from the tourist trade in views of Yosemite but also by his investments in San Francisco real estate. Although he continued to paint, he exhibited very little and the eastern art establishment increasingly ignored him. In the late 1860s he returned to New York, married, and traveled to Europe, visiting California only once, in 1871.

References

Arkelian, *Kahn Collection,* 30–31; Evans, "Some Letters of Jewett," 149–246; idem, "William S. and William D. Jewett," *California Historical Society Quarterly* 33 (December 1954): 309–20.

Kaufmann, Theodor

1814 Uelzen, Germany–1896 New York
Painter

Kaufmann developed his talent as a portrait and history painter while studying in his native Germany. After participating in the revolution of 1848, he immigrated to New York, where he taught painting and drawing

to, among others, THOMAS NAST. At the outbreak of the Civil War he enlisted in the Union army. He became known for his military scenes, especially of the campaigns of Admiral David Glasgow Farragut and General William Tecumseh Sherman. In 1869 his work appeared in international fairs in Vienna and Munich, and in the early 1870s publisher Louis Prang printed his paintings as chromolithographs. From 1870 to 1883 Kaufmann lived in Washington, D.C., where he taught WILLIAM HENRY HOLMES.

References

Cosentino and Glassie, *Capital Image,* 264; Ludwig Kaufmann Hoffman, *Theodor Ludwig Kaufmann: Maler und Freiheitskämpfer* (Uelzen, Germany: Heimatverein des Kreises Uelzen, 1977); Rick Stewart, *The American West: Legendary Artists of the Frontier* (Fort Worth, Tex.: Hawthorne, 1986), 40–41.

Keith, William

1838/39 Old Meldrum, Scotland–1911 Berkeley, Calif.
Painter

When he was twelve, Keith and his family emigrated from Scotland to New York, where he apprenticed to a wood engraver. In 1858 he began working at *Harper's,* which sent him to California to illustrate western scenes. After visiting England, where he produced engravings for the *London Daily News,* he settled in San Francisco, opening his own engraving firm. During the 1860s he studied painting under CHARLES NAHL. In 1868 the Oregon Navigation and Railway Company commissioned Keith to produce paintings of its route. Keith later went to Düsseldorf to study painting, returning to America in 1871. In Boston he shared a studio with WILLIAM HAHN and in 1872 moved to San Francisco with Hahn. While working in Yosemite, Keith became friends with naturalist John Muir. Around 1890, after sharing a studio with painter George Inness, Keith's style changed, influenced by tonalism. In the San Francisco earthquake of 1906 he lost around two thousand paintings—many from his early period. His later work and those images painted from memory of the lost canvases are moodier, indicating his interest in the old masters.

References

Fidelis Cornelius, *Keith: Old Master of California* (New York: Putnam, 1942); Alfred C. Harrison, Jr., *William Keith: The Saint Mary's College Collection* (Moraga: Saint Mary's College of California, 1988); Paul Mills, *An Introduction to the Art of William Keith* (Oakland, Calif.: Oakland Art Museum, 1956).

King, Charles Bird

1785 Newport, R.I.–1862 Washington, D.C.
Painter; HM 1827

Following the lead of his fellow artists working in early America, King specialized in portraiture. He studied under Edward Savage in New York, then with Benjamin West in London. He returned to America in 1812 and worked in Baltimore, Philadelphia, and Washington, D.C. In 1818 he settled permanently in the nation's capital. There he painted portraits of many prominent figures, including John Quincy Adams, John Calhoun, Henry Clay, James Monroe, and Daniel Webster. Commissioned by the federal government, King painted more than one hundred portraits of Indian delegates, representing at least twenty tribes, who visited the capital from 1821 to 1842. His work stands today as a valuable record of early Indian leaders.

References

Cosentino, *King;* James D. Horan, *The McKenney-Hall Portrait Gallery of American Indians* (New York: Crown, 1972); Herman J. Viola, *The Indian Legacy of Charles Bird King* (Washington, D.C.: Smithsonian Institution Press; New York: Doubleday, 1976).

Krans, Olof

Also known as Olaf Olofson
1838 Selja, Sweden–1916 Altoona, Ill.
Painter

In 1850 Krans and his family emigrated from Sweden to the religious colony of Bishop Hill, Illinois. While working in the community paint shop, he learned the rudiments of sign painting. During the Civil War he served the Union but after injuring his leg returned to Bishop Hill. A photographer hired him to operate a portable portrait gallery, an experience that was to in-fluence his later art. Krans made his living primarily as a house, sign, and ornamental painter in small towns near Bishop Hill. In 1894, when he formally retired, he was commissioned to paint a stage curtain for a local community center, thus embarking on his career as a view painter. In 1896, for the fiftieth anniversary of the founding of Bishop Hill, he created a series of paintings chronicling the community's early years and prominent citizens. Between 1896 and 1916 he made more than 110 paintings, including many portraits based on photographs and daguerreotypes.

References

Margaret E. Jacobson, "Olof Krans," in Jean Lipman and Alice Winchester, eds., *Primitive Painters in America, 1750–1950* (1950; Freeport, N.Y.: Books for Libraries Press, 1971), 97–105; Esther Sparks, "Olof Krans, 1838–1916," in Jean Lipman and Tom Armstrong, eds., *American Folk Painters of Three Centuries* (New York: Hudson Hills for Whitney Museum of American Art, 1980), 203–6; idem, "Olof Krans: Prairie Painter," *Historic Preservation* 24 (October–December 1972): 8–12.

Lee, Joseph

1827 Oxfordshire, England–1880 San Francisco
Painter

Beginning in 1858, Lee is listed in the San Francisco city registers as a sign and ornamental painter; in 1872 his occupation changes to "artist." His paintings exhibit painstaking detail, suggesting that he was largely self-taught. This attention to detail makes his work important for understanding early California history, especially of Alameda County. He included in his work town views, specific buildings, named ships (for example, the ship on which Robert Louis Stevenson sailed to the South Seas), local railroad lines, and prominent citizens. During the 1860s–70s he produced landscapes, seascapes, and pictures of yachts. He exhibited frequently at the Mechanics' Institute and San Francisco Art Association.

References

Alice Putnam Erskine, "Joseph Lee, Painter," *Antiques* 95 (June 1969): 805–11; Hough, *California's Western Heritage,* 54.

Leutze, Emanuel Gottlieb
1816 Schwäbisch-Gmünd, Germany–1868
Washington, D.C.
Painter; NA 1860

Leutze grew up in Philadelphia, where in 1834 he enrolled in John Rubens Smith's art class. In 1841 he traveled to Germany to study under Carl Friedrich Lessing. Leutze eventually became an influential figure among the group of Americans (including ALBERT BIERSTADT, GEORGE CALEB BINGHAM, WORTHINGTON WHITTREDGE, and CARL WIMAR) studying in Düsseldorf. Leutze used history painting to express patriotic feelings for his adopted country. Many of his major works, such as *Washington Crossing the Delaware,* 1851 (The Metropolitan Museum of Art, New York), were produced in Düsseldorf, but in 1859 he returned to America to paint a large fresco, *Westward the Course of Empire* [100], for the United States Capitol.

References
Groseclose, *Leutze;* Raymond L. Stehle, "Five Sketchbooks of Emanuel Leutze," *Quarterly Journal of the Library of Congress* 21 (April 1964): 81–93; idem, *"Westward Ho!"*

MacNeil, Hermon Atkins
1866 Chelsea, Mass.–1947 Queens, N.Y.
Sculptor, painter; NA 1906, NSS

During the mid-1880s MacNeil was appointed the first drawing instructor at Cornell University. In 1888 he went to Paris to study at the Ecole des Beaux-Arts and Académie Julien. Returning to America in 1891, he settled in Chicago, where he sculpted works for the World's Columbian Exposition and taught at the Art Institute. Dissatisfied with available models and inspired by Buffalo Bill's Wild West Show, he traveled west several times in search of "authentic" native Americans. In 1895 he won a scholarship financing three years of study at the American Academy in Rome, where he executed what is perhaps his most famous work, *The Sun Vow,* 1898 (The Metropolitan Museum of Art, New York). He also spent a year in Paris before returning to New York, where he taught occasionally at the Art Students League, National Academy of Design, and Pratt Institute. His work includes murals in Buffalo,

Chicago, and Paris; World War I monuments; the frieze on the Missouri State House in Jefferson City; and the design for the Columbia quarter issued before World War I.

References
Tom Armstrong et al., *Two Hundred Years of American Sculpture* (New York: Godine for Whitney Museum of American Art, 1976), 115, 117, 139–40, 291; Broder, *Bronzes of the American West,* 24, 84–91, 93, 193, 223–34, 237, 246, 254, 378; Craven, *Sculpture in America,* 516–21.

Matteson, Tompkins Harrison
1813 Petersboro, N.Y.–1884 Sherburne, N.Y.
Painter; ANA 1848

Although little known today, Matteson was relatively prominent during his lifetime. At age sixteen, he set up a portrait studio in Cazenovia, New York (the traditional birthplace of Hiawatha). In 1833 a city patron financed his year of study at the American Academy of Fine Arts in New York, where, after several relocations, he established a studio. Matteson exhibited his portraits and genre and history paintings at the American Art-Union and National Academy of Design and sold his drawings to magazines. During the 1850s he also taught artist Elihu Vedder. Although he may not have traveled west, he painted many Indian subjects. *The Last of the Race* [144] illustrates an early theme frequently depicted in his paintings and prints. In 1850, perhaps to escape a cholera epidemic in the city, he and his family moved to Sherburne, New York. He lived there for the rest of his life, except for one year in Albany as a state representative.

References
Groeschel, "Matteson"; Barbara Slavin, "A Study and Classification of the Illustrations of Tompkins H. Matteson between 1845 and 1855" (masters thesis, State University of New York at Oneonta, 1970); Sherburne Art Society, *Tompkins H. Matteson* (Sherburne, N.Y., 1949).

Melrose, Andrew W.
1836 Selkirk, Scotland–1901 West New York, N.J.
Painter

A prolific artist, Melrose painted landscape views of the Berkshire Mountains, Tyrolean Alps, and Hudson River Valley as well as scenes of Cornwall, Ireland, North Carolina, and Turkey. Many of his paintings also depict western themes and locations, suggesting that he may have traveled west, but some scholars attribute these subjects to photographic sources. From 1868 to 1883 he exhibited landscapes and genre paintings at the Brooklyn Art Association and National Academy of Design. His *Westward the Star of Empire* [20] commemorates the completion of the Chicago-Northwestern Railway to the Missouri River.

References
Gerdts, *Painting and Sculpture in New Jersey,* 157–58; Glanz, *How the West Was Drawn,* 82–83; Koke, *American Landscape and Genre Paintings* 2:322.

Miller, Alfred Jacob
1810 Baltimore–1874 Baltimore
Painter

After studying under Thomas Sully in Philadelphia, Miller attended the Ecole des Beaux-Arts in Paris and in 1833–34 toured Italy. He returned to Baltimore, then moved to New Orleans, where he established a studio in 1837. During his first year in Louisiana he met Sir William Drummond Stewart, who invited Miller to accompany him to the Rocky Mountains. On their six-month hunting trip they met explorer William Clark in Saint Louis and followed the Oregon Trail to Fort Laramie, Wyoming, with a caravan from the American Fur Company. When the expedition ended, Miller—one of the few artists to witness the annual trappers' rendezvous in Wyoming—returned to New Orleans. There he worked his sketches into finished works, completing eighteen oils and dozens of wash drawings. The former were exhibited at the Apollo Association in New York before they were shipped to Stewart's hunting lodge, Murthy Castle, in Scotland. Miller visited Stewart in 1840 and also traveled to London, where he met GEORGE CATLIN and viewed his Indian Gallery. In

1842 Miller returned to Baltimore. For nearly thirty years he painted portraits and western subjects, based on sketches he had made in 1837.

References
Marvin C. Ross, ed., *The West of Alfred Jacob Miller* (Norman: University of Oklahoma Press, 1951); Tyler, *Miller;* Robert C. Warner, *The Fort Laramie of Alfred Jacob Miller* (Laramie: University of Wyoming, 1980).

Moran, Thomas
1837 Bolton, England–1926 Santa Barbara, Calif.
Painter, illustrator; ANA 1881, NA 1884

At age seven, Moran and his family emigrated from England to Philadelphia, where he was apprenticed briefly to a wood engraver. Although best known as a painter, Moran was also a prolific illustrator. In 1862, after a trip to Lake Superior, which inspired a series of views related to Henry Wadsworth Longfellow's "Hiawatha," he and his brother Edward traveled to England. In 1871 Moran accompanied F. V. Hayden's geological survey of Yellowstone as a guest artist, with funding from *Scribner's* and railroad financier Jay Cooke. During the expedition Moran worked closely with photographer WILLIAM H. JACKSON. In 1872 Moran visited Yosemite and in 1873 joined John Wesley Powell's geological survey of the Grand Canyon and Colorado River. In 1874 he was again with Hayden in Colorado, where he visited the newly discovered Mount of the Holy Cross. Although most of his life was spent in the East, he traveled west frequently, often as a guest artist of the Santa Fe Railway.

References
Carol Clark, *Thomas Moran: Watercolors of the American West* (Fort Worth, Tex.: Amon Carter Museum, 1980); Kinsey, "Moran and the Surveying of the West"; Wilkins, *Moran.*

Mount, William Sidney
1807 Setauket, N.Y.–1868 Setauket, N.Y.
Painter; ANA 1831, NA 1832

Around 1830, after a year of study at the National Academy of Design, Mount began to paint genre scenes of rustic life on Long Island. It was presumably on the strength of these images that he was elected to the National Academy, where he exhibited regularly for nearly forty years. Unlike many of his contemporaries, Mount did not visit Europe nor move far from his hometown. Although he produced only about five paintings a year, his anecdotal pictures were extremely popular and were reproduced as engravings and lithographs, inspiring a generation of genre painters.

References

Bartlett Cowdrey and Herman Warner Williams, *William Sidney Mount: An American Painter* (New York: Columbia University Press for Metropolitan Museum of Art, 1944); Alfred Frankenstein, *Painter of Rural America: William Sidney Mount, 1807–1868* (Stony Brook, N.Y.: Suffolk Museum, 1968); idem, *William Sidney Mount* (New York: Abrams, 1975).

Mozier, Joseph

1812 Burlington, Vt.–1870 Faido, Switzerland
Sculptor

After working successfully for five years as a New York clothing merchant, Mozier embarked on a career as a full-time artist. In 1845 he moved to Europe to study in Florence and Rome, with sculptor Hiram Powers. In Italy he joined the circle of JOHN GADSBY CHAPMAN, Thomas Crawford, Horatio Greenough, William Wetmore Story, and other American expatriate artists. Influenced by the neoclassic sculpture of Antonio Canova and Bertel Thorvaldsen, Mozier produced idealized sculpture groups with classical, religious, and literary themes. His work reveals especially the close relationship between literature and the subject matter of neoclassic sculpture. The source of one of his most famous compositions, *The Wept of Wish-ton-Wish*, 1839 (Arnot Art Gallery, Elmira, New York), was a novel by James Fenimore Cooper. Nathaniel Hawthorne mentioned Mozier's *Pocahontas* [73] in his *French and Italian Note-Books* (1871).

References

Gerdts, *American Neo-Classical Sculpture*, 42, 59, 68–71, 120–21, 130–31, 134–35; Rodman Scheirr, "Joseph Mozier and His Handiwork," *Potter's American Monthly* 6 (January 1876): 24–28; Margaret Farrand Thorp, *The Literary Sculptors* (Durham, N.C.: Duke University Press, 1965), 55, 136.

Nahl, Charles Christian

1818 Kassel, Germany–1878 San Francisco
Painter, illustrator

In 1849, after extensive training in Germany and Paris, Nahl, along with FREDERICK A. WENDEROTH, immigrated to New York. In 1851, with his younger half-brother, Arthur, and Wenderoth, he set out for California via Panama to find his fortune in the mines. When that failed to happen, the three men opened a studio in Sacramento, but the great fire that destroyed much of the town in 1852 forced them to move to San Francisco. There the partnership continued, with each artist contributing his specialty to a single work. Wenderoth left the group by 1856, but the two brothers remained together, with Charles achieving the most acclaim. Nahl found a ready market for his animal studies, genre paintings of California life, photographs, portraits, and even classical scenes. During the 1850s–60s he exhibited regularly at the Mechanics' Institute in San Francisco. He also taught WILLIAM KEITH, who was to become a prominent California landscape painter. Nahl's patrons, such as Judge E. B. Crocker, were among the state's leading citizens.

References

Joseph Armstrong Baird, Jr., "Charles Christian Nahl: Artist of the Gold Rush," *American Art Review* 3 (September–October 1976): 56–70; Erwin G. Gudde, "Carl Nahl: California's Pioneer of Painting," *American German Review* 7 (October 1940): 18–21; Stevens, *Nahl*.

Narjot, Ernest

Also known as Erneste-Etienne de Franceville Narjot
1826 Saint-Malo, France–1898 San Francisco
Painter

Another California gold rush artist, Narjot grew up in a family of painters and studied in France before traveling west with the forty-niners. In San Francisco he established a successful studio specializing in genre scenes, landscapes, and portraits. From 1849 to 1865 he spent much of his time in the gold mines of Arizona and Mexico. Returning to San Francisco in 1865, he painted portraits and murals of mining towns and military scenes. His most important commission may have been his mural decorations for the tomb of Leland Stanford, Jr., son of the railroad financier. While painting the murals, he severely injured his eyes, and in 1887 many San Francisco artists donated their work to an auction on Narjot's behalf. Despite his disabilities, in 1888–89 he received high acclaim and several medals for paintings sent to the California State Fair in Sacramento. Like that of many other artists working in San Francisco, much of his work was lost in the great earthquake of 1906.

References

Albert Dressler, *California's Pioneer Artist: Ernest Narjot, a Brief Résumé of the Career of a Versatile Genius* (San Francisco: Albert Dressler, 1936); Orr-Cahall, *Art of California,* 50.

Nast, Thomas
1840 Landau, Germany–1902 Guayaquil, Ecuador
Painter, illustrator, cartoonist

The first American political cartoonist of consequence, Nast arrived in New York from Germany when he was six years old. Around 1855 he studied briefly under THEODOR KAUFMANN but was largely self-taught. At age fifteen, he began selling sketches to *Leslie's Illustrated Weekly Newspaper.* In 1860–61 the *New York Illustrated News* sent him to Europe on assignment, and on his return he began work as a battlefield artist for *Harper's,* his employer for the next twenty-five years. Nast invented the symbols of the donkey and elephant for the Democratic and Republican parties as well as the popular representations of Santa Claus and Uncle Sam. His illustrations appeared in *Beyond the Mississippi* (1867), an early western travel guidebook by Albert D. Richardson [112]. In the mid-1880s editorial changes at *Harper's* as well as developments in image reproduction and competition from other cartoonists brought about a decline in Nast's prominence. In 1887 he lost his fortune in a Colorado mining venture and attempted without success to establish a publishing enterprise. In 1902 he accepted President Theodore Roosevelt's offer of a position as consul general to Ecuador. Six months after his arrival in Guayaquil, Nast died of tropical fever.

References

Morton Keller, *The Art and Politics of Thomas Nast* (New York: Oxford University Press, 1968); Albert Bigelow Paine, *Th. Nast: His Period and His Pictures* (New York: Macmillan, 1904); *Th. Nast: An Exhibition of His Work* (Boston: Northeastern University Press, 1983).

Nehlig, Victor
1830 Paris–1909 New York
Painter; ANA 1863, NA 1870

Nehlig immigrated to New York in 1856. Trained in France, where he absorbed the academic tradition, he exhibited at the Brooklyn Art Association, National Academy of Design, and Pennsylvania Academy of the Fine Arts. He may have returned to Europe in the 1870s. Critics favorably compared his work to that of the best history painters of the day. Instead of depicting European scenes, however, Nehlig chose American subjects having what he considered epic or heroic qualities. Many of his works are of Civil War subjects, but increasingly his paintings—such as *Pocahontas and John Smith* [71]—focused on Indians and their encounters with whites.

References

Groce and Wallace, *New-York Historical Society's Dictionary,* 467; Koke, *American Landscape and Genre Paintings* 3:4; Tuckerman, *Book of the Artists,* 492.

O'Sullivan, Timothy
1840 Staten Island, N.Y.–1882 Staten Island, N.Y.
Photographer

O'Sullivan learned photography in Mathew Brady's studio in New York. By his twentieth birthday he had become a valued member of Brady's staff, first in New York and then in Washington, D.C., where he worked under Alexander Gardner. In 1861, as a member of Brady's Photographic Corps, O'Sullivan recorded Civil War battle scenes. In 1862 he joined Gardner when he opened his studio and gallery in Washington. In 1867–69 O'Sullivan accompanied Clarence King's geological survey of the fortieth parallel, which began at Virginia City, Nevada, where he made the first photographs of interior mining operations. In 1869 he journeyed to

Panama as photographer for the Darien canal survey and in 1871 joined Lieutenant George Wheeler's survey west of the one-hundredth meridian. The grueling conditions of the party's travels through the deserts of Arizona and Nevada in the heat of summer are chronicled in the haunting starkness of his views. In 1872 O'Sullivan was again with King for a brief tour of Utah. In 1873–75 he photographed native Americans living in the Four Corners area. In 1880 he was appointed chief photographer of the Department of the Treasury.

References

Rick Dingus, *The Photographic Artifacts of Timothy O'Sullivan* (Albuquerque: University of New Mexico Press, 1982); James D. Horan, *Timothy O'Sullivan, America's Forgotten Photographer* (Garden City, N.Y.: Doubleday, 1966); Joel Snyder, *American Frontiers: The Photographs of Timothy O'Sullivan, 1867–1874* (New York: Aperture for Philadelphia Art Museum, 1981).

Otter, Thomas Proudly

1832 Montgomery Square, Pa.–1890
Doylestown, Pa.
Painter, engraver

In 1849–51 Otter worked in Philadelphia at the engraving firm of Daniel Scattergood and then studied under painter James Hamilton. By 1855 he was exhibiting regularly at the Athenaeum in Boston, National Academy of Design in New York, and Pennsylvania Academy of the Fine Arts in Philadelphia. Although in 1860 he was listed as a student at the Pennsylvania Academy, he was also at that time teaching his own students and painting his best-known work, *On the Road* [109]. In 1865 he moved to New Britain, Pennsylvania. He remained there until 1870, when he accepted a teaching position at the Linden Female Seminary in Doylestown, Pennsylvania. Active in community affairs, Otter was a founding member of the Bucks County Historical Society. In 1876 he illustrated W. W. H. Davis's *History of Bucks County* with approximately forty views of local subjects, some of which may have been based on the artist's photographs.

References

Gemmill, "Ferreting Out Thomas P. Otter"; idem, "Thomas P. Otter," *Antiques* 114 (November 1978): 1028–35; Hassrick, *Way West*, 188–89.

Palmer, Frances (Fanny) Flora Bond

1812 Leicester, England–1876 Brooklyn
Watercolorist, lithographer

Born to a well-to-do English family, Palmer immigrated to America in the early 1840s with her husband, Edward Seymour Palmer, a lithographer, their two children, and her brother and sister, also artists. As a husband-and-wife team, the Palmers worked from their home in Brooklyn, specializing in railroad and riverboat scenes. In 1849, because of her husband's alcoholism, Palmer assumed full responsibility for her family. For a time she and her sister taught singing, painting, and wax-flower making and also worked as governesses and chaperons. Around 1850 Fanny joined the publishing firm of Currier and Ives. Unlike many other artists working for the firm, she became a permanent employee and was regarded as perhaps the most reliable and versatile artist in the Currier and Ives stable. Although she preferred landscapes, she also painted animal figures and numerous railroad and steamship scenes.

References

Peters, *Currier & Ives,* 27–29; Walton Rawls, *The Great Book of Currier & Ives' America* (New York: Abbeville, 1979), 51–92, 112, 206, 291, 330; Charlotte Streifer Rubenstein, "The Early Career of Frances Flora Bond Palmer (1812–1876)," *American Art Journal* 17 (Autumn 1985): 71–88.

Persac, Marie-Adrien

1823 near Lyon, France–1873 near Manchac, Louisiana
Painter, lithographer

Persac led a varied career not only as a landscape and genre painter but also as an architect, cartographer, surveyor, and teacher. He emigrated from France in the 1840s, lived for a time in Indiana, and by the 1850s was active in Baton Rouge and New Orleans. In 1856 he was a partner with photographer William G. Vail and also worked closely with lithographer B. M. Norman, who in 1858 published Persac's illustrated maps of the Mississippi River Delta. Persac's technique of including figures in his landscape views and scenes of southern plantations of 1860–61 is unusual. Instead of painting them freehand, he cut figure illustrations from popular magazines, pasted them onto a canvas, and then painted them to blend with the rest of the picture.

References

Groce and Wallace, *New-York Historical Society's Dictionary*, 501; John A. Mahé and Rosanne McCaffrey, eds., *Encyclopedia of New Orleans Artists, 1718–1918* (New Orleans: Historic New Orleans, 1987), 299; Tyler, *Visions of America*, 104–5, 108–9, 201 n. 44.

Pettrich, Frederick Augustus Ferdinand
Also known as Ferdinand Pettrich
1798 Dresden, Germany–1872 Rome
Sculptor; HM 1837

Pettrich studied under his father, Franz Pettrich, court sculptor to the king of Saxony. Quickly absorbing the neoclassic manner of Antonio Canova, he studied for a time under Bertel Thorvaldsen. In Rome, Pettrich gained a reputation for his portrait busts and allegorical figures. In 1835 he moved to America, settling in Washington, D.C., where he hoped to obtain government contracts. Despite his talent, his only work from this period is the allegorical sculpture *Charity*, 1836 (unlocated), and portrait busts of leading citizens. In search of commissions, Pettrich moved to Philadelphia. He lived there for several years, sculpting portrait busts and a large statue of George Washington resigning his commission as military commander (Customhouse, New York). To obtain the likeness, Pettrich used the life mask made by sculptor Jean-Antoine Houdon at Mount Vernon. Frustrated by a lack of significant commissions, Pettrich left America in 1843 to become the court sculptor to Emperor Dom Pedro II of Brazil, where he carved *The Dying Tecumseh* [145].

References

Craven, *Sculpture in America*, 68–69; Hugh Honour, *The New Golden Land: European Images of America from the Discoveries to the Present Time* (New York: Pantheon, 1975), 233–36; Raymond L. Stehle, "Ferdinand Pettrich in America," *Pennsylvania History* 33 (October 1966): 389–411.

Proctor, Alexander Phimister
1862 Bozanquit, Canada–1950 Palo Alto, Calif.
Sculptor, painter; ANA 1901, NA 1904, NSS

An acclaimed sculptor of animal figures and Indian subjects, Proctor grew up in Denver, surrounded by the myth and lore of the Old West. In 1888 he went to New York to study sculpture at the Art Students League and National Academy of Design. Beginning in 1891 he spent two years in Chicago, making animal models, equestrian statues, and the bronze sculpture *Charging Panther,* circa 1892 (The Corcoran Gallery of Art, Washington, D.C.), for the World's Columbian Exposition. He then traveled to Paris, where his work impressed Augustus Saint-Gaudens. The elder sculptor commissioned Proctor to return to New York to model the horses for his equestrian statues of Generals John Logan and William Tecumseh Sherman, intended for Central Park. Proctor produced a variety of bronzes, including *The Indian Warrior,* 1898 (The Brooklyn Museum), which was awarded a gold medal at the Exposition Internationale of 1900 in Paris. He also contributed to the Pan-American Exposition of 1901 in Buffalo. His important commissions include lions for the McKinley Monument in Buffalo; bison heads for a fireplace in the White House, requested by President Theodore Roosevelt; and the monumental bison of Dumbarton Bridge in Washington, D.C. His last work was *Monument to the Mustangs,* unveiled at the University of Texas in Austin, two years before his death.

References

Broder, *Bronzes of the American West,* 107–23, 181, 193, 240, 272, 360, 383, 387–88; Michael A. Jacobsen, "Some Visual Sources for the Sculpture of Alexander Phimister Proctor," *Apelles: The Georgia Arts Journal* 1 (Spring 1980): 16–23; Hester Elizabeth Proctor, ed., *Alexander Phimister Proctor, Sculptor in Buckskin: An Autobiography* (Norman: University of Oklahoma Press, 1971).

Ranney, William Tylee
1813 Middletown, Conn.–1857
West Hoboken, N.J.
Painter; ANA 1850

Ranney's fascination with the West was in large part due to his experiences in Texas, where, during the late

1830s, he served in the war for independence. In the early 1840s he exhibited at the National Academy of Design in New York, where he had studied before traveling west. Frontier themes first appeared in his paintings around 1846, perhaps sparked by the outbreak of the Mexican War and Texas's entry into the Union the year earlier. In 1853 Ranney moved permanently to West Hoboken, New Jersey, where he decorated his studio with guns, saddles, and Indian artifacts. He never returned west. His work features the characters and drama of the frontier rather than the western landscape. He painted for a popular audience, emphasizing the heroism and romanticism of figures such as trappers and homesteaders. Much of his work was distributed as lithographs and engravings by the American Art-Union, Currier and Ives, and Western Art-Union.

References

Linda Ayres, "William Ranney," in Amon Carter Museum, *American Frontier Life*, 79–108; William H. Goetzmann, Joseph Porter, and David Hunt, *The West as a Romantic Horizon* (Omaha: Joslyn Art Museum, 1981), 15, 99, 102, 112; Grubar, *Ranney*.

Remington, Frederic Sackrider

1861 Canton, N.Y.–1909 Ridgefield, Conn.
Painter, sculptor, illustrator; ANA 1891

Remington had a privileged upbringing, attending prep school and Yale University, where he studied art and distinguished himself in football. He worked briefly in upstate New York and on a sheep farm in Kansas. In 1885 he returned east, married, and, after settling in New York, began submitting illustrations to *Harper's, Outing,* and other popular magazines. By 1890 he had achieved fame not only as an illustrator and painter but also as a writer of western stories. In these he presented himself as a veteran of cavalry campaigns. He cultivated this western persona along with his friends, fellow easterners, Theodore Roosevelt and novelist Owen Wister. They glorified the West's rugged past, creating much of the nostalgia about the region that persists today. Remington frequently traveled west for his publishers and was sent to cover the Spanish-American War of 1898 as a correspondent and artist. Enormously prolific, during the last twenty years of his life he produced more than

twenty-seven hundred paintings and twenty-four editions of bronze sculpture.

References

Peter H. Hassrick, *Frederic Remington* (Fort Worth, Tex.: Amon Carter Museum, 1973); Samuels and Samuels, *Remington;* Shapiro and Hassrick, *Remington.*

Rindisbacher, Peter

1806 Emmental, Switzerland–1834 Saint Louis
Painter

The son of a Swiss veterinary surgeon, Rindisbacher was among the first artists to paint scenes of American Indian life. In 1821 he immigrated with his parents to Winnipeg, in a colonialization effort by the Hudson's Bay Company to settle the Canadian prairies. Although he had taken drawing lessons for only one summer in Switzerland, he diligently sketched the landscape he saw along the way to his new home. In 1822–23 his views of British forts appeared as lithographs in the London publication *Views in Hudson's Bay* (c. 1825). The harsh winter of 1825–26 prompted his family to move south to Wisconsin, where the young artist sold several paintings of native Americans to United States Indian Commissioner Caleb Atwater. These appeared in Thomas L. McKenney and James Hall's multivolume *The Indian Tribes of North America* (1837–44). In 1829 Rindisbacher moved to Saint Louis, where he painted Indian subjects, portrait miniatures, sporting scenes for *American Turf Register and Sporting Magazine,* and western landscapes. By the time of his death at age twenty-eight, he had achieved a significant reputation.

References

Michael Benisovich and Anna M. Heilmaier, "Peter Rindisbacher, Swiss Artist," *Minnesota History* 32 (1951): 155–62; Alvin M. Josephy, Jr., *The Artist Was a Young Man: The Life Story of Peter Rindisbacher* (Fort Worth, Tex.: Amon Carter Museum, 1970); John F. McDermott, "Peter Rindisbacher: Frontier Reporter," *Art Quarterly* 12 (Spring 1949): 129–44.

Rothermel, Peter Frederick
1817 Nescopeck, Pa.–1895 near Linfield, Pa.
Painter; HM 1847

Rothermel worked as a sign painter in Philadelphia, then enrolled in the Pennsylvania Academy of the Fine Arts, which he later directed. Although early in his career he painted portraits, historical subjects increasingly occupied his attention. His first great success was *De Soto Discovering the Mississippi* [65], purchased by the American Art-Union in 1844, and his *Patrick Henry in the House of Burgesses,* 1851 (Patrick Henry Memorial Shrine Foundation, Brookneal, Virginia), hung for a time in the United States Capitol. He spent the years 1856–59 in Europe, exhibiting several paintings at the Paris Salon. During the 1860s he was active in Philadelphia, where he painted his most ambitious work, *The Battle of Gettysburg—Pickett's Charge,* 1867–70 (William Penn Memorial Museum, Harrisburg, Pennsylvania), a sixteen-by-thirty-two-foot canvas that was exhibited at the Centennial Exposition of 1876 in Philadelphia.

References
Edwin B. Coddington, "Rothermel's Paintings of the Battle of Gettysburg," *Pennsylvania History* 27 (January 1960): 1–27; Gerdts and Thistlethwaite, *Grand Illusions,* 32, 47–48, 52, 67, 82, 103; Mark Thistlethwaite, "Peter F. Rothermel: A Forgotten History Painter," *Antiques* 124 (November 1983): 1016–22.

Russell, Andrew Joseph
1830 Nunda, N.Y.–1902 New York
Photographer

Russell began his career in New York, combining painting and photography, but virtually none of his early work has survived. During the Civil War he earned his living as a photographer. In 1868 he was hired by the Union Pacific Railroad to record roadbed construction progress. He frequently produced works in a series, showing bridges, tracks, and trestles in various stages of construction. His most famous photograph—misattributed for many years to the Salt Lake City photographer Charles Savage—depicts the golden spike ceremony celebrating the completion of the transcontinental railroad in 1869 [10]. Russell's prints appeared in *Leslie's Illustrated Weekly Newspaper, Scribner's,*

and other popular periodicals. THOMAS MORAN used his images as the basis for several engravings reproduced in *Picturesque America* (1872–74). In 1869 Russell joined Clarence King's geological survey of the fortieth parallel and the Union Pacific issued *The Great West Illustrated,* with fifty albumen prints of his work. Neither these images nor the hundreds of negatives he produced in the West brought him fame, however. In 1869 he returned east to establish a studio in New York, where he continued to produce images for magazines and newspapers.

References
Susan Danly, "Andrew Joseph Russell's *The Great West Illustrated,*" in Danly and Marx, *Railroad in American Art,* 93–112; Naef and Wood, *Era of Exploration,* 79–123; Susan Danly Walther, "The Landscape Photographs of Alexander Gardner and Andrew Joseph Russell" (Ph.D. diss., Brown University, 1983).

Russell, Charles Marion
1864 Saint Louis–1926 Great Falls, Mont.
Painter, sculptor

Hoping to cure him of his romantic notions of the West, Russell's father sent him to Montana just before his sixteenth birthday. Instead the young boy stayed on, working as an itinerant ranch hand for the next eleven years. During this time, after taking only three drawing lessons, Russell began sketching his surroundings and making small clay models of animals. In 1887–88 he traveled to Alberta, Canada, where he lived among the Blackfeet, learning their language and customs. In 1888 *Harper's* published one of his drawings, the first of his many magazine illustrations. Like his contemporary FREDERIC REMINGTON, Russell painted the Wild West as it was fading into history. Although he sold his paintings to fellow cowhands and received an occasional commission, it was not until 1896 that he began seriously to pursue art as a career. He was extremely prolific and handled watercolor, oil, and clay with ease. After the turn of the century he exhibited widely in America and in London. In 1911 he painted a mural for the Montana State House in Helena.

References
Dippie, *Looking at Russell;* Peter H. Hassrick, *Charles M. Russell* (New York: Abrams, 1989); Frederic G. Renner,

Charles M. Russell: Paintings, Drawings, and Sculpture in the Amon G. Carter Collection (1966; New York: Abrams for Amon Carter Museum, 1974).

Schreyvogel, Charles
1861 New York–1912 Hoboken, N.J.
Painter; ANA 1901

Schreyvogel's early artistic experience came as an apprentice to a goldsmith and later to a lithographer. In 1887 he managed to find financial support for study in Munich, and on his return to America in 1893 he traveled to the West. He spent five months at a Ute reservation in Colorado and then journeyed to Arizona to paint cowboys. In 1900 his first western painting, *My Bunkie,* circa 1899 (The Metropolitan Museum of Art, New York), won the Thomas B. Clarke Prize at the National Academy of Design. The painting brought him immediate success and the opportunity to return west, to Dakota Territory, where he concentrated on cavalry and Indian scenes. He researched his paintings thoroughly, making numerous clay models and studies from life. Because of his insistence on accuracy, preference for large canvases, and early death at age forty-nine, he left few finished paintings. Many of these, however, appeared as prints and photographs.

References
Hassrick, *Way West,* 102–3; Horan, *Schreyvogel;* Charles Schreyvogel, *My Bunkie and Others: Pictures of Western American Life* (New York: Moffat, Yard, 1909).

Shaw, Joshua
1776 Bellingborough, England–1860 Burlington, N.J.
Painter; HM 1838

Largely self-taught, Shaw exhibited in London at the Royal Academy and Royal Institute of Painters. He immigrated to America in 1817 at the urging of Benjamin West, whose *Christ Healing the Sick in the Temple,* 1815 (Pennsylvania Hospital, Philadelphia), he escorted to Philadelphia, where Shaw settled. With artist Thomas Birch, he is credited with originating in America a landscape movement several years before the rise of the

Hudson River school. Shaw took advantage of the increasing popularity of landscape painting and toured widely with his friend the engraver John Sartain, sketching scenes of the American South and Indians on the frontier. In 1820 he published *Picturesque Views of American Scenery.* Sold by subscription, it was among the first series of printed landscape views of America. Many of his images are allegories alluding to literary and historical themes. Others, however, are straightforward views, which were favored by his patrons. Shaw exhibited at the Athenaeum in Boston, National Academy of Design in New York, and Pennsylvania Academy of the Fine Arts in Philadelphia. He was also an inventor, having devised the percussion cap and other firearm improvements.

References
Miriam Carroll, "Joshua Shaw: A Study of the Artist and His Paintings" (master's thesis, University of California, Los Angeles, 1971); Albert Ten Eyck Gardner and Stuart P. Feld, *American Paintings: A Catalogue of the Collection of the Metropolitan Museum of Art* (New York: Metropolitan Museum of Art, 1965), 1:130–33; Edward J. Nygren, *Views and Visions: American Landscape before 1830* (Washington, D.C.: Corcoran Gallery of Art, 1986).

Sommer, Otto
Active 1860s New Jersey
Painter

Almost unknown today, Sommer worked in Newark and Belleville, New Jersey, and exhibited landscapes of the Catskill Mountains. Sometimes listed as being born in Germany, he has been confused with an artist who signed his paintings "A. Sommer." Otto Sommer copied Thomas Cole's series The Voyage of Life, 1842 (Munson-Williams-Proctor Institute, Utica, New York), and produced several paintings of the West, including *Beef for the Troops,* 1867 (unlocated), and *Westward Ho!* [106].

References
Gerdts, *Painting and Sculpture in New Jersey,* 66, 80; Robert Melville, "Galler: A Symposium on Painting, Sculpture, and the Applied Arts," *Architectural Review* 155 (May 1974): 311; Rudolph G. Wunderlich, "Western Words: An Exhibition of Important Paintings of the American West," *Kennedy Quarterly* 9 (June 1969): 8.

Stanley, John Mix

1814 Canandaigua, N.Y.–1872 Detroit
Painter

During the 1830s Stanley was an itinerant sign and portrait painter, traveling between Detroit and Chicago. In 1839, while in Fort Snelling, Minnesota, he painted Indian subjects and landscapes. Three years later he was at Fort Gibson, Oklahoma, gathering Indian material and painting portraits, which he exhibited in Cincinnati in 1846. In that year he also accompanied Colonel Stephen Kearny from Santa Fe, New Mexico, to San Diego, producing images for Kearny's official expedition report. In 1847 Stanley traveled up the Pacific Coast to sketch native Americans. For the next two years he lived in Hawaii, painting portraits of the native inhabitants. In 1849–50 he toured his Indian Gallery in the East. Although Congress declined to purchase his 150 canvases, the paintings remained in the Smithsonian Institution in Washington, D.C., where they were destroyed by fire in 1865. Another collection of his work was lost under similar circumstances at P. T. Barnum's museum in New York. In 1853–54 Stanley accompanied Isaac Stevens's Pacific Railway Survey as photographer and artist. Stanley spent the rest of his life repainting his lost works and organizing their exhibition, sale, and reproduction.

References

Kinietz, *Stanley;* Charles H. Sawyer, *John Mix Stanley: Traveler in the West* (Ann Arbor: University of Michigan Press, 1970); Schimmel, "Stanley."

Tait, Arthur Fitzwilliam

1819 near Liverpool, England–1905 Yonkers, N.Y.
Painter, illustrator; ANA 1853, NA 1858

A popular illustrator of western subjects, Tait began his career at age twelve, in the employ of a Manchester art dealer. Although he studied art at night at the Royal Manchester Institute, he was largely self-taught. Some sources report that he assisted with the exhibition of GEORGE CATLIN's Indian Gallery in London and Paris, and this experience may have prompted him to immigrate to America in 1850. In 1852 he began work for Currier and Ives, producing genre scenes of hunters and animals in the Adirondack Mountains. In subsequent years the publishers reproduced his illustrations in their finest format, the large-scale folio, using their most skilled lithographers and etchers. For a series on native Americans and life in the West, with which he collaborated with artist Louis Maurer, his source material included prints by KARL BODMER and Catlin in the collection of the Astor Library in New York. Although Tait never traveled further west than Chicago, he, like his contemporary WILLIAM RANNEY (whose western artifacts he sometimes borrowed for his paintings), considerably influenced contemporary perceptions about the West.

References

Adirondack Museum, *A. F. Tait: Artist in the Adirondacks* (Blue Mountain Lake, N.Y., 1974); Warder H. Cadbury, "Arthur F. Tait," in Amon Carter Museum, *American Frontier Life,* 109–29; Warder H. Cadbury and Henry R. Marsh, *Arthur Fitzwilliam Tait, Artist in the Adirondacks: An Account of His Career [and] A Checklist of His Works* (Newark: Associated University Presses, 1986).

Tavernier, Jules

1844 Paris–1889 Honolulu
Painter, illustrator

Tavernier began his studies in Paris with Félix Barrias, an instructor at the Ecole des Beaux-Arts, and from 1865 to 1870 exhibited regularly at the annual Salon. At the conclusion of the Franco-Prussian War in 1871 Tavernier left France, going first to London, where he worked briefly as an illustrator, and then to America with the engraver Allen Meason. In New York they worked as a team, producing illustrations for *Harper's Weekly, Leslie's Illustrated Weekly Newspaper, New York Graphic,* and *Scribner's* as well as for *Picturesque America* (1872–74). In 1873 *Harper's* commissioned Tavernier to travel with PAUL FRENZENY on an overland tour of the West. This experience not only broadened Tavernier's view of America but also provided him with a wealth of subject matter. He settled in California and became active in the art communities of Monterey and San Francisco. The state's most prominent citizens were among his clients, including banker William C. Ralston and railroad financier Leland Stanford. Tavernier remained in California until 1884, when he moved to Hawaii to escape financial problems, perhaps brought on by the acute alcoholism that would eventually cause his death at age forty-five. His published illustrations are numerous, but relatively few of his paintings have survived.

References

Robert Nichols Ewing, "Jules Tavernier (1844–1889): Painter and Illustrator" (Ph.D. diss., University of California, Los Angeles, 1978); Taft, *Artists and Illustrators of the Old West*, 95–116, 315–22; Van Nostrand, *First Hundred Years of Painting in California*, 72, 125.

Tirrell, George
Also known as John Tirrell
Born circa 1826 Massachusetts
Painter

According to Tirrell, he constructed "the longest panorama ever painted" (unlocated), a monumental undertaking that pictured the California landscape from Monterey to Yosemite. The work took three years to complete with the assistance of a painter named T. J. Hagemann and was first exhibited in San Francisco in April 1860 before touring the East in 1861–62. Tirrell taught the painter Alfred Lambourne, who, after 1866, painted scenery for the Salt Lake City Theater, suggesting that Tirrell also spent time in Utah.

References

Groce and Wallace, *New-York Historical Society's Dictionary*, 631: Museum of Fine Arts, *American Paintings in the Museum of Fine Arts, Boston* (Boston, 1969), 269; Trenton and Hassrick, *Rocky Mountains*, 388, 389 n. 21.

Tojetti, Domenico
1807 Rome–1892 San Francisco
Painter

Tojetti did not arrive in the United States until 1871, when he was sixty-four. A well-respected artist in Italy, he was a professor at the Accademia di San Luca in Rome, having received commissions and awards from the Vatican and European royalty. In 1867, at the request of the Guatemalan minister to Italy, Tojetti established a fine arts academy in Guatemala but finding the

climate disagreeable moved north, first to Mexico City, then to San Francisco. He and his sons created many frescoes for churches and mansions, including an altarpiece for Saint Ignatius Church, which was destroyed in the earthquake of 1906. His portraits were also popular. Most notable, however, are his allegorical paintings related to his adopted country. Variously titled *America*, *California*, and *Progress of America* [123], his compositions are painted in the Renaissance-inspired style he had learned in Italy. Tojetti's frequent exhibitions at the San Francisco Art Association suggest that he was prolific, but much of his work was lost in 1906.

References

Arkelian, *Kahn Collection*, 47; Orr-Cahall, *Art of California*, 56; University of San Francisco, *Domenico Tojetti* (San Francisco, 1959).

Trousset, Leon
Born France; active 1870s–80s California
Painter

Little known today, Trousset painted landscapes and historical scenes of California and New Mexico. His painting of Mission Santa Cruz, perhaps dated 1853, now on display in the mission, suggests that he was on the West Coast as early as the 1850s. Most of his works, however, place him in San Francisco in the 1870s. Along with JULES TAVERNIER and others, he was active in the Monterey Peninsula art community.

References

Hughes, *Artists in California*, 468; Van Nostrand, *First Hundred Years of Painting in California*, 127.

Walker, James
1819 Northamptonshire, England–1889
Watsonville, Calif.
Painter

Walker came to America at a young age and grew up in New York, where he studied painting. In his early twenties, he moved to New Orleans and then to Mexico City, where he was living when American troops invaded in 1847. He escaped over the mountains to join

General William Jenkins Worth, whom he served as an interpreter during the Mexican War. Walker witnessed and sketched most of the major battles and campaigns of the war, including the capture of Mexico City. After a trip to South America he returned to the United States and established a studio in New York in 1848. He received several government commissions for military scenes, and his *Storming of Chapultepec* [61] hung for many years in the Senate wing of the United State Capitol. He served the Union in the Civil War, and his later large-scale works were based on sketches made during this time. By 1870 he had established a studio in San Francisco. With particular attention to costumes and detail, he painted vaquero scenes, which are today considered unique observations of life in Spanish California. In the late 1870s he was again in New York; in 1884 he settled permanently in California.

References

Hassrick, *Way West,* 146–47; Marion R. McNaughton, "James Walker: Combat Artist of Two American Wars," *Military Collector and Historian* 9 (Summer 1957): 31–35; Sandweiss, Stewart, Huseman, *Eyewitness to War.*

Watkins, Carleton Eugene

1829 Oneonta, N.Y.–1916 Imola, Calif.
Photographer

Arriving in San Francisco in 1851, Watkins worked first as a shopkeeper. By 1854 he had learned photography in the studio of the prominent daguerreotypist Robert Vance. In 1856 he was working with photographer James M. Ford, who probably introduced him to the wet-plate collodion method. In 1861 Watkins made the first of many trips to Yosemite. His photographs were in direct competition with those of his colleague C. L. Weed, who had preceded him to the area in 1859. Watkins was again in Yosemite in 1865–66, this time with Josiah Whitney's survey party, which included the geologist Clarence King. Watkins's photographs from this expedition brought him lasting renown. As a result, in 1867, he established in San Francisco his Yosemite Art Gallery and also began exhibiting city views. In 1867 he traveled up the West Coast to Oregon, making photographs that are considered among his best. He was with King again in 1870 for his ascent of Mount Shasta. The financial panic of 1873 forced the closing of Watkins's studio, and his only series of negatives ultimately went to his competitor I. W. Tabor. This same year, however, he traveled to Utah with WILLIAM KEITH. Watkins later reshot many of his earlier images. Most of his glass-plate negatives were destroyed in the San Francisco earthquake of 1906.

References

James Alinder, ed., *Carleton E. Watkins: Photographs of the Columbia River and Oregon* (Carmel, Calif.: Friends of Photography, 1979); Naef and Wood, *Era of Exploration,* 79–123; Palmquist, *Watkins.*

Weir, John Ferguson

1841 West Point, N.Y.–1926 Providence
Painter; ANA 1864, NA 1866

An elder half-brother of artist Julian Alden Weir and one of ROBERT WEIR's sixteen children, John Ferguson grew up in West Point. His *Gun Foundry* [54], conceived and modeled after a foundry near West Point during the height of the Civil War, brought him great acclaim when it was exhibited at the National Academy of Design in New York in 1866 as well as in the Exposition Universelle of 1867 in Paris and Centennial Exposition of 1876 in Philadelphia. During the 1860s Weir also painted small-scale interior scenes, such as *An Artist's Studio* [52], the sales of which enabled him to study abroad in 1868–69. After returning to America, he was appointed the first dean of the art school at Yale University, a position he held until 1913.

References

Betsy Fahlman, "John Ferguson Weir: Painter of Romantic and Industrial Icons," *Archives of American Art Journal* 20 (1980): 2–9; Spassky, *American Paintings in the Metropolitan* 2:566–74; John Wilmerding, Linda Ayres, and Earl A. Powell, *An America Perspective: Nineteenth-Century Art from the Collection of Jo Ann and Julian Ganz, Jr.* (Washington, D.C.: National Gallery of Art, 1981), 58–59, 82, 169–70.

Weir, Robert Walter

1803 New York–1889 New York
Painter; ANA 1829, NA 1831

Weir was born into the prosperous household of a shipping merchant who had come to America from Scotland in 1795. The War of 1812, however, brought the family to bankruptcy, and at age ten, Weir was apprenticed to a cotton manufacturer. He was largely self-taught, as there were, in 1820, few means available for artistic training outside Europe. Eventually he found a patron and in 1824 traveled to Rome, where he shared rooms with the sculptor Horatio Greenough. While in Europe, Weir painted religious scenes and landscapes. He returned to America in 1827 and soon achieved success, exhibiting and teaching at the newly established National Academy of Design. In 1834 he become a professor of art at the United States Military Academy in West Point, New York, where he remained for forty-two years. Weir's remarkably varied work encompasses genre scenes, history paintings, landscapes, and portraits. His *Embarkation of the Pilgrims at Delft Haven* [57] is displayed in the rotunda of the United States Capitol.

References

Jacob Edward Kent Ahrens, "Robert Walter Weir (1803–1889)" (Ph.D. diss., University of Delaware, 1972); idem, "Robert Weir's *Embarkation of the Pilgrims*," *Capitol Studies* 1 (Fall 1972): 59–71; Cadet Fine Arts Forum, *Weir;* Irene Weir, *Robert W. Weir, Artist* (New York: Field-Doubleday, 1947).

Wenderoth, Frederick August

1819 Kassel, Germany–1884 Philadelphia
Painter

Known primarily for his close association with CHARLES NAHL, Wenderoth studied in Germany in 1845, then traveled to Paris and Algiers, perhaps in the company of the French painter Horace Vernet. Wenderoth's experiences may have lured Nahl to Paris in 1846. The two artists immigrated to New York in 1849 and then traveled together to California in 1851. Wenderoth appears to have contributed landscape backgrounds to compositions of the Nahl-Wenderoth partnership.

Wenderoth married Nahl's sister Laura, and the two moved east by 1856, settling in Philadelphia by 1857. Although his wife died in childbirth shortly after their arrival, Wenderoth stayed in Philadelphia, where he achieved success as a painter and photographer.

References

Groce and Wallace, *New-York Historical Society's Dictionary,* 672–73; Stevens, *Nahl,* 21, 26, 29, 32, 51, 53–54, 66.

Whittredge, Thomas Worthington

1820 Springfield, Ohio–1910 Summit, N.J.
Painter; ANA 1860, NA 1861

Whittredge began his career at age seventeen in Cincinnati as a sign and house painter. In 1846 his canvases came to the attention of Asher B. Durand, then president of the National Academy of Design. In 1849 Whittredge traveled to Europe, where he stayed ten years. In Düsseldorf he studied under Andreas Achenbach and associated with ALBERT BIERSTADT and EMANUEL LEUTZE. In 1866 he joined John Pope's expedition at Fort Leavenworth, Kansas, and traveled to Colorado and New Mexico, returning via the Santa Fe Trail. He was in the West again in 1870 (with SANFORD R. GIFFORD and John F. Kensett) and 1871. His landscapes, generally painted along western rivers, with mountains in the background, are more bucolic than those by Bierstadt and Moran. Whittredge was elected president of the National Academy in 1876.

References

Cheryl A. Cibulka, *Quiet Places: The American Landscapes of Worthington Whittredge* (Washington, D.C.: Adams Davidson Galleries, 1982); Edward H. Dwight, *Worthington Whittredge (1820–1910): A Retrospective Exhibition of an American Artist* (Utica, N.Y.: Munson-Williams-Proctor Institute, 1969); Anthony F. Janson, *Worthington Whittredge* (New York: Cambridge University Press, 1990).

Wimar, Carl Ferdinand
Also known as Charles or Karl Wimar
1828 Siegburg, Germany–1862 Saint Louis
Painter

A contemporary of GEORGE CALEB BINGHAM, Wimar was also a Missouri artist, although his roots were in Germany, where he lived until 1843. After settling in Saint Louis, Wimar studied under the local painter Léon Pomarede. In 1849 Pomarede, with Wimar as apprentice, produced a panorama of the upper Mississippi that enabled the young artist to study the landscape and Indian inhabitants along the river. The painting was exhibited in New Orleans and in the East before it was destroyed by fire in Newark. Wimar established his own studio in Saint Louis in 1851, before leaving for Europe to study under EMANUEL LEUTZE in Düsseldorf. While in Germany, Wimar painted scenes from contemporary frontier literature, several of which appeared as prints. In 1856 he returned to America and in 1858–59 traveled up the Missouri River, photographing and sketching Indians and scenes of western life. After completing a series of murals for the Saint Louis County Courthouse, Wimar died of tuberculosis at age thirty-four.

References
William R. Hodges, *Carl Wimar* (Galveston, Tex.: Charles Reymershoffer, 1908); Joseph D. Ketner, Rick Stewart, and Angela Miller, *Carl F. Wimar: Chronicler of the Missouri River Frontier* (forthcoming); Rathbone, *Wimar.*

Woodville, Richard Caton
1825 Baltimore–1855 London
Painter

Woodville may have first studied art at Saint Mary's College, an exclusive boys' school in Baltimore. In 1842 he enrolled briefly as a medical student at the University of Maryland but soon abandoned his studies in favor of art. Woodville focused on genre scenes, which he painted in the refined style of the seventeenth-century Flemish and Dutch masters. By age twenty, he was exhibiting at the National Academy of Design. In 1845 he joined the large number of American artists in Düsseldorf. Until the end of his short life (he died at age thirty), he lived in Europe, only returning twice to America. An engraving of Woodville's *War News from Mexico* [87] and *Old '76 and Young '48* [91] were shown at the American Art-Union.

References
Bartlett Cowdrey, "Richard Caton Woodville: An American Genre Painter," *American Collector* 13 (April 1944): 6–7, 14, 20; Francis Grubar, *Richard Caton Woodville: An Early American Genre Painter* (Washington, D.C.: Corcoran Gallery of Art, 1967); Hills, *Painters' America,* 48, 50, 53, 55.

Wyeth, Newell Convers
1882 Needham, Mass.–1945 Chadds Ford, Pa.
Painter, illustrator; NA 1941

A popular book illustrator and the father of artist Andrew Wyeth, N. C. Wyeth was among a select group chosen to study under illustrator Howard Pyle in Wilmington, Delaware. Wyeth produced hundreds of images for *Colliers, Saturday Evening Post, Scribner's,* and numerous other periodicals. His two trips to the West in 1904 and 1906 were sponsored by popular magazines. His strong narrative style and dramatic compositions made him a favorite for these commissions. In 1908 he moved his young family to Chadds Ford, a rural area that would figure in many of his paintings and remain his home for the rest of his life. He also produced a variety of murals, including those for the Missouri State House in Jefferson City and the National Geographic Society Headquarters and National Cathedral in Washington, D.C.

References
David Allen and David Allen, Jr., *N. C. Wyeth: The Collected Paintings, Illustrations, and Murals* (New York: Crown, 1972); Duff, *Wyeth;* Betsy James Wyeth, *The Wyeths: The Letters of N. C. Wyeth, 1901–1945* (Boston: Gambit, 1971).

References

Listed here are sources cited in abbreviated form in the artists' biographies, captions, and notes.

Allen, James Logan. *Passage through the Garden: Lewis and Clark and the Image of the American Northwest.* Urbana: University of Illinois Press, 1975.

Amon Carter Museum. *American Frontier Life: Early Western Painting and Prints.* New York: Abbeville, 1987.

Andrews, Ralph W. *Photographers of the Frontier West: Their Lives and Works, 1875–1915.* New York: Bonanza, 1965.

Appleton, Carolyn M., and Natasha S. Bartalini. *Henry Farny, 1847–1916.* Austin: Archer M. Huntington Art Gallery, University of Texas, 1983.

Arkelian, Marjorie Dakin. *The Kahn Collection of Nineteenth-Century Paintings by Artists in California.* Oakland, Calif.: Oakland Museum, 1975.

———. *Thomas Hill: The Grand View.* Oakland, Calif.: Oakland Museum, 1980.

———. *William Hahn, Genre Painter, 1829–1887.* Oakland, Calif.: Oakland Museum, 1976.

Baird, Joseph Armstrong, Jr. *Catalogue of Original Paintings, Drawings, and Watercolors in the Robert B. Honeyman, Jr., Collection.* Berkeley: Friends of the Bancroft Library, University of California, 1968.

Baker, Charles E. "The American Art-Union." *See* Cowdrey.

Barter, Judith A., and Lynn E. Springer. *Currents of Expansion: Painting in the Midwest, 1820–1940.* Saint Louis: Saint Louis Art Museum, 1977.

Barthes, Roland. *Mythologies.* Translated by Annette Lavers. New York: Hill & Wang, 1972.

Bercovitch, Sacvan, and Myra Jehlen, eds. *Ideology and Classic American Literature.* New York: Cambridge University Press, 1987.

Berkhofer, Robert F., Jr. *Salvation and the Savage: An Analysis of Protestant Missions and American Indian Response, 1787–1862.* Lexington: University of Kentucky, 1965.

———. *The White Man's Indian: Images of the American Indian from Columbus to the Present.* New York: Knopf, 1978.

Bickerstaff, Laura M.. *Pioneer Artists of Taos.* 1955. Denver: Old West, 1983.

Billington, Ray Allen. *Westward Expansion: A History of the American Frontier.* 1949, 1967, 1974. New York, 1982.

Bloch, E. Maurice. *George Caleb Bingham: The Evolution of an Artist.* Berkeley: University of California Press, 1967.

———. *The Paintings of George Caleb Bingham: A Catalogue Raisonné.* Columbia: University of Missouri Press, 1986.

Bowditch, Nancy Douglas. *George de Forest Brush: A Joyous Painter.* Peterborough, N.H.: Noone House, 1970.

Bowles, Samuel. *Across the Continent: A Summer's Journey to the Rocky Mountains, the Mormons, and the Pacific States, with Speaker Colfax.* Springfield, Mass., 1865.

———. *Our New West.* Hartford: Hartford Publishing, 1869.

Broder, Patricia Janis. *Bronzes of the American West.* New York: Abrams, 1974.

———. *Taos: A Painter's Dream.* Boston: New York Graphic Society, 1980.

Brooklyn Museum. *Buffalo Bill and the Wild West.* Pittsburgh: University of Pittsburgh Press, 1981.

Browne, Charles Francis. "Elbridge Ayer Burbank: A Painter of Indian Portraits." *Brush and Pencil* 3 (October 1898): 16–35.

Burbank, Elbridge A. *Burbank among the Indians.* Edited by Frank J. Taylor. Caldwell, Idaho: Caxton, 1944.

Cadet Fine Arts Forum of the United States Corps of Cadets. *Robert Weir: Artist and Teacher of West Point.* Essays by William H. Gerdts and James T. Callow. West Point, N.Y., 1976.

Carter, Denny. *Henry Farny.* New York: Watson-Guptill for Cincinnati Art Museum, 1978.

Cassedy, David, and Gail Shrott. *William Sidney Mount: Works in the Collection of the Museums at Stony Brook.* Stony Brook, N.Y.: Museums at Stony Brook, 1983.

Catherwood, Frederick. *Views of the Ancient Monuments in Central America, Chiapas, and Yucatán.* 1844.

Chan, Sucheng. *This Bitter-sweet Soil: The Chinese in California Agriculture, 1860–1910.* Berkeley: University of California Press, 1986.

Cosentino, Andrew J. *The Paintings of Charles Bird King (1785–1862).* Washington, D.C.: Smithsonian Institution Press for National Collection of Fine Arts, 1977.

Cosentino, Andrew J., and Henry H. Glassie. *The Capital Image: Painters in Washington, 1800–1915.* Washington, D.C.: Smithsonian Institution Press, 1983.

Cowdrey, [Mary] Bartlett, ed. *The American Academy of Fine Arts and American Art-Union.* New York: New-York Historical Society, 1953.

Craven, Wayne. *Sculpture in America.* 1968. Newark: University of Delaware Press; New York: Cornwall, 1984.

Crofutt, George A. *Crofutt's New Overland Tourist and Pacific Coast Guide.* Chicago: Overland, 1878–79.

Cronon, William. "Revisiting the Vanishing Frontier." *Western Historical Quarterly* 18 (April 1987): 157–76.

Culin, Stewart. "Games of the North American Indians." In *Twenty-fourth Annual Report of the Bureau of American Ethnology.* 1902–3. New York: Dover, 1975.

Current, Karen, and William R. Current. *Photography and the Old West.* New York: Abrams for Amon Carter Museum, 1978.

Dana, C. W. *The Garden of the World, or the Great West: Its History, Its Wealth, Its Natural Advantages, and Its Future. Also, Comprising a Complete Guide to Emigrants, with a Full Description of the Different Routes Westward by an Old Settler, with Statistics and Facts, from Hon. Thomas H. Benton, Hon. Sam Houston, Col. John C. Frémont, and Other "Old Settlers."* Boston: Westworth, 1856.

Danly, Susan, and Leo Marx, eds. *The Railroad in American Art: Representations of Technological Change.* Cambridge, Mass.: MIT Press, 1988.

Darrah, William Culp. "Beaman, Fennemore, Hillers, Dellenbaugh, Johnson, and Hattan." *Utah Historical Quarterly* 16–17 (1948–49): 491–503.

———. *Powell of the Colorado*. Princeton: Princeton University Press, 1951.

Dippie, Brian W. *Looking at Russell*. Fort Worth, Tex.: Amon Carter Museum, 1987.

———. *Remington and Russell*. Austin: University of Texas Press, 1982.

Drinnon, Richard. *Facing West: The Metaphysics of Indian-Hating and Empire-Building*. Minneapolis: University of Minnesota Press, 1980.

Duff, James H. *The Western World of N. C. Wyeth*. Cody, Wyo.: Buffalo Bill Historical Center, 1980.

Dutton, Clarence E. *Atlas to Accompany the Monograph on the Tertiary History of the Grand Cañon District*. 1882.

Eisenhower, John S. D. *So Far from God: The U.S. War with Mexico, 1846–1848*. New York: Random House, 1989.

Ekirch, Arthur Alphonse, Jr. *The Idea of Progress in America, 1815–1860*. 1944, 1951. New York: AMS Press, 1969.

Eldredge, Charles C., Julie Schimmel, and William H. Truettner. *Art in New Mexico, 1900–1945: Paths to Taos and Santa Fe*. New York: Abbeville for National Museum of American Art, 1986.

Evans, Elliot. "Promised Land." *Society of California Pioneers* (November 1957): 1–11.

———, ed. "Some Letters of William S. Jewett, California Artist." *California Historical Society Quarterly* 23 (June 1944): 148–77; and (September 1944): 226–46.

Ewers, John. *Artists of the Old West*. 1965, 1973. Garden City, N.Y.: Doubleday, 1982.

Fairman, Charles E. *Art and Artists of the Capitol of the United States of America*. Washington, D.C.: Government Printing Office, 1927.

Fifer, J. Valerie. *American Progress: The Growth of the Transport, Tourist, and Information Industries in the Nineteenth-Century West, Seen through the Life and Times of George A. Crofutt, Pioneer and Publicist of the Transcontinental Age*. Chester, Conn.: Globe Pequot, 1988.

Foner, Eric. *Free Soil, Free Labor, Free Men: The Ideology of the Republican Party before the Civil War*. New York: Oxford University Press, 1970.

Gemmill, Helen H. "Ferreting Out Thomas P. Otter." *Bucks County Historical Society Journal* 10 (Fall 1976): 19–40.

Gerdts, William H. *American Neo-Classical Sculpture: The Marble Resurrection*. New York: Viking, 1973.

———. *Painting and Sculpture in New Jersey*. Vol. 24 of *The New Jersey Historical Series*. Princeton: Van Nostrand, 1964.

Gerdts, William H., and Mark Thistlethwaite. *Grand Illusions: History Painting in America*. Fort Worth, Tex.: Amon Carter Museum, 1988.

Glanz, Dawn. *How the West Was Drawn: American Art and the Settling of the Frontier*. Ann Arbor: University of Michigan Press, 1982.

Goddard, Frederick B. *Where to Emigrate and Why: Describes the Climate, Soil, Productions, Minerals and General Resources, Amount of Public Lands, the Quality and Price of Farm Lands in Nearly All Sections of the United States and Contains a Description of the Pacific Railroad, the Homestead and Other Land Laws, Rates of Wages throughout the Country*. New York: Goddard, 1869.

Goetzmann, William H. *Exploration and Empire: The Explorer and the Scientist in the Winning of the American West*. New York: Knopf, 1966.

Goetzmann, William H., and William N. Goetzmann. *The West of the Imagination*. New York: Norton, 1986.

Groce, George C., and David H. Wallace. *The New-York Historical Society's Dictionary of Artists in America, 1564–1860*. New Haven, Conn.: Yale University Press, 1957.

Groeschel, Harriet Hoctor. "A Study of the Life and Work of the Nineteenth-Century Genre Artist Tompkins Harrison Matteson (1813–1884)." M.A. thesis, Barnard College, 1985.

Groseclose, Barbara S. *Emanuel Leutze, 1816–1868: Freedom Is the Only King.* Washington, D.C.: Smithsonian Institution Press for National Collection of Fine Arts, 1975.

Grubar, Francis S. *William Ranney: Painter of the Early West.* Washington, D.C.: Corcoran Gallery of Art, 1962.

Hales, Peter B. *William Henry Jackson and the Transformation of the American Landscape.* Philadelphia: Temple University Press, 1988.

Hassrick, Peter H. *The Way West: Art of Frontier America.* New York: Abrams, 1977.

Hendricks, Gordon. *Albert Bierstadt: Painter of the American West.* New York: Abrams for Amon Carter Museum, 1974.

Hills, Patricia. *The American Frontier: Images and Myths.* New York: Whitney Museum of American Art, 1973.

———. *The Painters' America: Rural and Urban Life, 1810–1910.* New York: Praeger, 1974.

Horan, James D. *The Life and Art of Charles Schreyvogel: Painter-Historian of the Indian-Fighting Army of the American West.* New York: Crown, 1969.

Hough, Katherine Plake. *California's Western Heritage.* Palm Springs, Calif.: Palm Springs Desert Museum, 1986.

Hughes, Edan M. *Artists in California, 1786–1940.* San Francisco: Hughes Publishing, 1986.

Hutchings, James Mason. *Scenes of Wonder and Curiosity in California.* New York: Roman, 1876.

Israel, Fred L., ed. *State of the Union Messages of the Presidents of the United States.* New York: Chelsea House in association with Bowker, 1967.

Jackson, Donald, and Mary Lee Spence, eds. *The Expeditions of John Charles Frémont.* Urbana: University of Illinois Press, [1970–80].

James, Edwin. *Account of an Expedition from Pittsburgh to the Rocky Mountains, Performed in the Years 1819 and '20 . . . under the Command of Major Stephen H. Long.* Philadelphia: Carey & Lea, 1823.

Jennings, Francis. *The Invasion of America: Indians, Colonialism, and the Cant of Conquest.* 1975. Norton, 1976.

Johannsen, Robert W. *To the Halls of the Montezumas.* New York: Oxford University Press, 1985.

Karnes, Thomas L. *William Gilpin: Western Nationalist.* Austin: University of Texas Press, 1970.

Kelly, Franklin. *Frederic Edwin Church and the National Landscape.* Washington, D.C.: Smithsonian Institution Press, 1988.

Kendall, George Wilkins. *The War between the United States and Mexico Illustrated.* New York: Appleton, 1851.

Kinietz, W. Vernon. *John Mix Stanley and His Indian Paintings.* Ann Arbor: University of Michigan Press, 1942.

Kinsey, Joni Louise. "Creating a Sense of Place: Thomas Moran and the Surveying of the American West." Ph.D. diss., Washington University, 1989.

Koke, Richard J., comp. *American Landscape and Genre Paintings in the New-York Historical Society.* Vol. 3 of *A Catalog of the Collection, Including Historical, Narrative, and Marine Art.* New York: New-York Historical Society, 1982.

Lamar, Howard R. *The Far Southwest, 1846–1912: A Territorial History.* New Haven: Yale University Press, 1966.

Lears, T. J. Jackson. *No Place of Grace: Antimodernism and the Transformation of American Culture.* New York: Pantheon, 1981.

Limerick, Patricia. *The Legacy of Conquest: The Unbroken Past of the American West.* New York: Norton, 1988.

Ludlow, Fitz Hugh. *The Heart of the Continent: A Record of Travel across the Plains and in Oregon, with an Examination of the Mormon Principles.* 1870. New York: AMS Press, 1971.

McCracken, Harold. *George Catlin and the Old Frontier.* New York: Dial, 1959.

McDermott, John F. *George Caleb Bingham: River Portraitist.* Norman: University of Oklahoma Press, 1959.

———. *Seth Eastman: Pictorial Historian of the Indian.* Norman: University of Oklahoma Press, 1961.

Malone, Dumas. *Jefferson the President, First Term, 1801–1805.* Boston: Little, Brown, 1970.

Mann, Maybelle. *The American Art-Union.* Otisville, N.Y.: ALM, 1977.

Maxwell, Everett. "The Art of Elbridge A. Burbank." *Fine Arts Journal* 22 (January 1910): 3–8.

Merk, Frederick. *Manifest Destiny and Mission in American History: A Reinterpretation.* New York: Knopf, 1963.

Miller, Dwight. *California Landscape Painters around Keith and Hill (1850–1900).* Palo Alto: Stanford University Department of Art, 1979.

Miller, Lillian B. *Patrons and Patriotism: The Encouragement of the Fine Arts in the United States, 1790–1860.* Chicago: University of Chicago Press, 1966.

Moorhead, Max L. *New Mexico's Royal Road: Trade and Travel on the Chihuahua Trail.* Norman: University of Oklahoma Press, 1958.

Morgan, Joan B. *George de Forest Brush, 1855–1941: Master of the American Renaissance.* New York: Berry-Hill Galleries, 1985.

Naef, Weston J., and James N. Wood. *Era of Exploration: The Rise of Landscape Photography in the American West, 1860–1885.* Buffalo and New York: Albright Knox Gallery and Metropolitan Museum of Art, 1975.

Nash, Roderick. *Wilderness and the American Mind.* 1967. New Haven: Yale University Press, 1982.

Nelson, Clifford M. "William Henry Holmes: Beginning a Career in Art and Science." *Records of the Columbia Historical Society of Washington, D.C.* 50 (1980): 252–78.

Orr-Cahall, Christina, ed. *The Art of California: Selected Works from the Collection of the Oakland Museum.* Oakland, Calif.: Oakland Museum, 1984.

Palmquist, Peter E. *Carleton E. Watkins: Photographer of the American West.* Albuquerque: University of New Mexico Press for Amon Carter Museum, 1983.

Paul, Rodman Wilson. *California Gold: The Beginning of Mining in the Far West.* Cambridge, Mass.: Harvard University Press, 1947.

———. *Mining Frontiers of the Far West, 1848–1880.* New York: Holt, Rinehart, & Winston, 1963.

Percival, Walter, ed. *Friendship's Gift: A Souvenir for 1848.* Boston: John P. Hill, 1848.

Peters, Harry T. *Currier & Ives: Printmakers to the American People.* Garden City, N.Y.: Doubleday, Doran, 1942.

Prescott, William H. *History of the Conquest of Mexico.* 1843. Philadelphia: McKay, 1891.

Prucha, Francis Paul. *American Indian Policy in the Formative Years: The Indian Trade and Intercourse Acts, 1790–1834.* Cambridge, Mass.: Harvard University Press, 1962.

———. *The Indians in American Society from the Revolutionary War to the Present.* Berkeley: University of California Press, 1985.

Rathbone, Perry T. *Charles Wimar, 1828–1862: Painter of the Indian Frontier.* Saint Louis: City Art Museum of Saint Louis, 1946.

Richardson, Albert D. *Beyond the Mississippi: From the Great River to the Great Ocean. Life and Adventure on the Prairies, Mountains, and Pacific Coast.* Hartford: American Publishing, 1867.

Rogin, Michael Paul. *Fathers and Children: Andrew Jackson and the Subjugation of the American Indian.* New York: Knopf, 1975.

Rohe, Randall. "The Geography and Material Culture of the Western Mining Town." *Material Culture* 16, no. 3 (1984): 99–115.

Rollins, C. B., ed. "Letters of George Caleb Bingham to James S. Rollins, Pt. 2: October 3, 1853–August 10, 1856." *Missouri Historical Review* 32, no. 2 (January 1938).

Sabin, Edwin L. *Building the Pacific Railway: The Construction-Story of America's First Iron Thoroughfare between the Missouri River and California, from the Inception of the Great Idea to the Day, May 10, 1869, When the Union Pacific and the Central Pacific Joined Tracks at Promontory Point, Utah, to Form the Nation's Transcontinental.* Philadelphia: Lippincott, 1919.

Said, Edward W. *Orientalism.* New York: Random, 1979.

Samuels, Peggy, and Harold Samuels. *Frederic Remington: A Biography.* Garden City, N.Y.: Doubleday, 1982.

———. *The Illustrated Biographical Encyclopedia of Artists of the American West.* Garden City, N.Y.: Doubleday, 1976.

Sandweiss, Martha, Rick Stewart, and Ben W. Huseman. *Eyewitness to War: Prints and Daguerreotypes of the Mexican War, 1846–1848.* Washington, D.C.: Smithsonian Institution Press for Amon Carter Museum, 1989.

Satz, Ronald N. *American Indian Policy in the Jacksonian Era.* Lincoln: University of Nebraska Press, 1975.

Saum, Lewis O. *The Fur Trader and the Indian.* Seattle: University of Washington Press, 1965.

Schimmel, Julia Ann. "John Mix Stanley and the Imagery of the West in the Nineteenth Century." Ph.D. diss., New York University, 1983.

Sekula, Allan. "The Body and the Archive." *October* 39 (Winter 1986): 3–64.

Shapiro, Michael, et al. *George Caleb Bingham.* New York: Abrams for Saint Louis Art Museum, 1990.

Shapiro, Michael, and Peter H. Hassrick. *Frederic Remington: The Masterworks.* New York: Abrams for Saint Louis Art Museum and Buffalo Bill Historical Center, 1988.

Sheehan, Bernard W. *Seeds of Extinction: Jeffersonian Philanthropy and the American Indian.* 1973. New York: Norton, 1974.

Slotkin, Richard. *The Fatal Environment: The Myth of the Frontier in the Age of Industrialization, 1800–1890.* 1985. Middletown, Conn.: Wesleyan University Press, 1986.

———. "Nostalgia and Progress: Theodore Roosevelt's Myth of the Frontier." *American Quarterly* 35 (Winter 1981): 608–37.

———. *Regeneration through Violence: The Mythology of the American Frontier, 1600–1800.* Middletown, Conn.: Wesleyan University Press, 1973.

Smith, Henry Nash. *Virgin Land: The American West as Symbol and Myth.* 1950. Cambridge, Mass.: Harvard University Press, 1970.

Spassky, Natalie. *American Paintings in the Metropolitan Museum of Art.* Vol. 2. Princeton: Princeton University Press for Metropolitan Museum of Art, 1985.

Starr, Kevin. *Americans and the California Dream, 1850–1915.* New York: Oxford University Press, 1973.

Stegner, Wallace. *Beyond the Hundredth Meridian: John Wesley Powell and the Second Opening of the West.* Boston: Houghton Mifflin, 1954.

Stehle, Raymond L. "*Westward Ho!:* The History of Leutze's Fresco in the Capitol." *Records of the Columbia Historical Society of Washington, D.C.* 60–62 (1963): 306–22.

Stevens, Isaac I. *Narrative and Final Report of Explorations for a Route for a Pacific Railroad, near the Forty-seventh and Forty-ninth Parallels of North Latitude from Saint Paul to Puget Sound–1855* (1860). Vol. 12, bk. 1, of United States War Department, *Reports of Explorations and Surveys, to Ascertain the Most Practicable and Economical Route for a Railroad from the Mississippi River to the Pacific Ocean.* Washington, D.C., 1855–60.

Stevens, Moreland L. *Charles Christian Nahl: Artist of the Gold Rush.* Sacramento: Crocker Art Gallery, 1976.

Szasz, Margaret Connell. *Indian Education in the American Colonies, 1607–1783.* Albuquerque: University of New Mexico Press, 1988.

Taft, Robert. *Artists and Illustrators of the Old West, 1850–1900.* 1953. Princeton: Princeton University Press, 1982.

———. *Photography and the American Scene: A Social History, 1839–1889.* 1938. New York: Dover 1964.

Taylor, Joshua C. *America as Art.* Washington, D.C.: Smithsonian Institution Press for National Collection of Fine Arts, 1976.

Thomas, Davis, and Karin Ronnefeldt, eds. *People of the First Man: Life among the Plains Indians in Their Final Days of Glory.* New York: Dutton, 1976.

Trenton, Patricia, and Peter H. Hassrick. *The Rocky Mountains: A Vision for Artists in the Nineteenth Century.* Norman: University of Oklahoma Press, 1983.

Truettner, William H. "The Art of History: American Exploration and Discovery Scenes, 1840–1860." *American Art Journal* 14 (Winter 1982): 4–31.

———. *The Natural Man Observed: A Study of Catlin's Indian Gallery.* Washington, D.C.: Smithsonian Institution Press for Amon Carter Museum and National Collection of Fine Arts, 1979.

Tuckerman, Henry T. *Book of the Artists.* New York, 1867.

Tyler, Ron. "George Caleb Bingham: The Native Talent," 25–49. *See* Amon Carter Museum.

———. *Visions of America: Pioneer Artists in a New Land.* New York: Thames & Hudson, 1983.

———, ed. *Alfred Jacob Miller: Artist on the Oregon Trail.* Fort Worth, Tex.: Amon Carter Museum, 1982.

Unruh, John D., Jr. *The Plains Across: The Overland Emigrants and the Trans-Mississippi West, 1840–60.* Urbana: University of Illinois Press, 1979.

Utley, Robert M. *The Indian Frontier of the American West, 1846–1890.* Albuquerque: University of New Mexico Press, 1984.

Van Nostrand, Jeanne. *The First Hundred Years of Painting in California, 1775–1875.* San Francisco: Howell, 1980.

Weinberg, Albert K. *Manifest Destiny: A Study of Nationalist Expansionism in American History.* 1935. New York: AMS Press, 1979.

Weiss, Ila. *Poetic Landscapes: The Art and Experience of Sanford Gifford.* Cranbury, N.J.: Associated University Presses, 1987.

Welling, William. *Photography in America: The Formative Years, 1839–1900.* 1978. Albuquerque: University of New Mexico Press, 1987.

White, G. Edward. *The Eastern Establishment and the Western Experience: The West of Frederic Remington, Theodore Roosevelt, Owen Wister.* Austin: University of Texas Press, 1985.

White, Richard. *The Roots of Dependency: Subsistence, Environment, and Social Change among the Choctaws, Pawnees, and Navajos.* Lincoln: University of Nebraska Press, 1983.

Wilkins, Thurman. *Thomas Moran: Artist of the Mountains.* Norman: University of Oklahoma Press, 1966.

Willumson, Glenn Gardner. "Alfred Hart: Photographer of the Central Pacific Railroad." *History of Photography* 12 (January–March 1988).

Wooster, Robert. *The Military and United States Indian Policy, 1865–1903.* New Haven: Yale University Press, 1988.

Worster, Donald. *Rivers of Empire: Water, Aridity, and the Growth of the American West.* New York: Pantheon, 1985.

Index

Contributors

William H. Truettner is curator of painting and sculpture at the National Museum of American Art. He is the author of *The Natural Man Observed: A Study of Catlin's Indian Gallery* and coauthor of *Art in New Mexico, 1900–1945: Paths to Taos and Santa Fe.*

Nancy K. Anderson is assistant curator of American art at the National Gallery of Art in Washington, D.C. She is the principal author of *Albert Bierstadt: Art & Enterprise* and is preparing a catalogue of the George Catlin collection at the National Gallery.

Patricia Hills is professor of art history at Boston University. Her exhibitions and catalogues include *Eastman Johnson, Turn-of-the-Century America, John Singer Sargent,* and *Social Concern and Urban Realism: American Painting of the 1930s.*

Elizabeth Johns is Silfen Term Professor of the History of Art at the University of Pennsylvania. She is the author of *Thomas Eakins: The Heroism of Modern Life, Ordering the Sovereignty: Genre Painting in the Antebellum United States* and numerous catalogue essays and journal articles.

Joni Louise Kinsey is visiting professor at Washington University in Saint Louis. Her dissertation, "Creating a Sense of Place: Thomas Moran and the Surveying of the American West," will be published by the Smithsonian Institution Press in 1991.

Howard R. Lamar is Sterling Professor of History at Yale University. His books include *The Far Southwest, 1846–1912: A Territorial History* and *The Readers' Encyclopedia of the American West.*

Alex Nemerov is a doctoral candidate in art history at Yale University and a Smithsonian Institution Fellow. His dissertation topic is "Making History: Representations of the American West, 1885–1916."

Julie Schimmel, assistant professor of humanities and religious studies at Northern Arizona University, has written *The Art and Life of W. Herbert Dunton, 1878–1936* and coauthored *Art in New Mexico, 1900–1945: Paths to Taos and Santa Fe.*

389

Photography Credits

Alinari/Art Resource [69]; Berry-Hill Galleries, New York [105, 310]; Brandywine River Museum, Chadds Ford, Pa. [265, 276]; Buffalo Bill Historical Center, Cody [95, 306]; Michael Cavanaugh/Kevin Montague [180]; © Jacques Gael Cressaty [195]; Denver Public Library [201]; M. Lee Fatherree [9]; Bill Finney [27, 183]; Gallery Fumi, Tokyo [64]; Giraudon/Art Resource [46, 309]; Judy Goffman Fine Art, New York [291]; Helga Photo Studio, Upper Montclair, N.J. [73, 83, 120, 310]; Patricia Hills [99]; Kennedy Galleries, New York [277]; Library of Congress, Washington, D.C. [221]; Marburg/Art Resource [307]; James O. Milmoe [31, 297]; The New Orleans Museum of Art [167]; The Oakland Museum, History Department, Calif. [117]; Lawrence Reynolds [106]; Clive Russ, Charlestown, Mass. [33]; The Saint Louis Art Museum [313]; Julie Schimmel [150]; ©1989 Sirlin Commercial Photographers, Sacramento [198]; Julia V. Smith [153]; Society of California Pioneers, San Francisco [237]; Joseph Szaszfai [175]; Taylor & Dull, Inc., Paramus, N.J. [277]; *Visión del Mundo Maya* (Mexico City, 1978) [49–50]; Vose Galleries, Boston [33]; Rynda White [274]; Daniel Wolf, Inc., New York [244]; Yale Collection of Western Americana, Beinecke Rare Book and Manuscript Library, New Haven [232].

For permission to reproduce illustrations appearing in this book, please correspond directly with the owners of the works as listed in the individual captions. The Smithsonian Institution Press does not retain reproduction rights for these illustrations or maintain a file of addresses for photo sources.

George Fiske, *Kitty Tatch and Friend on Overhanging Rock, Glacier Point, Yosemite, California,* ca. 1890s, photograph. Albumen Cabinet Mount #287, Yosemite National Park Collections, negative no. YM-18,194.

Typeset in Bembo by Maryland Composition
Company, Inc., Glen Burnie, Maryland
Printed on 128 gsm Matt Art by
South China Printing Co., Hong Kong
Copyedited by Kathleen Preciado
Production management by Kathleen Brown
Designed by Lisa Buck Vann